Educational Media and Technology Yearbook

For further volumes:
http://www.springer.com/series/8617

Michael Orey • Stephanie A. Jones
Robert Maribe Branch

Editors

Educational Media and Technology Yearbook

Volume 37

Springer

LB
1028.3
.E37
2012

Editors
Michael Orey
Educational Psychology
   and Instructional Technology
University of Georgia
Athens, GA, USA

Stephanie A. Jones
Department Leadership
   Technology and Development
Georgia Southern University
Statesboro, GA, USA

Robert Maribe Branch
Educational Psychology
   and Instructional Technology
University of Georgia
Athens, GA, USA

ISSN 8755-2094
ISBN 978-1-4614-4429-9   ISBN 978-1-4614-4430-5 (eBook)
DOI 10.1007/978-1-4614-4430-5
Springer New York Heidelberg Dordrecht London

Springer is part of Springer Science+Business Media (www.springer.com)

Preface

The audience for the *Yearbook* consists of media and technology professionals in schools, higher education, and business contexts. Topics of interest to professionals practicing in these areas are broad, as the Table of Contents demonstrates. The theme unifying each of the following chapters is the use of technology to enable or enhance education. Forms of technology represented in this volume vary from traditional tools such as the book to the latest advancements in digital technology, while areas of education encompass widely ranging situations involving learning and teaching which are idea technologies.

As in prior volumes, the assumptions underlying the chapters presented here are as follows:

1. Technology represents tools that act as extensions of the educator.
2. Media serve as delivery systems for educational communications.
3. Technology is *not* restricted to machines and hardware, but includes techniques and procedures derived from scientific research about ways to promote change in human performance.
4. The fundamental tenet is that educational media and technology should be used to:

   (a) Achieve authentic learning objectives
   (b) Situate learning tasks
   (c) Negotiate the complexities of guided learning
   (d) Facilitate the construction of knowledge
   (e) Aid in the assessment/documenting of learning
   (f) Support skill acquisition
   (g) Manage diversity

The *Educational Media and Technology Yearbook* has become a standard reference in many libraries and professional collections. Examined in relation to its companion volumes of the past, it provides a valuable historical record of current ideas and developments in the field. Part 1, "Trends and Issues in Learning, Design and Technology," presents an array of chapters that develop some of the current themes listed above, in addition to others. Part 2, "Trends and Issues in Library and Information Science," concentrates upon chapters of special relevance to K-12 education, library science education, school learning resources, and various types of library and media centers—school, public, and academic among others. In Part 3, "Leadership Profiles," authors provide biographical sketches of the careers of instructional technology leaders. Part 4, "Organizations and Associations in North America," and Part 5, "Graduate Programs in North America," are, respectively, directories of instructional technology-related organizations and institutions of higher learning offering degrees in related fields. Finally, Part 6, the "Mediagraphy," presents an annotated listing of selected current publications related to the field.

The editors of the *Yearbook* invite media and technology professionals to submit manuscripts for consideration for publication. Contact Michael Orey (mikeorey@uga.edu) for submission guidelines.

For a number of years we have worked together as editors and the ninth with Dr. Michael Orey as the senior editor. Within each volume of the Educational Media and Technology Yearbook (EMTY) we try to list all the graduate programs, journals, and organizations that are related to both Learning, Design, and Technology (LDT) and Library and Information Science (LIS). We also include a section on trends in LDT, trends in LIS, and we have a section profiling some of the leaders in the field. Beginning with the 2007 volume, we have attempted to generate a list of leading programs in the combined areas of LDT and LIS. One year, we were able to compose an alphabetical list of 30 of the programs that people told us were among the best. However, each year we have worked on being more systematic. Instead of following the *US News and World Report* model and have one top program list, we decided to use some of the same numbers that they use and generate a collection of top 20 lists, rather than attempt to generate a statistical model to generate the rankings list. One thought was to rank programs according to the number of publications that were produced; however, deciding which journals to include was an issue. We have decided to use a 5-year span, in this case 2007 through 2010, as the years to count (since at the time of writing, it is still 2011 and so we do not have a complete year). Furthermore, we decided to only count actual research reports that appeared in one of two journals, *Educational Technology Research and Development* and the *Journal of the Learning Sciences*. These two journals were primarily selected based on the general sense that they are the leading journals in the area of LDT. Noticeably absent is the area of information and library science. So, while these numbers are pretty absolute, choosing to only count these journals is somewhat arbitrary.

The other top 20 lists are based on self-report data collected as part of the program information in the Educational Media and Technology Yearbook. Every year, we collect general information about programs in LDT and LIS and publish this information in the Yearbook. Each year we also collect some additional data. We asked the representatives of each of the institutions to enter the US dollar amount of grants and contracts, the number of PhD graduates, the number of Masters graduates, and the number of other graduates from their programs. We also asked them for the number of full-time and part-time faculty. We then generated a top 20 list for some of these categories. The limitation in this case is that it is self-report data and there is no real way of verifying that the data is accurate. So, while the list of the 30 top programs from the first year lacked hard data, and the lists this year are based on numbers, those numbers may be just as unreliable. In the end, we have a collection of lists that we hope will be of use to our readers. Many of the universities that appeared in the list last year are here again, in addition to many others. More information about many of these universities can be found in part 5 of this edition.

There are five top 20 lists in this preface. The first of these top 20 lists is based on a count of publications. We used every issue from the 2007 through 2010 volume years of the *Educational Technology Research and Development* journal and the *Journal of the Learning Sciences*. We eliminated all book reviews and letters-to-the-editor and such. We only used the primary academic articles of these journals. Each publication counted 1 point. If the article had two authors, then each author's institution received 0.5 points. If there were three authors, then 0.33 was spread across the institutions. Also, as an additional example, if there were three authors and two of them were from the same institution, then that institution received 0.66 points and the institution of the remaining author received 0.33. Finally, the unit receiving the points was the University. So, in some cases, you might have publications from two completely different departments in the same journal. Table 1 shows our results. The University of Georgia came out as the top LDT program in the world. They were number 1 last year too; in fact, the top 5 are exactly the same as last year. A big change from last year is Brigham Young University who jumped from 16th to 7th. Another big move was the University of Maryland who was not on the top 20 list last year, but who is number 9 this year. Also, please note that because there was a three way tie at 19, the next university to be on the list would be at 22nd place. Therefore, there is no 20th place on the list.

We would love to hear your feedback on this approach for the future. Are there other journals that ought to be included?; Is it unfair that there are more publications in ETRD than IJLS?; What about recent graduates publishing with their new institution when the work was done at their previous institution? I am certain there are many other issues, and we welcome constructive feedback.Table 1 Top 20 Graduate Programs in the area of Learning, Design, and Technology as measured by the number of publications in *Educational Technology Research and Development* and the *Journal of the Learning Sciences*

Rank	Institution	Points
1	University of Georgia	10.48
2	Indiana University	7.66
3	Arizona State University	7.32
4	Nanyang Technological University	4.83
5	University of Wisconsin	4.52
6	Stanford University	4.51
7	Brigham Young University	4.13
8	University of Toronto	3.9
9	University of Maryland	3.86
10	SRI International	3.69

(continued)

Rank	Institution	Points
11	University of Northern Colorado	3.25
12	Open University of the Netherlands	3.1
13	University of Colorado	3.03
14	Aristotle University of Thessaloniki	3
14	University of Missouri	3
16	Purdue University	2.96
17	Utrecht University	2.94
18	San Diego State University	2.85
19	Florida State University	2.5
19	University of Illinois	2.5
19	University of New Mexico	2.5

The two primary measures of research achievement are publications and grants. While choosing ETRD and IJLS was somewhat arbitrary, the numbers are verifiable. In Table 2, we present the top 20 programs according to the dollar amount of grants and contracts for that program over the academic year of 2010–2011. While Table 1 was constrained to LDT, Table 2 has both LDT programs and LIS programs which resulted in the University of Calgary being number 1 in the grants and contracts list, but not appearing at all in the publication list. In fact, the only institutions that are both on the list for publications and grants are the University of Georgia (1 for publications and 19 for grants), Indiana University (2 for publications and 12 for grants), and University of Missouri (14 for publications and 7 for grants)..

The only shake up in the top 5 is that the University of North Carolina failed to report their data this year. They were replaced in the top 5 by the University of Louisville.Table 2 Top 20 LDT and LIS programs by the amount of grant and contract monies

Rank	University	Department	Total
1	University of Calgary	Office of Graduate Programs, Faculty of Education	20,000,000
2	University of Massachusetts, Amherst	Learning, Media and Technology Masters Program/Math Science and Learning Technology Doctoral Program	10,700,000
3	University of Louisville	Workforce and Human Resource Education Program	4,500,000
4	Virginia Tech	College of Liberal Arts and Human Sciences	3,500,000
5	George Mason University	Instructional Technology Programs	2,500,000
6	Utah State University	Department of Instructional Technology & Learning Sciences, Emma Eccles Jones College of Education and Human Services	1,800,000
7	University of Missouri-Columbia	School of Information Science & Learning Technologies	1,585,885

(continued)

Rank	University	Department	Total
8	University of Virginia	Instructional Science & Technology Program, Department of Curriculum & Instruction, Curry School of Education	1,500,000
8	New York University	Educational Communication and Technology Program (PhD) and Digital Media Design for Learning Program (MA, Adv. Cert.), Steinhardt School of Culture, Education, and Human Development	1,500,000
10	The University of Texas at Austin	Curriculum & Instruction	1,306,456
11	Georgia State University	Middle-Secondary Education and Instructional Technology	1,250,000
12	Indiana University	Instructional Systems Technology, School of Education	1,237,755
13	The Ohio State University	Cultural Foundations, Technology, & Qualitative Inquiry	1,200,000
14	University of North Carolina, Wilmington	Master of Science in Instructional Technology--Department of Instructional Technology, Foundations & Secondary Education	1,199,546
15	Université de Poitiers	Ingénierie des médias pour léducation	1,000,000
15	Lehigh University	Teaching, Learning, and Technology	1,000,000
15	University of Houston	Curriculum & Instruction	1,000,000
18	University of Memphis	Instructional Design and Technology	750,000
19	University of Georgia	Department of Educational Psychology and Instructional Technology, College of Education	600,000
20	Rutgers-The State University of New Jersey	School of Communication and Information	500,000
20	University of Geneva	TECFA—Master of Science in Learning and Teaching Technologies	500,000
20	Ohio University	Instructional Technology	500,000

Tables 1 and 2 are measures of research productivity. The remaining three tables are more related to teaching than research. The first, Table 3, shows the top 20 programs in terms of the number of full-time faculty. You will notice that the list is ordered by the number of full-time faculty (FT), but number 3, The University of Hong Kong has 110 total faculty members. We decided that full-time faculty was more important than part-time as a measure and so only generated one list for number of faculty. We just thought it would be interesting to see the total number of faculty as well. For example, it is interesting to see The University of Hong Kong and the University of Calgary with very large numbers (110 and 80, respectively) while the University of Georgia and the University of Oklahoma both have 11 full-time faculty and no part-time faculty.Table 3 Top 20 LDT and LIS programs by the

number of full-time faculty (also shown is the total faculty which includes
both full- and part-time faculty)

Rank	University	Department	FT	Total
1	Université de Poitiers	Ingénierie des médias pour léducation	25	50
2	Rutgers-The State University of New Jersey	School of Communication and Information	22	37
3	The University of Hong Kong	Faculty of Education	20	110
3	Middle East Technical University	Computer Education & Instructional Technology	20	60
5	Towson University	College of Education	17	22
6	University of Bridgeport	Instructional Technology	14	35
7	Valdosta State University	Curriculum, Leadership, & Technology	12	16
7	Valley City State University	School of Education and Graduate Studies	12	17
7	Anadolu University	Computer Education and Instructional Technology	12	21
7	Fordham University	MA Program in Public Communications in the Department of Communication and Media Studies	12	16
7	Utrecht University	Educational Sciences	12	19
12	University of Louisville	Workforce and Human Resource Education Program	11	25
12	University of Georgia	Department of Educational Psychology and Instructional Technology, College of Education	11	11
12	The University of Oklahoma	Instructional Psychology and Technology, Department of Educational Psychology	11	11
15	Taganrog State Pedagogical Institute	Media Education (Social Pedagogic Faculty)	10	30
15	Hacettepe University	Computer Education and Instructional Technology	10	22
15	Utah State University	Department of Instructional Technology & Learning Sciences, Emma Eccles Jones College of Education and Human Services	10	11
15	University of Missouri-Columbia	School of Information Science & Learning Technologies	10	18
15	Indiana University	Instructional Systems Technology, School of Education	10	22
20	University of Calgary	Office of Graduate Programs, Faculty of Education	8	80
20	University of Massachusetts, Amherst	Learning, Media and Technology Masters Program/Math Science and Learning Technology Doctoral Program	8	10
20	Georgia Southern University	College of Education	8	9

(continued)

Rank	University	Department	FT	Total
20	California State University Monterey Bay (CSUMB)	Master of Science in Instructional Science and Technology (IST)	8	20
20	Western Illinois University	Instructional Technology and Telecommunications	8	11

The next top 20 list is the number of PhD graduates. This list might be a good measure of research productivity as well as teaching productivity. The number of graduates is self-reported. The number of publications is verifiable, so it is interesting to compare who is on both lists. None of the three number ones are on top 20 publications list, but there are five institutions on both lists. University of Georgia, University of Missouri, Indiana University, Florida State University, and Ultrecht University are on both of these lists. The top school in terms of PhD graduates is also on the top school for amount of grant monies, University of Calgary.Table 4 Top 20 LDT and LIS programs by the number of PhD graduates. Please note that the list only goes to 17, but since there was a seven way tie for 17th, the next university would be 24th place

Rank	University	Department	Total
1	University of Calgary	Office of Graduate Programs, Faculty of Education	15
1	George Mason University	Instructional Technology Programs	15
1	University of Bridgeport	Instructional Technology	15
4	Wayne State University	Instructional Technology	11
4	University of Georgia	Department of Educational Psychology and Instructional Technology, College of Education	11
6	University of Missouri-Columbia	School of Information Science & Learning Technologies	10
6	Indiana University	Instructional Systems Technology, School of Education	10
6	Rutgers-The State University of New Jersey	School of Communication and Information	10
6	Ohio University	Instructional Technology	10
6	Middle East Technical University	Computer Education & Instructional Technology	10
11	University of Houston	Curriculum & Instruction	8
11	The University of Texas at Austin	Curriculum & Instruction	8
13	University of Central Florida	College of Education—ERTL	7
14	Florida State University	Educational Psychology and Learning Systems	6
14	Georgia State University	Middle-Secondary Education and Instructional Technology	6
14	Virginia Tech	College of Liberal Arts and Human Sciences	6
17	Texas Tech University	Instructional Technology	5
17	University of Louisville	Workforce and Human Resource Education Program	5

(continued)

Rank	University	Department	Total
17	Utrecht University	Educational Sciences	5
17	University of Virginia	Instructional Science & Technology Program, Department of Curriculum & Instruction, Curry School of Education	5
17	Kent State University	Instructional Technology	5
17	The Ohio State University	Cultural Foundations, Technology, & Qualitative Inquiry	5
17	Anadolu University	Computer Education and Instructional Technology	5

Our last top 20 list is based on the number of master's graduates. In our mind, we might consider this an indication of whether the program is more practitioner oriented than say the number of PhD graduates. Interestingly, University of lCalgary is second here, and is first in both grants and PhDs. So, this differentiation may be meaningless. It is interesting to note that last year we had six schools that produced more than 100 graduates and this year we have seven. While the economy has not done so well, several schools have attracted fairly large numbers of masters students to their programs and successfully graduating some pretty large numbers of graduates. Some people seek degrees during these economic downturns.Table 5 Top 20 LDT and LIS programs by the number of master's graduates

Rank	University	Department	Total
1	University of Bridgeport	Instructional Technology	294
2	University of Calgary	Office of Graduate Programs, Faculty of Education	250
3	Towson University	College of Education	180
4	Rutgers-The State University of New Jersey	School of Communication and Information	161
5	New York Institute of Technology	Department of Instructional Technology and Educational Leadership	130
5	George Mason University	Instructional Technology Programs	130
7	Utrecht University	Educational Sciences	100
8	University of Central Florida	College of Education—ERTL	75
9	Bloomsburg University	Instructional Technology & Institute for Interactive Technologies	60
9	Michigan State University	College of Education	60
11	University of Missouri-Columbia	School of Information Science & Learning Technologies	59
12	Georgia Southern University	College of Education	50
13	Wayne State University	Instructional Technology	48
14	California State University, East Bay	Online Teaching & Learning	45
14	Boise State University	Instructional & Performance Technology	45
16	University of Nebraska at Kearney	Teacher Education	44

(continued)

Rank	University	Department	Total
17	University of Texas at Brownsville	Educational Technology	42
18	University of Georgia	Department of Educational Psychology and Instructional Technology, College of Education	40
18	Lehigh University	Teaching, Learning, and Technology	40
18	University of Central Arkansas	Leadership Studies	40

We acknowledge that any kind of rankings of programs is problematic. We hope you find our lists useful. If you have suggestions, please let us know and we will try to accommodate those changes in future publications of the *Yearbook*. If your program is not represented, please contact one of us and we can add you to the database so that you can be included in future issues.

Athens, GA, USA   Michael Orey
Statesboro, GA, USA   Stephanie A. Jones
Athens, GA, USA   Robert Maribe Branch

Contents

Contributors

Carrie Bailey Department of Leadership, Technology, and Human Development, Georgia Southern University, Statesboro, GA, USA

Daisyane Barreto Learning, Design, and Technology Program, The University of Georgia, Athens, GA, USA

Robert Maribe Branch Department of Educational Psychology and Instructional Technology, University of Georgia, Athens, GA, USA

Abbie Brown Department of Mathematics, Library Science and Instructional Technology, East Carolina University, Greenville, NC, USA

Lori A. Brown University of Northern Colorado, Greeley, CO, USA

Yonjoo Cho Department of Instructional Systems Technology, Indiana University, Bloomington, IN, USA

Nancy Everhart School of Library and Information Studies, College of Communication & Information,, The Florida State University, Tallahassee, FL, USA

James E. Gall University of Northern Colorado, Greeley, CO, USA

Gabrielle Garner University of Georgia, Athens, GA, USA

Tim Green Department of Elementary and Bilingual Education, California State University, Fullerton, CA, USA

Ray K. Haynes Department of Instructional Systems Technology, Indiana University, Bloomington, IN, USA

Stephanie A. Jones Instructional Technology, Georgia Southern University, Statesboro, GA, USA

Kathryn Kennedy Department of Leadership, Technology and Human Development, Georgia Southern University, Statesboro, GA, USA

Jason LaFrance Department of Leadership, Technology, and Human Development, Georgia Southern University, Statesboro, GA, USA

Linda L. Lohr University of Northern Colorado, Greeley, CO, USA

Marcia Mardis School of Library and Information Studies, College of Communication & Information, The Florida State University, Tallahassee, FL, USA

Michael Orey Learning, Design, and Technology Program, The University of Georgia, Athens, GA, USA

Daniella Smith Department of Library and Information Sciences, College of Information, University of North Texas, Denton, TX, USA

Douglas Tedford Fundacion Rigoberta Menchu Tum of Guatemala, Teaching Services Latin America, Mexico City, Mexico

Jinn-Wei Tsao Learning, Design, and Technology Program, The University of Georgia, Athens, GA, USA

Dawn Tysinger Department of Leadership, Technology, and Human Development, Georgia Southern University, Statesboro, GA, USA

Anna Ursyn University of Northern Colorado, Greeley, CO, USA

Part I
Trends and Issues in Learning, Design, and Technology

Chapter 1
Trends and Issues in Learning, Design, and Technology

Daisyane Barreto and Michael Orey

1.1 Introduction

Lately, the influence of digital technologies in people's daily lives has become unquestionable. Devices, such as computers and smartphones, are now part of individuals' interpersonal communication, work, entertainment, and even learning. Interestingly, learning with these technologies can occur on a formal basis, such as students using simulations to understand complex content in physics, or an informal basis, with learners watching tutorials online to learn the basic skills of an image editing software.

As technology becomes more affordable, the number of individuals acquiring these devices grows. A recent study conducted by *Pew Research Center* indicated that approximately 85% of Americans own a cell phone, 52% a laptop computer, and 42% a game console (Zickuhr 2011). The "easy access" to these technologies (i.e., we are in an era when most individuals have access to everything, everywhere, any time) allows people to quickly communicate, gather information, and learn from one another. Therefore, technology is providing new spaces where learning can happen, which means learning is becoming mobile and can occur in many different ways.

Thus, avoiding technology is not an option anymore, and the question now is how to use these tools in a way that can be effective for education. Educators and scholars should consider not only the affordances of technology, but also the theories and practices to be used to improve educational contexts and technology use. This section of the book will introduce a collection of essays on current topics and issues related to educational technology. The topics vary from aesthetics in instructional design to online videogames. Overall, the purpose of the essays is (a) to present and

D. Barreto (✉) • M. Orey
Learning, Design, and Technology Program, The University of Georgia, Athens, GA, USA
e-mail: daisyane@uga.edu

M. Orey et al. (eds.), *Educational Media and Technology Yearbook*, Educational
Media and Technology Yearbook 37, DOI 10.1007/978-1-4614-4430-5_1,
© Springer Science+Business Media New York 2013

promote a discussion around the latest and future trends in the field as well as (b) to provide examples and cases of the use of technology in education.

In the first chapter, Lori Brown, Linda Lohr, James Gall, and Anna Ursyn explored the importance of aesthetics in instructional design. Although there has been an emergent interest on this topic lately, the authors highlighted that there are still criticisms regarding the value of aesthetics in instructional design. These criticisms are usually grounded on the lack of evidence of aesthetics' effectiveness on learning. Because of this, the authors proposed a framework to investigate aesthetics in instructional design, including five components. Four of these components compose the *design actions* part of an instructional program, i.e., contrast, alignment, repetition, and proximity. The last component of the framework is the *learning experience*, which involves the change or improvement of learners' attitude as a result of the design of the learning content as well as the visual aesthetics of an instructional program. In summary, the visual aesthetics is what makes the learning resources function properly, providing learners with visual elements that will guide and enhance their learning experience throughout an instructional program.

In the second chapter, Ray Haynes and Yonjoo Cho introduced theoretical diversity by exploring the pluralistic theories and approaches applied to current studies in the *Instructional System Technology* (IST) program at the University of Indiana. The studies discussed in this chapter involve: (a) learning strategies grounded on situational perspectives and traditional instructional methods, (b) learners' cognitive structures, intentions, and emotions, (c) design knowledge and practices, (d) digital resources that support educators and preservice teachers in the use of problem-based instruction, (e) unconventional methods and strategies that individuals use to "learn or teach with technology," (f) professional development and career mentoring, and (g) examining previous work and publications to identify trends on the field. In other words, the authors presented an educational environment in which students can find multiple theoretical perspectives and learn to connect theory, research, and practice.

In the third chapter, Gabrielle Garner explored the sociocultural, economic, and technological systems that frame cutting-edge artifacts. The author introduced online gaming as a case study, examining current popular online games and research studies related to online games in the field. The chapter focuses on: (a) general aspects of gaming industry and its development, and (b) game features that can support current trends in the field, such as establishing communities of practice or promoting innovative and collaborative environments.

In the fourth chapter, Abbie Brown and Tim Green examined the recent trends and issues in educational technology. According to the authors, funding availability has been one of the main issues in the past few years for K-12 and higher education settings. In order to overcome this problem, these sectors have been using the available technologies to share open content and resources. Regarding the current trends in the field, electronic books, mobile devices, cloud computing, and augmented reality are technologies to pay attention to as the number of users increases as well as their use in educational contexts.

Given the chapters presented in this section of the book, the current trends for educational technology in 2012 include: (a) investigating visual aesthetics as part of the instructional design process, (b) considering different theories and approaches to guide research and practice, (c) analyzing the sociocultural, economic, and technological systems that bound artifacts such as online games, and (d) an overview of the recent trends and issues in educational settings regarding the purpose and use of technology for teaching and learning. Overall, the use of technology for education should not target exposing students to a wide range of content, instead it should allow students to participate in the production of content as they interact, share, and collaborate with each other. Nevertheless, not all technologies were developed with an educational purpose in mind, which means that integrating technology in educational settings might pose a challenge to educators. That is, teachers and instructors may need to adjust, change, and control technology's use in the classroom according to their educational objectives. Thus, assessing the use and effectiveness of these tools is crucial to better learning environments. Moreover, the design and development of learning experiences must be founded in sound theories and guided by research and practices in the field. In this process, the structure and content of instruction are not the only key factors that contribute to the learning experience. The visual elements of instructional artifacts create a system that allows students to navigate the learning environment and take control of their own learning experience.

Reference

Zickuhr, K. (2011). Generations and their gadgets. *Pew Research Center's Internet & life project*. Retrieved from http://pewinternet.org/Reports/2011/Generations-and-gadgets.aspx.

Chapter 2
Where is the *Design* in Instructional Design? The Role of Visual Aesthetics in the Field

Lori A. Brown, Linda L. Lohr, James E. Gall, and Anna Ursyn

Where is the Design in Instructional Design? The Role of Visual Aesthetics in the Field (Design 1989).

This dialogue on the role of visual aesthetics in instructional design opens with a simple query and a simple play on the word—design, with the simple purpose of rousing interest in the idea and, perhaps, intimating a challenge in the nomenclature of instructional design. According to the Oxford English Dictionary (1989), our English word *design* originated with the fifteenth to the sixteenth century French word *desseing* meaning purpose or project. The same source makes note that in modern French, *dessein* is used to indicate "purpose or plan" and *dessin* is "design in art," but English uses the word *design* for both senses. One's prior knowledge and/or preconceived notions of the discipline may lead one to look at this dual semantic nature of design as mutually exclusive, complementary, or for some possibly not worthy of discussion.

Regardless of the perception of aesthetics as integral or negligible in the creation of effective instruction at large, it behooves us to take into account certain unavoidable implications about instructional design due to its association with the term *design*. This is arguably a far better position than an absence of design. For example, Donald Norman has recently noted that the current emphasis on STEM education (science, technology, engineering, and math) could specifically benefit from the addition of a letter D for design (Talbot 2011). Depending upon the diversity of influence, such as prior learning and/or partiality, one may expect a corresponding array of thoughts and practices among prominent scholars and instructional design professionals in interpreting and identifying design in instructional design. However, one may expect reactions to fall within a spectrum of

L.A. Brown (✉) • L.L. Lohr • J.E. Gall • A. Ursyn
University of Northern Colorado, Greeley, CO, USA
e-mail: lori.brown@unco.edu

M. Orey et al. (eds.), *Educational Media and Technology Yearbook*, Educational Media and Technology Yearbook 37, DOI 10.1007/978-1-4614-4430-5_2, © Springer Science+Business Media New York 2013

opinions that range from the absolute and resolute to the unaware and uninformed. The notions on either end of the spectrum may represent either a positive or a negative reception of design and aesthetics' role in the field. Yet, those who relate design with plan and strategy, more likely, discern the design in instructional design in the procedural tasks based on analysis and evaluation. Whereas, individuals inclined to detect the design in instructional design according to artistic or creative impressions likely have a heightened concern for the aesthetic in the discipline. Their concern may be manifest in terms of best practices and research on designers' consideration and implementation of aesthetic ideals and/or artistic and creative expediencies.

Substantive research on the treatment of visual aesthetics in instructional design compels the building of an historical, theoretical, and practical framework. An exploration of the foundational circumstances and premises of instructional design as they relate to aesthetics, along with current influences, provides the context for a productive and relevant dialogue. In addition, a concise treatise on the theoretical notion of aesthetics from its roots in philosophy, art, and education supports further exploration. A broad understanding and appreciation of the background also establishes the expertise needed to substantiate the thematic categories that comprise the definition of visual aesthetics in instructional design. Ultimately, the detailed and comprehensive explanation of visual aesthetics reveals strong ties to dynamic aspects of the affective domain, thereby indicating its potential contribution to the learning experience.

2.1 Visual Aesthetics in Instructional Design

As a discipline, most agree that instructional design largely originated from the demand for military training materials in the USA due to the crisis of World War II (Reiser 2001a, b). Given the urgency to disseminate vital information among a diverse, often distant, and sizeable population of troops and auxiliary personnel, the majority of designers and theorists in the field may not have considered or made aesthetics a priority in the early stages of the field. The government employed instructional designers who used some of the latest media, such as film, to reach their target audience of learners, the soldiers and other individuals who contributed to the war effort. Behaviorist principles, research, and theories prevailed at the time of World War II and in the years immediately following the war and guided the design and development of much of the instructional materials (Skinner 1954). Many terms, created by wartime instructional designers to service military needs, formed the basis of contemporary instructional designers' educations.

The publication of the taxonomy of Benjamin Bloom (1956) and its subsequent revisions (Anderson et al. 2000) influenced current understanding of the connection between learning experience and aesthetics by means of what Bloom termed the affective domain. Aesthetics seems to easily fit within the domain of learning that is expressive of learners' feelings and attitudes. While the identification of experiential learning and the corresponding placement of aesthetics as a dynamic feature in the affective domain generated interest and triggered some debate, it may have also contributed to (or been reflective of) modern compartmentalization of aesthetics in instructional design.

Subsequent researchers, such as Jean Piaget, a cognitive psychologist, further affected the precept of aesthetics and instructional design. Piaget insisted that all behaviors and states of being are mutually dependent on both the cognitive and affective (Clark and Fiske 1982). The factors of attention, relevance, confidence, and satisfaction in the ARCS motivation model reflected evolution in the study of the affective domain (Keller 1997). However, Keller (as cited in Shellnut 1998) also noted the absence of motivational considerations among popular design models during the 1980s. Having identified motivation as the neglected heart of the instructional design process, Keller acknowledged several measures related to motivation, such as "curiosity, expectancy, relevancy, and satisfaction" (Shellnut 1998, Significant Contributions section, para. 2). Keller's model does not directly address aesthetics; yet, consideration of the facets that relate to motivation provides insight beyond a strictly functional view of instruction.

Influential constructivist theories in the late 1980s and 1990s challenged instructional designers to consider learners' unique experiences and attitudes (Bull 2009; Huitt 2003). However, attention to all the varied experiential and attitudinal components of learning (including aesthetics) did not develop, as one might expect given the underlying philosophy of constructivist thought.

Investigation on the effects of affective elements ceded to an even stronger surge in cognitive learning theory in the late twentieth century (Baddeley 1992; Pass et al. 2003). Researchers delved into a line of investigation of mental processes that led to twenty-first century advances in function-oriented learning concepts, such as cognitive load theory (CLT) (Pass et al. 2004).

Tracing some of the most discernible influences and prevailing premises in the development of the discipline sheds light on the rationale behind current research agendas. Renewed interest in overlooked or under-investigated ideas points toward possible biases in the field and poses contemporary challenges and future developments.

Certainly, among the significant developments in and aspects of instructional design are the models that exemplify the theoretical pedagogies and inspirations of the authors at a given time. Most models tend to reflect to varying degrees is the generic standard for instructional design models that are based on the principles of analysis, design, development, implementation, and evaluation (ADDIE). Notable in absence is any reference or integration of aesthetics. The most common models neither tie visual aesthetics to instructional design in terms of certain design actions nor in any artistic sense. The want of aesthetics in typical, modern, instructional design models may enlighten a corresponding deficiency in research on the influence of aspects of the affective domain on the learning experience.

2.2 Contemporary Influences

Present-day discourse in academic journals and online editorials reveals a growing interest in support for innovative research that pertains to aesthetics' value and function in the design of effective instruction (Parrish 2009). The ways in which scholars and instructional designers connect aesthetics with the instructional design process are as numerous as they are disparate. Some critics uphold a perception of aesthetics as merely decorative (Wilson 2005) or as an afterthought—something designers may take into account, time and money permitting.

Parrish (2005) notes that aesthetics as a superficial attribute permeates the views of many designers and researchers. Parrish speculates that aesthetics among our society in general and among instructional design enthusiasts in particular is commonly and negatively associated with triviality and shallowness. No identified empirical study has established that attention to design actions (stemming from some aesthetic core) equates to a focus on superficial attributes rather than substantive qualities of effective instruction. Yet, other fields of design embrace and promote visual aesthetics. For example, there does not appear to be any conflict among graphic designers' realization of their goal to present information both effectively and aesthetically.

Visual aesthetics is an obvious and integral part of fashion design, interior design, graphic design, product design, industrial design, etc. The graphic designer translates principles of visual aesthetics into action toward the creation of meaningful, memorable, accessible, effective images (illustrations, graphics, typographic elements, etc.). Other design-based professions consider the achievement of a visual aesthetic to be a principle pursuit with no conflict between the characteristics that denote quality or value in relation to either the aesthetic or the didactic purpose. The use of these fields as examples should not imply that they view design in a uniform way that can be easily translated to learning. However, the pervasive use of design in an aesthetic sense in our culture does create a stark contrast with its educational use. It is also significant to note a growing and persistent expression of interest in visual aesthetics and learning consequences that pertain to affective, experiential, and emotional stimuli.

Simonson and Maushak (2001) are among those who argue on behalf of emotional affect and learning benefits. Parrish (2005) validates their argument, insisting that aesthetics is an integral component of a "high-level instructional design model" that is both ideal and attainable. Those who believe that aesthetics can be and should be a dynamic part of the instructional design process may be comparably small in number. But, their adamancy that visual aesthetics merits investigation and possibly equal consideration, if not total integration, amidst usability and other traditional and tested steps in instructional design models, makes their cause difficult to ignore. However, the case for visual aesthetics in instructional design has not moved forward—beyond recent, demonstrable, stimulation in awareness and interest (Kirschner et al. 2004). Wide-ranging ideas, far-reaching definitions of aesthetics, and lack of a general understanding of the question among leading scholars in the field may also hinder empirical research and inhibit the productive discussion of potentially beneficial learning outcomes (Hokanson et al. 2008; Parrish 2005; Wilson 2005).

2.3 Aesthetics' Philosophical, Artistic, and Educational Roots

The subsequent treatise on aesthetics from its roots in philosophy, art, and education reveals the extensive value the concept has enjoyed throughout recorded history and establishes it as a pillar of great importance in the study of any creative and design-related field. Aesthetics is a philosophy, a literary and artistic movement, a design ideal, and a practical consideration. The idiom itself derives from the Greek, αἰσθητικός, and conveys man's proper or good understanding through the senses. The etymology of the term is significant for the comprehension of more contemporary definitions and uses in reference to beauty and good taste. The Greek expression, particularly in Aristotle's (Trans. 1996) discussion of aesthetics in his *Poetics*, refers to perception in relation to form. A study of the ancient Greek lexicon inextricably ties perception to the representation, formation, and conception of that which was perceived, whether in reference to a physical (external) object or some concept or the mental (internal) process of perceiving, apprehending, or sensing with proper or "good" understanding. As a persuasive response to Plato's denigration of representative art as an imperfect and, therefore, corrupt copy of reality, Aristotle implicates human emotion within the framework of literary and illustrative art, and ultimately glorifies the act of imitation in both an artistic and metaphysical sense (Else 1986). Aristotle's explanation of aesthetics is valuable in that he places the notion firmly within the realm of human experience and designates certain exceptional sensory qualities of comprehension in its proper form.

Contemporary critics find a more fitting derivation of aesthetics in the discourse of German and British philosophers. Alexander Gottlieb Baumgarten and Immanuel Kant in the eighteenth century and G.W.F. Hegel in the nineteenth century were concerned with aesthetics as judgment in matters of taste and beauty (Baumgarten 1954; Crawford 1974; Hegel 1977). Even Friedrich Nietzsche ultimately identified an undeniable transformational potential in art and the aesthetic (Rampley 2000). The British theorist, Edmund Burke (1968), exerted a profound influence on aesthetic perceptions with his book, *A Philosophical Enquiry into the Origin of Our Ideas of the Sublime and Beautiful*, published in 1757. These philosophers took Aristotle's elucidation of aesthetics, as a profound appreciation, deep perception, heightened awareness through proper interaction of the senses, and delivered the notion, smoothly, first into the psychological realm and second into the contemporary conversation in the sphere of formal educational discourse. They discussed the promise of aesthetics in relation to the beauty of proper or good mental processes and physical responses. John Dewey's discussion of aesthetics in the early twentieth century extended the psychological and emotional perimeters of aesthetics and knowledge found in early German philosophy by relating aesthetic feelings to an experiential ideal, a mental response to feelings generated from encounters perceived as beautiful or unattractive (Dewey 1934). Dewey insisted upon the limitless potential of aesthetics beyond the conventional delineation in areas such as fine art, basing aesthetic appreciation on principles of subjectivism.

Currently, Patrick Parrish, a staunch advocate of aesthetics as a central and consequential concern in the field, breathes new life into much of Dewey's work and develops a compelling argument that instructional design research should put aesthetic ideals into practice, thereby realizing the opportunity to perceive the hitherto theorized learning benefits of instruction designed as aesthetic experiences. Parrish (2005) defines aesthetic experience as "a quality that exists equally in the experiences of everyday life as in the fine arts, and the one that certainly applies to the learning experiences we design as instructional designers" (p. 3).

Enthusiasts of aesthetics in instructional design corroborate recent denouncements of the field's inattentiveness to aesthetics by contextualizing it amidst the importance and interest garnered in the past. Evidence of the dissemination of aesthetics in early Aristotelian philosophy throughout succeeding centuries survives in the consistent depiction of it as a genuine sensorial experience, including response to stimuli that is emotional, attitudinal, motivational, etc. Traditionally, the quality or goodness of an aesthetic experience relates to a proper sensorial understanding, considered beautiful for the fulfillment of its potential and actualization of its natural purpose. Numerous areas of study, including psychology, fine art, industrial art, graphic and instructional design, etc., depend upon the precepts set forth in Aristotelian aesthetics to achieve more comprehensive and gratifying experiences (Wilson 2005). Comprehension and implementation of these philosophical principles help bring about an emotional experience or enhanced understanding when an individual encounters or interacts with some object or stimulus that involves the senses.

It is also possible to trace the aesthetic experience in relation to education (Dewey 1934; Parrish 2005, 2009). Wilson (2005), directly, connects instructional designers to the task of designing not only educational materials but also to educational experiences. His regard for aesthetics as "the immediate experience of learning" prompts an appeal to instructional designers that they "move beyond purely technical issues of theory application and enter into the realm of aesthetics" (The Fourth Pillar section, para. 1). It is within this sphere of influence that instructional designers have the opportunity to transform "available resources to help learners have a particular kind of effective learning experience" (The Fourth Pillar section, para. 1).

2.4   The Role of Visual Aesthetics in a Design-Dense Definition of Instructional Design

The preceding qualifies aesthetics as a cultural and historical ideal that permeates many contemporary disciplines. This background information provides a basis upon which we may construct and expand an appreciation of aesthetics in the field. Aesthetics, as a design action, principle or ideal, endures and advances in literary, philosophical, theoretical, and pedagogical areas. The long and productive tradition of aesthetics in other subjects, some with aims and activities comparable to instructional design, substantiates the call of aesthetics' advocates in the field to investigate its place in instructional design. Such an investigation needs to proceed, scientifically, and requires a breakdown of specific components of the definition proposed for visual aesthetics so that scholars and instructional design practitioners may deliberate, discuss, and come to an understanding of what aspects require further discussion or debate, and what aspects form the substance and merit of consequent research.

There is a need to bring together the various pieces to define the experience of visual aesthetics in instructional design. A delineation of the concept by identifying relevant language of the field offers critics and researchers a starting point to investigate visual aesthetics in an empirical study. Five thematic categories stand out and encompass the definition of visual aesthetics we propose: learning experience and four design actions—contrast, alignment, repetition, and proximity (CARP). The CARP design actions provide broad categories that are among the most universally recognized visual actions that designers can use to affect instructional material. If the theories that build the definition of visual aesthetics in instructional design hold true to their promise, designers realize the aim of creating effective instruction when the design decisions they make lead to proper use of design actions (CARP) that stir learners' senses. The emotive sensory experience is the effect of visual aesthetics in enhanced instructional material.

The thematic categories of visual aesthetics and the language classified within do not form the basis for determining the attractiveness of some educational unit, nor do they indicate the extent to which some arbitrary standard of beauty may confirm an aesthetic instructional design. CARP principles pertain to designers' deliberate utilization of contrast, alignment, repetition, and proximity or secondary actions toward the design of an enhanced learning experience. Design actions are distinct from other principles and considerations in the instructional design process in intent and effect. Contrast, alignment, repetition, and proximity produce visible changes or movements that designers apply "to instructional information or to the elements of information assembled to convey an idea" (Lohr 2008, p. 80).

The four key design actions of CARP are not new to designers. Individually, they have long histories in the visual arts. Williams (2008) brought the application of contrast, alignment, repetition, and proximity as a group to the attention of designers in the first edition of *The Non-Designer's Design Book* in 1994. Lohr (2008) directed them specifically to visual learning experiences. Both Williams (2008) and Lohr (2008) provide the basis for considering CARP design actions as definitive expressions of visual aesthetics in the field. Quantifying successful and visually stimulating educational material, relating it to visual aesthetics, and demonstrating consequential enhanced learning experience calls for a straightforward approach.

2.5   Contrast

"Contrast is a tool the designer uses to draw attention to the important features of a message and make the figure/ground distinctions clear" (Lohr 2000b, p. 48). Contrast for an instructional designer is an action that results in the distinction of elements on a page or screen by causing certain aspects either to intensify to diminish visually.

Information designers refer to chart junk and data ink, as negative contrast, detractions rather than enhancements (Tufte 1990). Appropriate use of contrast, as part of visual aesthetics, includes instructional designers' decisions to employ type, font, size (weight), depth, thickness, texture, dimension, shadow, tone (brightness—light to dark value), line, shape and style (italics, bold, and underline), etc. so as to inspire effective learning experiences. Effective learning experiences enhanced by proper use of contrast may take place when contrast occurs for emphasis or the lack of emphasis. Emphasis pertains to the elements or design on a page or layout that contribute to a material's visibility and/or readability and to the formation of a focal point—the element that makes the most intense impression (Carter 2003). When put into action, correctly, the tool of bold directs the attention of a learner. The notion of figure/ground is another design concept that pertains to contrast for the potential effect it may have on making important information distinct from less important information. The figure "refers to an item that is essential and should be noticed or perceived immediately," while the ground relates to "items of less importance" and should not "interfere with the perception of what is important" (Lohr 2000b, p. 48). Emphasis, therefore, is part of visual aesthetics in that it refers to the overall effect of contrast design decisions that become design actions and lead to the learners' enhanced experience.

Value refers to degree of lightness and darkness. The value of a given design element may occur in relation to the contrast of shades, tints of color, or even grayness. Similarly, size shows contrast in terms of largeness or smallness in type, objects, etc. Use of color for the sake of contrast relates to designers' decisions in selecting harmonious/complementary or opposite colors and shades, that is, colors that are adjacent to one another on the color wheel or opposite one another. Other contrastive design tools identified by various instructional designers include color, type, shape, depth, and space. Color can draw attention to specific information. Tufte (1990) suggests that color is useful from a learning standpoint for representing size, measure, and degree/differentiation. Shape results in similar design consequences under the influence of appropriately used CARP design actions. Designers interested in creating material in consideration of visual aesthetics use a circular shape to represent a cyclical process and a line between two ideas to demonstrate a connection. Such design actions are examples of visual aesthetics in that they employ the design action, aptly, with a resulting learning experience that enhances communication of the ideas in terms of both significance and context (Lohr 2008).

Space is another tool that designers with an understanding of visual aesthetics employ to affect learning experience. Depending upon the consequence of its use, space is a design element that falls within any of the four categories of design actions of CARP. When a designer chunks information or other visual elements to create depth and weight, resulting in learners' understanding of greater or less importance, the action is contrast, alignment, and proximity.

The most fundamental denotation of contrast involves designers' decisions to focus the attention of learners to help their recognition of similar and dissimilar information. Contrast in this capacity is part of visual aesthetics when it occurs by representing elements that are different in such a way that they look distinct and when similar ideas or concepts are visually consistent.

Williams (2008) considers contrast to be one of the most important visual design actions since instructional designers can use it to direct learners' attention to certain elements on a page. There are a variety of tools, such as type, color, shape, size, space, and thickness of lines, that form part of visual aesthetics based on their contrastive results. Correct contrast contributes to the learning experience and is an aesthetic element when it enhances readability, directs learners' attention, makes content more interesting or important, emphasizes differences, and shows continuity among related elements. Contrast helps learners create meaning given its nature of revealing and comparing "fundamental opposites: dark/light, soft/hard, fast/slow" (Rutledge 2007, para. 9). Even alignment can create contrast. Designers may implement changes in alignment, bold, color, depth, direction, italics, kerning, movement, orientation, position, shade, shape, size, space, texture, type, value, etc. Designers can achieve an overall visual aesthetic with contrast when the effect adds variety without destroying unity. As Rutledge (2007) explains, "design is largely an exercise in creating or suggesting contrasts, which are used to define hierarchy, manipulate certain widely understood relationships, and exploit context to enhance or redefine those relationships … all in an effort to convey meaning" (Contrast section, para. 1).

2.6   Alignment

Alignment and repetition both commonly appear in document design literature (Mullet and Sano 1995). Researchers and critics describe alignment as a critical element in the creation of appropriately balanced interfaces and instructional materials (Lohr 2008; Tufte 1990). Lohr (2008) defines alignment as the design action of "lining elements up along an edge or imaginary path" (p. 72). Williams (2008) refers to alignment as the logical and purposeful placement of all items in a layout toward the creation of visual associations among the elements in a design. Among the more obvious terms that belong in the category of alignment are edge, center, horizontal, and vertical. Other terms in this category refer to the arrangement of elements, such as alleys, balance, grid, gutters, justification (left-aligned, ragged right, top, bottom, centered, wrapped, and fully justified), layout, margins, order, outline, overlap, placement, structure, tension, text block, and white space.

Tufte (1990) recommends that designers create appropriately balanced interfaces by maintaining simplicity in the design and complexity in the critical details. Balance is an important consideration of designers in creating materials that represent visual aesthetics. The action of creating balance requires that instructional designers go beyond simplicity in presentation. They must distribute the visual elements in any instructional material in such a way that neither bores learners nor overwhelms them. By modifying or transforming the balance among elements aligned along an edge or imaginary path to varying degrees of equal or unequal weight, designers enhance instructional material and affect learners' experience by managing their attention (Carter 2003). Balance, as a tool for alignment, is distinct from contrast in that its use affects direction of attention rather than difference in proportion or strength.

Grids are also useful tools of alignment that facilitate balance. Grids help designers keep complicated alignments, orderly. Howard Bear (2009) suggests that designers take advantage of the options for automatic alignment in computer software programs when the need to arrange objects or elements is uncomplicated. However, more complex arrangements or layouts may necessitate the use of guidelines and grids in order to achieve precise placement of elements.

The codification of alignment also includes "commodity, firmness and delight" (Hokanson et al. 2008, Balance section, para. 1). Commodity relates to "the structuring of the interface design" (Hokanson et al. 2008, Balance section, para. 6). Gutters can provide a certain commodity when used to "separate type and pictures from one another," giving a design "a repetitious visual element" (Saw 2000, para. 6). Firmness refers to the strength of a design based on implementation of balance through unity in design structure. Delight is the beauty of cohesion in instructional information. Closely related ideas are rhythm and movement. Carter (2003) identifies movement as principle of visual concern that relates to the flow or rhythm with which learners visually address elements and ideas on a page or layout. The placement or positioning of objects, justified (left, right, center, top, and bottom) elements or text along an imaginary line or path, visual connection of all elements on the page, overall balance within the visual field, and symmetry are other considerations for this category.

The main purposes of alignment, as a design action frequently employed by instructional designers, are unification and connectivity. An example of the use and consequential learning experience of alignment in action is aligning an object, icon, or text in a given instructional material with the edges of a background, thereby demonstrating conceptual connection via the invisible line created by proper alignment (Lohr 2008). Items in any lesson may be connected or made to appear connected, balanced, sequential, and even directional through designers' use of rulers, grids, guidelines, and simple alignment along vertical or horizontal planes of a screen or printed page.

2.7 Repetition

Repetition in an instructional design sense is "the reuse of elements or the use of similar elements" (Lohr 2008, p. 72). Instructional designers may repeat colors, fonts/type, images, shapes, alignments, patterns, etc. in order to achieve unity and harmony in an instructional design. Inclusive in the category definition for repetition, a third aspect of the CARP design action is the steps and procedures of an instructional material as demonstrated in terms of recurring typefaces, visuals, backgrounds, and borders. Designers may repeat many of the same principles and tools suitable in quantifying visual aesthetics in the categories of contrast and alignment, including: font, size, shape, color, justification, structure, type, graphic styles, line thicknesses, graphic concepts, textures, spatial relationships, icons, style sheets, imagery, theme, etc. Appropriate classification under the thematic category of repetition is contingent upon the understanding of repetition as consistency with which designers represent and utilize elements. Additionally, consistency and visual similarity are fundamental elements for repetition (Williams 2008). Decoration or decorative design elements fall within the category of repetition when designers make use of them in a consistent and repetitive way.

Visually, repetition can provide symmetry to an instructional unit. Symmetrical information, objects, and images are easier to recall than asymmetrical elements (Sweller 1999). Thus, in addition to lending to a pleasing appearance, there are obvious instructional benefits for using repetition in the design of instruction. Gestalt theory helps explain the mind's ability "to perceive organize wholes by understanding relations between otherwise unconnected physical stimuli" (Pearsal and Trumble 1996, p. 584).

Proponents of visual aesthetics in instructional design indicate that all CARP design actions, used properly, can enhance instructional material and create a learning experience. Lohr (2000b) recommends the use of repetition to create a theme in a design, using the same or alike images, fonts, colors, etc. throughout a design that prepares the learner to receive new information. Designers can help learners perceive connections or relationships among repeated and grouped items or information.

Designing instruction in such a way that makes it more memorable for learners through repetition in style, content, and dual coding is of interest to cognitive psychologists as well as instructional designers (Gyselinck et al. 2002). Baddeley's (1992) interest in understanding the processes involved in working memory draws attention to repetition as a cognitive support. Because designers must understand how learners process information in order to create the most effective instruction, the discoveries regarding working memory and its use in organizing, contrasting, comparing, etc. are of primary importance (Kirschner 2002).

CLT presents instructional designers with ways they may achieve cognitively sound instruction. The CARP design actions help keep the limits of working memory from negatively affecting learners. Material that presents information in a highly connected format by taking advantage of the design actions may greatly reduce learners' working memory load (Kirschner 2002). Researchers have shown that designing educational interfaces that utilize repetitious multimedia results in a reduction in confusion (Brunyé et al. 2007). According to Good and Brophy (1990), the development of cognitively sound instruction can be achieved by repeating elements or styles in an instructional material resulting in the creation of contiguity that helps learners connect associated information. However, it is appropriate to mention Moreno and Mayer's (1999) cognitive theory of multimedia learning as relevant to instructional design and the design action of repetition. Moreno and Mayer (1999) base their theory on ideas of constructivist learning, cognitive load theory, and dual coding theory. They demonstrated that learners benefit from receiving information from two sources, such as text and images, and provide good reason to investigate design actions for the learning experiences they inspire. Essentially, consistency in design (principles, actions, and tools) within a given instructional material provides learners with additional clues in understanding relationships by reinforcing themes, making connections, and knowing how to proceed or navigate through a lesson (Howard Bear 2009).

2.8   Proximity

Proximity, as a part of visual aesthetics, includes order (hierarchy), grouping (closeness of related items), physical integration (text and visual materials), and spatial depth (differentiations between foreground and background). Proximity is the "placement of elements close together or far apart" (Lohr 2008, p. 72). Space and shape are proximal terms based on the contrastive capability when their function and appearance affects the portrayal of organizational and hierarchical information and comprehension of information. There are at least four distinct types of proximity relationships relevant to visual aesthetics in instructional design: close edge, touch, overlap, and combine (Saw 2000).

Mayer (2001) addresses proximity in relation to research in the field of educational psychology, but it also finds support for design-based learning benefits according to Gestalt principles. Purposeful placement of subordinate text close to the main titles/headings it supports and through careful arrangement of associated elements help learners perceive that they belong to the same group (Lohr 2008). As previously mentioned regarding repetition and cognitive theory, the contiguity principle "holds that it is better to present corresponding words and pictures simultaneously rather than separately" (Kirschner 2002, p. 8). This research validates the split-attention hypothesis that working memory has distinct and additive visuo-spatial registers and auditory registers. This principle is significant for design actions that utilize proximity since studies show that spatially separated information increases extraneous cognitive load. Based on CLT, instructional designers can facilitate and increase learning by utilizing design actions that reduce cognitive load. Instructional designers may consider using certain media or activities as part of the instructional content in an effort to minimize extraneous cognitive load. They may, also, take into account the CARP design actions in order to lighten the germane cognitive load. Attention to design decisions that affect the germane cognitive load not only enhances learning but also results in task resources being used for schema acquisition and automation (Sorden 2005). CARP in a broad sense and proximity in particular attend to CLT by structuring instructional material so as not to overload working memory.

Proximity is distinct from alignment in that the spatial considerations involve a relationship between ideas or elements that is less implicit than the association created with alignment (Williams 2008). Bullets, lists, and numbers clearly convey order and hierarchy. However, other design elements, such as fonts and font size (headings and labels) become elements that indicate proximity when used to convey order, importance, and/or direction (Lohr 2008). Thanks in large part to the work of

Mayer (2001) and other cognitive theorists, Gestalt principles of figure/ground and hierarchy are among the most represented elements in instructional design. Another principle of Gestalt relates the idea of the whole design being greater than the sum of the elements that constitute the whole.

Certainly, there is value in considering the components of visual aesthetics beyond superficial implementation and appreciation. Researchers need to consider the whole concept of visual aesthetics, the details of the definition proposed in order to ascertain whether "aesthetics is design beyond done, the essence of the design process which continues after the completion of operational and technical requirements" (Hokanson et al. 2008, Methods section, para. 5). Just as art and culture are inextricably tied and demonstrate a meaningful relationship, the design actions of CARP (and other elements such as color and shape that fall within the four main categories) must be bound together in order to create a learning experience, an experience in the affective domain, that is deeply and personally engaging for the learner. It is unification of the four design actions that paves the way toward the perception of aesthetics as an experience that is a natural and essential element of the instructional design process.

2.9   Learning Experience

The review of the CARP design action shows that there is support in the literature of the field for the contribution of these visual components to learning experience. Contrast is significant for drawing attention, guiding, or directing interest, and "because the meaningful essence of anything is defined by its value, properties, or quality relative to something else" (Rutledge 2007, Contrast section, para. 1). Contrast, alignment, repetition, and proximity are present everywhere in nature and art. These design actions are "a part of everything we see, do, experience, and understand" (Rutledge 2007, In Closing section, para. 1). Like contrast, alignment is "something you see and use every day" (Saw 2000, p. 3). Yet, despite being an "obvious design concept," there are complexities to its effective use in learning environments (Saw 2000, p. 3). The placement of elements in an instructional material "determines the structure of our designs and affects the overall readability," as well as determining the effectiveness with which a "design communicates the desired message" (Howard Bear 2009, p. 1). Part of what facilitates the learners' ability to make appropriate connections is unity. Williams (2008) describes unity in relation to alignment as the link between different items. She credits alignment with the potentiality of affecting the learners' experience by facilitating the cognitive processes that connect and mentally organize information. While Williams (2008) and Lohr (2008) encourage designers' attention to proximity concerning similar elements, they agree that designers may help learners' experience, causing them to make connections between related ideas or to grasp a unifying concept by attending to the placement of items. The potential contribution of repetition to learning experience pertains to the simplification of the overall design so that learners may sense associations among elements in instructional material (Lohr 2008). Furthermore, cognitive psychology insists that repetition is a powerful design action, based on the potential advantages of using it to make instruction not only more pleasing but also more memorable (Brunyé et al. 2007).

Proximity, as a design consideration of visual aesthetics, produces both unity and variety. Proximity, as an aesthetic consideration, helps designers and learners manage and arrange (physically and mentally) instructional content. Appropriate use of proximity, also, results in a more structured and orderly presentation that may help reduce learners' confusion when faced with new ideas (Williams 2008). The act of proximity in design can influence learning experience profoundly, since close placement of related items provides a visually unified instructional material. Learners comprehend unified concepts better when the instructional designer takes actions that help them make visual connections between separated units (Williams 2008).

The heart of the definition of visual aesthetics in instructional design is the learning experience in the affective domain. Dewey (1934) and Bloom (1956) make known in an educational arena this important idea, now championed by modern scholars, such as Mayer and Moreno (1998). The connection between learning experience and the affective domain lies in the emotional nature of what Dewey (1938) and Bloom (1956) refer to as experience and emotion, respectively. Whether or not a learning experience is positive or negative is less important in instructional design than whether the instruction is effective due to the enhancement through the design actions implemented.

As referenced above in the discussion of Bloom's (1956) influential taxonomy, a characteristic of the affective domain is an enhancement in emotional areas, such as feelings and attitude. Parrish (2008) describes learning experience similarly to the description of the affective domain as inclusive of all emotionally charged internal and external reactions or attitudes in relation to instruction. Examples of attributes related to attitudes in the affective domain include but not limited to learners' interest/disinterest, cooperation/resistance, satisfaction/dissatisfaction, appreciation/disapproval, and enthusiasm/disappointment. Recently, researchers have argued on behalf of the affective domain, noting that research and scholarly emphasis has neglected its merit and suggesting that it is the "gateway to learning" (Pierre and Oughton 2007, p. 1). Instruction designed with the affective domain in mind can affect and influence learners' values, beliefs, and attitudes (Pierre and Oughton 2007). Attitude is an acquired/learned response. As such, it is possible to alter attitude in predictable ways depending upon the instructional technology utilized. Attitudes are "not directly observable in themselves, but they act to organize or provide direction to actions and behaviors that are observable" (Simonson and Maushak 2001, p. 985). Bednar and Levie (1993) base attitudes in learning upon four qualities: affective responses, cognitions, behaviors, and behavioral intentions. They may be positive or negative and vary in intensity. Attitudes (attention, motivation, and satisfaction) are a driving force behind actions and behaviors; therefore, their contribution is manifest through the observation of actions. Ultimately, there is significant interaction between the emotional, affective, and cognitive domains with regard to learning and instruction (Martin and Briggs 1986).

Affective learning falls within the category of learning experience in that it helps instill or fortify learning in an enhancing or engaging fashion. Affective learning experiences are experiential learning in that they correspond directly with our "attitudes and willingness to take part in new things, and ability to make decisions about how we operate and behave in a variety of circumstances" (Pierre and Oughton 2007, p. 1). Attitudes are like experiences; while they may not be directly observable, it is possible to identify behavioral references and manipulate them to the benefit of learning or performance improvement (Bednar and Levie 1993; Simonson and Maushak 2001). While it may be challenging, it is most definitely possible to perceive explicitly the contributions of certain design actions toward the enhancement of learners' attitudes and experiences regarding their instruction.

Critics who encourage research in the affective domain and practical integration in teaching and design of instructional material insist, "There is seldom cognition or psychomotor activity not accompanied by some emotion or affect" (Pierre and Oughton 2007, p. 2). They acknowledge the need to reorient the driving forces in the field "toward design work that engages learners more meaningfully and effectively" and to shift instructional designers' focus toward "creating experiences, as opposed to simply developing products or processes" (Hokanson et al. 2008, Methods section, para. 2).

The quantity of terminology for learning experience is greater than the terms associated with and identified for the four design actions of CARP due to the inclusion of terms related to subjective experiences, subjective responses, basic emotions, and descriptive adjectives appropriate for attitudes, values, opinions, beliefs, and assessments of worth. Learning experience is, essentially, the change, measure, or enhancement of learner attitude, opinion, or sentiment after having undergone some instructional encounter and regarding expected outcomes and/or concerns about interface or textual design. Therefore, "aesthetic experiences are integral, but they don't disregard what [a] person brings to them and where they might lead" (Parrish 2005, p. 8). It is a pervasive and persuasive quality to consider in any design. Defining and putting to use visual aesthetics in the field of instructional design necessitate understanding the learning experience. The learning experience is a product of the affective domain, created thanks to designers' harmonious implementation of "elements of interactive design which are focused primarily on enhancing and heightening the learner's experience, as opposed to elements that merely satisfy the pedagogical or technological needs of the instructional objective" (Hokanson et al. 2008, Methods Section, para. 4).

2.10 Conclusion

That is the design in instructional design. Visual aesthetics in the field is an observable quality of instruction based on the emotion and experience that result from implementation of certain design actions. The role of visual aesthetics, in part, depends upon a productive dialogue and empirical research. Design is at the core of many definitions of aesthetics. It is the creative approach of considering and combining outward appearance with content (subject matter) so that the complexity of the design is not visible in the simplicity of the product (Rand 1985). The philosophy on aesthetics as an experience from Aristotle to Dewey provides the basis for later scholars to envision aesthetics in relation to instructional design as a "pleasant experience" (Hokanson et al. 2008, Methods section, para. 6). Visual aesthetics is "at the core of design, intertwined with utility and usability" (Hokanson et al. 2008, Methods section, para. 6). Ideally, these experiences contribute meaningfully to the manner with which learners employ technology (Kirschner et al. 2004).

Consideration of aesthetics in instructional design requires designers to go beyond current pedagogical biases or technological constraints to keep in mind a new objective of engaging the learner to the greatest extent. The definition of visual aesthetics is a preliminary response to the challenge intimated by champions of aesthetics in instructional design toward innovative research (Hokanson et al. 2008; Parrish 2005, 2009). Such innovation may appear chaotic and challenging, but the potential benefits make the adventure worthwhile (Hokanson et al. 2008). To go beyond utility, it is necessary to explore how the field portrays aesthetics by examining the frequency and form with which scholars and researchers represent it. This article presents the basis for defining visual aesthetics as a learning experience that enhances the instructional design process by incorporating the CARP design actions. An accurate appraisal of the assumptions and the notions—the driving forces that shape the dogma of our field—insofar as they relate to visual aesthetics is a timely and appropriate endeavor. Instructional design is no longer a new discipline—after nearly 70 years, now is the time to reflect on established doctrine. Reflection and debate revitalizes fields of study and in our case, it may be necessary to encourage rather than marginalize the innovative and creative advocates of visual aesthetics in effective learning design. It may be time to declare a draw in the debate on form vs. function. Based on the historical, theoretical, and philosophical framework provided, there is good reason to consider that form and function are not mutually exclusive and that they may interconnect in the design of effective instruction.

There are strong and valid arguments for design as a deliberate and procedural method and as an artistic and creative enhancement. It is the instructional focus that distinguishes our field. During and following WWII, the meaning of design in the field of instructional design, most likely and understandably, reflected a planning and strategic connotation. While the design of modern training may or may not have life or death consequences that compel efficient production, most would agree that the field's emphasis on access has filled the sense of urgency that surrounded wartime training. Numerous technological advances since WWII have impacted the field significantly. A number of pedagogical theories and cognitive discoveries have also influenced the practice of instructional design. The relationship between the two main connotations of design, the strategic and the aesthetic, is similar in that both are subject to the instructional aspect of the field. If they are not mutually exclusive, it may be time to consider a symbiotic association of strategic and aesthetic concerns.

References

Design. (1989). *Oxford English dictionary* (2nd ed.). Oxford: Oxford University Press.

Anderson, L. W., Krathwohl, D. R., Airasian, P. W., Cruikshank, K. A., Mayer, R. E., Pintrich, P. R., & Wittrock, M. C. (2000). *Taxonomy for learning, teaching, and assessing: A Revision of Bloom's taxonomy of educational objectives*. Boston, MA: Allyn & Bacon.

Aristotle. (1996). *Poetics* (M. Heath, Trans.) London, England: Penguin Books.

Baddeley, A. D. (1992). Working memory. *Science, 255*, 556–559.

Baumgarten, A. G. (1954). *Reflections on poetry; Alexander Gottlieb Baumgarten's Meditationes philosophicae de nonnullis ad poema pertinentibus* (K. Aschenbrenner & W. B. Holther, Trans.). Berkeley, CA: University of California Press.

Bednar, A., & Levie, W. H. (1993). Attitude-change principles. In M. Fleming & W. H. Levie (Eds.), *Instructional message design: Principles from the behavioral and cognitive sciences* (pp. 283–304). Englewood Cliffs, NJ: Educational Technology.

Bloom, B. S. (1956). Taxonomy of educational objectives: The classification of educational goals. In *Handbook I, cognitive domain* (pp. 201–207). New York, NY: David McKay.

Brunyé, T. T., Taylor, H. A., & Rapp, D. N. (2007). Repetition and dual coding in procedural multimedia presentations. *Applied Cognitive Psychology, 22*, 877–895. Retrieved from, http://ase.tufts.edu/psychology/spacelab/pubs/Brunye_Taylor_Rapp_ACP_impress.pdf.

Bull, P. (2009). Cognitive constructivist theory of multimedia design: A theoretical analysis of instructional design for multimedia learning. In G. Siemens & C. Fulford (Eds.), *Proceedings of World Conference on Educational Multimedia, Hypermedia and Telecommunications* (pp. 735–740). Chesapeake, VA: Association for the Advancement of Computing in Education. Retrieved from http://www.editlib.org/p/31581.

Burke, E. (1968). *A philosophical enquiry into the origin of our ideas of the sublime and beautiful* (J. T. Boulton, Ed.). Notre Dame, IN: University of Notre Dame Press.

Carter, R. (2003). Teaching visual design principles for computer science students. *Computer Science Education, 13*(1), 67–90.

Clark, M. S., & Fiske, S. T. (1982). *Affect and cognition*. Hillsdale, NJ: Erlbaum.

Crawford, D. (1974). *Kant's aesthetic theory*. Madison, WI: University of Wisconsin Press.

Dewey, J. (1934). *Art as experience*. Carbondale, IL: Southern Illinois University Press.

Dewey, J. (1938). *Experience and education*. New York: Simon & Schuster.

Else, G. F. (1986). *Plato and Aristotle on poetry*. Chapel Hill, NC: University of North Carolina Press.

Good, T. L., & Brophy, J. E. (1990). *Educational psychology: A realistic approach* (4th ed.). White Plains, NY: Longman.

Gyselinck, V., Cornoldi, C., Dubois, V., De Beni, R., & Ehrlich, M. F. (2002). Visuospatial memory and phonological loop in learning from multimedia. *Applied Cognitive Psychology, 16*, 665–685.

Hegel, G. W. F. (1977). *Phenomenology of spirit (A. V. Miller, Trans.)*. Oxford, England: Clarendon.

Hokanson, B., Miller, C., & Hooper, S. (2008). Commodity, firmness, and delight: Four modes of instructional design practice. In L. Botturi (Ed.), *Handbook of visual languages for instructional design: Theories and practices* (pp. 1–17). Hershey, PA: IGI Global. Retrieved from http://hokanson.cdes.umn.edu/publications/vidl_FourModels021907.pdf.

Howard Bear, J. (2009). *Introduction to the principles of design: The big picture*. Retrieved from Scribd website: http://www.scribd.com/doc/25325758/Principles-of-Graphic-Design.

Huitt, W. (2003). Piaget's theory of cognitive development. *Educational Psychology Interactive*. Retrieved from Valdosta State University, GA, website: http://www.edpsycinteractive.org/topics/cogsys/piaget.html

Keller, J. M. (1997). Motivational design and multimedia: Beyond the novelty effect. *Strategic Human Resource Development Review, 1*(1), 188–203.

Kirschner, P. (2002). Cognitive load theory: Implications of cognitive load theory on the design of learning. *Learning and Instruction, 12*, 1–10.

Kirschner, P., Strijbos, J., Kreijns, K., & Beers, P. J. (2004). Designing electronic collaborative learning environments. *Educational Technology Research and Development, 52*(3), 47–66.

Lohr, L. (2000a). Designing the instructional interface. *Computers in Human Behavior, 16*(2), 161–182.

Lohr, L. (2000b). Three principles of perception for instructional interface design. *Educational Technology, 40*(1), 45–52.

Lohr, L. (2008). *Creating graphics for learning and performance: Lessons in visual literacy.* Upper Saddle River, NJ: Merrill.

Martin, B. L., & Briggs, L. J. (1986). *The cognitive and affective domains: Integration for instruction and research.* Englewood Cliffs, NJ: Educational Technology.

Mayer, R. (2001). *Multimedia learning.* Cambridge, England: Cambridge University Press.

Mayer, R., & Moreno, R. (1998). A cognitive theory of multimedia learning: Implications for design principles. Retrieved from University of New Mexico website: http://www.unm.edu/~moreno/PDFS/chi.pdf.

Moreno, R., & Mayer, R. E. (1999). Cognitive principles of multimedia learning: The role of modality and contiguity. *Journal of Educational Psychology, 91*(9), 358–368.

Mullet, K., & Sano, D. (1995). *Designing visual interfaces.* Englewood Cliffs, NJ: SunSoft.

Parrish, P. (2005). Embracing the aesthetics of instructional design. *Educational Technology Magazine, 45*(2). Retrieved from Comet, UCAR Community Programs website: http://homes.comet.ucar.edu/~pparrish/.

Parrish, P. (2008). Plotting a learning experience. In L. Botturi & S. T. Stubbs (Eds.), *Handbook of visual languages for instructional design: Theories and practices* (pp. 91–111). Hershey, PA: IGI Global.

Parrish, P. (2009). Aesthetic principles for instructional design. *Educational Technology Research and Development, 57*(4), 511–528.

Pass, F., Renkl, A., & Sweller, J. (2003). Cognitive load theory and instructional design: Recent developments. *Educational Psychologist, 38*(1), 1–4.

Pass, F., Renkl, A., & Sweller, J. (2004). Cognitive load theory: Instructional implications of the interaction between information structures and cognitive architecture. *Instructional Science, 32*, 1–8.

Pearsal, J. M., & Trumble, W. R. (Eds.). (1996). *Oxford encyclopedic English dictionary.* Oxford: Oxford University Press.

Pierre, E., & Oughton, J. (2007). The affective domain: Undiscovered country. *The College Quarterly, 10*(4), 1–7.

Rampley, M. (2000). *Nietzsche, aesthetics, and modernity.* Cambridge, England: Cambridge University Press.

Rand, P. (1985). *Paul Rand: A designer's art.* New Haven, CT: Yale University Press.

Reiser, R. A. (2001a). A history of instructional design and technology: Part I: A history of instructional media. *Educational Technology Research and Development, 49*(1), 53–64.

Reiser, R. A. (2001b). A history of instructional design and technology: Part II: A history of instructional technology. *Educational Technology Research and Development, 49*(2), 57–67.

Rutledge, A. (2007). *Contrast and meaning.* Retrieved April 24, 2007 from A List apart website: http://www.alistapart.com/articles/contrastandmeaning/.

Saw, J. T. (2000). *Design notes, Art 104: Design and composition.* Retrieved from http://daphne.palomar.edu/design/align.html.

Shellnut, B. (1998). *John Keller: A motivating influence in the field of instructional design.* Retrieved October 15, 1998 from Keller's ARCS Model of Motivational Design website: http://www.arcsmodel.com/pdf/Biographical%20Information.pdf.

Simonson, M., & Maushak, N. (2001). Instructional technology and attitude change. In D. H. Jonassen (Ed.), *Handbook of research for educational communications and technology* (pp. 984–1016). Mahway, NJ: Lawrence Erlbaum. Retrieved from http://www.aect.org/edtech/ed1/pdf/34.pdf.

Skinner, B. F. (1954). The science of learning and the art of teaching. *Harvard Educational Review, 24*, 86–97.

Sorden, S. D. (2005). A cognitive approach to instructional design for multimedia learning. *Informing Science Journal, 8*, 263–279.

Sweller, J. (1999). *Instructional design in technical areas.* Camberwell, VIC: Australian Council for Educational Research.

Talbot, D. (2011). The problem with design education. *Technology Review*. Retrieved April 6, 2011 from http://www.technologyreview.com/business/37216/.

Tufte, E. R. (1990). *Envisioning information.* Cheshire, CT: Graphics.

Williams, R. (2008). *The non-designer's design book.* Berkeley, CA: Peachpit.

Wilson, B. G. (2005). Broadening our foundation for instructional design: Four pillars of practice. *Educational Technology, 45*(2), 10–15. Retrieved from http://carbon.ucdenver.edu/~bwilson/Pillars.html.

Chapter 3
Improving Learning and Performance in Diverse Contexts: The Role and Importance of Theoretical Diversity

Ray K. Haynes and Yonjoo Cho

The department of Instructional Systems Technology (IST) at Indiana University evolved from an Audio-Visual Education program that offered Master's and doctoral degrees by 1946. This academic program grew out of a campus service program where courses were taught by Audio-Visual Center staff with academic qualifications. Increased support by the federal government for education in science and technology led to adoption of the name Educational Media in 1959; this name change reflected the term favored by the US government.

The Educational Media division at Indiana University adopted a *systems view* of education in 1969 and changed its name to IST (Molenda 2010). By 1972, the IST curriculum was organized around several emphasis areas: message design, instructional design/development, evaluation and integration, systems design and management, and diffusion/adoption—all elements in a *systems view* of education. These themes persist in the research-and-theory emphasis areas of IST today and converge in the research and teaching enterprise of improving learning and performance. Currently, IST's emphasis is manifest in our collective efforts towards advancing the field through theoretical diversity: "We improve human learning and performance in diverse contexts."

Theoretical diversity is highly valued in advancing an applied field such as instructional technology. The goal of applied research is the discovery of new relationships in the knowledge within the domain to which the research is applied, whereas the goal of basic research purports the discovery of knowledge and the production of new knowledge (Torraco 2004). An important role for theory development

This chapter was created by the individual contributions of Indiana University's current Department of Instructional Systems Technology faculty and the historical perspective offered by Michael Molenda, Associate Professor Emeritus.

R.K. Haynes (✉) • Y. Cho
Department of Instructional Systems Technology, Indiana University,
201 N. Rose Avenue, Bloomington, IN 47405, USA
e-mail: rkhaynes@indiana.edu

M. Orey et al. (eds.), *Educational Media and Technology Yearbook*, Educational Media and Technology Yearbook 37, DOI 10.1007/978-1-4614-4430-5_3, © Springer Science+Business Media New York 2013

in applied research, therefore, is to bridge gaps in knowledge that exist along the research continuum from basic to applied (Lynham 2002). For an applied field to grow and gain recognition, advancing science (i.e., theory and research) and technology (i.e., process and conceptual tools, design, and evaluation) is crucial (Merrill and Wilson 2007). Good theory is practical because it advances knowledge in a field, guides research toward crucial questions, and enlightens the profession through evidence-based practices (Van de Ven 1989).

To improve learning and performance in diverse contexts, we must adhere to sound research practices. Our continued effort towards pushing and collapsing boundaries through theoretical diversity has fostered innovation in IST since its inception. In this chapter, we describe some of the diverse theories that underlie current research in IST at Indiana University. Included are Reigeluth's theory of instruction, Frick's theory of totally integrated education (TIE), Boling's design research, Brush, Ottenbreit-Leftwich, and Glazewski's collaborative research on problem-based learning in teacher education, Bonk's extreme learning, Haynes' discussion of social cognitive theory (SCT) and developmental networks (DN) in mentoring and appreciative inquiry (AI) in change interventions, and Cho's use of citation network analysis in the field.

3.1   An Information-Age Theory of Instruction[1] (Charles Reigeluth)

Reigeluth has described the Information-Age paradigm of education as being based principally on active learning, intrinsic motivation, customization, attainment-based student progress, collaborative learning, and self-directed learning (Reigeluth 1994; Reigeluth and Garfinkle 1994). His research group at Indiana University is pursuing the belief that the Information-Age paradigm of education will utilize the synthesis of two lines of instructional theory: project-based instruction (defined broadly to include problem-based and inquiry-based instruction) and more traditional instructional theory based on constructivism, cognitivism, and behaviorism.

3.2   A Theory of Project-Based Instruction

There is much validated guidance for the design of the "project space," including universal and situational principles for the project space (see e.g., Barrows 1986; Barrows and Tamblyn 1980; Duffy and Raymer 2010; Savery 2009). They include guidance for selection of a good problem or project, formation of groups, facilitation

---

[1] Parts of this section are taken from Reigeluth (2012).

of higher learning by a tutor, use of authentic assessment, and use of thorough debriefing activities. Computer-based simulations are often highly effective for creating and supporting the project environment, and seem likely to predominate by 2020. STAR LEGACY (Schwartz et al. 1999) is a good early example of a computer-based simulation for the project space.

For a high-tech vision of the project space, imagine a small team of students working on an authentic project in a computer-based simulation. Soon they encounter a learning gap (knowledge, skills, understandings, values, attitudes, dispositions, etc.) that they need to fill to proceed with the project. Imagine that the students can "freeze" time and have a virtual mentor in the form of an avatar appear and provide customized tutoring, based on traditional (nonproject-based) instructional theory, to foster the needed learning individually for each student. Then, as soon as the students have mastered the necessary learning (just-in-time), they unfreeze time in the project space and continue working on the project.

3.3 Traditional Instructional Theory

Selection of instructional strategies in the instructional space is primarily based on the type of learning (the ends of instruction) involved (see Unit 3 in Reigeluth and Carr-Chellman 2009). For *memorization*, drill and practice are most effective (Salisbury 1990), including chunking, repetition, prompting, and mnemonics. For *application* (skills), tutorials with generality, examples, practice, and immediate feedback are most effective (Merrill 1983; Romiszowski 2009). For *conceptual understanding*, connecting new concepts to existing concepts in a student's cognitive structures requires the use of such methods as analogies, context (advance organizers), comparison and contrast, analysis of parts and kinds, and various other techniques based on the dimensions of understanding required (Reigeluth 1983). For *theoretical understanding*, causal relationships are best learned through exploring causes (explanation), effects (prediction), and solutions (problem solving); and natural processes are best learned through description of the sequence of events in the natural process (Reigeluth and Schwartz 1989).

These sorts of instructional strategies have been well researched for their effectiveness, efficiency, and appeal. And they are often best implemented through computer-based tutorials, simulations, and games in the "instructional overlay." Each student continues to practice until she or he reaches the standard of mastery for the learning. Upon reaching the standard, the student returns to the project space where time is unfrozen, to apply what has been learned to the project and continue working on it until the next learning gap is encountered, and this learning–doing cycle is repeated.

Reigeluth's research team is currently working on the design of a new kind of Learning Management System, called a Personalized Integrated Educational System, that offers tools for record keeping, planning, instruction, and assessment for student learning (Reigeluth et al. 2008).

3.4 TIE Theory (Theodore Frick)

When we learn something new, we are able to connect it to what we already know. The desired outcome of successful learning attempts is to form appropriate mental schemata. Such mental structures allow us to act intelligently as we go through life and carry out complex tasks (cf. Kandel 1989, 2001; Squire and Kandel 1999; van Merriënboer and Kirschner 2007).

Frick's recently developed theory of TIE predicts that mental structures formed by learners are expected to be stronger when *knowing-that-one*, *knowing-how*, and *knowing-that* are integrated with learner *emotions* and *intentions*. Such whole, completely connected mental structures are expected to be less vulnerable to forgetting.

Socrates identified "will" or "intent" as a part of mind, as distinguished from the intellect and emotion (cf., *The Republic of Plato* (Cornford 1945)). Greenspan and Benderly (1997) have noted that since the ancient Greek philosophers, the rational or cognitive aspect of mind has often been viewed as developing separately from emotion. They argue that this view has blinded us to the role of emotion in how we organize what we have learned: "In fact, emotions, not cognitive stimulation, serve as the mind's primary architect" (p. 1). They identify the importance of emotion during human experience: "… each sensation … also gives rise to an affect or emotion … . It is this *dual coding* of experience that is the key to understanding how emotions organize intellectual capacities … " (p. 18). In a similar vein, Goleman (2011) articulates this idea from the framework of 'emotional intelligence' (see Fig. 3.1).

Given the importance of emotion and intention in learning, it is discouraging that the majority of US high school students are bored every day in school. Yazzie-Mintz (2007) summarizes results from a survey of 81,499 students in 110 high schools across 26 US states. Approximately two out of three students said that they were bored in class every day. When asked why they were bored, the top reasons were that learning materials were uninteresting, irrelevant, and not challenging enough.

If emotion is the architect of mental structures, as mounting evidence appears to support (cf., Greenspan and Shanker 2004), then it follows that many students are likely to be developing ill-formed mental schema for the subject matter they are expected to learn—mental structures which are weakened or disconnected from existing mental structures due to feelings of meaninglessness, irrelevance, boredom, and even disdain with respect to the content of their education.

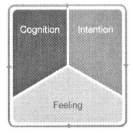

Fig. 3.1 Schema for integration of thinking, willing, and feeling. (Graphic by Colin Gray)

Ideally, students should instead be developing mental structures that are strengthened through real purpose in life and positive emotion. If so, then those positive feelings and the relevant purpose of learning activities will facilitate organization of mental structures that constitute long-term memory. Metaphorically speaking, once we have a solidly built house on a good foundation, then it is easier to add or remodel a room. We build on what is already there in terms of the existing structure.

To focus only on student cognitive development at the expense of emotion will result in weaker or disconnected mental schemata. Such schemata will lack wholeness and hence would be poorly integrated into existing mental structures, much like an uninvited guest at a party who stands in the corner of the room and does not interact with other invited guests.

TIE theory builds on seminal work of John Dewey, Charles Sanders Peirce, Elizabeth Steiner, George Maccia, Stanley Greenspan, Kenneth Thompson, Myrna Estep, David Merrill, and Jeroen van Merriënboer. Implications from TIE theory include a strategy for reconceptualization of curriculum that is based on authentic learning tasks selected from existing culture. These tasks are predicted to help students integrate nine kinds of knowing with emotions and intentions: recognitive, acquaintive, appreciative, imitative, adaptive, creative, instantial, relational, and criterial (cf. Maccia 1988; Frick 1997).

For further explanation see: http://educology.indiana.edu/Frick/TIEtheory.pdf.

3.5 Design Knowledge and Design Pedagogy (Elizabeth Boling)

Design (the entire enterprise, under which making strategy decisions is subsumed) uses and creates generalized knowledge in the scientific sense. Generalized knowledge in design falls into two categories: first, knowledge about people, materials, and phenomenon that provide potentially fruitful avenues of design action and that warn designers off directions not likely to be productive (Krippendorf 2006); and second, knowledge about how design is carried out, what designers do, how they think, and other aspects of designing itself (Cross 2007). The first category includes what are called in the instructional design (ID) field "prescriptive theories" (Reigeluth and Carr-Chellman 2009), or principles (Silber 2007). These are necessary for effective design of instruction, whether employed explicitly or absorbed and used implicitly by designers, but they are not sufficient to instantiate individual designs, the "ultimate particular" which designs must become in order to exist as more than ideas (Stolterman 2008), and the extent to which any but the most broad of these can be generalized is arguable (Lawson 2005). This category also includes bodies of knowledge drawn upon across fields of design, including ID, psychology, sociology, physiology, and others that describe human characteristics, abilities, limitations, and universally or locally shared behaviors. The most pervasive form of the second category in this field is process knowledge expressed as models of designing (Smith and Boling 2009), whereas in other fields of design extensive empirical studies of designers in the act of designing are carried out using rigorous methods amenable to the production of generalized findings (see for example: Cross and Christiaans 1997; Goldschmidt 1991; Lawson 2004) and treat the issue of research on design as a serious area of study (Margolin 2010).

Research on designing shows that at least two other forms of knowledge are required to move beyond the choice of an instructional strategy and effect an instantiation of that strategy (Nelson and Stolterman 2003; Rowe 1987; Vincenti 1990). Precedent, the experienced record of designs and design moves, is a dispersed form of knowledge that is not complete until it is used (Boling 2010; Lawson 2004). Design judgment, the ability to recognize and discriminate patterns and properties, and to assess their appropriateness, in a specialized area of action, is a form of knowledge recreated anew in each individual who develops it and not amenable to explicit transfer from one individual to another (Nelson and Stolterman 2003). Developing expertise in designing requires prolonged and varied exposure to precedent (Lawson and Dorst 2009), reflection in action (Schön 1983), and individual development of the human instrument (Boling and Smith 2010; Boling 2008).

3.6   Using Technology to Support Problem-Based Learning in Teacher Education (Thomas Brush, Anne Ottenbreit-Leftwich and Krista Glazewski)

Problem-based learning (PBL) represents a widely recommended best practice in which effective technology integration can make a tangible difference. PBL provides learners with authentic ill-structured problems without a clear solution path. Using this student-centered approach, the teacher guides students through the problem-solving process (Barrows 2002). Several meta-analyses have shown PBL to be more effective than traditional instruction in increased student achievement and engagement (Ravitz 2009; Strobel and van Barneveld 2009; Walker and Leary 2009). Strobel and van Barneveld (2009) found that "PBL was superior when it comes to long-term retention, skill development and satisfaction of students and teachers, while traditional approaches were more effective for short-term retention as measured by standardized board exams" (p. 44).

New technology tools have the capacity to make the implementation of PBL in both university and K-12 classrooms much more effective. Collaboration is a large component of PBL, and many "Web 2.0" technology tools have recently been leveraged to facilitate collaboration among learners. For example, wikis can facilitate PBL implementation and practice by providing an environment in which instructors and students can collaborative, discuss, and reflect. In addition, students can take full advantage of linking to research, images, and videos to support their solutions. One vocational teacher education course used wikis to facilitate PBL; preservice teachers were provided a case and used a template wiki page that included guidance for each section that needed to be addressed (e.g., design considerations, recommendations, record of meetings, references) (Robertson 2008). Other teacher education programs have used online resources such as electronic resources, threaded discussion, PBL scenarios, videoconferencing, and distance tutorial support to facilitate PBL (Wheeler et al. 2005).

Based on the demonstrated effectiveness of PBL, more K-12 school models are implementing technology-enhanced PBL to target twenty-first century skills. For example, the "New Tech High" model currently in place in high schools across the country uses technology-enhanced PBL as a foundation. Some teacher education programs have attempted to address the need for teachers prepared to meet the instructional needs of these new school models by incorporating more PBL into their courses. A study of one program that introduced technology integration in a PBL environment found that preservice teachers' intentions to use technology for PBL increased (Park and Ertmer 2008). In another study, 96 preservice teachers collaborated on PBL lessons that integrated technology (So and Kim 2009). Results indicated that the preservice teachers demonstrated increased knowledge of PBL theory and practice.

Unfortunately, many teacher education programs still approach preservice classrooms with conventional practices (Feiman-Nemser 2008; Kiggins and Cambourne 2007), and few preservice teachers have clear conceptions of designing and implementing technology-enhanced PBL instruction (So and Kim 2009). However, more teacher education programs are beginning to recognize the potential for PBL and the need for support in order to integrate PBL (Murray-Harvey and Slee 2000; Edwards and Hammer 2006). In order for PBL to be successfully adopted by preservice teachers, teacher education faculties need to be comfortable with technology-enhanced PBL (Vannatta and Beyerbach 2001). Our current research efforts are focused on both identifying and developing web-based tools and resources that teacher educators and preservice teachers at institutions across the nation can utilize to develop effective PBL curricula. This happens in tandem with fostering opportunities for teacher educators to collaborate with experts in the integration of Web 2.0 tools and PBL strategies to use these resources and implement curriculum reform in their own teacher education programs. To learn more about our work, please visit http://education.indiana.edu/pbltech.

3.7   Extreme Learning (Curtis Bonk)

For the past two decades, Curt Bonk has been exploring online and blended learning as well as emerging technology tools for learning and collaboration. Recently, this research has involved aspects of the Web 2.0 and participatory e-learning such as blogging in China and Korea (Kang et al. in press), the creation and use of shared online video such as found in YouTube (Bonk, in press), TeacherTube, Academic Earth, and dozens of other places, and wikis in education. His wiki research has stretched from national surveys of elementary teacher use of wikis to the creation of cross-institutional wikibooks in higher education (Bonk et al. 2009) to the endorsement and use of wikis in corporate training environments (Lee and Bonk 2010) to the challenges, frustrations, and opportunities of wikibooks in the world community (Lin et al., in press). As detailed below, this research has both widened and narrowed during the past couple of years.

Using his recent book, *The World Is Open: How Web Technology Is Revolutionizing Education* (Bonk 2009b), as a base, his research camp is now focused on aspects of open education (Iiyoshi and Kumar 2008). In particular, they have coined a new term, "extreme learning," to represent their main focus. Akin to nontraditional or informal learning, extreme learning entails how people learn or teach with technology in unusual ways. It encompasses any technology-based learning not traditionally included in schools, universities, or corporate and military training centers. Think "not school." Extreme types of learning occur in or from planes, trains, boats, mountain tops, islands, icebergs, space stations, parks, monuments, war zones, religious missions, retreats, vacation resorts, submarines, camps, research stations (e.g., Antarctica), outdoor classrooms, grocery stores, museums, zoos, conferences, institutes, and summits, cafes, bookstores, nursing homes, hospital beds, shopping malls, virtual worlds, online communities or groups, webinars, webcam experiences, text messaging, mobile devices, virtual schools, open educational resources and open courseware, open universities, free universities or courses, etc. As such a list illustrates, humans not only learn in classrooms, we learn far beyond them such as on a ship at sea, in the air, and when in remote lands (Bonk 2009a). Each place, tool, and resource listed above offers countless people new hope for an education; often information rich, free, and on-demand.

As noted in Bonk's *World is Open* book, anyone can now learn anything from anyone else at any time. The above listing of environments for such learning is just a starting point. Bonk's research team is chronicling a wide array of extreme learning Web resources from which to learn. As the list has grown to over 200 such online resources, programs, and initiatives, four subteams have developed; namely (1) virtual education, (2) online language education, (3) adventure learning and environment education (Doering 2006; Doering and Veletsianos 2008), and (4) social change and global education. These four subteams are currently conducting an evaluation of these 200+ Websites using an eight-part coding scheme. This scheme includes the following criteria: (1) Content richness; (2) Functionality of technology; (3) Extent of technology integration; (4) Novelty of technology (Coolness Factor #1); (5) Uniqueness of environment/learning (Coolness factor #2); (6) Potential for learning; (7) Potential for life changing; and (8) Scalability of audience.

As part of these efforts, the Extreme Team is attempting to record "empowerment moments" wherein people's lives, and, in effect, their identities, were changed due to their use of Web-based technology. The team intends to document human development and growth as it pertains to life-changing moments involving learning technology. The world is open for learning and it is time to collect human interest stories that prove it and that can serve an inspiration for others.

3.8   Social Cognitive Theory, Developmental Networks, and Appreciative Inquiry (Ray Haynes)

Social cognitive theory (SCT) and developmental networks (DN) can be used to understand and structure mentoring in work organizations. The appreciative inquiry (AI) perspective can be useful in structuring and evaluating change interventions. There are numerous definitions of mentoring however, a central defining feature of organizational mentoring is that it is an interpersonal developmental relationship embedded in the career context (Higgins and Kram 2007). SCT is an extension of social learning theory (SLT) and it suggests that human functioning (behavior) including performance (required behavior) is not driven by internal forces or external stimuli. Rather, it is shaped by triadic reciprocality that involves: (a) personal factors, (b) external environmental factors, and (c) overt behavior (cf., Bandura 1986). SCT is considered a core theory in mentoring research because it takes a cognitive–constructivist approach to the mentoring dimension of career development. Cognition is concerned with thought processes and constructivists view people as proactive shapers of the environment rather than mere responders to it (Lent and Brown 1996). Triadic reciprocality drives individual functioning; thus, it plays a central role in determining individual, group, and ultimately organization performance. The individual factors in the triad operate interactively as determinants of each other; reciprocal determinism (Bandura 1986).

Many scholars and thought leaders in the areas of human resource development (HRD), organizational development (OD), and human performance technology (HPT) align in the view that personal factors and the environment interact to create a byproduct that is behavior or performance. This is evident in Lewin's field theory equation $B = F\ (P, E)$ which asserts that behavior is a function of an interaction between the person and the environment (see, Lewin 1998). Further, Gilbert's notion of worthy performance, at its core, includes the person—environment interaction (cf., Gilbert 1978). SCT acknowledges this interaction but goes further by suggesting that behavior is also a codeterminant of the person environment interaction (Lent et al. 1994). SCT enables a paradigm shift from the stimulus–response view of learning and individual behavior to a cognitive–constructivist view of learning and individual behavior. Further, SCT offers a broad explanatory base for adult learning (Merriam and Caffarella 1999) and HRD subsets such as workplace learning, employee development, and organizational socialization (Gibson 2004).

As a core theory, SCT provides an explanatory base for mentoring. However, recent work in theory building has advanced thinking and research on mentoring in the career context. The construct of developmental networks (DNs) is now a prevailing perspective in mentoring research (Molloy 2005). DNs have come of age due to changes in the contractual nature of work, technological innovation, the impermanence of organizational structure, and workforce diversity (Higgins and Kram 2001). The DN perspective hinges on two core concepts: network diversity and developmental relationship strength. These are core concepts in social network theory and research (Brass 1995, Ibarra 1993 as cited in Higgins and Kram 2001).

DNs consist of a set of people (mentors) whom the protégé describes as actively interested and takes action to advance the protégés career by providing developmental assistance consisting of career and psychosocial support. Molloy (2005) describes (DNs) as concurrent dyadic developmental relationships. Researchers can draw on SCT and the DN perspective to produce research and contribute to theory building germane to mentoring at work (see Haynes and Ghosh 2008; Haynes and Petrosko 2009; Ghosh et al. 2010). The next logical extension of this work is to apply the DN perspective in K-12 and higher education settings.

In addition to SCT and the DN perspective, appreciative inquiry theory (AI) can be used in evaluating performance interventions as well as developing them (see Haynes and Ghosh 2011). AI is a positive approach to effect change in social systems; it can be viewed as a form of action research (Cooperrrider and Srivastva 1987; Marques et al. 2011). One of the core assumptions in AI is the perspective that organizations have positive aspects about them even when they are malfunctioning. The key is to drive change and or evaluate it by focusing first on those positive aspects.

3.9 The Use of Citation Network Analysis for Interdisciplinary Collaboration (Yonjoo Cho)

Previous reviews published in *Educational Technology Research and Development* (*ETR&D*) have revealed the rankings of individual authors and institutions in instructional technology (IT) but have not provided qualitative details on relations and networks of scholars (Anglin and Towers 1992; Gall et al. 2010; Hannafin 1991; Klein 1997; Ku 2009). Citation network analysis is an answer that solves limitations of previous reviews in the field and opens possibilities for interdisciplinary collaboration.

A distinctive feature of citation network analysis is that it has a theoretical framework borrowed from social network analysis (Jo et al. 2009). Social network analysis is a methodology for examining structures among actors, groups, and organizations, with some patterns of interaction or ties between them (Borgatti et al. 2009; Hatala 2006). Analysis of a citation network built among publications allows us to have a better grasp of how a scholarly community has evolved in the field (Fernandez-Alles and Ramos-Rodríguez 2009; Jo et al. 2009). Citation network analysis has been used in IT cognate fields such as HPT (Cho et al. 2011) and HRD (Jo et al. 2009) as well as in IT itself (Cho et al. in press).

For example, Cho and colleagues (in press) identified the research trends in IT by analyzing the citation network of 803 articles published in *ETR&D* from 1989 to 2011. On the basis of the citation network analysis, Cho et al. (in press) identified five key themes of IT. The five themes were not totally separate and distinctive but overlapped in many respects compared to those of HPT (Cho et al. 2011) and HRD (Jo et al. 2009) (see Table 3.1).

Table 3.1 Comparison of key themes of IT, HPT, and HRD

Field	IT	HPT	HRD
Key research themes	Instructional design	Performance	Learning and performance
	Learning environments	Instructional design	Theory building
	The role of technology	Performance support	Training transfer
	IT research	Organization/workplace	
	Psychological foundations	Transfer of training	

The results of thematic analysis in Cho et al.'s (in press) study are in contrast with those of HRD discovered by Jo et al.'s (2009) citation network analysis. The themes of HRD appear to be more theoretical and distant from immediate needs of practices than those of IT. In other words, the IT field is a more narrowly focused field than HRD. Instructional design, however, has been recognized as an important intervention for planning processes and practice of HRD and has also played a critical role in decision-making on training strategies and in the instructional nature of the field (Hardré 2003; Korth 1997).

ID was also among the five key themes in the HPT field, indicating that IT and HPT are closely related (Cho et al. 2011). The two fields, however, had different emphases in ID research. The IT field has produced studies on conceptual frameworks (e.g., Jonassen and Rohrer-Murphy 1999), instructional design models (e.g., Jonassen 1997), and designing learning environments (e.g., Hannafin et al. 1997), whereas HPT's studies emphasized instructional designers' practices and activities from the lens of experts and novices (e.g., Rowland 1992). This is presumably due to each field's emphasis on theory or practice and because HPT claims to be a "field of practice" (Foshay et al. 1999, p. 896).

In Cho et al.'s (in press) study, the subfields (five themes) of the *ETR&D* network were less distinctive and, rather, interrelated in direct or indirect ways. One possible reason is that conceptual frameworks in IT research were mostly borrowed from psychology (Weinstein and Shuck 2011). Although the IT field has always claimed its interdisciplinary nature that is influenced by diverse fields such as psychology, communication, and computer science, Cho et al. (in press) did not identify evidence of the field's interdisciplinary efforts for expanding the scope of IT research, except with psychology. As the unit of analysis in IT research becomes larger and it becomes more complex to investigate learning environments in diverse organizational settings, multiple perspectives and innovative approaches to IT research are called for in the field. Theory development efforts as in HRD will help advance the field by providing more explanatory power and insights to existing IT research (Cho and Egan 2009; Cho and Yoon 2010).

The use of citation network analysis has expanded the limited landscape of IT, HPT, and HRD. Identifying whose scholarly works are the most influential and what relationships are the most impactful in the field is definitely a timely intellectual discourse that we need to possess in order to make the scholarly community strong and sustainable, as well as to expand our interdisciplinary efforts to advance the field.

3.10   Conclusion

The foregoing discussions of the theories undergirding current research in IST provide the department's history, its current state, and future directions in improving learning and performance in diverse contexts. Theoretical diversity plays a central role in IST's enterprise of improving learning and performance. The lack of theory makes for great difficulty when attempting to solve problems in applied or practical settings. Kurt Lewin's statement "There is nothing so practical as a good theory." (see, Marrow 1969) underscores the importance of theoretical grounding in design, instruction, learning, and performance. Brevity precludes elaboration of the theoretical range in IST; however, it is necessary to point out that the *systems view* still prevails as an orienting and feedback source. Consequently, as IST at Indiana University produces outputs in the form of teaching students, research, and service it does so cognizant of the inextricable link between theory, research, and application within the context of existing systems. It is an exciting time for IST. We are engaged in the timely and timeless pursuit of improving learning and performance in diverse contexts. What this means for students is that they can find a place within our diverse theoretical range. This theoretical diversity enables faculty and students to work across disciplines to improve design, instruction, learning, and performance. Our interdisciplinary collaboration facilitates theory building, which in turn begets theoretical diversity.

References

Anglin, G. J., & Towers, R. L. (1992). Reference citations in selected instructional design and technology journals, 1985–1990. *ETR&D, 40*(1), 40–43.

Bandura, A. (1986). *Social foundations of thought and action: A social cognitive theory.* Englewood Cliffs, NJ: Prentice Hall.

Barrows, H. S. (1986). A taxonomy of problem-based learning methods. *Medical Education, 20*(6), 481–486.

Barrows, H. S. (2002). Is it Truly Possible to Have Such a Thing as dPBL? *Distance Education, 23*(1), 119–122.

Barrows, H. S., & Tamblyn, R. M. (1980). *Problem-based learning: An approach to medical education.* New York: Springer.

Boling, E. (2008, October). *Design is not systematic: Alternative perspectives on design—Designer as human instrument.* Panel session organized by David Jonassen at Association for Educational Communications and Technology, Orlando, FL.

Boling, E. (2010). *The need for design cases: Disseminating design knowledge. International Journal of Designs for Learning, 1*(1). http://www.scholarworks.iu.edu/journals/index.php/ijdl/article/view/919.

Boling, E., & Smith, K. M. (2010, July 7–9). Intensive studio experience in a non-studio masters program: Student activities and thinking across levels of design. Design Research Society: Montreal, QC.

Bonk, C. J. (2009a). The wide open learning world: Sea, land, and ice views. *Association for Learning Technology (ALT) Online Newsletter*, Issue 17. Retrieved September 22, 2011, from http://archive.alt.ac.uk/newsletter.alt.ac.uk/newsletter.alt.ac.uk/1h7kpy8fa5s.html.

Bonk, C. J. (2009b). *The world is open: How Web technology is revolutionizing education*. San Francisco: Jossey-Bass.

Bonk, C. J. (in press). YouTube anchors and enders: The use of shared online video content as a macrocontext for learning. *Asia-Pacific Collaborative Education Journal, 7*(1).

Bonk, C. J., Lee, M. M., Kim, N., & Lin, M.-F. (2009). The tensions of transformation in three cross-institutional wikibook projects. *The Internet and Higher Education, 12*(3–4), 126–135.

Borgatti, S. P., Mehra, A., Brass, D. J., & Labianca, G. (2009). Network analysis in the social sciences. *Science, 323*, 892–895.

Cho, Y., & Egan, T. M. (2009). Action learning research: A systematic review and conceptual framework. *Human Resource Development Review, 8*, 431–462.

Cho, Y., & Yoon, S. W. (2010). Theory development and convergence of human resource fields: Implications for human performance technology. *Performance Improvement Quarterly, 23*(3), 39–56.

Cho, Y., Jo, S. J., Park, S., Kang, I., & Chen, Z. (2011). The current state of human performance technology: A citation network analysis of *Performance Improvement Quarterly*, 1988–2010. *Performance Improvement Quarterly, 24*(1), 69–95.

Cho, Y., Park, S., Jo, S. J., & Suh, S. (in press). The landscape of educational technology viewed from the ETR&D journal. *British Journal of Educational Technology, 43*(6).

Cooperrrider, D. L., & Srivastva, S. (1987). Appreciative inquiry in organization life. In R. Woodman & W. Pasmore (Eds.), *Research in organization change and development* (Vol. 1, pp. 129–169). Greenwich, CT: JAI.

Cornford, F. M. (Transl, 1945). *The Republic of Plato*. New York: Oxford University Press.

Cross, N. (2007). *Designerly ways of knowing*. London: Springer.

Cross, N., & Christiaans, H. (Eds.). (1997). *Analysing design activity*. Chichester, UK: John Wiley & Sons.

Doering, A. (2006). Adventure learning: Transformative hybrid online education. *Distance Education, 27*(2), 197–215.

Doering, A., & Veletsianos, G. (2008). Hybrid online education: Identifying integration models using adventure learning. *Journal of Research on Technology in Education, 41*(1), 23–41.

Duffy, T. M., & Raymer, P. L. (2010). A practical guide and a constructivist rationale for inquiry based learning. *Educational Technology, 50*(4), 3–15.

Edwards, S., & Hammer, M. (2006). Laura's story: Using problem based learning in early childhood and primary teacher education. *Teaching and Teacher Educator, 22*(4), 465–477.

Feiman-Nemser, S. (2008). From preparation to practice: Designing a continuum to strengthen and sustain teaching. *Teachers College Record, 103*(6), 1013–1055.

Fernandez-Alles, M., & Ramos-Rodríguez, A. (2009). Intellectual structure of human resource management research: A bibliometric analysis of the journal *Human Resource Management*, 1985–2005. *Journal of the American Society for Information Science and Technology, 60*(1), 161–175.

Foshay, W. R., Moller, L., Schwen, T. M., Kalman, H. K., & Haney, D. S. (1999). Research in human performance technology. In H. D. Stolovitch & E. I. Keeps (Eds.), *Handbook of human performance technology* (2nd ed., pp. 895–915). San Francisco: Jossey-Bass Pfeffer.

Frick, T. W. (1997). Artificially intelligent tutoring systems: What computers can and can't know. *Journal of Educational Computing Research, 16*(2), 107–124.

Gall, J. E., Ku, H. Y., Gurney, K., Tseng, H. W., Yeh, H. T., & Chen, Q. (2010). Citations of *ETR&D* and related journals, 1990–2004. *ETR&D, 58*(3), 343–351.

Ghosh, R., Haynes, R. K., & Kram, K. E. (2010). Developmental networks as holding environments for growing leaders: An adult development perspective. *Academy of Management Annual Meeting Proceedings, USA*, pp. 1–6. Doi: 10.5465/AMBPP.2010.54500728.

Gibson, S. K. (2004). Social learning (cognitive) theory and Implications for human resource development. *Advances in Developing Human Resources, 6*, 204–210.

Gilbert, T. F. (1978). *Human competence: Engineering worthy performance*. New York: McGraw-Hill.

Goldschmidt, G. (1991). The dialectics of sketching. *Creativity Research Journal, 4*(1), 123–143.

Goleman, D. (2011). *The brain and emotional intelligence: New insights* (Kindleth ed.). Northhampton, MA: More Than Sound LLC.

Greenspan, S. I., & Benderly, B. L. (1997). *The growth of the mind and the endangered origins of intelligence.* Reading, MA: Addison-Wesley.

Greenspan, S. I., & Shanker, S. G. (2004). *The first idea: How symbols, language, and intelligence evolved from our primate ancestors to modern humans.* Cambridge, MA: Da Capo (Kindle edition).

Hannafin, K. M. (1991). An analysis of the scholarly productivity of instructional technology faculty. *ETR&D, 39*(2), 39–42.

Hannafin, M. J., Hannafin, K. M., Land, S. M., & Oliver, K. (1997). Grounded practice and the design of constructivist learning environments. *ETR&D, 45*(3), 101–117.

Hardré, P. L. (2003). Beyond two decades of motivation: A review of the research and practice in instructional design and human performance technology. *Human Resource Development Review, 2*(1), 54–81.

Hatala, J. P. (2006). Social network analysis in human resource development. *Human Resource Development Review, 5*(1), 45–71.

Haynes, R. K., & Ghosh, R. (2008). Mentoring and succession management: An evaluative approach to the strategic collaboration model. *Review of Business, 28,* 3–12.

Haynes, R. K., & Petrosko, J. M. (2009). An investigation of mentoring and socialization among law faculty. *Mentoring & Tutoring: Partnership in Learning, 17,* 41–52.

Haynes, R. K., & Ghosh, R. (2011). Dialogue Circle: An exercise in Gendered introspection and reflection. In J. Marques, S. Dhiman, & J. Biberman (Eds.), *Managing in the twenty-first century: Transforming toward mutual growth* (pp. 135–145). New York: Palgrave Macmillan.

Higgins, M. C., & Kram, K. E. (2001). Reconceptualizing mentoring at work: A developmental network perspective. *Academy of Management Review, 26,* 264–268.

Higgins, M. C., & Kram, K. E. (2007). The roots and meaning of mentoring. In B. R. Ragins & K. E. Kram (Eds.), *The handbook of mentoring at work: Theory, research, and practice* (pp. 349–372). Thousand Oaks, CA: Sage.

Iiyoshi, T., & Kumar, M. S. V. (2008). *Opening up education: The collective advancement of education through open technology, open content, and open knowledge.* Retrieved from http://mitpress.mit.edu/catalog/item/default.asp?ttype=2&tid=11309.

Jo, S. J., Jeung, C. W., Park, S., & Yoon, H. J. (2009). Who is citing whom: Citation network analysis among HRD publications from 1990 to 2007. *Human Resource Development Quarterly, 20*(4), 503–537.

Jonassen, D. H. (1997). Instructional design models for well-structured and ill-structured problem-solving learning outcomes. *ETR&D, 45*(1), 65–94.

Jonassen, D. H., & Rohrer-Murphy, L. (1999). Activity theory as a framework for designing constructivist learning environments. *ETR&D, 47*(1), 61–79.

Kandel, E. R. (1989). Genes, nerve cells, and the remembrance of things past. *Journal of Neuropsychiatry, 1*(2), 103–125.

Kandel, E. R. (2001). The molecular biology of memory storage: A dialogue between genes and synapses. *Science, 294,* 1030–1038.

Kang, I., Bonk, C. J., & Kim, M-C (in press). A case study of blog-based learning in Korea: Technology becomes pedagogy. *The Internet and Higher Education.*

Kiggins, J., & Cambourne, B. (2007). The knowledge building community program: A partnership for progress in teacher education. In T. Townsend & R. Bates (Eds.), *Handbook of Teacher Education* (pp. 365–380). Netherlands: Springer.

Klein, J. D. (1997). *ETR&D*-development: An analysis of content and survey of future direction. *ETR&D, 45*(3), 57–62.

Korth, S. J. (1997). Planning HRD interventions: What, why, and how. *Performance Improvement Quarterly, 10*(4), 51–71.

Krippendorf, K. (2006). *The sematic turn: A new foundation for design.* New York: Taylor & Francis.

Ku, H. Y. (2009). Twenty years of productivity in *ETR&D* by institutions and authors. *ETR&D, 57*(6), 801–805.

Lawson, B. (2004). *Schemata, gambits* and *precedent:* Some factors in design expertise. *Design Studies, 25*(5), 443–457.

Lawson, B. (2005). *How designers think* (3rd ed.). London: Elsevier Press.

Lawson, B., & Dorst, K. (2009). *Design expertise*. London: Taylor & Francis.

Lee, H., & Bonk, C. J. (2010, October). The use of wikis for collaboration in corporations: Perceptions and implications for future research. *Proceedings of E-Learn 2010—World conference on E-learning in corporate, government, healthcare, and higher education* (pp. 2581–2587). Chesapeake, VA: AACE.

Lent, R. W., Brown, S. D., & Hackett, G. (1994). Toward a unifying social cognitive theory of career and academic interest, choice and performance. *Journal of Vocational Behavior, 45,* 79–122.

Lent, R. W., & Brown, S. D. (1996). Social cognitive approach to career development: An overview. *The Career Development Quarterly, 44*, 310–321.

Lewin, M. A. (1998). Kurt Lewin: His psychology and a daughter's recollections. In G. A. Kimble & M. Wertheimer (Eds.), *Portraits of pioneers in psychology* (Vol. 3, pp. 105–118). Mahwah, NJ: Lawrence Earlbaum.

Lin, M.-F., Sajjapanroj, S., & Bonk, C. J. (in press). Wikibooks and Wikibookians: Loosely-coupled community or the future of the textbook industry? *IEEE Transactions on Learning Technologies.*

Lynham, S. A. (2002). The general method of theory-building research in applied disciplines. *Advances in Developing Human Resources, 4*(3), 221–241.

Maccia, G. S. (1988). *Genetic epistemology of intelligent natural systems: Propositional, procedural and performative intelligence.* Paper presented at Hangzhou University, Hangzhou. Retrieved July 17, 2011 from http://educology.indiana.edu/Maccia/GeneticEpistemologyOfIntelligentSystems_propositionalProceduralPerformativeIntelligence1988.pdf.

Margolin, V. (2010, July 7–9). *Design research: Towards a history.* Design Research Society: Montreal, QC.

Marques, J., Dhiman, S., & Biberman, J. (Eds.). (2011). *Managing in the twenty-first century: Transforming toward mutual growth.* New York: Palgrave Macmillan.

Marrow, A. J. (1969). *The practical theorist: The life and work or Kurt Lewin.* New York: Basic books.

Merriam, S. B., & Caffarella, R. S. (1999). *Learning in adulthood: A comprehensive guide* (2nd ed.). San Francisco: Jossey-Bass.

Merrill, M. D. (1983). Component display theory. In C. M. Reigeluth (Ed.), *Instructional-design theories and models: An overview of their current status* (pp. 279–333). Hillsdale, NJ: Lawrence Erlbaum Associates.

Merrill, M. D., & Wilson, B. (2007). The future of instructional design. In R. A. Reiser & J. V. Dempsey (Eds.), *Trends and issues in instructional design and technology* (2nd ed., pp. 335–351). Upper Saddle River, NJ: Pearson Education, Inc.

Molenda, M. (2010). Origins and evolution of instructional systems design. In K. H. Silber & W. R. Foshay (Eds.), *(2010), Handbook of improving performance in the workplace* (Instructional design and training delivery, Vol. one, pp. 53–92). San Francisco: Peiffer.

Molloy, J. C. (2005). Developmental networks: Literature review and future research. *Career Development International, 10*, 536–548.

Murray-Harvey, R., & Slee, P. (2000, December). *Problem based learning in teacher education: Just the beginning!* Sydney, Australia: Paper presented at the Australian Association for Research in Education.

Nelson, H. G., & Stolterman, E. (2003). *The design way: Intentional change in an unpredictable world: Foundations and fundamentals of design competence.* Englewood Cliffs, NJ: Educational Technology Publishers.

Park, S. H., & Ertmer, P. A. (2008). Impact of problem-based learning (PBL) on teachers' beliefs regarding technology use. *Journal of Research on Technology in Education, 40*(2), 247–267.

Ravitz, J. (2009). Summarizing findings and looking ahead to a new generation of PBL research. *The Interdisciplinary Journal of Problem-based Learning, 3*(1), 4–11.

Reigeluth, C. M. (1983). Meaningfulness and instruction: Relating what is being learned to what a student knows. *Instructional Science, 12*(3), 197–218.

Reigeluth, C. M. (1994). The imperative for systemic change. In C. M. Reigeluth & R. J. Garfinkle (Eds.), *Systemic change in education* (pp. 3–11). Englewood Cliffs, NJ: Educational Technology.

Reigeluth, C. M. (2012). Instructional theory and technology for a post-industrial world. In R. A. Reiser & J. V. Dempsey (Eds.), *Trends and issues in instructional design and technology* (3rd ed., pp. 75–83). Boston: Pearson Education.

Reigeluth, C. M., & Carr-Chellman, A. A. (Eds.). (2009). *Instructional-design theories and models: Building a common knowledge base (Vol. III).* New York: Routledge.

Reigeluth, C. M., & Garfinkle, R. J. (1994). Envisioning a new system of education. In C. M. Reigeluth & R. J. Garfinkle (Eds.), *Systemic Change in Education* (pp. 59–70). Englewood Cliffs, NJ: Educational Technology.

Reigeluth, C. M., & Schwartz, E. (1989). An instructional theory for the design of computer-based simulations. *Journal of Computer-Based Instruction, 16*(1), 1–10.

Reigeluth, C. M., Watson, S. L., Watson, W. R., Dutta, P., Chen, Z., & Powell, N. (2008). Roles for technology in the information-age paradigm of education: Learning management systems. *Educational Technology, 48*(6), 32–39.

Robertson, I. (2008). Learners' attitudes to wiki technology in problem based, blended learning for vocational teacher education. *Australian Journal of Educational Technology, 24*(4), 425–441.

Romiszowski, A. (2009). Fostering skill development outcomes. In C. M. Reigeluth & A. A. Carr-Chellman (Eds.), *Instructional-design theories and models: Building a common knowledge base* (Vol. III, pp. 199–224). New York: Routledge.

Rowe, P. (1987). *Design thinking.* Boston: MIT Press.

Rowland, G. (1992). What do instructional designers actually do? An initial investigation of expert practice. *Performance Improvement Quarterly, 5*(2), 65–86.

Salisbury, D. F. (1990). Cognitive psychology and Its implications for designing drill and practice programs for computers. *Journal of Computer-Based Instruction, 17*(1), 23–30.

Savery, J. R. (2009). Problem-based approach to instruction. In C. M. Reigeluth & A. A. Carr-Chellman (Eds.), *Instructional-design theories and models: Building a common knowledge base* (pp. Vol. III, pp. 143–165). New York, NY: Routledge.

Schön, D. (1983). *The reflective practitioner: How professionals think in action.* London: Temple Smith.

Schwartz, D. L., Lin, X., Brophy, S., & Bransford, J. D. (1999). Toward the development of flexibly adaptive instructional designs. In C. M. Reigeluth (Ed.), *Instructional-design theories and models: A new paradigm of instructional theory* (Vol. II, pp. 183–213). Mahwah, NJ: Lawrence Erlbaum.

Silber, K. (2007). A principle-based model of instructional design: A new way of thinking about and teaching ID. *Educational Technology, 47*(5), 5–19.

Smith, K. M., & Boling, E. (2009). What do we make of design? Design as a concept in educational technology. *Educational Technology, 49*(4), 3–17.

So, H., & Kim, B. (2009). Learning about problem based learning: Student teachers integrating technology, pedagogy and content knowledge. *Australasian Journal of Educational Technology, 25*(1), 101–116.

Squire, L. R., & Kandel, E. R. (1999). *Memory: From mind to molecules.* New York: Henry Holt and Co.

Stolterman, E. (2008). The nature of design practice and implications for interaction design research. *International Journal of Design, 2*(1), 55–65.

Strobel, J. & van Barneveld, A. (2009). When is PBL more effective? A meta-synthesis of meta-analyses comparing PBL to conventional classrooms. *Interdisciplinary Journal of Problem-based Learning, 3*(1). http://docs.lib.purdue.edu/ijpbl/vol3/iss1/4.

Torraco, R. J. (2004). Challenges and choices for theoretical research in human resource development. *Human Resource Development Quarterly, 15*, 171–188.

Van de Ven, A. H. (1989). Nothing is quite so practical as a good theory. *Academy of Management Review, 14*, 486–489.

van Merriënboer, J. J., & Kirschner, P. A. (2007). *Ten steps to complex learning: A systematic approach to four-component instructional design.* Mahwah, NJ: Lawrence Erlbaum Associates.

Vannatta, R., & Beyerbach, B. (2001). Facilitating a constructivist vision of technology integration among education faculty and preservice teachers. *Journal of Research on Computing in Education, 33*(2), 132–148.

Vincenti, W. (1990). *What engineers know and how they know it: Analytical studies from aeronautical history.* Baltimore, MD: The Johns Hopkins University Press.

Walker, A., & Leary, H. (2009). A problem based learning meta analysis: Differences across problem types, implementation types, disciplines, and assessment levels. *The Interdisciplinary Journal of Problem-based Learning, 3*(1), 12–43.

Weinstein, M. G., & Shuck, B. (2011). Social ecology and worksite training and development: Introducing the social in instructional system design. *Human Resource Development Review, 10*(3), 286–303.

Wheeler, S., Kelly, P., & Gale, K. (2005). The influence of online problem-based learning on teachers' professional practice and identity. *Research in Learning Technology, 13*(2), 125–137.

Yazzie-Mintz, E. (2007). Voices of students on engagement: A report on the 2006 high school survey of student engagement. Retrieved July 14, 2011 from http://www.eric.ed.gov/PDFS/ED495758.pdf.

Chapter 4
Trends and Issues: The Consumption and Sustainability of Digital Media in the Modern Global Economy

Gabrielle Garner

4.1 Introduction

Currently, much of the developed human world works, plays, shops, learns, and manages personal relationships online. As a socially constructed technological system (Hughes 1983), the Internet has become a digital repository of human arti-fact and activity. Facilitating an increase in the momentum of participation across the online space (Callon 1999), human access to technological tools and a global knowledge base has catalyzed the creation, proliferation, convergence, and con-sumption of digital media within a vast and diverse community of media-making professionals and consumer creators (Banks and Humphreys 2008; Consalvo 2006; Jenkins 2006).

Digital media artifacts have been legislative (laws of copyright for media and intellectual property distribution); architectural (dial-up, DSL, or Broadband con-nections); educational (information search engines, instructional media, online edu-cation platforms, web-based academic journals, etc.); recreational (massively multiplayer online games, humorous images, entertainment programming, etc.); personal (weblogs, videos, photographs, etc.); and ground-breaking (coal mines that generate energy to power the system). As long as media makers and system developers continue to engineer and update diverse artifacts that facilitate human regulation (legislative), access (architectural), education (educational services and media), recreation (entertainment media), expression (personal media exchange), participation (retention of public/private utilities and acquisition of natural resources), and a multitude of other activities and processes in the world wide web, the Internet, as a system, is likely to continue growing, changing, and enduring through persistent social, economic, and technological construction.

G. Garner (✉)
University of Georgia, 216 Rivers Crossing, Athens, GA 30602-7144, USA
email: ggarner@uga.edu

M. Orey et al. (eds.), *Educational Media and Technology Yearbook*, Educational
Media and Technology Yearbook 37, DOI 10.1007/978-1-4614-4430-5_4,
© Springer Science+Business Media New York 2013

This essay aims to clarify the sociocultural, economic, and technological mechanisms that shape modern artifacts, which have been innovated, disseminated, and sustained within a seemingly durable, yet constantly changing online network of Internet users. The ways in which digital media has been consumed and sustained in today's global economy are exemplified in the case of online videogames, specifically those that have shown evidence of sustainability in the global marketplace over time.

4.2 Online Videogames and Artifacts of Innovation

Online videogames are modern artifacts that have appeared in technological form at some point between the turn of the twentieth and twenty-first centuries (1990–2011). They represent a recent development and production of a new or seemingly new human idea. Like most forms of digital media, the design of a videogame is constrained by the desires of a target consumer audience (social force) and stakeholders (economic, social, and technological influence) (Schell 2008). Its architecture is constrained by the specifications and capabilities of technological tools and platforms (technological and economic influence), along with the varied expertise of its engineers (social influence) (Schell 2008; Salen and Zimmerman 2004). Social, technological, and economic forces have the power to shape algorithms, codes, design methodologies, resource allocation, and a multitude of other factors that, ultimately, affect the player experiences and the lifespan of a game's popularity (Consalvo 2006; Hunicke et al. 2004; Montfort and Bogost 2009; O'Donnell 2011; Schell 2008). Successful online videogames are technological systems that sustain the practices of collaborative innovation and play among a diverse group of media makers.

The lasting success of online videogames, like *Ultima Online*, has resulted from stakeholders' collective ability to continuously innovate, update, hybridize, experiment with, and disseminate new media within the online game space over the course of years and decades. With a successful trajectory of continued innovation, *Ultima Online* was released in 1996 as the first massively multiplayer online role-playing game (MMORPG), and nearly 15 years later, this artifact of innovation is still being played. Five years after its original release, Origin Systems of Electronic Arts reported that "with the release of its latest expansion pack, *Ultima Online: Age of Shadows*, *Ultima Online* (UO) has surpassed 250,000 subscribers" (BusinessWire 2003). The press release explained that the achievement of such a high number of active players was the result of players' perceived enthusiasm for the dissemination of the aforementioned expansion packs, or new and updated game content, which allowed players to design and build their own houses, provided two new in-game player professions, and introduced a new realm for players to "explore and settle" (BusinessWire 2003).

With the financial support of Electronic Arts,[1] Origin Systems' production team became a community of persistent, shared innovation through its continued production of innovation artifacts (expansion packs) over time. This example demonstrates the social awareness of its stakeholders, who were able to adapt their business model (dissemination of expansion packs) in ways that grew with in-game cultural trends and exer-game technological advancements.

As the case of *Ultima Online* demonstrates, among videogames emerging from the late 1990s, sustained play over time was due to continued financial support (EA Inc. supported Origin Systems production team), sustained innovation (release of expansion packs generate increased player subscription), and the timely dissemination of innovation artifacts (release of expansion packs during the fifth year of operation), which was influenced by producers' awareness of social, economic, and technological trends as well as the availability of financial support and the ability to continually innovate. Over time, the practice of collaborative innovation in the making of these games has generated a similar, consistent impact on the nature of professional media work (Deuze 2007).

In light of the complex external forces that have affected the innovation, distribution, and sustained consumption (play) of MMOGs, like *Ultima Online*, the work of designing and developing these artifacts can be macroscopically simplified as an input-process–output system: game developers engage in the process of innovating and produce an online video game. Expertise and technology serve as the input that initiates a process of envisioning, designing, and developing a new product. At the end of the input-process–output system, an online videogame is produced. However, this process of game production is complicated by the fact that teams that have produced videogames include highly diverse teams of designers, artists, engineers, producers, project managers, executives, financiers, transdisciplinary subject matter experts, and even players (Consalvo 2006; O'Donnell 2011; Postigo 2007; Salen and Zimmerman 2004). In addition, as a result of improved communication technologies, cultural diversification within and among production teams has increased tremendously (Earley and Mosakowski 2000; Hitt et al. 1999a, b). Given the complexity of managing dynamic, multicultural groups, team members, managers, and producers survive in their roles by continually adapting to change with a sensible awareness of each others' strengths and weaknesses.

Callon (1999) described the approach to "technological development as a succession of steps from the birth of an idea (invention) to its commercialization (innovation) by way of its development," but questioned "the claim that it is possible to distinguish during the process of innovation phases or activities that are distinctly technical or scientific from others that are guided by economic or commercial logic" (p. 84). Callon (1999) further explains:

> For example, it is often believed that at the beginning of the process of innovation, the problems to be solved are basically technical, and that economic, social, political, or indeed

---

[1] According to the company's website, Electronic Arts Incorporated is "a leading global interactive entertainment software company" (as of June 6, 2011) with over eight thousand employees worldwide (as of March 31, 2010) (http://aboutus.ea.com/home.action, accessed June 6, 2011).

cultural considerations come into play only at a later stage. However, more and more studies are showing that this distinction is never as clear-cut. This is particularly true in the case of radical innovations: Right from the start, technical scientific, social, economic, or political considerations have been inextricably bound up in an organic whole. Such heterogeneity and complexity, which everyone agrees is present at the end of the process, are not progressively introduced along the way. They are present from the beginning (p. 317).

Considering the reality that sociological, technological, and economic analyses are woven into technological systems through the communities that collaboratively innovate these artifacts, knowing more about their social construction would not only inform our understanding of the practice of innovation, but it would also reveal the nature of durable (Hughes 1999) online videogames and game developers' expertise about players' desires and needs in online videogame play.

Hughes (1999) suggested that socially constructed artifacts have been "durable" when they "project into the future the socially constructed characteristics acquired in the past when they were designed" (p. 77). Considering the diversity of experts employed in the making of videogames, it may be possible to determine the strength, or projected durability, of an online videogame by drawing connections between its "social construction" and the extent to which they continue to exist over time. Law (1999) explained, "The stability and form of artifacts should be seen as a function of the interaction of heterogeneous elements as these are shaped and assimilated into a network. In this view, then, an explanation of technological form rests on a study of both the conditions and the tacts of the system building" (Law 1999, p. 113). Online videogames have been comparable to the engineering of other technological systems because of their capacity to give life to networked communities of collaborative innovation through the process of production.

4.3   Communities of Collaborative Innovation

From the perspective of the stakeholders, the Internet facilitates an opportunity for the continued growth of online videogame environments, which in turn helps to extend the livelihood and collaborative practice of innovation within and among production teams. Like many evolving technological systems, "the reality of games is they're never done, especially online games" (Anonymous Videogame Producer, personal communication, November 11, 2010). Theory from the fields of learning sciences and educational psychology has suggested that professional groups which engage in shared social practice, such as the collaborative innovation of videogame production teams, have been socially constructed (Vygotsky 1978), and over time, the formation of these socially constructed work communities, or communities of practice, facilitates the development of skills and competencies among adults (Lave and Wenger 1991).

Because successful online videogames have "never" been done (Anonymous Videogame Producer, personal communication, November 11, 2010) and have been continually adapted to meet the needs of technological, economic, and social change (Schell 2008), team members' continual innovation and adaptation to environmental change has emerged over time within a socially constructed context, further influencing the sustainability of the game(s) they make. If videogame production teams do operate similarly to communities of practice (Lave and Wenger 1991) and of innovation (West 2009), then there is a strong likelihood that teams engaged in the persistent practice of videogame innovation have been or were able to strategically develop themselves as professional communities that systematically generated new or adapted skills and competencies through some combination of these activities, which have facilitated the processes of both innovation (West 2009) and learning among group members: social interaction and experience (Bandura 1986), cultural participation (Wenger 1998), apprenticeship (Brown et al. 1989), inquiry (Engestrom 1999), knowledge creation (Hakkarainen et al. 2004), flow (Csikszentmihalyi 1990), creativity (Montuori and Purser 1999), and creative group thought processes of convergent and divergent thinking (Kaner and Karni 2007; Larey 1995).

Based on theoretical arguments and previous empirical research from studies of creativity (Csikszentmihalyi 1990; Kaner and Karni 2007; Larey 1995; Montuori and Purser 1999) and social learning (Bandura 1986; Brown et al. 1989; Engestrom 1999; Hakkarainen et al. 2004; Vygotsky 1978; Wenger 1998; West 2009), I question whether game developers of successful online videogames were more or less equipped to sustain continued innovation when they operated within a context that promoted collaborative learning and knowledge creation.

Due to the critical need for persistent and sustained innovation, game developers of successful online videogames continually produced new game content with a keen sociological awareness of the consumer market, which means that many have had to engage in sociological inquiry within and outside of the workplace through play. While further ethnographic study is recommended to define, from observed practice, the activities, tools, strategies, or characteristics of these communities, which most directly support innovation (and thus, sustainability of the videogame), the characteristics of successful MMOGs have been delineated as a way of generating an understanding of the socially constructed expertise of game developers.

4.4   Sustainable Innovation

In sustainable MMOGs, such as *World of Warcraft*, *Everquest*, and *Ultima Online*, players participated in communities of play within the context of a designed adventure. Closely resembling the designed experiences of successful MMOGs, Campbell's (1949) description of the monomyth has served as a common source of creative inspiration for writers and designers of the entertainment industry (Vogler 1998), including game developers:

> A hero ventures forth from the world of common day into a region of supernatural wonder. Fabulous forces are there encountered and a decisive victory is won. The hero comes back from this mysterious adventure with the power to bestow boons on his fellow man (Campbell 1949, p. 23).

As sustainable online videogames have been consistently innovated, updated, mashed up, hybridized, played with, and disseminated over time, the underlying narrative of successful MMOGs has been based on this concept of an evolving adventure, which is seemingly endless and also reflective of one's experiences in life.

Through innovated, animated, and life-like adventures, game developers have engaged players in the meaning-making activities of inquiry, discovery, cooperation, mentor-apprenticeship, problem-solving, language use, and personal expression have appeared as core features of these communities. Empirically and theoretically oriented reports of research in games and game environments have emphasized game design features and their influences on the cognitive and social development of players (Dickey 2005, 2007; de Freitas et al. 2010; Fields and Kafai 2009; Girvan and Savage 2010; Gros 2007; Kriz 2003; Rosas et al. 2003; Steinkuehler 2006; Wideman et al. 2007). To explore the influence of collaborative interaction on young teenagers' cognitive development, Fields and Kafai (2009) investigated players' activity in the context of an after-school club and popular virtual world, called *Whyville*, where knowledge diffusion, learning, and free play were central to community participation. Supported by the methodological approach of "connective ethnography," Fields and Kafai (2009) documented patterns of social interaction and communication in players' knowledge-sharing activities within real and virtual spaces. In research aiming to draw connections between player psychology and design features of virtual worlds and videogames, ethnographic methods of inquiry have shown that these games have engaged players in cooperation, language use, social interaction, self-expression, and the obvious use of modern technology.

Given the narrative, text-heavy quality of many virtual worlds and MMORPGs of the 1990s and early 2000s, discourse analysis arose as a practical approach to qualitative and ethnographic methods among cognitive, developmental, and educational researchers of player interactivity and communication (Dickey 2007; Fields and Kafai 2009; Steinkuehler 2006). Through "cognitive ethnography," Steinkuehler (2006) applied rigorous discourse analysis to the study of language expressed in the MMORPG, *Lineage*. Influenced by research findings in functional linguistics (citing Clark 1996; Gee 1999; Halliday 1978; Levinson 1983; Schiffrin 1994), Steinkuehler (2006) interpreted the cognitive activity of players in the context of their interaction and communication. Steinkuehler's analysis of discourse expressed among members of the *Lineage* community, conceived as a culture-sharing group, involved an analysis of *Lineage* language (morphology and syntax) and patterns of *Lineage* practices (activities, interaction, and communication) that revealed shared goals, values, and identity construction among *Lineage* players. The study exemplifies a nuanced application of discourse analysis in the landscape of a globally networked society, where research traditions found in anthropology, sociology, and developmental psychology have converged in the socially responsive, scientific exploration of digital media artifacts. The extent to which game developers engage in rigorous sociological inquiry is unknown; however, the case of *Lineage* shows that game developers had engineered in-game opportunities for the development of shared meaning and a sense of community as seen in player identity development (through role-playing) and in the development of shared goals and values (through communication, interaction, collaborative activity, and language use).

Dickey's (2007) work inadvertently highlighted game developers' awareness of player needs by emphasizing the potential influences of MMORPG character design and narrative environment on players' intrinsic motivation in a critical analysis of *World of Warcraft*. Based on a discursive analysis of players' communicative expression and response to multimedia, or multimodal features of videogames, Dickey (2007) aimed to draw connections between game design features and player psychology, specifically the aspect of intrinsic motivation, as a way of generating practical knowledge that may inform instructional designers' approaches to the design of interactive learning environments.

Shaped by game developers' awareness of players' desires along with their own access to technological resources, the MMORPG is described as "a flexible design which allows players choice, collaboration, challenge, and achievement, while at the same time it is a design which provides scaffolding for players to progress and learn. The design of small quests in MMORPGs may provide a model of how to design learning tasks within an interactive learning environment" (Dickey 2007, p. 263). Although the purpose of the MMORPG was "to entertain" and the purpose of instructional design was "to foster learning," Dickey (2007) suggested that both MMORPGs and interactive learning environments were designed to expose players to various forms of information, while intrinsically motivating them to use new knowledge to formulate future plans of action. Information about the potential impact of these design features on learners was intended to provide useful fodder for instructional designers seeking to incorporate intrinsic motivation in designed learning environments.

In the context of game development, selections of previous research from the field of education (Dickey 2007; Fields and Kafai 2009; Steinkuehler 2006) have shown that successful, sustainable MMOGs expose players to intrinsically motivational activities, which primarily involve acquiring and using knowledge to formulate and carry out future plans of action through inquiry, language use, communication, role play, identity development, and self-expression in the context of strategically designed adventures, or monomyths. The common nature of play within *Ultima Online*, *Whyville*, *Lineage*, and *World of Warcraft* demonstrates that game developers of recent decades have developed a shared perspective and expertise about what appeals to player-consumers from a sociological, technological, and economic standpoint.

4.5   Conclusion

It is argued that the livelihood of modern artifacts, including tools, services, environments, games, and digital media, can be sustained over long periods of time to the extent that they have been developed and adapted with continually up-to-date knowledge of what the consumer market, or society, is and is not doing. Because they appear to respond to and emerge from the activities of an increasingly globalized, inquisitive, and networked human population, the innovation, dissemination, and endurance of digital media artifacts can provide insight into the uniquely constructed needs, desires, skills, and competencies of today's digital citizens (Callon 1999; Deuze 2007; Fischer 2007; Jenkins 2006).

Based on this review of previous empirical research, user-generated wiki content, MMOGs that have sustained popularity and use over time (*Ultima Online, Whyville, Lineage,* and *World of Warcraft*), and an interview with a professional videogame producer, these trends were observed:

- Online videogames were poised for sustainability in the global marketplace when they were continually shaped over time by communities of persistent innovation and play, including a diverse professional workforce and their direct experience with the target consumer audience.
- Drawn from the fields of anthropology and cognitive psychology, the meaning-making activities of inquiry, discovery, cooperation, apprenticeship, problem-solving, language use, and personal expression appeared as integral features of player activity in successful MMOGs, which highlights a shared perspective among game developers about what appeals to consumers (sociologically) and the (technological) platform capabilities needed (via adequate financial support) to facilitate in-game activities that appeal to consumers.

Supported by these indications, I argue that communities engaged in the persistent innovation and play of online videogames are likely to sustain a durable trajectory of innovation within corporate contexts when they continually adapt to sociological, technological, and economic changes over time. Successful and well-designed online videogames, particularly massively multiplayer online (role-playing) games, require a workforce that is able to engage in the practice of innovation with a persistent awareness of consumer, or player, needs (sociological awareness) and available resources (technological and economic awareness).

As this essay has explained, the sustainability of artifacts, including tools, services, environments, games, and digital media, is dependent upon the social awareness of its stakeholders, which could include engineers, financiers, analysts, executives, and producers. Collaborative innovation and inquiry were at the core of game development. In the case of sustainable online videogames emerging throughout the last 20 years, game developers' sociological, technological, and economic awareness has led them to design environments that have engaged players in the socially constructed, meaning-making activities of inquiry, discovery, cooperation, apprenticeship, problem-solving, language use, and personal expression. The implication of this finding is that these kinds of MMOGs present a unique opportunity for players to develop skills in the activities of inquiry, discovery, cooperation, mentor-apprenticeship, problem-solving, language use, and personal expression.

References

Bandura, A. (1986). *Social foundations of thought and action: A social cognitive theory.* Englewood Cliffs, NJ: Prentice Hall.

Banks, J., & Humphreys, S. (2008). The labor of user co-creators: Emergent social network markets? *Convergence: The International Journal of Research into New Media Technologies, 14*(4), 401–418. doi:10.1177/1354856508094660.

Brown, J. S., Collins, A., & Duguid, P. (1989). Situation cognition and the culture of learning. *Educational Researcher, 18*(1), 32–42.

BusinessWire (2003, March 14). ORIGIN Systems announces record number of subscriptions in *Ultima Online* franchise history: Popularity of the latest expansion pack, *Age of Shadows*, drives up sales. Retrieved on June 14, 2011 from http://news.ea.com/portal/site/ea/?ndmViewId=news_view&newsId=20030314005303&newsLang=en.

Callon, M. (1999). Society in the making: The study of technology as a tool for sociological analysis. In W. E. Bijker, T. P. Hughes, & T. J. Pinch (Eds.), *The social construction of technological systems: New directions in the sociology and history of technology* (pp. 83–106). Cambridge, MA: MIT.

Campbell, J. (1949). *The hero with a thousand faces.* Princeton, NJ: Princeton University Press.

Clark, H. H. (1996). *Using language.* Cambridge: Cambridge University Press.

Consalvo, M. (2006). Console video games and global corporations: Creating a hybrid culture. *New Media & Society, 8*(1), 117–137. doi:10.1177/1461444806059921.

Consumers Union of U.S., Inc. (n. d.). About us: Our history. Retrieved June 14, 2011 from http://www.consumerreports.org/cro/aboutus/history/interactive/index.htm.

Csikszentmihalyi, M. (1990). *Flow: The psychology of optimal experience.* New York, NY: Harper Collins.

de Freitas, S., Rebolledo-Mendez, G., Liarokapis, F., Magoulas, G., & Poulovassilis, A. (2010). Learning as immersive experiences: Using the four-dimensional framework for designing and evaluating immersive learning experiences in a virtual world. *British Journal of Educational Technology, 41*(1), 69–85. doi:10.1111/j.1467-8535.2009.01024.x.

Deuze, M. (2007). *Media work.* Cambridge, MA: Polity.

Dickey, M. D. (2005). Engaging by design: How engagement strategies in popular computer and video games can inform instructional design. *Educational Technology Research and Development, 53*(2), 67–83.

Dickey, M. D. (2007). Game design and learning: A conjectural analysis of how massively multiple online role-playing games (MMORPGs) foster intrinsic motivation. *Educational Technology Research and Development, 55*, 253–273. doi:10.1007/s11423-006-9004-7.

Earley, P. C., & Mosakowski, E. (2000). Creating hybrid team cultures: An empirical test of transnational team functioning. *Academy of Management Journal, 43*, 26–49.

Engestrom, Y. (1999). Innovative learning in work teams: Analyzing cycles of knowledge creation in practice. In Y. Engestrom, R. Miettinen, & R.-L. Punamaki (Eds.), *Perspectives on activity theory* (pp. 377–404). Cambridge, MA: Cambridge University Press.

Fields, D. A., & Kafai, Y. B. (2009). A connective ethnography of peer knowledge sharing and diffusion in a tween virtual world. *Computer-Supported Collaborative Learning, 4*, 47–68. doi:10.1007/s11412-008-9057-1.

Gee, J. P. (1999). *An introduction to discourse analysis: Theory and method.* New York: Routledge & Kegan Paul.

Girvan, C., & Savage, T. (2010). Identifying an appropriate pedagogy for virtual worlds: A communal constructivism case study. *Computers in Education, 55*, 342–349.

Gros, B. (2007). Digital games in education: The design of games-based learning environments. *Journal of Research on Technology in Education, 40*(1), 23–38.

Hakkarainen, K., Palonen, T., Paavola, S., & Lehtinen, E. (2004). *Communities of networked expertise: Professional and educational perspectives.* Amsterdam: Elsevier.

Halliday, M. A. K. (1978). *Language as a social semiotic.* London: Edward Arnold.

Hitt, M. A., Nixon, R. D., Hoskisson, R. E., & Kochhard, R. (1999a). Corporate entrepreneurship and cross-functional fertilization: Activation, process and disintegration of a new product design team. *Entrepreneurship: Theory and Practice, 23*, 145–167.

Hitt, M. A., Nixon, R. D., Hoskisson, R. E., & Kochhard, R. (1999b). Corporate entrepreneurship and cross-functional fertilization: Activation, process and disintegration of a new product design team. *Entrepreneurship: Theory and Practice, 23*, 145–167.

Hughes, T. P. (1983). *Networks of power: Electrification in western society, 1880-1930.* Baltimore, MD: Johns Hopkins University Press.

Hughes, T. P. (1999). The evolution of large technological systems. In W. E. Bijker, T. P. Hughes, & T. J. Pinch (Eds.), *The social construction of technological systems: New directions in the sociology and history of technology* (pp. 51–82). Cambridge, MA: MIT.

Jenkins, H. (2006). *Convergence culture: Where old and new media collide.* New York, NY: New York University.

Kaner, M., & Karni, R. (2007). Engineering design of a service system: An empirical study. *Information Knowledge Systems Management, 6*(3), 235–263.

Kriz, W. C. (2003). Creating effective learning environments and learning organizations through Gaming Simulation Design. *Simulation & Gaming, 34*, 495–511. doi:0.000000000000009664 64000776276.

Larey, T. S. (1995). *Convergent and divergent thinking, group composition, and creativity in brainstorming groups.* Ann Arbor, MI: ProQuest Information & Learning.

Lave, J., & Wenger, E. (1991). *Situated learning: Legitimate peripheral participation.* Cambridge, MA: Cambridge University Press.

Law, J. (1999). Technology and heterogeneous engineering: The case of Portuguese expansion. In W. E. Bijker, T. P. Hughes, & T. J. Pinch (Eds.), *The social construction of technological systems: New directions in the sociology and history of technology* (pp. 111–134). Cambridge, MA: MIT.

Levinson, S. C. (1983). *Pragmatics.* Cambridge: Cambridge University Press.

Montfort, N., & Bogost, I. (2009). *Racing the beam: The Atari video computer system.* Boston, MA: MIT.

Montuori, A., & Purser, R. E. (1999). *Social creativity.* Cresskill, NJ: Hampton.

O'Donnell, C. (2011). The *Nintendo Entertainment System* and the 10NES chip: Carving the video game industry in silicon. *Games and Culture, 6*(1), 83–100. doi:10.1177/1555412010377319.

Postigo, H. (2007). Of mods and modders: Chasing down the value of fan-based digital game modifications. *Games and Culture, 2*(4), 300–313. doi:10.1177/1555412007307955.

Rosas, R., Nussbaum, M., Cumsille, P., Marianov, V., Correa, M., Flores, P., Grau, V., Lagos, F., Lopez, X., Lopez, V., Rodriguez, P., & Salinas, M. (2003). Beyond Nintendo: Design and assessment of educational video games for first and second grade students. *Computers in Education, 40*, 71–94.

Salen, K., & Zimmerman, E. (2004). *Rules of play: Game design fundamentals.* Cambridge, MA: MIT.

Schell, J. (2008). *The art of game design: A book of lenses.* New York, NY: Elsevier.

Schiffrin, D. (1994). *Approaches to discourse.* Oxford: Blackwell.

Steinkuehler, C. A. (2006). Massively multiplayer online videogaming as participation in a discourse. *Mind, Culture & Activity, 13*(1), 38–52.

Vygotsky, L. S. (1978). *Mind in society: The development of higher psychological processes.* Cambridge: Harvard University Press.

Wenger, E. (1998). *Communities of practice: Learning, meaning and identity.* Cambridge, MA: Cambridge University Press.

West, R. E. (2009). What is shared? A framework for understanding shared innovation within communities. *Educational Technology Research and Development, 57*, 315–332. doi:10.1007/s11423-008-9107-4.

Wideman, H. H., Owston, R. D., Brown, C., Kushniruk, A., Ho, F., & Pitts, K. C. (2007). Unpacking the potential of educational gaming: A new tool for gaming research. *Simulation & Gaming, 38*(1), doi: 10.1177/104687810629765.

Chapter 5
Issues and Trends in Instructional Technology: Despite Lean Times, Continued Interest and Opportunity in K-12, Business, and Higher Education

Abbie Brown and Tim Green

We continue the tradition of reporting the issues and trends of instructional technology that have continued or arisen within the past year. This chapter is comprised of four sections: Overall Developments, Corporate Training and Development, Higher Education, and K-12 Settings.

5.1   Overall Developments

As with the previous year, the nation's economy was less than robust. Funding for K-12 and higher education took a sizeable hit throughout the nation. Federal funding for technology in K-12 and higher education was significantly reduced. Private sector funding for technology, however, remained relatively stable in comparison to the previous year. Although funding remained an issue, all sectors maintained an innovative approach to integrating instructional technology. The K-12 and higher education sectors looked to reduce costs by sharing resources through cloud computing, collaborative online environments, e-books, and open content resources. Mobile devices (specifically, tablet computing and smart phones), online learning, cloud computing, and augmented reality are this year's significant trends to watch.

A. Brown (✉)
Department of Mathematics, Science Instructional Technology Education,
East Carolina University, Flanagan Hall, Greenville, NC 27858, USA
e-mail: brownab@ecu.edu

T. Green
Department of Elementary and Bilingual Education, California State University,
Fullerton, CA, USA

M. Orey et al. (eds.), *Educational Media and Technology Yearbook*, Educational
Media and Technology Yearbook 37, DOI 10.1007/978-1-4614-4430-5_5,
© Springer Science+Business Media New York 2013

5.2 Corporate Training and Development

As we have done in previous issues and trends chapters of the yearbook (e.g., Brown and Green 2010, 2011), we continue to track corporate application of instructional technologies primarily by referring to the American Society for Training and Development's (ASTD's), *State of the Industry Report,* (Patel 2010). The current ASTD annual report is based on data collected from the ASTD's Forum organizations, ASTD BEST award winners, and responses from users of ASTD's WLP (Workforce Learning and Performance) Scorecard. The report describes the activities of organizations recognized as exemplary in their approach to workplace learning and performance as represented by the BEST award winners; larger, global organizations typically represented by Forum members; and data collected from users of ASTD's WLP Scorecard benchmarking and decision support tool.

5.2.1 Expenditure for Learning

ASTD reports that organizational expenditures for learning remained relatively stable over the past year Patel 2010. Organizations surveyed report employees accessed an average of 31.9 h of formal learning content in 2009; this is 3.1 h less than was accessed on average in 2008 (Patel 2010). The average annual learning expenditure per employee rose slightly (1.2%) from \$1,068 in 2008 to \$1,081 in 2009. Patel observes the increase, however, is at least in part due to the fact that learning functions were serving a diminished workforce. For the first time in 5 years, the ratio of learning staff to employees increased, with each learning staff member serving approximately 13 fewer employees in 2009 than in 2008 (Patel 2010). Thus, expenditure per employee increased even though overall expenditures for learning decreased.

The percentage of learning expenditure relative to business organizations' revenue and profit increased in 2009; from 0.59 to 0.071 of revenue and from 8.75 to 10.88% of profit (Patel 2010). Patel states that maintaining a commitment to learning functions, even though revenue and profit decreased, caused these increases.

It is particularly interesting to note that the ASTD report indicates increased spending on external providers of instruction (i.e., consultants and training providers) by almost 5%. For the first time in 5 years, organizations increased spending on outsourcing Patel 2010. It should be noted, however, that Forum and BEST organizations spent less on external services and increased spending on internal services by approximately 7.5% over the previous year Patel 2010.

5.2.2 Instructional Content

The ASTD report suggests that learning content topics have remained stable for the past few years, with minor changes in percent distribution of topic areas in the most recent year's survey. The largest percentage of formal learning hours (17.2%) is related to profession or industry-specific content; managerial and supervisory training accounts for 10.4% of these learning hours; information technology and systems account for 9.3%; processes, procedures, and business practices account for 9.2%; and mandatory and compliance training accounts for 7.8% (Patel 2010). The most recent survey saw minor increases in executive development and new employee orientation, which Patel suggests may be due to increased change in personnel (Patel 2010).

5.2.3 Use of Technology: e-Learning Increases Significantly

According to the ASTD report, an average of 36.5% of learning hours were available through computing technology in 2009. This increase is a change from the previous annual report's finding of greater use of instructor-led classroom learning and is the highest report of technology-based learning hours in ASTD's 14-year history of the survey (Patel 2010).

In the past 5 years, e-learning has contributed to the reuse ratio of instruction. The most recent ASTD report indicates that the average reuse ratio is 56.3, which is to say the average hour of learning content was used 56.3 times (Patel 2010). Patel asserts that the reuse ratio is a strong indicator that learning functions are becoming increasingly efficient Patel 2010.

5.3 Higher Education

We examine higher education's information technology use and instructional technology application primarily by referring to the *EDUCAUSE Core Data Service Fiscal Year 2009 Summary Report* (Arroway et al. 2010), *The ECAR Study of Undergraduate Students and Information Technology, 2010* (Smith and Borreson Caruso 2010), and *The Horizon Report* (Johnson et al 2011a, b). Trends in online learning are further examined by referring to The Sloan Consortium's report, *Class Differences: Online Education in the United States* (Allen and Seaman 2011). Each of these is a large, ongoing study with significant resources allocated to measuring the technological climate of higher education. *The EDUCAUSE Core Data Service Fiscal Year 2009 Summary Report* is drawn from information supplied by over 875 participating institutions (Arroway et al. 2010); *The ECAR Study of Undergraduate Students and Information Technology, 2010*, compiles and summarizes responses provided by over 36,000 undergraduate students (Smith and Borreson Caruso 2010); *The Horizon Report* is a qualitative analysis that examines the use of emerging technologies in learning-focused organizations, produced in collaboration between the EDUCAUSE Learning Initiative and the New Media Consortium (Johnson et al 2011a, b); and the Sloan Consortium's report on online learning is based on the responses provided by over 2,500 colleges and universities (Allen and Seaman 2011).

An important trend mentioned by the ECAR study and *The Horizon Report* is that of cloud computing (Smith and Borreson Caruso 2010; Johnson et al. 2011a, b). Cloud computing helps students and faculty with collaborative activities (e.g. using Google Docs to collaborate on papers or presentations); it also decentralizes information technology support as the college or university is no longer solely responsible for maintaining the software and data repositories students and faculty are using.

5.3.1   Information Technology on Campus: Staffing and Compensation

Operating budgets, staffing, and staff compensation kept pace with student enrollment at most higher education institutions during 2009. With relatively small changes over the past 5 years, college and university information technology organizations received funding increases that reflect institutional growth (Arroway et al. 2010).

5.3.2   Campus Technology Support and Use of Technology for Instruction

Networked computing continues to improve on most campuses. As an example, Internet connectivity in residence halls is nearly ubiquitous (Arroway et al. 2010). While wired connectivity remains common in many classrooms, WiFi connectivity in classrooms and the campus in general (i.e. common areas, restaurants, residence halls) is growing steadily. Bandwidth to the Internet is continuing its steady increase at all colleges and universities responding to the *EDUCAUSE Core Data Survey* (Arroway et al. 2010); web-based videoconferencing capabilities in particular have grown dramatically in the past few years (Arroway et al. 2010). Use of web portals offering access to campus resources such as the registration, transcripts, and libraries is increasing at all colleges and universities responding to the EDUCAUSE survey (Arroway et al. 2010).

Classroom technologies such as computers, document and LCD projectors, smart boards, and clickers are increasing. Televisions are one technology that is diminishing in classrooms as it is viewed as a "legacy instructional delivery system" (Arroway et al. 2010).

Course-management systems (e.g. Blackboard) continue to increase in use. Though what that use specifically is was not measured by the *EDUCAUSE Core Data Survey*, a hybrid approach where a course-management system is used in conjunction with face-to-face instruction is employed for "all or nearly all courses" on campuses that support course-management systems (Arroway et al. 2010).

Learning online. The number of chief academic officers stating that online education is critically important to their institution increased in the past year (Allen and Seaman 2011); 63% of institutions responding in the Sloan Consortium's report indicate online learning to be a critical part of their institution's long term strategy with the increased interest greatest among for-profit institutions. Over 5.6 million students took at least one online course in Fall, 2009; this is an increase of almost one million students from the previous year (Allen and Seaman 2011). Almost 30% of higher education students currently take at least one course online (Allen and Seaman 2011).

In the past year, more academic leaders rated online education as being the same or better than face-to-face education; 66% of those surveyed perceive online education as equal or superior to face-to-face education (Allen and Seaman 2011).

5.3.3   *Faculty Use of Technology for Instruction*

Reporting the results of the Faculty Survey of Student Engagement (FSSE), Smith and Borreson Caruso (2010) note that the majority of college and university faculty are making use of course-management systems, but are not making use of other technologies such as collaborative editing software, student response systems, or plagiarism detection tools. Smith and Borreson Caruso suggest that many instructors continue to teaching using traditional, lecture-based instruction (Smith and Borreson Caruso 2010). It should be noted that results of the *ECAR Study of Undergraduate Students and Information Technology* have for the past 7 years consistently indicated that students prefer only a moderate amount of technology use from instructors.

5.3.4   *Student Computing*

Undergraduates continue to bring their own, relatively new desktop computers, laptops, or netbooks with them to campus (Smith and Borreson Caruso 2010). Eighty-nine percent of the undergraduates reported in the *ECAR Study of Undergraduate Students and Information Technology, 2010*, own a laptop or a netbook, and 70% report their newest computer is less than 2 years old (Smith and Borreson Caruso 2010). It should also be noted that a significant percentage of students own and use significantly older computing tools: 17% of the ECAR study respondents report their newest computer is 4 years old or older (Smith and Borreson Caruso 2010).

An increasing number of undergraduates own Internet capable, handheld devices (60%) and about half of them report accessing the Internet from these devices daily

(Smith and Borreson Caruso 2010). Students aged 25 and older are increasing their use of social-networking sites (SNS), catching up with the consistent use reported over the past 4 years by 18 and 19 year-olds (Smith and Borreson Caruso 2010). Facebook is by far the most popular and commonly used of the SNS (Smith and Borreson Caruso 2010).

The ECAR study results indicate that students are using networked computers for coursework. Ninety-four percent of students surveyed report using their college or university library website for school, work, or recreation; over one-third of respondents use their library website multiple times a week; more than 90% of the respondents report using presentation software and course-management software; and over 85% use spreadsheets (Smith and Borreson Caruso 2010). About 25% of students reported using e-books or e-textbooks in a course, and over 30% report using a course-management system daily (Smith and Borreson Caruso 2010). The use of e-texts is particularly noteworthy; *The Horizon Report* identifies electronic books and mobile devices (most of which have optional, e-reader software available) are "technologies to watch" (Johnson et al 2011a, b.

Undergraduates are making, using, or creating online content. About 25% report playing online multiuser games and using social bookmarking/tagging sites; over 33% contribute to blogs; 40% participate in wikis; and 42% contribute to video websites such as YouTube (Smith and Borreson Caruso 2010).

Over 90% of students surveyed reported using text messaging and accessing SNS; 40% make use of Voice over Internet Protocol (VoIP) (e.g. Skype) (Smith and Borreson Caruso 2010). A much smaller number of students report using SNS for course work; 30% are using SNS in their courses; over 50% of SNS-using students use it to communicate with classmates about their course or courses; less than 8% of SNS-using students communicate with instructors about the course via SNS (Smith and Borreson Caruso 2010).

5.4   K-12 Education

Three national annual reports were consulted in reporting the trends and issues for the K-12 Education section. The *Technology Counts 2011*, *The 2011 Horizon Report: K-12 Edition*, and *The New 3 E's of Education: Enabled, engaged, Empowered; How Today's Students are Leverage Emerging Technologies for Learning*. *Technology Counts 2011* are the 12th annual report published by *Education Week*. This report focuses on the overall state of educational technology in K-12 schools. *The Horizon Report*, produced by the New Media Consortium and the Consortium for School Networking (CoSN), focuses on emerging technologies or practices that are likely to gain use within K-12 over the next year to 5 years. The 2010 National Findings Report, *The New 3 E's of Education: Enabled, engaged, Empowered; How Today's Students are Leverage Emerging Technologies for Learning*, is part of a series of reports published by Project Tomorrow in conjunction with Blackboard Inc. This report examined data collected from "294,399 K-12 students, 42,267 parents, 35,525 teachers, 2,125 librarians, 3,578 school/district administrators and 1,391 technology leaders representing 6,541 public and private schools from 1,340 districts" (Project Tomorrow 2011, p. 4).

Many of the major issues regarding instructional technology use in K-12 have remained relatively consistent since the previous review. There are several issues that were key holdovers: online learning, use of mobile devices, and the use of Web 2.0 tools (Brown and Green 2010, 2011). Online learning in K-12 remained a growing area. Two major areas regarding the use of mobile devices rose to the forefront. These two were the use of smart phones and tablet devices (e.g. iPads). Funding for overall K-12 continued to be a major issue that, not surprisingly, had a direct effect on instructional technology use.

5.4.1 The Overall State of K-12 Technology

Last year's *Technology Counts* focused on how public school districts used technology to enhance and improve teaching and learning. This was a departure from previous years (2009 and prior) when the reports focused on indicators covering state technology policy and practice—specifically, technology use and technology capacity. With these reports, states were given grades on how well they were doing in relationship to these indicators. In 2009, the nation earned a B in technology use and a C+ in technology capacity for use. Nine states received A grades for technology use, while 11 received D+ grades and the District of Columbia received an F. Three states earned A grades in technology capacity for use, while seven earned D grades and five earned F grades (Hightower 2009). The 2010 *Technology Report,* due to a lack of sufficient state-level data, shifted its focus to how public school districts are using technology to enhance and improve teaching and learning. Letter grades were not provided in the 2010 report for states or the nation. The 2011 *Technology Report* does not focus on the overall nation or individual states. Teacher's use of technology is the focus (Education Week 2011, p. 40).

5.4.2 Funding

As occurred during the previous year's review, the overall funding for K-12 dropped—significantly in many states—as state budget deficits rose. In our last review, we wrote that market analysts predicted large deficits for states to continue for another 2–3 years (Devaney 2010). This prediction came true. Many states struggled to balance their budgets, and as a result funding for K-12 was reduced in many states. According to a report from the Center on Budget and Policy Priorities (2011), "At least 34 states and the District of Columbia are cutting aid to K-12 schools and various education programs" (Johnson et al. 2011). As with previous reviews, specific numbers on how much money states spent on K-12 educational technology remains difficult to obtain. Despite the cuts, there was some indication that spending on technology in education did occur. According to a survey report, *Schools Move Beyond The Basics: Competition Will Drive Technology Into The Education Market* (Belissent et al. 2011) decision-makers in education reported that they expected IT budgets to increase. The report indicated that 36% expected them to increase by at least 5 and 10% expected budgets to increase by 10% or more (Belissent et al. 2011).

The nation as a whole encountered a record high deficit. As of the writing of this review, federal funding for educational technology through the Enhancing Education Through Technology (EETT) program had been eliminated. Many programs that were previously under EETT were shifted to different programs because educational technology is being integrated into other programs (Nagel 2011).

5.4.3 Teacher Technology Availability and Use: Devices and Software

In last year's review, we provided a snapshot of the technology resources public school districts made available to their teachers and students as described in *Technology Counts 2010* (Education Week 2010). The data pointed to teachers having relatively good access to various technology tools. Access to electronic tools was 95% for all secondary teachers and 87% for all elementary teachers. Eighty-two percent of secondary teachers and 83% of elementary teachers had server space for posting a web page and class materials. Online student assessment tool access was 72% (secondary teachers) and 73% (elementary teachers). Online curricula access was 66% for both elementary and secondary teachers. Opportunity for distance learning was 65% (secondary) and 64% (elementary). Access to course-management and course-delivery software was 57% for all teachers. Finally, 44% (secondary) and 46% (elementary) have remote access to school or district software.

The 2011 *Technology Counts* report provided related statistics broken down again by elementary and secondary teachers; however, the focus was slightly different—specific educational technology tools teachers had access to and how often teachers used these tools, software usage by teachers, and the percentage of teachers reporting how students used educational technology. Overall, 97% of teachers (98% elementary; 95% secondary) surveyed had access to computers in the classroom every day. The percentage moves to 99% when including computers that could be brought into the classroom (via laptop carts). It is interesting to note that there are 5.3 students per computer in the classrooms with access to computers in them every day. The ratio drops to 1.7 students per computer for classrooms where access also includes computers that could be brought into the classroom (the percentage of these computers with Internet access was reported to be 95) (Education Week 2011, p. 40).

Table 5.1 Teacher availability of technology devices (Data from Education Week 2011, p. 40)

Technology device	Available in the classroom every day (%)	Available as needed (%)
LCD or DLP projectors	48	36
Interactive whiteboards	23	28
Document camera	17	22
Digital cameras	14	67
Classroom response systems	6	22
MP3 player/iPod	5	18
Handheld devices	4	8
Videoconference units	1	21

Table 5.2 Use of technology devices by elementary and secondary teachers (Data from Education Week 2011, p. 40)

Technology device	Use sometimes or often	
	Elementary teachers (%)	Secondary teachers (%)
LCD or DLP projectors	68	78
Interactive whiteboards	58	58
Document camera	60	48
Digital cameras	53	41
Classroom response systems	35	34
MP3 Player/iPod	34	37
Handheld devices	60	28
Videoconference units	12	15

Technology devices: The *Technology Counts 2011* report highlighted eight different technology devices: LCD or DLP projectors, videoconference units, interactive whiteboards, classroom response systems, digital cameras, MP3 Player/iPod, document camera, and handheld devices. The following chart shows the percentage of teachers surveyed who had access to these devices. There is no differentiation between elementary and secondary teachers because access for each device was similar (within 2–5%); exceptions were for the interactive whiteboards where elementary teachers had 31% availability as needed to 23% availability as needed for secondary teachers, and the LCD or DLP projectors where secondary teachers had 56% access every day to 44% access every day for elementary teachers. The LCD or DLP projectors were available to the highest percentage of teachers in the classroom every day. Digital cameras had the highest availability as needed for the teachers surveyed (Education Week 2011, p. 40).

Table 5.2 shows the percentage of teachers who indicated they *use or sometimes use* the devices listed in Table 5.1. The chart is divided into elementary and secondary use.

Teacher Software Use for Instruction and Administrative Tasks. The *Technology Counts 2011* report highlighted 14 software types (see Table 5.3). Word Processing (96%) and the Internet (94%) were the most reported types *sometimes or often used*

Table 5.3 Teacher Software use for instruction and administrative tasks (Data from Education Week 2011, p. 41)

	Software use	
Software type	Sometimes or often use (%)	Rarely use (%)
Word Processing	96	2
The Internet	94	5
Managing Student Records	80	9
Presentations	63	22
Spreadsheets and Graphing	61	25
Subject-Specific	59	19
Desktop Publishing	53	22
Drill and Practice/Tutorials	50	33
Database Management	44	24
Administering tests	44	24
Graphics, image-editing	40	30
Simulation and visualization	33	24
Blogs and Wikis	16	22
Social-networking sites	8	14

by the teachers surveyed. Social-networking Websites were reported as the lowest *sometimes or often used* at 8%. There were very few differences between software type use by elementary and secondary teachers except for presentation software (secondary: 73% *sometimes or often use*; elementary: 58%) and drill and practice/tutorials (elementary: 56% *sometimes or often used*; secondary: 40%). Table 5.3 shows the percentage of use of the various software types.

5.4.4 Teacher Technology Training and Professional Development

We expressed optimism in the past two reviews that the number of states with technology standards for teachers would increase (46 states had teacher technology standards, as of the 2009 review). We were also hopeful that additional states would implement technology requirements for teacher licensure. We predicted in previous reviews that the number of states requiring technology course work or the passing of a test to demonstrate competency would slightly increase (Brown and Green 2010). As of the 2010 review (Brown and Green), only 21 states required either technology course work or the passing of a test to demonstrate competency. Ten states required course work or a test for initial licensure for administrators (Hightower 2009).

Although data are not readily available to support our predictions from our previous reviews, there are data available, similar to last year's available data, which allow us to gain an understanding of the training teachers are receiving in educational technology. Two areas of data are available from the *Technology*

Counts 2011 report: (1) the various types of training teachers received for using educational technology for instruction, and (2) the amount of time teachers spent per year in professional development related to educational technology (Education Week 2011, p. 41).

Teachers reported (78%) that *independent learning* was the primary type (*moderate to major extent*) of training they engaged in for learning how to use educational technology for instruction. The next two types were training provided by staff who are responsible for technology support or integration at their school (61%) and various professional development activities (61%). Graduate teacher education program (33%) was reported as the next most engaged in type of technology training (Education Week 2011, p. 40).

Fifty-three percent of teachers reported spending 1–8 h per year in professional development on educational technology. Eighteen percent reported 9–16 h. Nine percent reported 17–32 h. Seven percent reported participating in 33 or more hours. Thirteen percent reported not participating in any professional development (Education Week 2011, p. 40).

5.5 Student Use and Ownership of Technology

Our previous reviews reported data from two Kaiser Foundation Family studies (Rideout et al. 2010; Rideout et al. 2005) describing 8- to 18-year-olds' use of media in and out of school. The two studies indicated that 8- to 18-year-olds spend a significant amount of hours each day engaged in media (6 ½ h in 2005; approximately 7 ½ h in 2010). The media ranged from watching television to reading print-based materials. The largest percentage of time was spent using digital media (e.g. watching live or recorded television 4 h a day). The 2010 study indicated that all media use increased except for movies (which remained at 25 min a day) and print-based (which dropped 5 min a day to 38 min). Music and audio had the greatest increase at 47 min a day for a total of 2 h and 31 min a day (Rideout et al. 2010).

Although there are no new studies (as of the writing of this review) that provide an updated perspective on media use by K-12 students *in and out of school,* data exist describing frequency of student use of educational technologies *in the classroom. Technology Counts 2011* (Education Week 2011) provides data on 13 student uses of educational technology in the classroom. The report indicates the percent of teachers reporting frequency (*rarely or sometimes/often*) of student use of educational technology. Sixty-nine percent of all teachers indicated that their students *sometimes or often* use educational technology to *learn or practice skills.* The next two most frequently reported uses were *conduct research* (66%) and *prepare written text* (61%). Table 5.4 provides data broken down by elementary and secondary teachers (Education Week 2011).

We believe that media use in and out of school has, at minimum, remained consistent. We predict that student use of media in and out of school will continue to increase slightly, as it did from 2005 to 2010, as more students gain access to

Table 5.4 Teacher reporting of student frequency of educational technology use in the classroom (Data from Education Week 2011, p. 41)

Educational technology use	Elementary		Secondary	
	Rarely use (%)	Sometimes or often use (%)	Rarely use (%)	Sometimes or often use (%)
Prepare written text	27	57	20	67
Create or use graphics of visual displays	29	49	24	59
Learn or practice basic skills	15	76	21	53
Conduct research	23	64	20	69
Correspond with others	20	26	24	20
Contribute to Blogs or Wikis	10	7	16	13
Use Social-Networking Websites	7	6	12	9
Solve problems, analyze data, or perform calculations	21	45	25	46
Conduct experiments or perform measurements	24	23	27	30
Develop and present multimedia presentations	26	35	24	53
Create art, music, movies, or websites	25	21	24	32
Develop or run demonstrations, models, or simulations	21	14	26	25
Design and produce a product	15	11	20	17

personal mobile devices. As a result, students and parents will continue to put pressure on administrators and teachers to allow the use of these devices as learning tools in and out of the classroom.

Student Access to Educational Technology. The major trend in student access to educational technology over the past two reviews has been mobile devices. In last year's review, we reported that according to the *Generation M2: Media in the Lives of 8- to 18-Year-Olds*, the percentages of ownership in this age range were 66% for cell phones, 76% for iPod/MP3 players, and 29% for laptops (Rideout et al. 2010). *Technology Counts 2010* reported 71% of teens owned a cell phone (Manzo 2010). When compared to available data from 2009, student ownership of mobile devices—especially cell phones—increased.

The Project Tomorrow's Speak Up National Findings Report (2011), *The New 3 E's of Education: Enabled, engaged, Empowered; How Today's Students are Leverage Emerging Technologies for Learning,* indicates an increase as well. The report points out two significant areas regarding students and mobile devices. The first is that from 2009 to 2010 smart phone access of middle and high school students increased by 42%. The second point is that "when the data for middle and high school students is analyzed for differences based upon school demographics such as qualification for Title 1 funding (as an indication of community poverty) or community type (urban, rural or suburban) there is relatively little or no difference in the data results" (Project Tomorrow 2011, p. 18).

Table 5.5 Percent of parents likely to purchase a mobile device for their child to use at school (Data from Project Tomorrow's Speak Up National Findings Report (2011) p. 6)

Grade of child	Likely to purchase (%)	School responsibility to purchase (%)	Unlikely to purchase (%)	Unsure (%)
K-5	63	14	11	10
6–8	69	13	10	8
9–12	70	12	8	7

The report also indicates that in addition to cell phone and smart phone access, students have access to other mobile devices such as a laptop, MP3, and a tablet device (specifically the iPad). In grades 9–12, 85% of students surveyed indicated having access to an MP3 player, 67% to a laptop, 44% to a smart phone, and 10% to an iPad. Students surveyed in grades 6–8 indicated the following access levels: 79% MP3 players, 60% laptops, 34% smart phone, and 13% iPad. Students in grades 3–5 surveyed indicated access levels of 55% for MP3 players, 42% for laptops, 19% for smart phones, and 8% for iPads. Students surveyed in grades K-2 indicated the following access levels: 37% MP3 players and laptops, 16% smart phones, and 10% iPad.

Mobile devices remain a major trend for this review. There has been a shift in focus, however, from schools providing access to mobile devices (i.e. laptops and other hand held devices) to student owned mobile devices — specifically cell phones and smart phones. With increased student access to cell phones and smart phones coupled with shrinking K-12 budgets, many schools have begun to consider how to most effectively leverage student owned mobile devices for learning. We predict this will remain as a trend. The *2011 Horizon Report: K-12 Edition* supports this prediction by indicating mobile devices as one of the technologies in the category of Time-to-Adoption: 1 Year or Less (New Media Consortium 2011).

We predicted in our last review that mobile devices and online learning would continue to be trends in 2011, and that cloud computing, collaborative environments, e-books, and game-based learning would emerge as trends.

Mobile devices: The use of mobile devices and online learning did continue as trends. Mobile devices, specifically smart phones and tablet devices, such as the iPad, gained increased traction during the review period. As indicated earlier in the chapter (see "Student Access to Educational Technology"), there has been a steady increase in the number of K-12 students who have personal access to mobile devices. This, along with data from the Project Tomorrow's *Speak Up* National Findings Report (2011) indicating how likely parents are to purchase a mobile device for their child to use at school (see Table 5.5), leads us to predict that the use of mobile devices will remain as a continuous trend.

Data exist indicating that teachers, parents, and students, in particularly, are willing and ready for these tools to be used in the classroom (Project Tomorrow 2011; Johnson et al. 2011a, b). Whether the full potential of mobile devices as learning tools will be realized or not, however, depends greatly on the actions of policy makers and administrators.

Table 5.6 Middle school and high school students who reported taking online classes (Data from Project Tomorrow's Speak Up National Findings Report 2011, p. 8)

Year	Middle school students (%)	Secondary students (%)
2010	19	30
2009	13	18
2008	9	10

Online learning. Online learning continued as a trend as well. Our last review (Brown and Green 2011) reported that, according to the Sloan Consortium, the growth of K-12 students using online courses significantly rose from 2008 to 2009; from 2005, the total number of students using online courses increased by 47%. We predicted in our last review that the number of students taking online courses would increase during this review period. Although there is no specific data available (at the time we wrote this review) for 2011 to explicitly support our prediction, based on data provided in Project Tomorrow's *Speak Up* National Findings Report (Brown and Green 2011), we believe our prediction was correct. Table 5.6 demonstrates the increase in students in middle school and high school who reported taking online classes.

During the review period (actually starting in late 2010), online learning has evolved into many different forms and filled various roles. Three specific trends for online learning occurred that we believe are trends to watch: (1) online learning being used for credit recovery for students to make up courses they did not complete, (2) an increase in blended learning (i.e., courses that include some components of online learning), and (3) universities running online K-12 programs such as college-level elective courses for high school students and courses for gifted students (Davis 2011; Ash 2011; Horn and Staker 2011; Picciano and Seamna 2010). A recurring theme with these trends is the personalization of instruction for students with varied needs. Online learning and blended learning, as does educational technology in general, hold a great deal of promise for being able to provide unique educational opportunities for a wide-range of students.

Additional innovative and emerging technologies and practices: In addition to mobile devices and online learning and blended learning, there is evidence of other innovative and emerging technologies and practices being used in K-12 during this review period. The most significant are cloud computing, collaborative environments, and e-books. Game-based learning and augmented realities made advances as well.

In our previous review, we reported that schools had begun to use cloud-based computing mostly for productivity and administrative purposes (Johnson et al. 2010, p. 9). We predicted that as schools become more familiar and comfortable with using cloud-based computing, there would be an increase in its use for teaching and learning. The 2011 Horizon Report: K-12 Edition indicated that cloud computing had a Time-to-Adoption of 1 year or less. The report indicated that, "Growing out of research in grid computing, cloud computing transforms once-expensive resources like disk storage and processing cycles into a readily available, cheap commodity" (Johnson et al. 2011a, b, p. 1). This allows for applications such as word processing, image-editing, and media creation tools to be made available to teachers and students through the Web (as a cloud-based application). Doing so, teachers and students have access to free or very low-cost alternatives to applications that are expensive and proprietary (Johnson et al. 2011a, b). Many who use these cloud-based applications do not realize they are even using them.

We also predicted in our previous review that the use of collaborative environments (e.g. Ning, VoiceThread, Wikis) would continue to increase for teaching and learning, if schools are able to manage security and safety issues while providing adequate access to these tools for teachers and students (Robinson et al. 2010). The data to support these predictions are not overwhelming, but do point to these tools being used. According to Project Tomorrow's *Speak Up* Survey Report (2011), 11% of the teachers indicated that on any given school day they are *Empowering collaboration between students using blogs, SNS, wikis, or GOOGLE docs*. We predict that a steady—albeit slight—increase in use will continue. The major obstacle will continue to be how IT and administrators will manage security and safety issues while providing the level of access in schools to collaborative environments that students and teachers desire.

The e-book is the third innovative and emerging technology from our pervious review that we predicted would be a major trend in K-12 in 2011. We wrote that we believe e-books—specifically digital textbooks—would gain more attention as schools continued to lower costs while at the same time provide teachers and students with access to the most current and useful content. Digital textbooks could find a great deal of traction if publishers provided content in ways that could be accessed on the various mobile devices students use. There is some evidence that e-books are increasing in use. Approximately one-third of school libraries have e-books, according to the *Survey of E-book Penetration and Use in U.S. School (K-12) Libraries* (Library Journal 2010). Of the two-thirds of school libraries not offering e-books, 25% indicated having a plan to offer e-books in the next 12 months, 42% indicated having a plan to offer e-books in the next couple of years, and 37% indicated having no plan to offer e-books (Library Journal). Elementary schools were the least likely to have indicated having a plan to offer e-books (Library Journal). According to Project Tomorrow's *Speak Up* report, 27% of middle school students and 35% of high school students are using online textbooks in their regular course work (Project Tomorrow 2011, p. 9). Based on available data, we predict an increase in the use of e-books as districts continue to cut costs and maximize technology schools and students have available; as tablet devices quality improves and costs decrease; and as increased content becomes available an electronic format. We believe that student desire to have access to course content in an electronic format will also be a driving force in the adoption of e-books in K-12.

In addition to the trends of cloud computing, collaborative environments, and e-books, there was some evidence of other innovative and emerging technologies being used in K-12 such as game-based learning and augmented reality. *The 2011 Horizon Report: K-12 Edition* identified nine innovative and emerging technologies as ones to watch over the next 2–5 years. The nine they identified as ones to watch were augmented reality, game-based learning, cellular networks, open content, gesture-based computing, learning analytics, personal learning environments, and wireless power. Of these, we predict that game-based learning and augmented reality will have the greatest near term effects on K-12.

5.6 Conclusion

We again predict, as we did in the 2011 review, that spending on instructional technology will remain relatively stable in all sectors with the exception of a possible decrease in the K-12 sector due to the lack of a full economic recovery. Despite this, we anticipate continued innovative uses of instructional technology and opportunities available for instructional technology specialists in corporate, higher education, and K-12 environments. Based on the trends observed in online learning, we predict an increase of use in all sectors—especially with the continued improvement of mobile devices, the availability of quality electronic content and resources, and the proliferation of cloud-computing environments. We also predict increased use of augmented realities based on both online learning's continued growth and the improvement and proliferation of mobile devices.

References

Allen, I. A., & Seaman, J. (2011). *Class differences: Online education in the United States, 2010.* Babson Park, MA: Babson Survey Research Group.

Arroway, P., Davenport, E., Xu, G. & Updegrove, D. (2010). *EDUCAUSE core data service fiscal year 2009 summary report.* Retrieved from http://net.educause.edu/ir/library/pdf/PUB8007.pdf.

Ash, K. (2011). Gaming goes academic. *Technology Counts, 30*(25), 24, 28.

Belissent, J., Mines, C., & Darashkevich, Y. (2011). *Schools move beyond the basics: Competition will drive technology into the education market.* Retrieved from http://www.forrester.com/rb/Research/schools_move_beyond_basics_competition_will_drive/q/id/58178/t/2.

Brown, A., & Green, T. (2010). Issues and trends in instructional technology: Growth and maturation of web-based tools in a challenging climate; Social networks gain educators' attention. In M. Orey, S. A. Jones, & R. M. Branch (Eds.), *Educational media and technology yearbook* (Vol. 35, pp. 29–44). New York: Springer.

Brown, A., & Green, T. (2011). Issues and trends in educational technology: Lean times, shifts in online learning, and increased attention to mobile devices. In M. Orey, S. A. Jones, & R. M. Branch (Eds.), *Educational media and technology yearbook* (Vol. 36). New York: Springer.

Davis, M. (2011). Credit-recovery lessons. *Technology Counts, 30*(25), 30, 32.

Devaney, L. (2010). Economy continues to batter schools. *eSchool News, 13*(2), 1, 38.

Education Week. (2010). *Technology Counts, 29*(26).

Education Week. (2011). *Teachers & technology, 30*(25), 40–41.

Hightower, A. M., (2009). Tracking U.S. trends: States earn B average for policies supporting educational technology use. *Technology Counts 2009, 28*(26), 30–33.

Horn, M., & Staker, H. (2011). *The rise of blended k-12 learning.* Retrieved from http://www.innosightinstitute.org/media-room/publications/education-publications/the-rise-of-k-12-blended-learning/.

Johnson, N., Oliff, P., & Williams, E. (2011). An update on state budget cuts. Retrieved from http://www.cbpp.org/cms/index.cfm?fa=view&id=1214.

Johnson, L., Smith, R., Levine, A., & Haywood, K. (2010). *The 2010 Horizon report: K-12 edition*. Austin, Texas: The New Media Consortium.

Johnson, L., Smith, R., Willis, H., Levine, A., & Haywood, K. (2011a). *The 2011 Horizon report*. Austin, TX: The New Media Consortium.

Johnson, L., Smith, R., Willis, H., Levine, A., & Haywood, K. (2011b). *The 2011 Horizon report: K-12 edition*. Austin, Texas: The New Media Consortium.

Library Journal (2010). *LJ/SLJ survey of ebook penetration & Use in U.S. school libraries*. Retrieved from http://c0003264.cdn2.cloudfiles.rackspacecloud.com/School%20Library%20Ebook%20Report_2.pdf.

Manzo, K. (2010). Educators embrace iPods for learning. Education Week: *Technology Counts 2010, 29*(26), 16–17.

Nagel, D. (2011). EETT eliminated in 2011 Obama budget proposal. *T.H.E. Journal*. Retrieved from http://thejournal.com/articles/2010/02/01/ed-tech-funding-eliminated-in-2011-obama-budget-proposal.aspx.

Patel, L. (2010). *2010 state of the industry report: ASTD's definitive review of workplace learning and development trends*. Alexandria, VA: American Society for Training & Development.

Picciano, A., & Seamna, J. (2010). Class connections: High school reform and the role of online learning. Retrieved from http://www3.babson.edu/ESHIP/research-publications/upload/Class_connections.pdf.

Project Tomorrow. (2011). *Speak up 2010*. Retrieved from http://www.tomorrow.org/SpeakUp/.

Rideout, V. J., Foehr, U. G., & Roberts, D. F. (2005). *Generation M: Media in the lives of 8- to 18-year-olds*. Menlo Park, CA: Henry J. Kaiser Family Foundation.

Rideout, V. J., Foehr, U. G., & Roberts, D. F. (2010). *Generation M2: Media in the lives of 8- to 18-year-olds*. Menlo Park, CA: Henry J. Kaiser Family Foundation.

Robinson, L. K., Brown, A. H., & Green, T. D. (2010). Security vs. Access: Balancing Safety and Productivity in the Digital School. *International Society for Technology in Education* (ISTE).

Smith, S. D., & Borreson Caruso, J. (2010). *The ECAR study of undergraduate students and information technology, 2010*. Boulder, CO: EDUCAUSE.

Chapter 6
Introduction to the Qualitative Inquiry Award

Robert Maribe Branch

The Qualitative Inquiry Award began one afternoon when Robert deKieffer and Andrew Yeaman were discussing the current state of scholarship. Bob was the President of the Educational Communications and Technology (ECT) Foundation and Andrew had been chairing the Young Researcher Award for a couple of years. The ECT Foundation is a non-profit organization for charitable and educational purposes that has made a substantial commitment in support of Association for Educational Communications and Technology (AECT). These purposes reflect the belief that instruction can be improved with new systems for learning and with assessment of techniques for the communication of information. The Foundation funds leadership-training programs for AECT in addition to awarding scholarships, internships, and fellowships. The ECT Foundation's Young Researcher Award is presented to the best paper reporting on a quantitative or qualitative study addressing a question related to educational technology. The winning paper receives special consideration for publication in Educational Technology Research and Development (ETR&D), the refereed scholarly research journal published by the AECT. However, a need had become apparent for recognizing and rewarding scholarship apart from quantitative research based in experimental psychology, which is what was being submitted for the Young Researcher Award at the time.

A special award was approved to run on a trial basis and in 1992 the competition was first offered. In 1995, the Foundation announced the creation of an on-going award. The prize was funded in perpetuity when Lida Cochran promised a bequest in memory of her late husband, Lee W. Cochran. The Award is only to be given when there is an outstanding application so there has not been a winner every year. However, reviewers have reported that the number of entries has continually

---

Based on an original narrative by Andrew R. J. Yeaman published in the 2011 Yearbook

R.M. Branch (✉)
Department of Educational Psychology and Instructional Technology,
University of Georgia, Athens, GA, USA
e-mail: rbranch@uga.edu

M. Orey et al. (eds.), *Educational Media and Technology Yearbook*, Educational
Media and Technology Yearbook 37, DOI 10.1007/978-1-4614-4430-5_6,
© Springer Science+Business Media New York 2013

increased over the years and the overall quality of the submissions continues to improve.

The Qualitative Inquiry Award recognizes qualitative insights into the social and cultural aspects of the professional field of ECT. This award encourages and recognizes qualitative understanding about ECT. The emphasis is on inquiry from disciplines such as anthropology, art criticism, cultural studies, history, literary criticism, philosophy, and sociology. The aim for the Award is to build awareness of the professional field's purposes and its position in the world. The intention is to augment existing professional knowledge of how to do things through asking deeper questions about what should be done, why should it be done, and who is involved in the doing. Award recipients have a session reserved for them to give a presentation at the annual AECT conference and the author has the opportunity to publish in this Yearbook.

The Qualitative Inquiry Award is open to all relevant instructional areas including training. The main criteria are the use of social or cultural theory for the on-going development of scholarship in ECT. Co-authored submissions are not accepted. This award recognizes the contributions of individuals to professional scholarship. Membership in AECT is required. Consult the AECT web site for more information about the Qualitative Inquiry Award.

Chapter 7
Social Capital Influences upon Internet Usage of Rural Guatemalan English Teachers

Douglas Tedford

7.1 Introduction

From 1960 to 1996, a civil war was waged in the mountain highlands and jungles of the Republic of Guatemala. Difficulties imposed by the war upon transportation and communication disrupted the development of information communication technology (ICT) infrastructures in remote areas, and of knowledge and practices for the use of ICT in education. This produced a digital divide between metropolitan and rural regions (Attewell 2001; Caniz 2006; Koss 2001). The 1996 Esquipulas Peace Accords (Conciliation Resources 2007) and subsequent agreements demonstrated a commitment by the Guatemalan government to support equal educational opportunities for its indigenous peoples. This commitment was enriched through the promise of enhancing educational opportunities by provision of equal Internet access throughout Guatemala (ITFORCEGT 2006; Ordoñez 2006; United Nations Educational, Scientific and Cultural Organization 2008, ¶ 2).

This objective has been followed up most effectively in the nation's capital and least successfully in mountainous, rural regions such as San Lucas, Toliman, the site of the study (Menchú 2007). Researchers postulate that providing Internet access does not guarantee usage (Crump and McIlroy 2003; Foth 2003), and raise questions of why the Internet is neglected when available (DiMaggio and Hargittai 2001; Natriello 2001). Although a digital divide has been noted between developed and developing nations (Leavey 2003; Rogers 2003), few research studies discuss disparities in third world online education. Creed and Joynes describe the situation:

> In general, distance education is an under-researched area and the need for improvement in the quality and quantity of research and evaluation is widely acknowledged ... What research exists tends to be strong on description but weak on evaluative data, both quantitative and qualitative, on which to make judgments about effectiveness and this is particularly

D. Tedford, Ed.D (✉)
Fundacion Rigoberta Menchu Tum of Guatemala, Teaching Services Latin America,
Mexico City, Mexico

M. Orey et al. (eds.), *Educational Media and Technology Yearbook*, Educational
Media and Technology Yearbook 37, DOI 10.1007/978-1-4614-4430-5_7,
© Springer Science+Business Media New York 2013

so in developing countries. What are the reasons behind this? The usual suspects, common to research in any area, are there: poor dissemination, limited research skills and constrained resources which often push research and evaluation to the bottom of the agenda. But there are also other reasons specific to distance education itself. (Creed and Joynes 2005, p. 6)

The lack of support for research on distance education in the developing world impedes the knowledge within and between third world cultures about their common concerns. The challenges to the spread of third world online education have been addressed through the promotion by intergovernmental organizations, such as the International Bank for Reconstruction and Development, of applying social capital to improve the quality of Internet access and usage in the developing nations (International Bank for Reconstruction and Development 2006, 2007a, 2008). Although journal articles and websites have advanced an agenda of interactivity between educators via the Internet and have suggested the value of social capital for the diffusion of the Internet in the developing world, specific research studies which investigate the contribution or influence of social capital for online education of any sort are not found. For instance, Eugene Kowch said in an interview:

[S]o far the education sector has little to say about (the) ... contribution (of) ... social capital at ... global levels. Little research is done to provide measures of social capital accretion and depreciation in the education sector ... Are we measuring this macro policy phenomenon in distance learning? I have seen no evidence of it ... While social capital concepts may seem abstract or disconnected from most educational technology leadership today ... technology-enhanced education offers more social capital capacity for our nations than do most sub-fields in education... (Lorenzetti 2004, p. 6)

What was known about the disparities of Internet access for rural sections of the developing world was tied to the mutually dependent factors of infrastructure and buying power, both of which are scarce in rural, remote sectors. Rutherford et al. (2004) defined the Internet as a principally urban technology:

The telecommunications infrastructures which support the Internet are predominantly deployed within and between major cities (and)....broadly speaking, core urban regions have significant advantages over peripheral rural regions in terms of access to telecommunications ... In large cities, the monetary and academic necessity of ICT skills, including facility with the Internet, is a given, driving achievement in higher education and business ...Infrastructure, pricing and training function (work) in tandem to expand the use of services for profit and public benefit. (p. 1)

Goodman et al. (2001) commented that, while satellite technologies make the Internet available in remote sectors, a question remains: "Who pays?" (p. 21). Apart from financial resources, the principle challenges for fomenting Internet usage in rural, remote sectors are the lack of Internet sophistication among potential users and a dearth of ICT experts to guide them. Goodman, Gottstein, and Goodman believe:

There are a number of divides even if only the Internet is considered, with distinctions between populations based on ....income, education, language, occupation, and ethnicity. Multiple distinctions make for stark gaps. Thus, poor, semiliterate, ethnic minorities in small, isolated rural villages in the world's poorest countries are not as likely ... to be frequent or sophisticated users as are people not characterized by any of these traits. (p. 21)

The ICT market has been identified as favoring the best quality of services in and between large urban centers (Rutherford et al. 2004). Perhaps the only way in which an online teacher development program could be successfully introduced in a rural sector of the developing world would be through the infusion of donated resources and a staff of experts in ICT and teacher training. These would be funded by government social welfare resources, nonprofit collaborations, private industry initiatives, or a combination of these sources, because wholly private, for-profit efforts would be considered unwise (Romo-Rodriguez 2005).

7.2   San Lucas Toliman and Environs

San Lucas Toliman is representative of many remote, rural towns in Guatemala which could benefit from this type of cooperative effort. In San Lucas, the Fundación Rigoberta Menchú Tum (FRMT) already operates a small school, the Centro Educativo Luciano Pavarotti, Programa Utzilal Tijonikel, which includes an Internet-connected community technology center (CTC). The education director oversaw all education initiatives of the FRMT from offices based in Guatemala City and traveled regularly to oversee progress of programs at the school, including utilization of the computer lab. An operations manager and headmaster locally governed the school and CTC. The researcher had functioned as a volunteer educational consultant to the FRMT since August 2006. With the intention of playing a more active role in the educational development of rural teachers throughout Guatemala, the FRMT education director invited the researcher to conduct seminars for English teachers at the Pavarotti school. Along with data for enhancing teacher involvement and persistence in online education, recommendations and refinements for practices in the management of the CTC resulted.

The ICT project was initiated in July 2007. At that time, and by invitation of the education director of the FRMT, comprised of 34 teachers who had participated in a teacher training program at the FRMT's school and led by the researcher, were offered free usage of the Internet to participate in follow-up training online with the researcher in a 26-week course. Of the 34, only 19 elected to try out free online access, and only 5 of them completed the course. This perplexed the FRMT education staff, local Ministry of Education leadership, and the researcher (Cifuentes 2007; Galvez 2007). In reaction to a comment that perhaps the nonparticipating teachers lacked motivation, the FRMT agreed to support the researcher in the role of facilitating a study to shed light on challenges and potential resolutions to teacher rejection of the Internet.

In order for the results of such a study to foment lasting change in practices tied to teacher Internet usage in San Lucas, it would be necessary to select a research approach which validated the norms and values of community-driven development, making the input of local leadership endemic to the research plan and its implementation (International Bank for Reconstruction and Development 2007a, b, ¶ 1). As suggested by multiple sources, the study should deflect its focus from issues of improving Internet access to questions of how to improve Internet usage (Crump and McIlroy 2003; Foth 2003) and should integrate learning about the effect of social capital for enhancing teacher involvement with ICT (International Bank for Reconstruction and Development 2007a; Lorenzetti 2004).

These goals were compatible with the Participatory Rural Appraisal (PRA) (Chambers 1990, 1992, 1994, 1998). It had been previously employed to study interactions between rural indigenous groups developing nations, including Guatemala (Dudwick et al. 2006; Ibañez et al. 2002). The PRA is known as "a growing family of participatory approaches and methods that emphasize local knowledge and enable local people to make their own appraisal, analysis, and plans… to enable (entities) to work together to plan context-appropriate programs (International Bank for Reconstruction and Development, 2007a, ¶ 2). Use of the PRA was found to eliminate distortions of data collection and findings (Chambers 1998) which could result from cultural differences between developed and developing nations (Laungani 2005), and to support culturally meaningful styles of collecting and evaluating data. The PRA foments community-driven identification of problems and involves the community in devising methods, conducting data collection, interpreting data, and developing solutions to be implemented locally (Gonsalves 2005).

Coleman explained that definitions of social capital could be molded to match a variety of needs or functions (1988). Sabatini (2007) provided a website gateway to diverse applications of social capital for research. Alsop et al. (2003) considered social capital as norms and values transmitted through social networks. Lin described social capital as "resources embedded in social relations" (2001, p. xi). Social capital was found to suggest a context for understanding needs for guidance to overcome barriers to the use of the Internet, as provision of the apparatus of Internet access does not guarantee usage (Crump and McIlroy 2003; Foth 2003). Woolcock (1998, 2002) favored viewing social capital as knowledge, norms, and values originating from three types of networks, namely bonding, bridging, and linking. In line with Woolcock's definitions, bonding social capital refers to close associations of equals, such as teachers. Bridging social capital connotes associations with locally accessible experts, such as ICT technicians. Linking social capital describes individuals originating from outside the immediate social setting, such as the researcher and the education coordinator of the FRMT.

Through this perspective, social capital in networks was particularly significant because it had been identified as both a medium for long-distance sharing of ICT knowledge, norms, and values and as a catalyst for local change in ICT skills and preferences (Van Bavel et al. 2007), empowering community-driven development of solutions to locally identified problems. The perspective of social capital was also seen valuable for identifying the effectiveness of opinion leaders and change agents in encouraging online participation (Rogers 1995, 2003).

In interviewing teachers during the summer of 2008, the researcher took the role of noninvasive facilitator, and relegated duties involving direct contact with the teachers to a culturally sensitive, native Spanish-speaking research assistant. Research questions addressed teacher concerns about using the Internet, teacher satisfaction with Internet resources, and social influences upon Internet usage. The native researcher reconstructed the questions into shorter units and met individually for interviews with 20 of the 34 teachers, who had been selected in a purposive sample, as in Table 7.1.

Table 7.1 Characteristics of 34 Teachers Invited to Enroll in a 26-Week Online Course

Sub-Group Size	Course Completion	Description of Participation	Interview Sample
5	Yes	consistent	5
6	no	consistent, then dropped out	5
8	no	logged on once or twice only	5
15	no	never logged on	5

Led by the research assistant, interviews were transcribed in Spanish at the end of each interview period. Representative statements were culled from the transcriptions and assigned response categories identical to the research questions. These representative statements were then copied in large print onto five sets of sentence strips for analysis after conclusion of the 20 interviews. Next, employing the principles of the permanent group interview (PGI) method within the PRA approach (Grenier 1998), 42 community educators attended an open-invitation meeting and dinner to review, prioritize, interpret, and discuss the representative estatements. The purpose was for them to present their suggestions for increasing the involvement and persistence of local teachers in online education. The PGI was led by the FRMT education director, and the meeting was facilitated through support of the researcher and research assistant.

This meeting crystallized the community's understanding of specific teacher ICT concerns and temporal ICT challenges. It brought to light how teacher decisions to use free Internet services for online professional development were influenced positively or negatively by bonding, bridging, and linking social capital. These data supported the FRMT, the researcher, and the community in its shared goals to increase participation of rural Guatemalan teachers in online learning. Evidence for the forms of social capital and their influence is cited through translated excerpts from the interviews and through descriptions of the community's evaluation of findings in the PGI. Comments of both types are presented as an English-language translation of the original Spanish. The interview data and community findings provide an example of the challenges and promises of online education for remote, rural towns in Guatemala, and demonstrate how such a study design could be of value in other regions of the developing world.

7.3   Temporal Impediments to Internet Access

Although the emphasis and value of the study was to learn about the influences of social capital upon usage, it was essential to provide brief background data covering the physical and economic context within which teachers made the choice to accept or reject free Internet services and coursework in San Lucas. Lack of buying power and of electrical and telecommunications infrastructures in communities impeded the purchase or usefulness of a home computer and of Internet services. Some of the interviewed teachers lived outside of town in small settlements located on hillsides or in forested areas. Buying power limited access to higher-priced dwellings within the town limits or in larger nearby settlements, where the presence of electricity lines could make home computer use with Internet service a remote possibility, if teachers were able to purchase them. Barriers to Internet usage were further exacerbated by the limited availability of landline telephones, requiring the purchase of satellite-based connections in place of lower-cost dial-up services.

Added to buying power and electrical and telecommunications infrastructures, distance to a public Internet-connected location represented another level of challenge for teachers seeking to obtain online educational resources or participate in online coursework. Travel into town was essential for accessing any public Internet site, and the price per hour at Internet cafes was prohibitive for all but a few, making free access through FRMT's CTC an attractive option. To get to an Internet café or the CTC, the teachers relied on public transportation for mobility from homes as far as 2 h from the center of town, while others walked. Transportation ranged from motorcycle, taxis, and small buses to flatbed trucks. Night travel was thought unsafe due to the possibility of crime requiring teachers to leave town in time to arrive home before dusk.

7.4 Influences of Bonding Social Capital upon Internet Usage

Bonding social capital is an essential resource for getting things done in rural Guatemalan communities (Durston 2002). This correlates with Fazio (2007) indicating that Guatemala's mountainous landforms provided the resources and infrastructure for building of an agricultural-based economy but also promoted close, bounded relationships which grew out of exclusion from the (metropolitan Spanish-speaking) host culture. Thereby, analysis and findings from the rural teachers of this study should manifest a bonding social capital effect of strong interdependence for using the Internet within the community of San Lucas and should reveal the presence of traditions or values which were distinct from larger city cultures. These were found to be present, and bonding social capital influences were found to both support and deter Internet usage of the interviewed teachers.

The interview excerpts bore clear witness to the positive and negative influences which bonding social capital associations can levy upon teacher attitudes and goals about using the Internet. As in all cultures, studying online requires the displacement of other activities, rearranging of task commitments, and negotiation in family units about how available resources will be applied. The 42 community educators which met in the PGI extolled teachers for managing their time to allow for online study, encouraged women to act independently, and recommended the exploration of methods for educating families about the importance of supporting all genders in a commitment to learn online. These injunctions represented the first stage of a plan for developing the social capital supports necessary to sustain online teacher professional development practices in the region.

7.5   Influences of Bridging Social Capital upon Internet Usage

Within this study, the concept of bridging social capital referred to seeking the involvement of expert resources for learning to use the Internet. Randolph and Krause (2002) emphasized, in addition to the need for effective ICT mentors, the important role students can play in providing mutual aid when learning how to utilize technology. They cited a "lack of knowledge about and discomfort with computers" as a precedent to the formation of negative attitudes leading to avoidance of the Internet. Rowe-Whyte et al. (2002) commented upon the potential reactions of novice adopters, including the holding of "negative attitudes that can undermine persistence and achievement" (p.2). Some Mayan teachers, for whom Spanish is a second language, struggled with poor adaptation to a technological innovation, which supplies advanced instructions in Spanish or English. Most teachers reported a need for in-depth guidance and sensitive follow up. For some, it was their first encounter with computers.

Most of the teachers of San Lucas had little or no previous experience with the Internet, only a few of those interviewed speak Spanish as the primary language, and many find English-language instructions online to be a significant challenge. From within the bonding social groups that teachers formed, some were esteemed for their skills in using the Internet and they serve a bridging social capital function. When teachers attended the CTC, they hope for guidance from the ICT technician, another potential source of bridging social capital. Because these technicians possess specialized knowledge about computers and the Internet and because they control access to the CTC, these individuals can levy considerable influence in the decision of a teacher to use the Internet for learning.

Contrasting experiences were related in the interviews. Anxiety about in-depth guidance over time for using the Internet was also tied to the weak ICT background knowledge presented by the teachers. Additionally, expectations of learning Internet usage in trial and error online activities without guidance in person were reported by teachers to be unrealistic, and consistent with assertions by a number of researchers that online learning is most effective when combined with face-to-face learning opportunities (Batane 2004; Chang 2004; Henning 2003; Olugebenga Ojo and Kayode Olakulehin 2006).

The comments of a group of community educators, assembled for the PGI meeting, included requests for the FRMT to enhance Internet training opportunities for teachers with no previous computer experience, and encouraged teachers to manage their time and priorities in order to utilize the free Internet services at the school. Although the Internet could provide a gateway for easing the transition to acquisition of Internet practices through contact with entities distant from the receiver, this was not at all found to be the case in San Lucas, where the best way to support Internet usage was found to be a combination of bonding and bridging influences in social networks. This finding in the PGI meeting was fully consistent with assertions by Kavanaugh et al. (2005) that a combination of bridging and bonding social capital sources makes for a dynamic environment for community change:

> Communities with "bridging" social capital … as well as "bonding" social capital … are the most effective in organizing for collective action … When people with bridging ties use …the Internet, they enhance their capability to educate community members and to organize, as needed, for collective action (p. 119).

Within the context of this study, linking social capital resources, transmitted through the conduit of the Internet to remote communities (Van Bavel et al. 2007), would be useless without the support of ICT experts, as a form of bridging social capital, to guide teachers supported by their associates in bonding social capital groups, for development as online learners.

7.6 Influences of Linking Social Capital Upon Internet Usage

Teacher interviews clearly demonstrated a general appreciation for the value of Internet resources originating from outside their community. While these resources were looked upon as valuable or even essential, the multiple barriers of buying power, infrastructure, and distance were viewed as insurmountable by most teachers. Of the 34 teachers invited to take advantage of free Internet usage for coursework under the auspices of the FRMT, only 11 persisted for one half of the 26-week course, with 5 completing. Although online resources were hosted by entities from outside the community, the definition of linking social capital in the context of the study is limited to individuals from outside of the immediate societal context which through direct human interaction could have influenced the Internet usage of the teachers. The researcher served as the chief source of linking social capital, as facilitator of the 26-week course in English teaching which spurred this study, joined by the FRMT education director who extended the offer of free Internet services for the teachers. Other linking social capital sources were academic and professional contacts via email, college online study colleagues, and prayer partners. However, in convergence with research by Woolcock and Narayan (2002), the paucity of references in teacher interviews to resources qualifying as linking social capital underlined the influence of bonding and bridging social capital as the key supports for using the Internet to learn online.

With so few teachers accepting the offer for free Internet usage and such a small percentage of enrolled teachers completing the coursework, it was essential that this quandary should be studied from the perspective of the community. An open invitation was extended to all members of the educational community to participate. The meeting followed PRA guidelines for group derivation of findings based on the interview data, and possibly eliminated the potential for distortion of findings and recommendations which could have resulted from cultural insensitivity by the researcher. This approach heightened the propensity of the study's findings to result in permanent systemic change driven by community decision making. The FRMT as provider of free Internet services, the FRMT education director as an agent of change and opinion leadership, and the researcher as an ongoing promoter of online teacher education worked together to support the implementation of a research project designed to meet the community's specifications.

7.7   Conclusion

The collaboration between the researcher, native-speaker research assistant, staff of the FRMT, teachers receiving training services, and community educational leadership resulted in the establishment of a new level of dialogue for developing a system of online professional development in rural, remote sections of Guatemala. After completion of just a few of the interviews, it became apparent that low responsiveness of teachers to the offer of free Internet usage was not due to a simple lack of motivation, as had been asserted. Specifically, the study advanced the cause of social justice for an underserved rural teacher population in a developing nation, by demonstrating:

1. Indicators for improving Internet availability per location and hours of access.
2. Community recommendations about how to develop new skills, habits, and priorities for online education.
3. Levels of interest for creation of specialized online coursework matching the community's needs.
4. Needs to address a general scarcity of resources to overcome challenges of buying power, infrastructure, and distance for gaining access to Internet hardware, connections, and training.

Local comments pointed up the essentiality of a cooperative agreement between private and public entities to coordinate pay scales, work schedules, and proximity of Internet services, so that all teachers of the region might benefit from equal opportunities for professional advancement with the Internet as a prime tool in the process. The potential integration of efforts between these entities represents a fusion of local bonding and bridging social capital sources and external, linking social capital. Most importantly, this study has brought to fruition findings based on an analysis of social capital forces which directly affect teacher decisions to study online, dispelling baseless assertions about their unresponsiveness.

The ideal solution, requiring the greatest commitment of funding and manpower, would be to equip the town of San Lucas with universal Internet access free of charge, supply all teachers and students with low-cost, solar-powered wirelessly connected laptop computers, and conduct Internet training for all recipients with regular follow-up training and individualized assistance to promote the development of a digitally literate population. In line with the evidence supplied by this study, systemic change to close the digital divide in rural sectors of the developing world such as San Lucas will depend upon the close collaboration of industry, government entities, and the nonprofit sector to support engagement and persistence in online teacher professional development.

References

Alsop, R., Chase, R., & Owen, D. (2003). *Social capital, empowerment, and community driven development: Presentation notes. PSIA Sourcebook.* World Bank: Geneva. Retrieved at http://info.worldbank.org/etools/bspan/PresentationView.asp?PID=936 &EID=482=936 &EID=482

Attewell, P. (2001). The first and second digital divides. *Sociology of Education, 74,* 252–259.

Batane, T. (2004). Inservice teacher training and technology: A case of Botswana. *Journal of Technology and Teacher Education, 12,* 387–410.

Caniz, E. (2006) Evaluation of technological needs and resources at five middle schools in Totonicapán, Guatemala. *CLASPO Report: Summer 2006.* Austin: Center for Latin American Social Policy at the University of Texas. Retrieved at www.utexas.edu/cola/insts/llilas/claspo/research/noformat/claspo/PDF/field reports/tzoc 06.pdf.

Chambers, R. (1990). *Rapid but relaxed and participatory rural appraisal: Towards applications in health and nutrition.* Retrieved at www.unu.edu/unupress/food2/UIN08E/uin08e 0u.htm

Chambers, R. (1992). Rural Appraisal: Rapid, Relaxed, and Participatory. *Institute of Development Studies Discussion Paper 311.* Sussex: HELP. Retrieved at www.worldbank.org/wbi/sourcebook/sba 104.htm

Chambers, R. (1994). Participatory rural appraisal: Challenges, potential, paradigms. *World Development, 22*(10), 1437–1454.

Chambers, R. (1998). Beyond "Whose reality counts?" New methods we now need? *Studies in Cultures, Organizations and Societies, 4,* 279–301.

Chang, T. (2004). Transborder tourism, borderless classroom: Reflections on a Hawaii—Singapore experience. *Journal of Geography in Higher Education, 28*(2), 179–195.

Cifuentes, W. (2007). Online chat with the Assistant Education Director of the Fundación Rigoberta Menchú Tum by Douglas Tedford. *December, 6,* 2007.

Coleman, J. (1988). Social capital in the creation of human capital. *American Journal of Sociology, 94*(Suppl), S95–S120.

Conciliation Resources. (2007). *Agreement on social and economic aspects and agrarian situation: 1996, Mexico City.* Conciliation Resources, website. Retrieved at http://www.c-r.org/ourwork/accord/guatemala/socio-economic-accord.php.

Creed, C. & Joynes, C. (2005). *Education for all global monitoring report: Improving the quality of primary school through distance education.* Study undertaken by IRFOL: Distance Learning and Improving the Quality of Education Report. International Research Foundation for Open Learning for the EFA Monitoring Team. Paris: UNESCO.

Crump, B. & McIlroy, A. (2003). The digital divide: Why the don't-want-to's won't compute —Lessons from a New Zealand ICT project. *First Monday, Peer Reviewed Journal on the Internet* 8(12). Retrieved at http://www.firstMonday.org/issues/issue8_12/crump/#c6.

DiMaggio, P. & Hargittai, E. (2001). *From the 'digital divide' to 'digital inequality': Studying Internet use as penetration increases.* Sociology Department, Princeton University. Princeton, NJ. Retrieved at http://www.princeton.edu/~arts pol/workpap/WP15%20-%20DiMaggio%2BHargittai.pdf.

Dudwick, N., Kuehnast, K., Nyhan Jones, V., & Woolcock, M. (2006). *Analyzing social capital in context: a guide to using qualitative methods and data.* Washington, DC: World Bank Institute. Retrieved at http://siteresources.worldbank.org/WBI/Resources/Analyzing_ Social_Capital_in_Context-FINAL.pdf.

Durston, J. (2002). *El capital social campesino en la gestión del desarrollo rural: Diadas, equipos, puentes y escaleras.* Santiago de Chile: CEPAL: Comisión Económica para America Latina y el Caribe. Retrieved at http://www.eclac.org/publicaciones/xml/0/11700/Capitulo_III.pdf.

Fazio, M. (2007, February). *Economic opportunities for indigenous peoples in Latin America: Guatemala, Conference Edition,* February 2007. Washington, DC: World Bank. Retrieved at http://web.worldbank.org/WBSITE/EXTERNAL/TOPICS/EXT EDUCATION/0,content MDK:21185632~menuPK: 282391~pagePK:64020865~piPK:51164185~theSitePK:2823 86,00.html.

Foth, M. (2003, December 15–17). *Connectivity does not insure community: on social capital, networks, and communities of place.* The International conference on information technology in regional areas, Caloundra, Queensland, Australia. Retrieved at http://www.mobilecommunitydesign.com/research/Foth-Connectivity_does_not_ensure_community-on_social_capital_networks_and_communities_of_place.pdf.

Galvez, O. (2007). *Telephone interview, September 20, 2007, between Douglas Tedford and Osbaldo Galvez, chief administrator of the Centro Educativo Luciano Pavarotti.* Guatemala: San Lucas Toliman.

Gonsalves, J. (2005). *Participatory research and development for sustainable agriculture and natural resource management: A sourcebook.* Ottawa: International Development Research Centre.

Goodman, S. E., Gottstein, J. B., & Goodman, D. S. (2001). International perspectives: wiring the wilderness in Alaska and the Yukon. *Communications of the Association for Computing Machinery, 44*(6), 21–25.

Grenier, L. (1998). *Working with indigenous knowledge: a guide for researchers.* Ottawa: International Development Research Centre.

Henning, E. (2003). 'I click,therefore I am (not)': is cognition 'distributed' or is it 'contained' in borderless e-learning programmes? *International Journal of Training and Development 7*(4), 303–317. Retrieved at EBSCO Host database.

Ibañez, A., Linder, K., & Woolcock, M. (2002). Social capital in Guatemala: A mixed methods analysis. *Guatemala Poverty Assessment Program, Technical Paper No. 12.* Geneva: International Bank for Reconstruction and Development.

International Bank for Reconstruction and Development (IBRD/World Bank). (2006). *Social capital, empowerment, and community driven development, description.* Retrieved at http://info.worldbank.org/etools/vod/PresentationView.asp?PID=936&EID=482

International Bank for Reconstruction and Development (IBRD/World Bank). (2007a). *Social capital and information technology.* Retrieved at http://www1.worldbank.org/prem/poverty/scapital/topic/info1.htm

International Bank for Reconstruction and Development (IBRD/World Bank). (2007b). *World Bank Participatory Sourcebook, Appendix 1: Methods and Tools.* Retrieved at http://www.worldbank.org/wbi/sourcebook/sba104.htm.

International Bank for Reconstruction and Development (IBRD/World Bank). (2008). *PovertyNet: Information and Communication Technology.* Retrieved at http://web.worldbank.org/WBSITE/EXTERNAL/TOPICS/EXTPOVERTY/EXTEMPOWERMENT/0contentMDK:20265884~menuPK:543261~pagePK:148956~piPK:2166~theSitePK:486411,00.html

ITFORCEGT. (2006). *India—Guatemala IT Education Centre of Excellence.* Retrieved at http://www.itforcegt.org/

Kavanaugh, A., Reese, D., Carroll, J., & Rosson, M. (2005). Weak ties in networked communities. *The Information Society, 21,* 119–131.

Koss, F. (2001). Children falling into the digital divide. *Journal of International Affairs, 55*(1), 75–90.

Laungani, P. (2005). Building multicultural counseling bridges: The holy grail or a poisoned chalice? *Counseling Psychology Quarterly, 18*(4), 247–259.

Leavey, T. (2003). The Internet remains a mystery to most people. *UN Chronicle, 4*(34), 34–35.

Lorenzetti, J. (2004). Strategic planning and social capital in distance education: a conversation with Eugene Kowch. *Distance Education Report, 8*(18), 5–7.

Menchú, P. (2007). Letter re: Douglas Tedford, Fundación Rigoberta Menchú Tum.

Natriello, G. (2001). Bridging the second digital divide: What can sociologists of education contribute? *Sociology of Education, 74,* 260–265.

Olugebenga Ojo, D., & Kayode Olakulehin, F. (2006). Attitudes and perceptions of students to open and distance learning in Nigeria. *International Review of Research in Open and Distance Learning, 7*(1), 1492–3831.

Ordoñez, A. (2006). *India abrira un centro de entratenimiento informatico (India will open an ICT training center)*. El Periodico: Guatemala. Retrieved September 30, from http://www.itforcegt.org/photos3.php.

Randolph, K. A., & Krause, D. J. (2002). Mutual aid in the classroom: An instructional technology application. *Journal of Social Work Education, 38*(2), 259–272.

Rogers, E. (1995). *Diffusion of Innovations* (4th ed.). New York: The Free Press.

Rogers, E. (2003). *Diffusion of innovations* (5th ed.). New York: The Free Press.

Romo-Rodriguez, G. (2005). Information and communication technologies and non-governmental organizations: Lessons learnt from networking in Mexico. *The Electronic Journal of Information Systems in Developing Countries, 21*(3), 1–29.

Rowe-Whyte, A., O'Sullivan, P. & Hunt, S. (2002). Immediacy on the web: Narrowing the digital divide. *Department of Communication, Illinois State University, Normal, Illinois. Retrieved from EBSCO Host Database.*

Rutherford, J., Gillespie, A. & Richardson, R. (2004, December). The territoriality of pan-European telecommunications backbone networks. *Journal of Urban Technology*, 1–34.

Sabatini, F. (2007). *Social capital gateway: resources for the study of social capital, website.* Retrieved at http://www.socialcapitalgateway.org/NV-eng-education.htm.

United Nations Educational, Scientific and Cultural Organization (UNESCO). (2008). Latin American and Caribbean ministers approved new plan of action for the information society 11-03-2008 (San Salvador). Communication and Information Resources, website. Retrieved at http://portal.unesco.org/ci/en/ev.php-URL_ID=26186&URL_DO=DO_TOPIC&URL_SECTION=201.html.

Van Bavel, R., Punie, E. & Tuomi, I. (2007). IPTSICT-enabled changes in social capital, in the IPTS Report. *Institute for Prospective Technological Studies (IPTS) of the European Commission, Directorate General, Joint Research Centre.* Retrieved at http://www.jrc.es/home/report/english/articles/vol85/ICT4E856.htm.

Woolcock, M. (1998). Social capital and economic development: toward a theoretical synthesis and policy framework. *Theory and Society, 27,* 151–208.

Woolcock, M. (2002). *Social capital and development: concepts, evidence and applications.* Power point presentation, Workshop on understanding and building social capital in Croatia, Zagreb, Yugoslavia. World Bank and Harvard University.

Woolcock, M., & Narayan, D. (2002). Social capital: Implications for development and theory, research, and policy. *World Bank Research Observer, 15*(2), 225–249.

Part II
Trends and Issues in Library and Information Science

Chapter 8
Trends and Issues in Library and Information Science

Stephanie A. Jones

8.1 Introduction

Events this year emphasize that education is continuing to embrace technology at a dramatically accelerated pace. In his third State of the Union Address, President Obama called for greater technological literacy among young people in the country (Birch 2012). He subsequently challenged states to meet the goal of adopting the use of digital textbooks for every student by 2017. States are taking measures to integrate digital learning and technology into the educational process as a means to help ensure that all students graduate from high school prepared for college and a career. The majority of states have some type of online learning programs for K-12 students and to date at least five states have laws requiring students to take virtual classes (Davis 2011). Across the country, schools are moving swiftly towards the ultimate goal of 1:1 computing and relying on digital resources for teaching and learning.

These ambitious goals come with huge challenges. Can we fund these changes in a time of economic hardships? Which technologies will be utilized and how will every student have access to the same information? How do we ensure that the needs of all students, including those who are physically, mentally, socially, emotionally, or financially disadvantaged, are being adequately addressed in a way that enables them to reach their fullest potential? Are education professionals prepared to meet the needs of all students in a virtual environment? What type of professional development do they need and who will provide it?

The three chapters in this section address topics pertinent to this discussion. They raise further questions and posit solutions for school librarians, teachers, administrators, and other stakeholders to consider.

S.A. Jones (✉)
Instructional Technology, Georgia Southern University,
Statesboro, GA, USA
e-mail: sjones@georgiasouthern.edu

M. Orey et al. (eds.), *Educational Media and Technology Yearbook*, Educational
Media and Technology Yearbook 37, DOI 10.1007/978-1-4614-4430-5_8,
© Springer Science+Business Media New York 2013

In their timely chapter, "From Paper to Pixel: The Promise and Challenges of Digital Textbooks for K-12 Schools," Marcia Mardis and Nancy Everhart describe the growing adoption of the digital textbook in all levels of education across the USA. They begin the chapter with a discussion of the educational benefits of digital textbooks and the advantages they have over their print counterparts. Besides their portability, obvious advantages of digital textbooks are that they can be customized, are available any time, and can be easily revised and updated. Additionally, some digital textbooks include enhancements such as video and audio to meet the various learning needs of all learners. Despite the many advantages afforded by digital textbooks, Mardis and Everhart acknowledge the difficulties to widespread implementation. Not surprisingly, the primary roadblock is cost. The implementation of digital textbooks will require many school districts to upgrade their existing technological infrastructure and increase bandwidth capacity, both costly propositions in a time of budget cutbacks. There are also corollary expenses involved such as the provision of toner, paper, and photoduplication for those students who do not have access to the Internet or a computer at home. Mardis and Everhart also discuss other considerations to adoption including the controversy over digital vs. print reading, the need for ongoing professional development for teachers, and the legal requirements for e-reading devices to accommodate visually impaired users. Finally, Mardis and Everhart include a lengthy explanation of the vital role school librarians can provide in supporting the school's transition to digital textbooks. They note that educators may not be prepared to integrate digital textbooks into the curriculum because they lack professional development and suggest that school librarians guide teachers in the design of online learning options that take advantage of the capabilities of digital textbooks.

Teaching in an online environment is substantively different than teaching in a face to face environment. Not only must online instructors have a thorough knowledge of subject matter content, they need to be proficient in writing and communication, instructional design, and technology integration. Such abilities are typically beyond the scope of teacher preparation programs, although that is beginning to change. The need for specialized training for online faculty is the premise of the chapter, "Preparing Education Professionals for K-12 Online Learning Programs." The chapter begins with an overview of the growth of K-12 virtual schools and a description of how preparatory and professional development programs were developed to train K-12 teachers for working in virtual schools. The rest of the chapter focuses on early efforts to prepare the other educational professionals who also will work in this online learning environment: school librarians, educational technologists, administrators, school psychologists, and school counselors. The chapter concludes with a list of suggested readings compiled by experts in the field of online learning.

There have been few studies on how school librarians can provide services to special education students in the media center. Daniella Smith helps to fill this gap with her study described in the chapter "The Web 2.0 Connection: An Exploratory Study of School Library Services for Students with Autism Spectrum Disorders." Smith explains how Web 2.0 tools can be used in effective interventions for students with Autism Spectrum Disorders (ASD) since these tools address their visual spatial learning strengths. The study of 508 school librarians at all school levels was designed to explore the relationship between the use of Web 2.0 tools and assistance to students with ASD, their teachers, and their parents and guardians. The results showed that school librarians who frequently use Web 2.0 tools believed they should provide these services and were more comfortable doing so. Those librarians who were less prone to provide these services pointed to Internet filtering which prevented them from using Web 2.0 tools. Additionally, the study revealed that many school librarians were unsure of the proper methods to provide assistance to special education students. Smith recommends that professional development and school library preparation programs should do more to prepare school librarians to serve special populations. She also suggests that school librarians advocate for unfiltered Internet access.

Digital technology has the potential to change the landscape of American schools. If President Obama's vision of digital technology implementation comes true, images of children carrying heavy backpacks full of textbooks to a brick and mortar school will be a thing of the past. We can only imagine what new image will take its place; however, it is incumbent upon all of us to work together to find solutions to the challenges we are facing as we progress in this remarkable venture.

References

Birch, B. A. (2012, February 3). Obama to push schools on digital textbooks. Retrieved from Education News, http://www.educationnews.org/technology/obama-to-push-schools-on-digital-textbooks/.

Davis, M. R. (2011, October 17) States, districts move to require virtual classes. Retrieved from Education Week, http://www.edweek.org/dd/articles/2011/10/19/01required.h05.html.

Chapter 9
From Paper to Pixel: The Promise and Challenges of Digital Textbooks for K-12 Schools

Marcia Mardis and Nancy Everhart

9.1 Introduction

Digital textbooks will soon be part of every classroom in the USA. This trend accompanies an imperative for schools to facilitate twenty-first century learning in which educators prepare students to learn and live productively in a global society where accurate and current information is a meaningful part of everyday learning. School librarians, especially those in Florida, can be key players in the successful implementation of digital textbooks to foster a sensible, balanced solution for educators and learners.

9.2 What Is a Digital Textbook?

Digital textbooks come in many forms ranging from:

- Electronic textbooks (e-textbooks) specially created for a reader like Amazon's Kindle or Apple's iPad
- Read-on-demand computer-based textbooks like those from Google Books and NetLibrary
- Print-on-demand e-textbooks
- Modular assemblages of audio, visual, interactive, and text resources presented via iTunesU, wikis, and digital applications

M. Mardis, Ed.D (✉) • N. Everhart, Ph.D
School of Library and Information Studies, College of Communication & Information,
The Florida State University, 252 Louis Shores Building,
Tallahasse, FL 32306-2100, USA
e-mail: mmardis@fsu.edu; everhart@fsu.edu

M. Orey et al. (eds.), *Educational Media and Technology Yearbook*, Educational
Media and Technology Yearbook 37, DOI 10.1007/978-1-4614-4430-5_9,
© Springer Science+Business Media New York 2013

In this chapter, we explore all types of digital textbooks and weigh the benefits and drawbacks of each format for schools. We examine the advantages and challenges of the growing use of digital textbooks and make recommendations for school librarians' roles in the digital textbook implementation process.

9.3   Textbooks and US Public Education

The textbook is the single greatest driver of the classroom experience in US public schools (Greaves and Hayes 2008; Schmidt et al. 1997; Tulley and Farr 1985) and the ways in which teachers and students interact with the information contained in textbooks is a key definer of the learning experience.

Textbook adoption is most often considered a statewide activity; all states mandate some sort of state-level review of materials used in the classroom (Hitchcock et al. 2010; Tulley 1989). State-level textbook adoption was formed in response to widespread practices in the early years of public education when children used the books available in their own homes. For the most part, textbook adoption processes are long-standing, often dating back to Civil War Reconstruction because "Southern states … did not want their children to read the Yankee version of what that conflict had been all about" (Mathews 2005, ¶10). Once graded instruction became standard practice in public schools, teachers and parents demanded uniform instructional materials. By 1925, textbook adoption had become a state-level activity in over half of the states and this adoption approach has remained stable in ensuing years (Follett 1985). Currently, in many instances, districts are given some discretion over some of the materials selected. While historically the local materials adoption process tended to result in disjointed curriculum that was both inconsistent from district to district and had unclear connections to state curriculum goals, state-level instructional materials adoption guidance has evolved (Dole et al. 1987).

In public schools in the USA, textbooks are important supports for a number of teaching and learning activities. Textbooks help to standardize the material teachers present in content areas; ensure that classroom content is aligned to mandated curricula; provide a focal point for instructional activities; support pedagogical approaches; and give structure to homework.

Momentum is growing for digital textbooks: As technology and the Internet have gained presence in classrooms, instructional materials and activities have become digitally rich and the use of digital textbooks is rapidly gaining ground in education at all levels. With an industry average of almost $56 million in wholesale sales in the USA in 2009 (Maneker 2010), the digital book is an unstoppable juggernaut. While colleges and universities have moved headlong into digital textbooks as a means to reduce costs for students, K-12 education is venturing cautiously, but steadily, into using digital textbooks.

State laws, many of which have been rewritten to include digital content as an acceptable use of state textbook funding, will serve as catalysts that spur the transition to digital textbooks. Already, major advancements in — and support for — digital textbooks have occurred in Indiana, Virginia, West Virginia, California, Texas, and Florida. The State Educational Technology Director's Association (SETDA) is currently surveying their members in an attempt to form a coalition that will identify and work to overcome policy and practice barriers to pursue the use of open digital content as part of a broader strategy to rethink textbook and traditional instructional materials policies and practices in a digital age (SETDA 2010).

9.4 Digital Textbooks: A Boon to Learning?

The interest in and growth of digital textbooks can be attributed to several perceived advantages for learners. Some possible advantages are obvious: digital textbooks are compact and light, making them easy to transport and store; many have search, highlight, and note-taking features convenient for studying and quick reference; content can be updated instantaneously; and digital textbooks are immediately available anytime, anywhere. Digital textbooks are also appealing for the ways in which they support learning, teaching, and technology integration as well as their potential to enhance the health and welfare of children.

9.5 Digital Textbooks Support Twenty-First Century Learners

There have been major changes in teaching and learning styles in today's digital world and in the way students engage with materials. Digital technology has transformed how our students communicate and should influence the way teachers teach. Differentiation of instruction demands that teachers adopt a more interactive approach to delivering content through the use of multimedia and collaboration. This approach to delivering content will help to keep students motivated and engaged in learning.

> Kids are wired differently these days …They're digitally nimble. They multitask, transpose and extrapolate. And they think of knowledge as infinite. They don't engage with textbooks that are finite, linear and rote
>
> (Sheryl R. Abshire, Chief Technology Officer, Calcasieu Parish School System, Lake Charles, LA).

Digital textbooks increase opportunities to learn: The use of digital textbooks can help teachers avoid wasted instruction time due to the distribution and collection of textbooks, students with forgotten or lost textbooks and incomplete homework. The convenience of the online format means that the student textbook is always at hand.

Digital textbooks can provide access to a wealth of information that is readily retrievable from the Internet. Digital texts can make access to information expeditious and mobile, and convenient for students who have been absent. The appeal of this convenience can be seen in higher education where many universities have provided digital textbooks to students. Princeton University began selling textbooks usable on Amazon's Kindle in 2008 (Taylor 2008). This move was so wildly popular that just 1 year later, in the Fall 2009 semester, Amazon partnered with Princeton and five other universities to provide new students with the devices (Williamson 2010). Other examples of digital textbook adoption have shown that whether in K-12 schools or higher education, users appreciate the convenience of digital textbooks because they use digital resources for the majority of their work (JISC 2009).

> It is convenient to not have to find a ride to the local library [and] it may not be necessary. Students, such as myself, do use the Internet for nearly every assignment because of online encyclopedias/databases, online texts, blogs and other Web sites and search engines
>
> (Hayley H., posted on the Room for Debate blog).

Rather than just providing versions of traditional textbooks, many companies are striving to provide schools with textbook reading devices that allow digitally enhanced interactive functionalities. Publishers, anxious to provide schools with enticements for children to read their books, often offer companion websites that are graphically rich and able to engage readers in numerous ways. Along with the content on the page, children can access online videos and games, win prizes, and engage in safe social networking (Lowman 2010).

9.6 Digital Textbooks Can Promote Good Teaching

While print textbooks are designed to support multiple state standards, forcing teachers to dissect and analyze the pages of textbooks to create lessons pertinent to their local needs (Schachter 2009), teachers can use digital textbooks and materials to receive customized curriculum to complement and extend their state's standards. Though information is ever-changing and can be quickly outdated in print textbooks, students using digital textbooks can access news about current events and link to information and media that enriches a learning encounter. And, teachers are encouraged to collaborate with one another to select complementary online resources and to update and refine classroom content.

> The students in my general chemistry class almost never open their textbook. My reason: The less I use the book, the more they learn ... Without a textbook, I can create curriculum [from digital resources] that engages students by relating science to their everyday lives. Lessons become clearer when I link the topic to an issue that affects them personally
>
> (Geoff Ruth 2005, Chemistry and Biology Teacher, Leadership High School, San Francisco).

Digital textbooks enable differentiation: All teachers have an imperative to differentiate their instruction to meet the needs of all learners, but often they lack the resources and skill to do so (Gable et al. 2000). Digital textbooks provide support for students with various learning needs through flexibility and multimedia. Those students who have low vision or who are physically unable to hold a book or turn pages may find a digital textbook easier to use and read. Students who are easily distracted can take advantage of the multimedia capabilities of the digital textbook to stay active and focused. This variety of supports is particularly helpful to English Language Learner students, a student population that has more than doubled in the past 15 years from approximately two million to well over five million students, or about 150% (Waters 2007). Students can use video and audio to augment the text, thus increasing the likelihood they will grasp concepts.

9.7 Digital Textbooks Can Promote Improved Technology Integration

Schools must show a return-on-investment with technology expenditures and digital textbooks help schools demonstrate the need for more and better technology and Internet connectivity (Lewin 2009). Adoption of digital textbooks may serve as an impetus for schools to invest in 1:1 computing because all students will require a device to access learning materials. Schools that already have 1:1 laptop initiatives can maximize their investment in laptops by also using digital textbooks. In schools where 1:1 computing is mature, teachers already have the skills they need to integrate digital content into their instruction (Drayton et al. 2010). The combination of laptops and textbooks proved effective in digital textbook forerunner, Forney Independent School District (TX), where teachers integrate technology seamlessly. Ubiquitous computing environments are uniquely suited for digital textbook adoption because ready access to digital content may already be ingrained in school culture (Greaves Group and Hayes Connection 2008) and part of the vision of almost all school administrators (Project Tomorrow 2010).

[There is] an urgent need for teachers and researchers to address the discrepancy between the types of literacy experiences students encounter at school (paper, pencil, and print texts), and those they practice in their daily lives outside the school environment (Web 2.0). One way to bridge such incongruity is to expand the types of texts students are exposed to and engaged with at school by turning attention to electronic books

(Lotta Larson 2009).

9.8 Digital Textbooks May Make Financial Sense

Billions of dollars are spent on print textbooks every year. Florida, California, and Texas accounted for more than $1.1 billion in textbook spending in 2009 (Baumann 2010). The National Association of College Stores stated the average price of a new textbook for the 2008–2009 school year as $64; the price of a used textbook as $57 (Riddle and Traylor 2010), though some textbooks can cost close to $200. As textbooks become more readily available in multiple formats, the difference in cost between the various formats can be quite significant.

We spend about $81 per student each year on textbooks but only $19 per student on all of the digital content we subscribe to—and that includes a broad collection of multimedia resources, databases, and interactive lessons

(Bailey Mitchell, Chief Technology and Information Officer,
Forsyth Schools (GA)).

While school districts vary, new textbooks for the K-12 curriculum are typically replaced every 5–6 years in each subject area (Tulley and Farr 1985). Textbooks must be replaced in order to obtain current information, particularly in the subject areas of health, science, and social studies. Student textbooks in use today, perhaps adopted in 2005, will not contain information about President Barrack Obama's first day in office in 2009, Hurricane Katrina in 2005, or the downgrade of Pluto from planet to dwarf planet in 2006. Schools using digital textbooks can receive updated information by the publisher, without having to replace the entire textbook series (Reynolds 2010).

Digital textbooks improve local control over curriculum: The textbook industry currently functions as an oligopoly in which a few companies control the market. In some instances, these companies are not operating in the best interests of the school districts and work to perpetuate the perception that their content is superior to any open content that may be available. They offer different pricing to different districts and force districts into replacement schedules and format limitations. Locked into long term relationships with textbook publishers based on long-standing replacement procedures and schedules, many states have been restricted to only review publishers' offerings rather than a wide range of material in a variety of media (Thevenot 2009).

Slick marketing campaigns, promises of convenience, and a familiar publisher's representative can sell textbook adoption committees on adopting a new series. As a result, large textbook producers continue to get larger and guard their market share fiercely. Seldom are the ways in which textbooks are actually used in the classroom studied or linked to student outcomes. So, in many ways, the ultimate impact of textbook adoption committees' decisions is never seen and classroom shortcomings might be attributed to any number of other factors (Follett 1985).

The tension between textbook rigor and textbook appeal is decades old and seemingly unresolvable. Efforts to standardize adoption of rigorous instructional materials have been blamed for constraining learning and narrowing curriculum. Even when curriculum developers and teachers are given the option to choose in-depth instructional materials over more visually appealing, engaging materials, they choose the less challenging content (Dutch 2005). On the other hand, the elimination of state-level controls, whether in favor of local control or no control, threatens to leave educational resources subject to the vagaries of community funding, local priorities, and socioeconomic variations among districts and students (Tulley and Farr 1985).

Digital content has the potential to offer better material and the expanded range of content (Ezarik 2005) while preserving the best practices of collaborative decision-making on quality content. With some digital textbook companies, students and teachers will have the ability to create custom textbooks in which they add chapters from a variety of selected books, other relevant articles and resources, and even their own materials (Fiorello 2010).

9.9   Digital Textbooks May Protect Children's Health and Safety

The Accreditation Council for Occupational Therapy Education (ACOTE) recommended that a child not carry more than 15% of his or her body weight (Hoffman 2009), yet studies have consistently found that children are carrying 17% or more of their body weight in backpacks up to 18.4 lb (Plank 2011)! Bookbags with textbooks that are too heavy or are worn incorrectly can cause physical harm for children and teenagers. In addition to poor posture, damage can be done to muscles and joints, leading to back, neck, and shoulder pain (American Academy of Pediatrics 2010; Dale 2004), back strain and altered gait (Forjuoh et al. 2004), and scoliosis and abnormal curvature of the spine (Sebastian 2006). The US Consumer

Product Safety Commission projected more than 13,260 injuries related to backpacks were treated at hospital emergency rooms, doctor's offices, and clinics in 2000 (Dale 2004). A study of backpack use and back pain in 1,122 children showed 74.4% of them were classified as having back pain associated with the use of backpacks (Sheir-Neiss et al. 2003). Digital textbooks would decrease the physical burden placed on students who use print textbooks. They are also accessible to students online at home or at school, eliminating the need to transport heavy print textbooks in their backpacks for use to do homework assignments.

Digital textbooks can protect the environment: A transition to digital textbooks may also have environmental benefits. The report, *Environmental Trends and Climate Impacts: Findings from the U.S. Book Industry* (Borealis Centre for Environment and Trade Research 2008) included estimates of environmental factors of publishing including high energy use and pollution related to printing and transporting books, deforestation, and other costs related to textbook production, disposal, and recycling.

9.10   The Challenges of Digital Textbook Adoption

Despite possible advantages, a move to digital textbooks poses many challenges. The cost of hardware and software licenses as well as updating the technology infrastructure and bandwidth capacity of schools is costly. Putting a laptop or other reader device in the hands of every student could cost millions of dollars. The executive director of the Association of American Publishers, Stephen Driesler, conceded that "it is likely to be funding, not logistical issues" that will prevent the adoption of digital textbooks in schools (Colin 2005). Many parents and educators feel that if a child does not have a traditional textbook, then learning cannot be taking place (Baker 2005). For now, the financial savings and educational advantages of digital textbooks remain aspirational and may pose hidden costs for learning, teaching, and implementation.

Digital textbooks may compromise comprehension and engagement: A decade of research has consistently supported the conclusion that children "perceive Web text reading as different from print text reading" (Sutherland-Smith 2002, p. 664). Digital media does not promote in-depth reading (Liu 2009). The reading of fixed text is the dominant form of reading in non-digital environments, but multimedia digital textbooks require a different kind of reading across interactive layers consisting of visual clues, hypertext, digital paper, and "image, audio or even ideogram" (Thomas 2005, ¶3). This balance of focal and peripheral attention while reading digital media is not easily accomplished (Liu 2009). And, despite improvements in e-reader devices, users read 20–30% more slowly; use more effort; and are more tired than when reading on paper (Aamodt 2009). Perhaps the greater reading effort required by digital texts explains why many students have remarked that digital textbook user interfaces do not seem designed for sustained reading (JISC 2009) and that they prefer to use them for shorter tasks like verifying facts.

> When we read from the screen of a multifunctional computing device, whether it's a PC, a Smartphone, a Kindle, or an iPad, we sacrifice that singlemindedness. Our attention is scattered by all the distractions and interruptions that pour through our computers and digital networks. The result, a raft of psychological and neurological studies show, is cursory reading, weak comprehension and shallow learning...We may not want to admit it, but the medium matters. When we tell ourselves that reading is the same whether done from a screen or a book, we're kidding ourselves — and cheating our kids
>
> (Nicholas Carr 2010).

Administrators, teachers, and school librarians will need to carefully consider students' reading levels in the selection of digital textbooks. The methods for calculating comprehension in digital reading are evolving and cannot be accurately calculated for measures like the Lexile Framework for Reading (Rowsell and Burke 2009).

Furthermore, a lack of comprehension can affect students' research and writing habits. Young readers seek immediacy when performing searches for answers to classroom assignments and homework. They may resort to copying, pasting, or plagiarizing text when attempting to synthesize ideas into writing (Sutherland-Smith 2002).

As one elementary school principal pointed out, there is a need to make adoption decisions based on learning improvement data. She says she'll wait for the next round of scores from the state standardized test given in the spring before spending more money on any devices (Perez 2010).

Digital textbooks can exclude visually impaired learners: Accessibility of learning materials remains a concern for persons with disabilities. The current e-reader devices present "significant barriers that keep people with disabilities from having full and equal access" (Bagnestos 2010, para. 4). The National Federation of the Blind (NFB) and the American Council for the Blind (ACB) successfully filed suit with the United States Department of Justice Civil Rights Division to intervene in e-reader textbook replacement pilot projects at six major American universities (Dorn and Stein 2010). While many e-readers have text-to-speech capabilities, other features like menu selection, voice activated navigation, note taking, and bookmarking features are not accessible to visually impaired users. Images are excluded from screen readers, thus obscuring a significant portion of digital content to low vision users. The settlement reached between the universities and the Department of Justice required an end to the recommendation, purchase, or promotion, of any e-reader devices until the e-readers are fully accessible to all students. E-reader manufacturers are required to bring the devices into compliance with the Americans with Disabilities Act (ADA) (United States Department of Justice 2010). In June 2010, the United States Department of Education affirmed the Department of Justice position and urged any schools considering the adoption of digital textbooks delivered via e-readers to seek for technical assistance from either agency (Schaffhauser 2010b).

> If we don't consider individuals with disabilities when we integrate new technologies into the educational environment, students with disabilities can and will be left behind as their non-disabled peers gain the benefits of learning that are enhanced by technological advances. This result would be inconsistent with our civil rights laws
>
> (Russlynn Ali, Assistant Secretary for Civil Rights, U.S. Department of Education).

Digital textbooks may perpetuate socioeconomic gaps in education: Former California Governor Schwarzennegger's 2009 *California Free Textbook Initiative* substitutes open source digital resources for state-adopted science and math textbooks. This move attracted national attention (Lewin 2009). One of the main concerns with this program is its potential to negatively impact students from low socioeconomic backgrounds or children who lack equipment and connectivity at home. Over a fifth of students (22%) find reading on a screen uncomfortable and may resort to printing partial or entire texts (Allen 2008). Printers, paper, and ink can be added to the list of hidden costs, that may, by necessity, shift to the school districts. Some less affluent districts may not be able to afford these costs, resulting in another type of digital divide for students from low-income families.

Ancillary costs of digital textbooks can erode savings: School administrators cite cost savings as the main reason to select digital textbooks over print and expect to see savings of 50% or more (Allen 2008). Even though this may be true, the cost of a digital textbook goes beyond this initial investment. Digital textbooks require student access to computers or other mobile devices, Internet connections, and hardware systems that require periodic upgrades and maintenance. And, in many instances, schools must absorb at least part of the cost of making materials accessible to all students through printing and reformatting. In *Eliezer Williams, et al., vs. State of California*, Superior Court officials found that districts were responsible for ensuring that "students receive printed instructional materials that are identical in content… or by providing those students with the electronic equipment and/or active Internet connections they need at home to access the materials" (Californina Learning Resource Network 2008, ¶3).

For many schools, investing in digital textbooks results in duplicate expenditures. Learning management systems (e.g., Blackboard and Moodle) are used by an increasing number of districts. They come populated with digital resources which are as comprehensive as digital textbooks (Greaves Group and Hayes Connection 2008). Teachers may already have integrated these systems into their teaching and may be reluctant to revise current pedagogy to switch to digital textbooks. Until a standard format for digital text is created, schools may have to invest in multiple readers. Some digital texts are formatted for specific e-reader devices; some others work on computers only. Reading devices, or e-readers, are available for netbooks, mobile devices, and tablets as well as dedicated e-book platforms and they continue to expand (JISC 2009), leading schools to invest in multiple devices to provide content to learners and educators.

Current Internet connectivity cannot support digital textbook use: Despite superintendents' support for 1:1 computing and digital curricula, curriculum directors reported skepticism that their technology infrastructures were ready to handle the demands of digital materials and the accompanying growth in devices (Greaves Group 2006). The majority of curriculum directors surveyed for the *America's Digital Schools 2006* report admitted that expenditure in digital materials was likely to triple in the next 5 years, but they did not see bandwidth and device availability keeping pace (Greaves Group 2006). That 5 year forecast is rapidly coming to fruition. The subsequent *America's Digital Schools 2008* report confirmed the growth of 1:1 and mobile computing as major trends in education, making bandwidth a continuing critical concern (Greaves Group and Hayes Connection 2008). Web-based learning resources demand high levels of bandwidth to ensure adequate speed and connectivity. Many schools are simply unprepared to handle the volume of network traffic volume and "experience the thwarting effect of inadequate connectivity on instructional innovation" (Everhart and Mardis 2012, p. 181).

Home connectivity is also an issue. It is estimated that about a third of Americans have no access to high speed Internet service because they cannot afford it or choose not to have it (Stelter and Wortham 2010). Although continuity of the school-to-home learning experience is essential when students do not have printed textbooks to rely upon, schools cannot afford to absorb this cost for parents and many parents do not understand the importance of the investment or are not in a position to make it (Greaves Group 2006).

Although some research has suggested that issues of broadband accessibility have been circumvented by the use of mobile devices like smartphones among urban poor and minority students, it is becoming clear that "not all digital experiences are created equal" (Watkins 2009, p. 68). Mobile devices are often limited in their educational use by small screen size, lack of display clarity, limited image size and complexity, restrictive keyboard and mouse functions, and diminished space for interactive elements (Churchill and Hedberg 2008). Although access to the Internet may be available through smartphones, data plans are expensive and some cell phone applications (apps) have an associated cost. Despite the fact that groups like Comcast are now making data plans accessible to low income users (Comcast 2011), the new "digital divide" may be an "app gap" in which high quality content cannot be used on mobile devices until a unique app is created for it.

> The growth in machines and the changing mix of applications are driving dramatic growth in required Internet bandwidth that most school districts and states have not yet predicted
>
> (America's Digital Schools 2008).

Many teachers are not prepared to make best use of digital content: Adequate professional development is key to the success of digital innovations in schools. The majority of school administrator respondents to the *America's Digital Schools 2006* survey reported that they were concerned about their teachers' and librarians' abilities to seamlessly integrate new digital technologies into the existing curriculum (Greaves Group and Hayes Connection 2008). At about $100 per student per year, districts often do not plan for the substantial time and investment in professional development they will need to make to ensure the success of their digital textbook programs (Greaves Group 2006). The successful integration of technology into everyday classroom practices must be sustained by ongoing professional development. The investment in infrastructure enhancements, hardware upgrades, and mobile learning initiatives has yet to be matched with an investment in human capital (Kirsch et al. 2007).

Digital textbooks will not resolve flaws in traditional curriculum: Regardless of format, on the whole, textbooks emphasize "familiarity with many topics rather than concentrated attention to a few" (Schmidt, et al. 1997, p. 2). This lack of content rigor has been linked to lackluster US performance on international tests of mathematics and science, declining student motivation, and even lack of high school completion (Koretz 2009). Before digital textbooks can be credited with enhancing learning, curricula must be reformed to focus in depth on key topics and give students a common set of educational concepts upon which to build. In the pressure of daily instruction in a high stakes environment, textbooks become an essential tool of enacted curriculum and, as a result, teachers cover numerous topics shallowly in an effort to complete the range of material contained in the textbook. Splintered adoptions of digital textbooks without national or even statewide agreement upon the uses for and content in digital textbooks may only exacerbate this issue further.

9.11 Florida: Digital Textbook Frontier?

In June 2011, the Florida Governor, Rick Scott, signed Senate Bill 2120 mandating that all public schools in the state use entirely digital textbooks and digital assessments by 2015. This move is significant because not only is Florida one of the states that benchmark textbook adoption for the nation, but also because the law is the first of its kind. Only two other states have similar laws. California's legislation encourages, but does not mandate, digital textbooks in public schools by 2020. In 2010, Illinois passed legislation that redefined textbooks to include digital formats. In Texas, Senate Bill 6 was recently signed into law allowing school districts greater flexibility to spend instructional materials funds on digital content, professional development, and technology support. However, Florida's mandate is the most ambitious measure, requiring full implementation of digital textbooks and state standardized assessments within 3 years. This move will put pressure on schools not only to provide adequate devices and digital resources, but also to ensure that school bandwidth is robust and that home access is possible (Everhart and Mardis 2012). These considerations are serious given that some reports find home broadband access uneven in Florida with rural areas especially unserved (Mardis 2011).

Despite a projected decline in enrollment from 2007–2008 to 2011–2012, Florida spent the fourth highest amount on instructional materials for its public schools behind California, Texas, and New York (Market Data Retrieval (MDR) 2009). With the passing of Florida legislation allowing school districts to use textbook funds to purchase digital content and other online educational resources (Manzo 2009), the nation will look to Florida as one of the states to take the lead. Currently, in many districts across the state, students and teachers access digital versions of their current textbooks (Surdin 2009). Florida educators will want to pay particular attention to discussions of digital textbooks because policymakers are often attracted to the perceived cost savings that are linked to their adoption. Although the textbook adoption process in Florida has had a long tradition and one that includes digital textbooks. An established state initiative, Orange Grove Texts Plus, provides textbook titles free to higher education students who go online to view them. Students can download and print the books, or they can buy bound volumes at about half the cost of normal textbooks. For example, students using an introductory calculus textbook can read, download, and print some or all of the pages for free while comparable textbooks retail for $100–160 at bookstores (Travis 2010). Orange Grove Texts Plus, geared to college students, proved enticing to Florida's high schools due to its free content. Clearwater High School in Pinellas County is a frontrunner in the digital textbook movement. They established a 1:1 initiative putting a wireless reading device into the hands of each of its 2,100 students for the 2010–2011 school year. The school issued e-readers to all of its teachers—who are pleased with them (Catalanello 2010).

However, the largest consumer of digital content in Florida, the Florida Virtual School (FLVS), relies on other forms of digital content, not digital textbooks, to date. Florida Virtual School is the largest in the nation and expanding rapidly. In 2008–2009, the school's enrollment climbed to over 124,000 which represented a 25% increase over the previous school year (Center for Digital Education 2009). According to the FLVS Chief Development Officer (Smith 2010),

> We use digital textbooks...only in our AP courses, when/if required. We really try to limit the amount of external resources we include in our courses because of recurring costs/licensing fees often associated with the resource. We also sell our courses outside the State of Florida and external resources can create licensing issues for our clients (i.e., the client would have to purchase a license to use the external resource in addition to purchasing the course) ... We do have a former [school librarian] on our team who works with our curriculum specialists, project managers, etc. to help us select, contract and license external resources.

In 2011, the Florida legislature passed House Bill 7197 which mandates that, as of the 2011–2012 school year, all Florida students must have taken an online course prior to high school graduation. The growth of virtual schooling exacerbates the challenges virtual school educators and learners face in accessing digital content. The results of a 2010 survey conducted by Blackboard, Inc., and Project Tomorrow

Table 9.1 Existing state-led virtual schooling programs (Center for Digital Education 2009)

Alabama	Kentucky	North Dakota
Arkansas	Louisiana	Oregon
Florida	Maryland	South Dakota
Georgia	Michigan	Texas
Hawaii	Mississippi	Utah
Idaho	Missouri	Virginia
Illinois	New Mexico	West Virginia
	North Carolina	Wisconsin

suggested that demand for online learning for credit forward, credit recovery, and curriculum supplementation is skyrocketing in all secondary grades (Blackboard Inc. & Project Tomorrow 2010). And, as Table 9.1 illustrates, virtual schooling is widespread and the lessons learned from FLVS' handling of digital content will set a noticeable example.

A big concern among Florida educators is how they will finance the devices for virtual schooling and digital textbooks. Many administrators are turning to "Bring Your Own Device" or BYOD policies to ensure that children have access to instructional material without the school district's incurring the massive expense of providing and maintaining a device for every student. BYOD policies do have the advantage of shifting much of the expense of technology to students and for creating a home–school technology continuum, but lingering concerns about broadband capacity (Roscorla 2011), professional development (Ray 2011), filtering (Schaffhauser 2011), lack of digital citizenship (Churches 2011), universality of access (Norris and Soloway 2011), and fidelity of content rendering across devices (Sullivan 2011) have many critics unsure that this approach is a viable long term solution. Still, developments in this area are constant and initiatives like Apple's iPad-based digital textbook program may force a single platform that will resolve many of the issues relating to managing a range of devices (Olivarez-Giles 2012; Thier 2012).

9.11.1 Digital Textbooks Can Extend School Librarians' Reach

Digital textbooks represent another opportunity for school librarians to enhance their vital leadership in teaching and learning. Librarians are experts at identifying, collecting, and organizing the best content, free or for a fee, and a move to open content learning resources may even free up funds to create stronger digital collections. In an age when many school librarians are not sure about the continued relevance of their promotion of reading and love of books, e-books and digital textbooks may represent a fresh way to continue advocacy for the importance of reading (Peters 2009) as well as for the school librarian's crucial leadership role in technology integration. Noted author–editor Marc Aronson wrote recently on his blog, *Nonfiction Matters*, "Out of the rubble of the economic crash is coming this great moment of opportunity, we just have to figure out how to seize it" (Aronson 2009, para. 3).

Librarians at Clearwater High School near Tampa, FL, were involved from the early stages of their school's move to digital textbooks. The librarians, with the aid of English teachers, use e-readers with their "Battle of the Books" team so that they can read the required books over the summer. The librarians are also hopeful that the e-readers will assist lower level students' reading of textbooks by using the read aloud feature. They are also going to keep detailed data on students' yearly gains in order to determine if this is the case. The US Department of Education has urged the district to seek technical assistance in their plan for deployment to remain in compliance with the Americans with Disabilities Act (ADA) (Schaffhauser 2010a)

Our good and passionate teachers have long deviated from the standard textbook to add or include additional info they felt was necessary. I have watched them skip over chapter after chapter of expensive textbooks because the content is not presented in a way that was conducive to teaching and learning in their classrooms…I can even see in the future where our high school teachers will be creating their own textbooks from the digital resources they have collected over the years just as many college professors have already done. The [school library] could easily provide digital support resources such as databases and e-books 'attached' to individual chapters in textbooks. [Use of the library] would skyrocket. Collaboration with teachers would move to a new level creating more of a partnership in the learning process

(Cana Nudi 2010, School Librarian, Chiles High School, Tallahassee, FL).

Perhaps pilot projects, like the one spearheaded by the school librarian at Park Vista Community High School in Palm Beach County are the answer. The librarian purchased five e-book readers to determine if students in an intensive reading class would demonstrate an increased interest in reading when using electronic readers as opposed to traditional books. The pilot project was evaluated using teacher observation and student comments through an end-of-year student survey. The teachers, reading coach, school librarian, and principal monitored the progress of the program, discussed challenges that arose, and brainstormed solutions (Table 9.2).

Students who participated in the pilot project were surveyed at its conclusion and an average of 80% enjoyed using an e-book more than a traditional book and it helped them to concentrate or raise their comprehension level (McTigue 2010). Teachers were also positive.

As for my observations, my students really enjoyed reading on the [e-reader]. They actually arrived early to class because they wanted one of the five I had.

Table 9.2 Challenges and solutions to e-reader adoption faced by Park Vista Community High School (FL)

Challenge	Solution
Students' ability to purchase additional e-books charged to the school	Load e-books and then unregister the device from credit card account
Devices freezing up	Keep devices charged between 35 and 95%, and set them to airplane mode to save power. When the devices freeze up, hold down the power button or take out the battery and plug into a power source
Providing classroom sets of e-books at a discount similar to print editions	E-book supplier is investigating solutions

Usually I have to remind the students that they should be reading their books, not looking around the room, but since they have been reading off of the [e-readers], I haven't had to remind them—they were engaged in the reading. I also liked that they could each put their own bookmarks for where they left off, whereas sometimes in class with the traditional books, some of their bookmarks get lost or removed. Another teacher noted that incorporating audio would be beneficial for students' fluency and students also wanted audio in future e-books. (McTigue 2010).

For school librarians who currently manage physical textbook circulation, digital textbooks will not eliminate this important duty or cause a shift to classroom resource collections over library collections. Digital textbooks will represent an important transformation in the way school librarians are involved with the resource base of the school. As *School Library Journal* editor Brian Kenney (2009) pointed out, "The digital textbook could be media specialists' Trojan horse, stealthily moving materials from the library into the classroom. We could infuse these textbooks with different points of view in multiple formats, customize them to address diverse learning styles, and make them the launching point of Guided Inquiry" (para. 3). The tedious work of inventorying and shifting piles of weighty texts will be replaced by carefully thought-out circulation strategies that integrate digital texts with the resources already available through the school library. Just imagine how a school's textbooks could be augmented with deep links to an array of content from database articles to streaming media to books (both "e" and print) to open-source content from resources like the Library of Congress. Digital textbooks will justify continued subscriptions to the high quality supplemental resources we promote to teachers and students every day. Marcia Mardis, an assistant professor at Florida State University's School of Library and Information Studies who studies how school librarians can successfully integrate digital content into their collections and services maintains, "Teachers don't have the time to spend searching websites for these resources and then learning how to use them in the classroom. They need a single integrated approach—the type that a school librarian can create" (Whelan 2009).

Two leaders in the digital book movements for schools, the aforementioned Forney Independent School District and Cushing Academy in Massachusetts, included their school librarians in the shift to digital texts. Forney, an early adopter of digital textbooks in 2004, included an extensive library of e-books on its district-purchased student laptops along with eight digital textbooks. Forney's technology director says district librarians helped review the over 2000 e-books, including novels, historical documents, and major speeches, to identify sources that related to the curriculum (Ishikuza 2004). Cushing Academy is a partner institution with the James Martin 21st Century School at Oxford University. They have transformed their library into a learning center complete with e-readers, flat screen TVs, and laptops (Block 2009). Surveys conducted by the school showed students were not turning to printed materials for research, instead they were going online. So, instead of a 20,000 volume collection of print books, Cushing now has a database of millions of digital textbooks from which students will access materials using e-readers or laptops. In an interview on National Public Radio's *All Things Considered*, Suzie Carlisle, Dean of Academics, stated, "Part of our desire to move in this direction is to meet the students where they are most comfortable, and it's our responsibility, as well, to help students understand the emerging technologies that they are going to be faced with" (Block 2009). According to Cushing Academy's headmaster, the change has already increased the library's circulation numbers (Block 2009).

When there is a school-wide initiative and technology is involved, school libraries can also benefit. Brophy Preparatory School in Phoeniz, Arizona began the mandatory tablet PC program in 2006. To support the PCs, the entire campus has become completely wi-fi accessible (Young 2007). Similar situations have been reported in Florida where broadband connectivity has been upgraded and school librarians provide tech coordination, support, and the leadership necessary to address access issues from district to desktop (Everhart and Mardis, in press)

School librarians, cognizant of these issues, can provide school-wide leadership to assist students, teachers, and parents to tackle these concerns when transitioning to digital textbooks. Working in collaboration with teachers, school librarians promote comprehension through questioning, clarifying, seeking meaning, and discussion. Librarians play a significant role in reading comprehension instruction in order to enable students' creation and application of new knowledge.

9.12   Recommendations

In addition to considering the possible benefits and drawbacks to digital textbooks outlined above, educational stakeholders have considerations unique to their roles.

9.12.1   For Educational Policymakers

- To the extent possible, allow districts to retain control over local adoption of digital materials. District officials have a much better read on the readiness of their teachers, students, and parents. Research has demonstrated that centralized state textbook adoption processes do not yield cost or time savings

(Tulley 1989; Tulley and Farr 1985) so nothing is lost by retaining local adoption. However, local adoption succeeds with technical assistance and this type of support should be provided.

- Create guidelines for the adoption of open content. Having no state guidance on content adoption threatens to return public education to the late 1800s-style of uncontrolled, unvetted, and often unrecorded educational resources. Open content or learning objects are digital resources that can offer the flexibility and currency that any textbook approach cannot. The two approaches can be combined to great benefit.
- Support the creation of a national or statewide clearinghouse of digital educational material. Many states already have digital libraries for educators. Support continued funding for these resources and development of tools that allow school librarians and teachers to access them more readily.
- Pilot the use of digital textbooks in a limited number of districts. Measure the kinds of learning that results from print textbook-based activities and compare those results to similar activities based on digital texts.
- Avoid adopting or promoting digital textbooks that require printing. Printing content from a digital textbook drives up costs for the district in toner, paper, and photoduplication. However, a printing option should be available for students without home access to the Internet or a computer.

9.12.2   For School Administrators

- Provide professional development to teachers to ease the transition to digital textbooks and ameliorate classroom management, instructional design, and technology implementation burdens that may result from the shift.
- Upgrade the district bandwidth to the maximum possible to ensure that content remains readily accessible, even in peak use times (JISC 2009).
- Integrate school libraries into the local adoption and distribution process. School librarians have the expertise to develop circulation strategies for digital textbooks and, in many cases, already support the devices that will be used to interact with the digital content (Oder 2009). Instead of attempting to find funding for new staff with resource selection expertise, empower the staff you have!

9.12.3   For School Librarians

- Become active in your district's efforts to adopt digital textbooks. After all, you have the expertise to select high quality resources. It's needed here and students and teachers are reassured by your "stamp of approval" (JISC 2009). Table 9.3 provides ideas for you to use digital textbooks to enhance your leadership activities.

Table 9.3 Leadership roles for school librarians in digital textbook implementation

	Teacher	Instructional partners	Resource specialist	Program leader	Even further
Access	Promote student awareness of digital textbooks and relevant resources available in the school and school library	Co-plan, co-teach, and co-assess assignments that make effective use of digital textbooks and relevant resources	Determine if the school library website can allow 24/7 access to digital textbooks from home and other locations	Develop partnerships to obtain funding and free resources that enhance digital textbook lessons	Guide teachers to develop and tailor online learning options that enhance digital textbooks
	Promote teacher awareness of digital textbooks and other relevant resources available in the school and school library	Ensure equal access for all students (including those with disabilities) and teachers via logon and password information, and effective ways for printing needed information	Locate sources of free, downloadable digital video, learning objects, and e-books that enhance digital textbooks and integrate objects into the OPAC	Facilitate the integration of online training in the use of digital textbooks	Design and facilitate online interactions with student, faculty, and experts in remote locations
		Ensure equal access for all students and teachers via curriculum mapping and sharing connections and overlap with teachers	Correlate physical and digital resources relevant to digital textbooks in the OPAC Serve as a testing and experimental center for hardware platforms	Conduct workshops for parents about the impact of digital textbooks on them and their children	Keep detailed data on issues dealing with access for further program development

(continued)

Table 9.3 (continued)

	Teacher	Instructional partners	Resource specialist	Program leader	Even further
Skill	Design professional development for teachers using digital textbooks	Co-plan, co-teach, and co-assess lessons that include digital textbooks, relevant resources, and twenty-first century skills	Make available digital textbook tutorials	Survey teachers on professional development needs	Promote a collection of professional learning digital videos and resources relevant to digital textbooks
	Facilitate after school learning communities in which teachers participate in online learning experiences	Provide support and professional development for effective use of digital textbooks and relevant resources	Build a collection of relevant resources that enhance the digital textbook curriculum	Seek professional development in network administration and new applications use	Incorporate digital media and digital textbook activities into school television production
		Serve as a model for using digital textbooks in your own instruction		Educate parents on copyright, safety, and use of digital textbooks	Facilitate the use of multiple sources of digital content to construct unique digital textbooks
Policy	Educate students and teachers on capacity limitations, copyright, and safety implications of digital textbook applications to promote digital citizenship	Collect information about instructional events that make use of digital textbooks and present in annual or quarterly reports to administration and school board	Ensure that the collection policy pertains to collecting and describing resources relevant to digital textbooks	Determine future digital textbook and application needs and communicate those to district personnel	Perform policy impact studies and adjust on an ongoing basis
		Participate on technology-planning committees that make decisions about technology, equipment, and resources	Develop Acceptable Use Policies that include digital textbooks		Get involved in state and national committees and legislative initiatives dealing with digital textbooks

Motivation	Promote activities that utilize digital textbooks effectively and efficiently, and are engaging for learners	Share co-teaching successes using digital textbooks and relevant resources with other teachers	Create an online repository of successful lessons and teacher feedback	Share research on student learning with digital textbooks	Facilitate an online community for student learners to share ideas and projects as a result of using digital textbooks
		Facilitate sharing of successful lessons with other teachers		Collect and share data on student success using digital textbooks	
		Set up stations in the library for individual and small group training		Develop school-wide celebrations that encourage a positive transition to digital textbooks	

- Look at the content in your collection from a granular perspective—that is, think of how a video, an podcast, an image, and text can work together to promote understanding of a concept. Think of how you can assemble from songs, audiobooks, podcasts, and videos that you choose into a playlist in iTunes. Enable your teachers and students to create playlists of high quality content you've selected.
- Catalog digital items in your collection for discovery. Annotate catalog records in the MARC 653 field for uncontrolled vocabulary and 658 field for curriculum objective. Start with the items in a key grade level in a particular subject and get the teachers and students to try out your cataloging system.
- If your catalog has a tagging feature, let everyone use it! Encourage kids and teachers to add their own tags so that they can find the digital content they need in your collection.

References

Aamodt, S. (2009, May 14). A test of character. Retrieved from http://roomfordebate.blogs.nytimes.com/2009/10/14/does-the-brain-like-e-books/.

Allen, N. (2008, August 1). Course correction: How digital textbooks are off track and how to set them straight. Retrieved June 15, 2010, from http://www.studentpirgs.org/textbooks/reports/course-correction.

American Academy of Pediatrics. (2010). Safety & prevention: Backpack safety Retrieved May 10, 2010, from http://www.healthychildren.org/English/safety-prevention/at-play/pages/Backpack-Safety.aspx.

Aronson, M. (2009, July 1). The future is now. Retrieved from http://blog.schoollibraryjournal.com/nonfictionmatters/2009/08/09/the-future-is-now/.

Bagnestos, S. (2010, April 22). Principal Deputy Assistant Attorney General for Civil Rights Samuel R. Bagenstos testifies before the House Judiciary Subcommittee on the constitution, civil rights and civil liberties. Retrieved June 30, 2010, from http://www.justice.gov/crt/speeches/2010/crt-speech-100422.html.

Baker, M. (2005, February). How to: Toss the text: Nine tips to help you get started teaching without textbooks. *Edutopia*. Retrieved from http://www.edutopia.org/how-toss-text.

Baumann, M. (2010, January/February). Bringing digital textbooks to the masses. *EContent*. Retrieved from http://www.econtentmag.com/Articles/ArticleReader.aspx?ArticleID=61152.

Blackboard Inc., & Project Tomorrow. (2010, June). Learning in the 21st century: 2010 trends update, from http://bb.blackboard.com/g/?H0W2FQH9KE.

Block, M. (2009, November 9). Digital school library leaves book stacks behind (transcript). *All Things Considered*. Retrieved June 16, 2010, from http://www.npr.org/templates/transcript/transcript.php?storyId=120097876.

Borealis Centre for Environment and Trade Research. (2008). Environmental trends and climate impacts: Findings from the U.S book industry. A research report commissioned by the Book Industry Study Group and Green Press Initiative. Retrieved September 30, 2011, from http://www.greenpressinitiative.org/documents/trends_summary.pdf.

Californina Learning Resource Network. (2008). Electronic instructional materials and the Williams Settlement's sufficiency requirements. Retrieved June 1, 2010, from http://www.clrn.org/fdti/williams.cfm.

Carr, N. (2010, June 1). The medium matters. Retrieved from http://roomfordebate.blogs.nytimes.com/2010/02/10/do-school-libraries-need-books/#nicholas.

Catalanello, R. (2010, June 2). Textbooks ditched at Clearwater High as students log on to Kindles, *St. Petersburg Times Online*. Retrieved from http://www.tampabay.com/news/education/k12/textbooks-ditched-at-clearwater-high-as-students-log-on-to-kindles/1099264.

Center for Digital Education. (2009). Online learning policy survey: A survey of the states. Retrieved September 30, 2011, from http://www.ecs.org/html/offsite.asp?document=http%3A%2F%2Fmedia%2Econvergemag%2Ecom%2Fdocuments%2FCDE09%2BREPORT%2BNacol%5FShort%5FV%2Epdf.

Churches, A. (2011). BYOD and DC. Retrieved from http://edorigami.edublogs.org/2011/11/24/byod-and-dc/.

Churchill, D., & Hedberg, J. (2008). Learning object design considerations for small-screen handheld devices. *Computers in Education, 50*(3), doi: 10.1016/j.compedu.2006.09.004.

Colin, C. (2005, October). Laptops take the lead. *Edutopia*. Retrieved from http://www.edutopia.org/no-more-books.

Comcast, I. (2011). Internet essentials. Retrieved September 30, 2011, from http://www.internetessentials.com/.

Dale, J. C. (2004). School backpacks: Preventing injuries. *Journal of Pediatric Health Care, 18*(5), 264–266.

Dole, J., Rogers, T., & Osborn, J. (1987). Improving the selection of basal reading programs: A report of the textbook adoption guidelines project. *The Elementary School Journal, 87*(3), 282–298.

Dorn, J., & Stein, J. (2010). *Kindling the flame for plaintiffs: Legal challenges to the use of the Kindle and e-readers in the classroom*. Washington, DC: Proskauer.

Drayton, B., Falk, J., Stroud, R., Hobbs, K., & Hammerman, J. (2010). After installation: Ubiquitous computing and high school science in three experienced, high-technology schools. *Journal of Technology, Learning and Assessment (JTLA), 9*(3). Retrieved from http://escholarship.bc.edu/cgi/viewcontent.cgi?article=1196&context=jtla.

Everhart, N., & Mardis, M. A. (2012). In the district and on the desktop: School libraries as essential elements of effective broadband use in schools. In M. Orey, S. A. Jones, & R. M. Branch (Eds.), *Educational Media and Technology Yearbook 2011* (pp. 173–186). New York, NY: Springer.

Ezarik, M. (2005, March). The textbook adoption mess—And what reformers are doing to fix it. *District Administration*. Retrieved from http://www.districtadministration.com/viewarticle.aspx?articleid=197.

Fiorello, P. (2010, April 21). Get ready for digital textbooks in K-12 education. Retrieved June 25, 2010, from http://drpfconsults.com/get-ready-for-digital-textbooks-in-k-12-education/.

Follett, R. (1985). The school textbook adoption process. *Book Research Quarterly, 1*(1), 19–23.

Forjuoh, S. N., Schuchmann, J. A., & Lane, B. L. (2004). Correlates of heavy backpack use by elementary school children. *Public Health, 118*(7), 532–535. doi:10.1016/j.puhe.2003.10.010.

Gable, R. A., Hendrickson, J. M., Tonelson, S. W., & Van Acker, R. (2000). Changing disciplinary and instructional practices in the middle school to address IDEA. *The Clearing House, 73*(4), 205–208.

Greaves Group. (2006). *America's digital schools 2006: A five year forecast: Mobilizing the curriculum*. Shelton, CT: Market Data Research [MDR].

Greaves Group & Hayes Connection. (2008). *America's digital schools 2008: Six trends to watch*. Shelton, CT: Market Data Research [MDR].

Greaves, T. W., & Hayes, J. (2008). *America's Digital Schools 2008: Six trends to watch*. Shelton, CT: Market Data Research [MDR].

Hitchcock, C., Hendricks, V., Johnson, M., Christensen, S., & Siller, M. A. (2010, July). Accessible textbooks in the K-12 Classroom: An educator's guide to the acquisition of alternate format core learning materials for pre-K-12 students with print disabilities (2010 Revision). Retrieved September, 2011, from http://aim.cast.org/sites/aim.cast.org/files/AccessibleTextbooksClassroom8.10.10.pdf.

Hoffman, A. O. (2009, December 8). Backpack awareness: One of many ways that occupational therapists serve students. Retrieved January 24, 2012, from http://www.aota.org/News/Consumer/Backpack08.aspx.

Ishikuza, K. (2004). A Texas district goes digital: Forney, TX, school is first in the nation to swap textbooks for digital versions. *School Library Journal, 50*(7), 14.

JISC. (2009, November). JISC national e-books observatory project: Key findings and recommendations. Retrieved June 1, 2010, from http://www.jiscebooksproject.org/wp-content/JISC-e-books-observatory-final-report-Nov-09.pdf.

Kenney, B. (2009, September 1). As goes California: A flawed initiative could become a fabulous opportunity. Retrieved July 1, 2010, from http://www.schoollibraryjournal.com/article/CA6685542.html.

Kirsch, I., Braun, H., Yamamoto, K., & Sum, A. (2007). *America's perfect storm: Three forces changing our nation's future.* Princeton, NJ: Educational Testing Service.

Koretz, D. (2009). How do American students measure up? Making sense of international comparisons. *America's High Schools, 19*(1). Retrieved from http://www.princeton.edu/futureofchildren/publications/journals/article/index.xml?journalid=30&articleid=36&sectionid=71.

Larson, L. C. (2009). e-Reading and e-Responding: New tools for the next generation of readers. *Journal of Adolescent & Adult Literacy, 53*(3), 255–258. doi:10.1598/JAAL.53.3.7.

Lewin, T. (2009, August 8). Moving into a digital future, where textbooks are history, *New York Times,* p. A1. Retrieved from http://www.nytimes.com/learning/teachers/featured_articles/20090914monday.html.

Liu, A. (2009, June 1). A new metaphor for reading. Retrieved from http://roomfordebate.blogs.nytimes.com/2009/10/14/does-the-brain-like-e-books/.

Lowman, S. (2010, March 21). The future of children's book publishing, *Washington Post.* Retrieved from http://www.washingtonpost.com/wp-dyn/content/article/2010/03/19/AR2010031901574.html.

Maneker, M. (2010, March 23). E-book sales took off in January, from http://www.thebigmoney.com/blogs/goodnight-gutenberg/2010/03/23/ebook-sales-take-january.

Manzo, K. K. (2009). Turning the digital page. *Education Week, 3*(1).

Mardis, M. A. (2011, August 7–11). *Home broadband adoption and student achievement: Scenes from an initial examination of households in rural Florida, USA.* Paper presented at the School libraries: Empowering the 21st Century Learner. IASL 2011 40th Annual Conference & 15th International Forum on Research in School Librarianship, Kingston, Jamaica.

Market Data Retrieval [MDR]. (2009). 2007–2008 public school expenditures. Retrieved June 10, 2010, from http://www.schooldata.com/pdfs/PubSchExp2007_2008.pdf.

Mathews, J. (2005). Why don't we fix our textbooks?, *The Washington Post.* Retrieved from http://www.wshingtonpost.com/wp-dyn/articles/A56501-2005March22.htm.

McTigue, B. (2010, June 10). [Our schools' move to digital resources].

Norris, C., & Soloway, E. (2011). Tips for BYOD K12 programs: Critical issue in moving to "Bring Your Own Device." *District Administration.* Retrieved from http://www.districtadministration.com/article/tips-byod-k12-programs.

Nudi, C. (2010, June 6). [The appeal of digital textbooks].

Oder, N. (2009, October 12). Google's Clancy wonders: What happens to libraries when ebooks predominate? *Library Journal.* Retrieved from http://www.libraryjournal.com/article/CA6701538.html.

Olivarez-Giles, N. (2012). Apple digital textbooks: Can Apple reinvent another industry? *Christian Science Monitor.* Retrieved from http://www.csmonitor.com/Innovation/2012/0119/Apple-digital-textbooks-Can-Apple-reinvent-another-industry.

Perez, L. (2010). Can iPod touch boost math scores? One Pinellas school tests theory, *St. Petersburg Times.* Retrieved from http://www.tampabay.com/news/education/k12/can-ipod-touch-boost-math-scores-one-pinellas-school-tests-theory/1084761.

Peters, T. (2009, November 1). The future of reading: As the book changes form, the library must wwchallenge its own power base—readers. *Library Journal.* Retrieved from http://www.library-journal.com/index.asp?layout=articlePrint&articleID=CA6703882.

Plank, W. (2011, August 31). How heavy can a backpack get? *The Wall Street Journal*, p. D1.

Project Tomorrow. (2010, May). Unleashing the future: Educators "Speak Up" about the use of emerging technologies for learning. Speak Up 2009 national findings from teachers, aspiring teachers, and administrators. Retrieved May 10, 2010, from http://www.tomorrow.org/speakup/pdfs/SU09UnleashingTheFuture.pdf.

Reynolds, R. (2010, April 28). Digital textbooks, open content, and critical literacies *Xplana*. Retrieved from http://blog.xplana.com/2010/04/digital-textbooks-open-content-and-critical-literacies/.

Riddle, E., & Traylor, J. (2010). Higher education retail market facts & figures 2010. Retrieved June 10, 2010, from https://www.nacs.org/Research/IndustryStatistics/HigherEdFactsFigures.aspx.

Roscorla, T. (2011). Wolf Creek Public Schools embraces BYOD, puts pedagogy first. *Converge*. Retrieved from http://www.convergemag.com/policy/Wolf-Creek-Public-Schools-BYOD.html.

Rowsell, J., & Burke, A. (2009). Reading by design: Two case studies of digital reading practices. *Journal of Adolescent & Adult Literacy, 53*(2), 106–118. doi:10.1598/JAAL.53.2.2.

Ruth, G. (2005, February 8). No books, no problem: Teaching without a text. *Edutopia*. Retrieved from http://www.edutopia.org/no-books-no-problem.

Salpeter, J. (2009). Textbook deathwatch. *Technology & Learning, 30*(1), 26–29.

Schachter, R. (2009, October 21). Digital classrooms take flight. *District Administration*. Retrieved from http://www.districtadministration.com/viewarticle.aspx?articleid=2161.

Schaffhauser, D. (2010a). Can higher ed tech support benefit from a tech makeover? *Campus Technology*. Retrieved from http://campustechnology.com/articles/2010/12/17/can-higher-ed-tech-support-benefit-from-a-tech-makeover.aspx.

Schaffhauser, D. (2010b). Department of Ed lays down law on Kindle e-Reader usage. *Campus Technology*. Retrieved from http://campustechnology.com/articles/2010/06/29/department-of-ed-lays-down-law-on-kindle-e-reader-usage.aspx.

Schaffhauser, D. (2011). Wolf Creek district deploys NAC to support BYOD. *THE Journal*. Retrieved from http://thejournal.com/articles/2011/12/12/wolf-creek-district-deploys-nac-to-support-byod.aspx.

Schmidt, W. H., McKnight, C. C., & Raizen, S. A. (1997). *A splintered vision: An investigation of U.S. science and mathematics education*. Boston: Kluwer.

Sebastian, S. (2006, November 15). Kids lug books in digital age, *Columbus Dispatch*. Retrieved from http://www.accessmylibrary.com/article-1G1-154469595/kids-lug-books-digital.html.

Sheir-Neiss, G., Kruse, R., Rahman, T., Jacobson, L., & Pelli, J. (2003). The association of backpack use and back pain in adolescents. *Spine, 28*(9), 922–930. doi:10.1097/00007632-200305010-00015.

Smith, J. (2010, April 4). [Digital textbook interview].

State Educational Technology Directors Association [SETDA]. (2010). National trends reports. Retrieved Report, from http://www.setda.org/web/guest/nationaltrendsreport.

State of Florida (2011). Senate Bill (SB) 2120: K-12 education funding.

Stelter, B., & Wortham, J. (2010, March 13). Effort to widen access sets off battle: A 10 year plan by FCC, *New York Times*. Retrieved from http://community.nytimes.com/comments/www.nytimes.com/2010/03/13/business/media/13fcchtml.

Sullivan, D. (2011). Why do Amazon & Apple hate families? Retrieved from http://daggle.com/amazon-apple-hate-families-2867.

Surdin, A. (2009). In some classrooms, books are a thing of the past: Digital texts gaining favor, but critics question quality, *The Washington Post*. Retrieved from http://www.washingtonpost.com.

Sutherland-Smith, W. (2002). Weaving the literacy web: Changes in reading from page to screen. *The Reading Teacher, 55*(7), 662–669.

Taylor, C. (2008, October 10). Editorial: Digital books can provide convenience Retrieved June 15, 2010, from http://www.baylor.edu/lariat/news.php?action=story&story=53559.

Thevenot, B. (2009, November 6). The tipping point: Texas textbook politics meets the digital revolution, *Texas Tribune*. Retrieved from http://www.texastribune.org/stories/2009/nov/06/tipping-point-texas-textbook-politics-meets-digital-revolution/.

Thier, D. (2012). Apple sold 350K digital textbooks in three days, but what comes next? *Forbes*. Retrieved from http://www.forbes.com/sites/davidthier/2012/01/23/apple-sold-350k-digital-textbooks-in-three-days-but-what-comes-next/.

Thomas, S. (2005, November). Transliteracy—Reading in the digital age. *The Higher Education Academy English Subject Centre Online Newsletter, 9*. Retrieved from http://www.english.heacademy.ac.uk/explore/publications/newsletters/newsissue9/index.htm.

Travis, S. (2010, April 26). Students get break on books: Some college titles offered free online, *Sun-Sentinel*. Retrieved from http://articles.sun-sentinel.com/2010-04-26/news/fl-fltl-cp-freebooksfla-20100426_1_textbook-advocate-textbook-affordability-state-study-showed-textbooks.

Tulley, M. A. (1989). The pros and cons of state-level textbook adoption. *Book Research Quarterly, 5*(2), 71–80.

Tulley, M. A., & Farr, R. (1985). Textbook adoption: Insight, impact, and potential. *Book Research Quarterly, 1*(2), 4–11.

United States Department of Justice. (2010, January 13). Justice Department reaches three settlements under the Americans with Disabilities Act regarding the use of electronic book readers. Retrieved June 30, 2010, from http://www.justice.gov/opa/pr/2010/January/10-crt-030.html.

Waters, J. (2007). The universal language. *THE Journal, 34*(1), 34–40.

Watkins, S. (2009). *The young and the digital: What the migration to social network sites, games and anytime, anywhere media means for our future*. Boston, MA: Beacon.

Whelan, D. L. (2009, August 31). Marcia Mardis explores digital resources in the library. *School Library Journal*. Retrieved from http://www.schoollibraryjournal.com/article/CA6678735.html.

Williamson, J. (2010, March 29). E-readers or traditional books: Which is better for education? Retrieved June 5, 2010, from http://www.distance-education.org/Articles/E-readers-or-Traditional-Books--Which-Is-Better-for-Education--232.html.

Young, T. (2007). Prep school students buy own tablet PCs for classroom work. *Phoenix Business Journal*. Retrieved from http://phoenix.bizjournals.com/phoenix/stories/2007/12/31/story4.html.

Chapter 10
Preparing Education Professionals for K-12 Online Learning Programs

Kathryn Kennedy, Dawn Tysinger, Carrie Bailey, and Jason LaFrance

10.1 Introduction to K-12 Online Learning Programs

Over the last two decades, K-12 online learning has become pervasive. All 50 states, plus Washington, DC, have K-12 online learning programs, ranging from fully online to more blended environments (Watson et al. 2011). Fully online programs deliver 80% or more of their course offerings online. Blended programs provide more of a mixture within single classrooms, so in one course, students are exposed to a mixture of face-to-face and online learning. Hybrid programs offer a choice of both solely online and solely face-to-face courses (Barbour and Kennedy, in press). New models are emerging on a daily basis, so programs that have both a blended and hybrid approach more than likely exist at this time.

Laws that require students to engage in online learning are being adopted more readily across the country. For instance, Michigan (2006), New Mexico (2007), Alabama (2008), and now Idaho (2011) require their K-12 students to experience online learning before they graduate high school. The Keeping Pace report states that virtual schools enrolled 450,000 students in the 2009–2010 academic year, a 40% increase since the previous year (Watson et al. 2010). By 2020, it is predicted that half of high school classes will be offered online (Christensen et al. 2010). Because K-12 online enrollments are continuing to increase exponentially, there is a critical need for preparatory and professional development programs to prepare all education professionals for these unique learning environments.

As early as 2003 (Irvine et al. 2003), researchers and practitioners called for teachers to learn how to teach online. Because of this early advocacy, today there are standards for online teachers to meet and follow, including the International Association for K-12 Online Learning's *National Standards for Quality Online*

K. Kennedy (✉) • D. Tysinger • C. Bailey • J. LaFrance
Georgia Southern University, Department of Leadership, Technology,
and Human Development, P.O. Box 8131, Statesboro, GA 30460, USA
e-mail: kmkennedy@georgiasouthern.edu

M. Orey et al. (eds.), *Educational Media and Technology Yearbook*, Educational
Media and Technology Yearbook 37, DOI 10.1007/978-1-4614-4430-5_10,
© Springer Science+Business Media New York 2013

Teaching (iNACOL 2008) and the International Society for Technology's National Education Technology Standards for Teachers (ISTE 2008), which are designed to help teachers meet technology integration benchmarks in all K-12 learning environments. These standards can be used to help teachers understand what they are responsible for when incorporating hybrid, blended, and purely online learning into their teaching.

In addition to the standards, teacher training for K-12 online learning often involves learning theories in online learning and pedagogy (Archambault 2011). Topics within this area include but are not limited to instructional design, communication, and student support for online learning environments. Currently, training for online teachers occurs in many venues. For instance, many virtual schools offer training for their own teachers as well as teachers who are new to K-12 online learning and those who are still in their preparatory programs. Examples of these schools include Virtual High School Global Consortium and the Florida Virtual School. Some teacher education programs, such as the University of Florida (Kennedy et al. 2012; Kennedy and Archambault, in press), University of Central Florida, University of South Florida, and Iowa State University (Compton et al. 2009) partner with virtual, hybrid, blended, and face-to-face schools to offer preservice and in-service teacher training for K-12 online learning. Several universities have started offering certificate programs in online teaching, including some of the ones mentioned above and Arizona State University. Georgia and other states have begun online teaching endorsements. Organizations like Online Teaching Associates, PBS TeacherLine, and EdTech Leaders Online also offer professional development for teachers who want to learn how to teach online. Despite these efforts, there are still only less than 2% of teacher education programs preparing teachers for K-12 online learning (Kennedy and Archambault, in press). Given the scarcity of training for teachers, it is not surprising that training for other education professionals has only recently begun to receive some attention.

10.2 School Librarians

School library media specialists play an integral role in K-12 online learning programs. Some take an embedded librarian approach, which is typically associated with postsecondary educational institutions; now this concept is growing in the K-12 online learning arena (Dale and Kellam 2012). Like their embedded counterparts in higher education, school librarians can offer many of the same services in the online learning environment as they do in the face-to-face library media center. Although school librarians typically are fluent in the use of many technologies, they have little experience with online delivery (Green and Jones 2012) and therefore need training for teaching in the online environment. Using the American Association of School Librarian (AASL) *Standards for the 21st Century Learner* and the American Library Association (ALA)/AASL and National Council for Accreditation of Teacher Education (NCATE) standards for school library media preparation, certification programs for school librarians have begun to offer field experiences in

K-12 online learning programs. Courses are being designed specifically for creating online resources. At Georgia Southern University, in particular, there is a course in virtual school libraries. This course, designed by Dr. Judi Repman, promotes the use of Web 2.0 tools to reach students in online learning environments. One method the school library candidates learn is how to develop online pathfinders as tools for students that organize resources around a specific topic. The program also encourages school media specialists to partner and collaborate with teachers in order to offer students a co-teaching experience where the teacher librarian infuses information literacy into the curriculum in online course modules. Georgia Southern University's program has connected some of their school library candidates with the state's virtual school after the candidates voiced interest in gaining more experience in K-12 online schooling. Florida Virtual School, Virtual Virginia, and Georgia Virtual School are three virtual schools who currently employ school library media specialists.

10.3   Educational Technologists/Technology Specialists

Educational technologists/technology specialists typically come from one or more of the following backgrounds: computer science, instructional technology, instructional design, and/or technology education. Depending on the focus of their instructional technology program, students can range in experience from networking-focus to instructional design, where a majority of training is spent on educational tools and their meaningful integration into the curriculum. The preparatory programs typically follow standards set forth by the International Society for Technology in Education (ISTE) (http://www.iste.org/standards/nets-refresh-project.aspx) and/or the Association for Educational Communications and Technology (AECT) (http://www.aect.org/standards/advstand.html). ISTE's standards are divided into two strands—Technology Leadership and Technology Facilitation. One of the ISTE standards revolves around "Digital Learning Environments." This standard states that candidates "Create, support, and manage effective digital learning environments" (ISTE). Educational technology/technology specialist preparatory programs are designed to prepare their graduates to help implement technology meaningfully into schools, and with the growth of online learning in all of its forms, it would be beneficial for some of the students' field work to be set in K-12 online learning programs so that they understand what it is like to support a virtual learning environment.

10.4   Administrators

The call for digital-age leadership requires administrators to develop their own technology skills and those of others. In school administration preparatory programs, there is still much work to be done in the area of K-12 online learning. As such, some K-12 online learning programs have taken on the task of training their own leaders internally. Training in the field of online leadership is available, for instance, through the Virtual Leadership Training program offered at the Florida Virtual School.

For K-12 administration preparatory programs, coordinators can begin to include curriculum specific to K-12 online leadership by looking at the iNACOL developed standards that program leaders can utilize to ensure a quality online program (http:// www.inacol.org/research/nationalstandards/index.php) and incorporate these standards into courses. In addition, ISTE's standards for administrators (http://www.iste.org/ standards/nets-for-administrators/nets-for-administrators-sandards.aspx) can be used as well. A final source is the iNACOL forum which covers topics such as recruiting, training, and retaining online teachers, as well as online programs, policies, and management (http://www.inacol.org/forum/index.php?act=idx).

In addition to training on standards, administrators need to understand the K-12 online learning concept of leading in an environment where learning is anytime, anywhere. This requires leaders to be networked and collaborative co-learners with colleagues around the world. One way to accomplish this is for preparatory programs to emphasize that their students harness the power of personal learning networks. Signing up for a Twitter account allows education professionals to follow experts in the field through social media, creating opportunities for ongoing learning and sharing of ideas (see Hakan Senturk's "Teach Me" blog, http://teach-me-tech.blogspot. com/2010/11/building-your-own-pln-with-twitter.html). A search on www.listorious. com for "edtech leaders" will help establish a great foundation for learning. Currently, a national survey is being administered to see what other models exist in terms of preparing administrators for K-12 online learning programs (LaFrance and Beck 2012).

10.5   School Psychologists

Currently, most school psychologists affiliated with virtual schools are either employees of the local education agency assigned to the virtual school or school psychologists in private practice who are contracting for service delivery. Although the 11 Domains of School Psychology Graduate Education and Practice as set forth in the Standards for Graduate Preparation of School Psychologists (NASP 2010a) could all apply to the practice of school psychology in the virtual school, few training programs or professional development opportunities address this unique need. This absence seems glaring when considering that School Psychology: A Blueprint for Training and Practice III (NASP 2006) highlights technology use and impact as one of the societal factors that define the context of school psychological practice.

Consistent with the Principles for Professional Ethics (NASP 2010b), school psychologists may increase their competence in any area by engaging in supervised practice by a professional already competent in that skill. Ideally, this would mean that a school psychologist would seek out professional experiences within the virtual school (e.g., consultation, behavior management, academic intervention, or crisis intervention), which would be supervised by a school psychologist already proficient in service delivery in that environment. However, given that few school psychologists have received training for competence in this area, the school psychologist wishing to expand his/her skills in providing services within K-12 online learning programs would be well advised to seek supervision from professionals in related fields where training models for service in virtual schools may exist (i.e., counseling or social work). School psychology preparation programs are currently in the process of examining the best ways to structure field experiences in order to prepare school psychologists for K-12 online learning programs (Tysinger et al. 2012).

10.6 School Counselors

While there is some research relating to models of online mental health counseling, little work has been done in the arena of virtual school counseling programs. The role of school counselors in such environments is vague, and examples are limited (Currie 2010). School counseling programs, whether serving students in traditional, hybrid, or fully online environments, need to align with national standards that address academic, career, and personal/social domains to best meet the needs of the students served. As highlighted by research in online mental health counseling, issues of confidentiality, counselor competence, crisis procedures, and research on the efficacy and limitations of such models must be addressed (Barnett 2005; Shaw and Shaw 2006).

However, frameworks are beginning to emerge with promise of more research and innovation to come. One such model to examine is that outlined for the newly developed Department of Defense Education Activity (DODEA) Virtual School (www.dodea.edu). Integral to the development of this new virtual high school was the structuring of a virtual school counseling department that aligned with the American School Counseling Association's (ASCA 2005) National Model and offers a "comprehensive developmentally appropriate guidance and counseling program designed to meet the needs of all students the school serves" (DODEA 2010). Other models include those outlined by programs such as Virtual Virginia (Virginia Department of Education (2009)) (http://www.virtualvirginia.org/) and Florida Virtual School (http://www.flvs.net/), which has partnered with the University of South Florida to provide virtual internships for school counselors.

10.7 Discussion

What else should those interested in preparation of these education professionals consider? A good place to start would be general readings that provide an overview of K-12 online learning. The following must-reads for those new to the field are recommended by K-12 online learning experts:

- *Keeping Pace with K-12 Online Learning* (http://kpk12.com/): This report provides an annual update on K-12 online learning around the USA (Watson et al. 2010).

- *Lessons learned from virtual schools: Experiences and recommendations from the field* (Ferdig and Cavanaugh 2011): This book offers insight into what practitioners and researchers have learned in the last 20 years about the field of K-12 online learning.
- The International Association for K-12 Online Learning (iNACOL) also offers a plethora of information (iNACOL 2011).
- Special issues of *Distance Learning Magazine* (Volume 7, Issue 2, 2010) and *Journal of Technology and Teacher Education* (Volume 17, Issue 4, 2009) share the latest information and research in the field.

In addition to these general readings, select studies should be included from the iNACOL database that is currently being designed. This database will include research on K-12 online learning and will incorporate the Virtual School Clearinghouse, a database that began organizing research in the field (http://www.vsclearinghouse.com). Training for education professionals, whether it is for teachers, school library media specialists, educational technologists/technology specialists, administrators, school psychologists, or school counselors, should also include guest lectures from professionals in virtual, blended, and hybrid programs. Most importantly, education professionals need practical experience in K-12 online learning programs, whether via field experiences, guided observations, internships, or immersions. During these experiences, the education professionals should be encouraged to reflect and engage in self-evaluations. In addition, these individuals should be provided mentors who can help guide their ongoing professional development.

K-12 online learning has been around since the early 1990s, and as each day passes, enrollments in virtual, hybrid, and blended programs grow exponentially. A growing trend now is district-level homegrown online learning initiatives, some of which function as blended learning environments that marry face-to-face with online learning (Watson et al. 2010). Because of these developments, we need to constantly think about how we prepare education professionals for these new learning environments. As mentioned here, a handful of virtual, hybrid, and blended schools, colleges and schools of education, international and national professional organizations, and businesses are offering training already. While this is a big step forward, we need to be taking a giant leap by focusing on twenty-first century reform and the preparation of education professionals who will be leaders in that movement.

References

Alabama State Board of Education. (2008). *Alabama Administrative Code (AAC) Rule 290-3-1-.02(12) for Online Courses*. Retrieved from http://www.adph.org/tpts/assets/schoolpolicy.pdf.
American Association of School Librarians (AASL 2007). Standards for the 21st century learner. Retrieved from http://www.ala.org/ala/mgrps/divs/aasl/guidelinesandstandards/learningstandards/standards.cfm.
American School Counseling Association. (2005). *The ASCA national model: A framework for school counseling programs* (2nd ed.). Alexandria, VA: Author.

Archambault, L. M. (2011). The practitioner's perspective on teacher education: Preparing for the K-12 online classroom. *Journal of Technology and Teacher Education, 19*(1), 73–91.

Barbour, M., & Kennedy, K. (in press). K-12 online learning: A worldwide perspective. In A. Hirumi (ed.) *Designing alternative environments to facilitate e-Learning: A systematic approach.* Washington, DC: International Society for Technology in Education (ISTE) (in press).

Barnett, J. E. (2005). Online counseling: New entity, new challenges. *The Counseling Psychologist, 33*, 872–880.

Christensen, C. M., Horn, M. B., & Johnson, C. W. (2010). *Disrupting class: How disruptive innovation will change the way the world learns* (2nd ed.). New York: McGraw-Hill.

Compton, L., Davis, N. E., & Mackey, J. (2009). Field experience in virtual schooling: To be there virtually. *Journal of Technology and Teacher Education, 17*(4), 459–477.

Currie, N. S. (2010). Virtual counseling for students enrolled in online educational programs. *Educational Considerations, 37*(2), 22–26.

Dale, J., & Kellam, L. (2012). The incredible embeddable librarian. *Library Media Connection, 30*(4), 30–31.

DoDEA. (2010). DoDEA launching virtual high school. *Synched: Department of Defense Education Activity Newsletter*, 1, 1–6. Retrieved from http://www.dodea.edu/VirtualSchool/VSNewsletterVersionOne.pdf.

Ferdig, R.E. & Cavanaugh, C. (Eds.) (2011). *Lessons learned from virtual schools: Experiences and recommendations from the field.* Vienna, VA: International Association for K-12 Online Learning (iNACOL).

Green, L. S. & Jones, S. A. (2012). Transforming collaboration: Student learning, anytime, anywhere (in press).

Idaho Senate. (2011). *Bill 1184.* Retrieved from www.legislature.idaho.gov/legislation/2011/S1184.pdf.

International Association for K-12 Online Learning (iNACOL). (2008). *National standards for quality online teaching.* Retrieved October 10, 2008, from http://www.inacol.org/resources/nationalstandards/NACOL%20Standards%20Quality%20Online%20Teaching.pdf

International Society for Technology in Education (ISTE). (2008). *National educational technology standards (NETS*T) and performance indicators for teachers.* Retrieved from http://www.iste.org/Content/NavigationMenu/NETS/ForTeachers/2008Standards/NETS_for_Teachers_2008.htm

Irvine, V., Mappin, D., & Code, J. (2003). Preparing teachers to teach online: The role of faculties of education. In D. Lassner & C. McNaught (Eds.), *Proceedings of World Conference on Educational Multimedia, Hypermedia and Telecommunications* (pp. 1978–1981). Chesapeake, VA: AACE.

Kennedy, K., & Archambault, L. (2012). Offering pre-service teachers field experiences in K-12 online learning: A national survey of teacher education programs. *Journal of Teacher Education, 63*(3), 185–200.

Kennedy, K., Cavanaugh, C., & Dawson, K. (2012). Pre-service teachers' experience in a virtual school. *Journal of Teacher Education, 63*(3), 185–200.

LaFrance, J. & Beck, D. (2012). The current state of educational leadership program field experiences in k-12 virtual school settings for pre-service administrators in the United States (in press).

Michigan Department of Education. (2006). *380. 1278a: Requirements for high school diploma.* Retrieved from http://www.legislature.mi.gov/%28S%285ti0q4avj23jrxj3hqvmvd45%29%29/mileg.aspx?page=GetObject&objectname=mcl-380-1278a

National Association of School Psychologists. (2006). *School psychology: A blueprint for training and practice III.* Bethesda, MD.

National Association of School Psychologists, (2010a). *Standards for graduate preparation of school psychologists.* Bethesda, MD.

National Association of School Psychologists (2010b). *Principles for professional ethics.* Bethesda, MD.

New Mexico Public Education Department. (2007). *SB209/HB201*. Retrieved from http://www. nmlegis.gov/lcs/_session.aspx?Chamber=H&LegType=B&LegNo=201&year=07.

Shaw, H. E., & Shaw, S. F. (2006). Critical ethical issues in online counseling: Assessing current practices with an ethical intent checklist. *Journal of Counseling & Development, 84,* 41–53.

Tysinger, D., Kennedy, K., Tysinger, J., & Diamanduras, T. (2012). Preparing school psychologists to work in K-12 online learning environments (in press).

Virginia Department of Education. (2009). Virtual Virginia school counselor handbook. Retrieved from http://www.virtualvirginia.org/counselors/handbook/downloads/counselor_handbook. pdf.

Watson, J., Murin, A., Vashaw, L., Gemin, B., & Rapp, C. (2010). *Keeping pace with K-12 online learning: An annual review of policy and practice.* Evergreen, CO: Evergreen Education Group.

Watson, J., Murin, A., Vashaw, L., Gemin, B., & Rapp, C. (2011). *Keeping pace with k-12 online learning: An annual review of policy and practice.* Evergreen, CO: Evergreen Education Group.

Chapter 11
The Web 2.0 Connection: An Exploratory Study of School Library Services for Students with Autism Spectrum Disorders

Daniella Smith

11.1 Introduction

Web 2.0 boasts a variety of interactive, multimedia driven tools such as blogs, wikis, picture slideshows, video sharing, social tagging, and social networking websites. These tools allow teachers and students to simultaneously engage in activities that were not imagined 30 years ago (Bolan, Canada, and Cullin, 2007). As such, these tools have become integral parts of classroom activities. They are implemented to build social skills, create and display projects, and to participate in activities without the restriction of time zones or physical boundaries (Norton and Hathaway 2008).

Another important aspect of Web 2.0 tools is that they afford opportunities for participatory learning instead of passive activities (Barlow 2008). This is appealing and empowering to students who may not be intrinsically motivated to learn when presented with traditional vehicles of learning such as lectures and reading (Barlow 2008; Hicks and Graber 2010). When Web 2.0 tools are incorporated into curriculums, students simultaneously become content creators and consumers of information (Bolan et al. 2007; Hicks and Graber 2010) who improve their literacy skills by reading, writing, analyzing, and interpreting information (Gooch and Saine 2011).

The resulting projects are collaborative environment catalysts that urge students to share their interests (Tattersall 2011) and opinions (Bolan et al. 2007). As editors, students develop a collective knowledge base that inspires communication while reflecting diverse perspectives. Bolan et al. further suggest that social tagging encourages students to contribute to the subject content by collectively working to classify information. This allows students to store and share content in a way that is familiar to them (Bolan et al. 2007).

D. Smith, Ph.D (✉)
Department of Library and Information Sciences, College of Information,
The University of North Texas, Denton, TX, USA
e-mail: Daniella.Smith@unt.edu

M. Orey et al. (eds.), *Educational Media and Technology Yearbook*, Educational
Media and Technology Yearbook 37, DOI 10.1007/978-1-4614-4430-5_11,
© Springer Science+Business Media New York 2013

School librarians are experts who teach school communities information literacy skills in order to access information. As such, Web 2.0 tools are becoming popular among school librarians who use them to classify information and teach technology-enhanced lessons. One particular group of students that can benefit from lessons designed with Web 2.0 tools are students with autism spectrum disorders (ASD).

According to Centers for Disease Control and Prevention (2011), ASD refer to a group of developmental disorders that impact the brain. The early signs of these disorders typically manifest by the time children are 3 years old. These signs are not physical in nature. Instead they reflect the way children with ASD communicate, behave, and learn. For example, children with ASD may prefer to be alone, avoid eye contact with others, and have delayed speech and language skills. While the symptoms of the disorders may improve with intervention, there is currently no cure for them.

Technology such as Web 2.0 tools is often used in interventions. Web 2.0 tools are beneficial to students with ASD because they are visual learners (D'Auria 2010). For example, Dr. Temple Grandin (2010) is a well-known, high-functioning autistic. Grandin affirms her memory functions much like a movie. According to Grandin, her conversations are translated to pictures. Much like many autistic learners, Grandin excels in visual spatial skills. Grandin is an example of how providing students who have ASD with Web 2.0 tools can enable them to function in environments that address their visual spatial learning strengths.

Still there is not an abundance of research pertaining to how school librarians use Web 2.0 tools with special needs students such as those with ASD. The purpose of this study was to explore the relationship between school librarians' use of Web 2.0 tools and their provision of services to students with ASD, the teachers of students with ASD, and the parents and guardians of students with ASD. The following questions guided the investigation.

11.2   Research Questions

1. Do school librarians feel their school libraries are equipped with technology to assist students with ASD?
2. Is there a relationship between the frequency of Web 2.0 use among school librarians and the belief that a school librarian should provide assistance to students with ASD, the teachers of students with ASD, and the parents and guardians of students with ASD?
3. Is there a relationship between the frequency of Web 2.0 use among school librarians and their comfort level with providing assistance to students with ASD, the teachers of students with ASD, and the parents and guardians of students with ASD?

11.3   Literature Review

11.3.1   Web 2.0 and School Libraries

There has been very little research discussing the impact of Web 2.0 tools in relation to school librarians (Branch and deGroot 2011; Smith 2010). Web 2.0 advocates assert school librarians must remain relevant by incorporating Web 2.0 tools with traditional services (Baumbach 2009; Farmer and Shontz 2009; Harris 2006). By doing so, school libraries can harness emerging trends to undertake traditional library services and attract current students who are digital natives. In addition, Web 2.0 tools provide a new way for school librarians to share their expertise while incorporating societal trends into their practice. Baumbach (2009) further advises school librarians to use Web 2.0 tools because they are in alignment with national standards, improve equitable access to information, save money, are versatile, encourage creativity, and teach information literacy skills.

School librarian efforts to adjust to societal trends such as Web 2.0 tools are reflected in the School Library Journal Spending Survey. For example, Farmer and Shontz (2009) observed several differences between the 2009 and 2008 spending surveys. The results revealed more school librarians were mentioning Web 2.0 tools than they did in previous years. These results signified computer instruction in school libraries was focused less on traditional classes and more on instruction and learning with Web 2.0 tools. But filtering, deficient budgets, a need for training for staff and students, a lack of knowledge about Web 2.0, and poor district support were listed as reasons why school librarians do not use Web 2.0 tools.

Baumbach (2009) completed another nationwide study to determine how school librarians were using Web 2.0 tools and their Web 2.0 professional development needs. The study had several significant findings similar to Farmer and Shontz's (2009) results. For instance, the main reasons the participants of Baumbach's study stated they were not using Web 2.0 tools were inaccessibility in schools, the absence of training relevant to school librarians, a lack of time to explore the tools, and a lack of knowledge about tools that are available. Lack of knowledge as a barrier was evidenced by the finding that less than 30% of the respondents were using Web 2.0 tools for library programming. Baumbach concluded that school librarians' use of these tools was in sharp contrast to K-12 students who incorporate them into their daily lives.

Similar to Baumbach's (2009) exploration of professional development needs, Smith (2010) conducted a survey of teacher leaders enrolled in a school librarianship degree program. Though the study participants had varying degrees of teaching experience, many of them were not aware of what Web 2.0 tools were before they began the program. The results indicated that once the participants learned about Web 2.0 through hands-on activities incorporated into the program, they used their new skills to practice leadership behaviors and act as role models for other educators.

The participants similarly confirmed that prior to beginning the school librarianship degree program, they participated in technology professional development in their school districts. Still, the professional development did not offer them practical ways to use the technology during lessons. The hands-on application of the technology helped them visualize the projects that were possible and be confident with their technology skills. Smith (2010) concluded that Web 2.0 tools can be used as facilitators for teaching preservice school librarians how to be leaders. In addition, technology professional development should be sustained, emphasize practical applications, and include feedback. However, school district administrators must be accepting of new techniques to integrate technology into learning environments.

Branch and deGroot (2011) had findings comparable to Smith's (2010). Like Smith, Branch-Mueller and deGroot's results noted that prior to coursework, many of the participants had not used Web 2.0 tools in their professional practice. Yet learning to use the tools improved their confidence and helped them become leaders as they became known for being technology experts. Through training, the participants were able to recognize the difference between traditional learning and active learning with Web 2.0 tools. Branch-Mueller and deGroot's summary also identified organizational cultures and restricted access to tools as barriers that prevented the participants from using technology.

11.3.2 The Educational Needs of Autistic Students

The education of students with ASD poses challenges for many reasons. The first challenge is that ASD symptoms range from mild to severe. According to the National Institute of Mental Health (2011), symptoms of ASD reflect one of three areas: social impairment, communication difficulties, and repetitive and stereotyped behaviors. Diagnosis is difficult because there are no two cases of the disease exactly the same.

The heterogeneous nature of the disease complicates the education of students with ASD because an intervention that is appropriate for one student may not meet the needs of another. Unfortunately, children with ASD tend to have difficulties verbally articulating their needs, and gestures are frequently substituted for words (Krebs et al. 2010). Consequently, forming relationships is problematic and can impact the overall effectiveness of their education (Emam and Farrell 2009).

The Individuals with Disabilities Education Act (U.S. Department of Education 2004) seeks to improve the educational outcomes of special needs students such as those with ASD. This law mandates that students with special needs be educated in the least restrictive environment. Nonetheless, inclusion is a notion that is often rejected for students with ASD because the symptoms of their disability create obstacles that impede peer interaction and social development (Poon 2011; Strain et al. 2011). In the classroom, these obstacles are accentuated because educating students with ASD requires curriculum adaptations. "Not all teachers were prone to commit wholeheartedly to exerting extra efforts to meet the needs of the pupils with ASD in their class" (Emam and Farrell 2009, p. 414).

The commitment that teachers exhibit towards meeting the needs of students with ASD is directly related to the perceptions that the parents of students with ASD have of the educational system. According to Lynch and Irvine (2009), parents of students with ASD often criticize schools for the deficient services offered to their children. Conversely, parents of ASD students who are included in the educational process tend to feel more satisfied with the services that are offered to their children. Simpson et al. (2010) maintain that the needs of ASD students can be met by preparing all educators with strategies to teach them. Educators can be prepared through ongoing professional development and degree programs that explain how to collaborate and instruct students in structured learning environments. Most importantly, it is recommended that teachers exhaust all available resources before placing students in restrictive environments.

One resource that addresses the strengths of students with ASD is technology (Wainer and Ingersoll 2011). Children with autism have been found to respond positively to technology for learning basic skills. Several researchers have used a combination of instruction and video modeling to strengthen the social skills of students with ASD (D'Ateno et al. 2003; MacDonald et al. 2005; Nikopoulos and Keenan 2007). Likewise, a computer-based program containing simulations of everyday activities helped children with ASD improve their speech in the classroom (Hetzroni and Tannous 2004). Resembling simulations, virtual reality technologies such as Second Life have been found to help students with ASD because the environments can be individualized and enable them to experience real-life scenarios (Strickland et al. 1996) while minimizing anxiety (Moore et al. 2000).

Research equally indicates that computers are instrumental for improving the reading skills of students with ASD. Interactive books with music have been shown to improve involvement in learning in small group environments (Carnahan et al. 2009). In another study, children with autism who were presented with book-based and computer-based reading instruction spent more time reading when they were using the computer-assisted learning. Comparably, they were less likely to resist learning when the instruction was offered by a computer (Williams et al. 2002).

11.4 Methodology

11.4.1 Population

Invitations were sent to 1,000 school librarians from a list compiled by searching online school directories. Responses were also solicited by posting to school librarian listservs. A purposive sample of 508 school librarians in the USA responded to the survey. The participants included one school librarian from a preschool, 83 from schools that combined elementary and secondary grade levels, 99 from middle schools, 129 from high schools, and 197 from elementary schools.

11.4.2   Data Collection and Analysis

An online survey was used to implement a mixed-method design. Since this topic was exploratory in nature, open-ended questions were included to gain a better understanding of the closed-ended questions on the survey. The survey was designed to collect demographic data and information about the services participants provide to students with ASD, the teachers of students with ASD, and the parents and guardians of students with ASD. The findings reported here relate specifically to Web 2.0 tools and their relationship with the services provided by school librarians.

Upon the completion of the data collection, the Statistical Package for the Social Sciences (SPSS) was used for the quantitative analysis of the research questions. The software Nvivo was used to code the qualitative data obtained from the open-ended questions into themes. Frequencies of responses were used to examine Research Question 1.

Research Question 2 was analyzed by using the Spearman rank correlation coefficient to determine the relationship between the frequency of Web 2.0 use and the belief that assistance should be provided to students with ASD, the teachers of students with ASD, and the parents and guardians of students with ASD. The Spearman rank correlation coefficient was used again for Research Question 3 to determine the relationship between the frequency of Web 2.0 use and the participants' comfort level with providing assistance to students with ASD, the teachers of students with ASD, and the parents and guardians of students with ASD.

11.5   Findings

11.5.1   Research Question 1

Do school librarians feel their school libraries are equipped with technology to assist students with ASD?

The participants were asked to list the technology they felt was available in their libraries to assist students with ASD. Most respondents (62%) reported that their library was equipped with technology to assist students with ASD. The list and frequency of these tools are presented in Fig. 11.1. The label "same for all" in Fig. 11.1 reflects responses that noted that additional technology that is specifically beneficial to special needs students such as those with ASD was not available. A response specifying "tools were available" did not necessarily equate to the tool being used with the ASD students. Several respondents commented they did not know how to use the technology with ASD students. For example, one participant wrote, "I believe that we have great technology available to us, but I am not sure of what would be best to use with autistic children." Another participant with a similar opinion wrote, "Ok. So I really don't know if I am equipped with this technology,

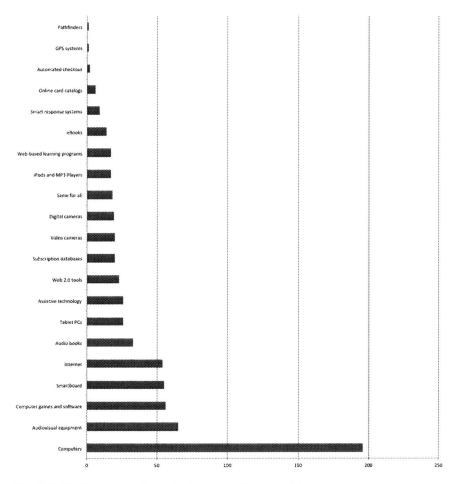

Fig. 11.1 The frequencies of technologies reported by the participants

but we do have student access to various electronic resources; computers, iPads with wireless, iPod touches, etc."

Web 2.0 tools were listed as a type of technology available in libraries. When asked the frequency of Web 2.0 use in their libraries, a total of 73% of the respondents agreed or strongly agreed they frequently use Web 2.0 tools. The participants were provided with a list of Web 2.0 tools and asked to select all of the tools they currently use in the school library. The results, as indicated in Fig. 11.2, were as follows: educational gaming sites (73%), slide shows and pictures (60%), blogs (50%), wikis (48%), social networking sites (35%), video sharing (34%), and social tagging sites (31%).

The survey responses indicate some of the study participants were not using Web 2.0 tools because of restriction to access. This finding is consistent with Farmer and Shontz's (2009) statement that librarians are not able to use Web 2.0 tools because

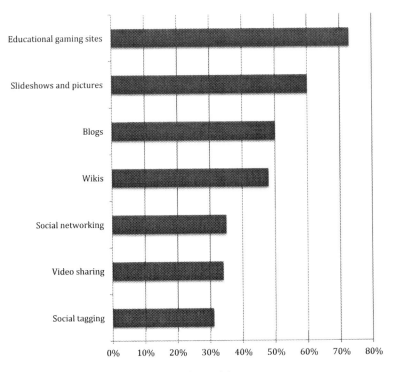

Fig. 11.2 The types of Web 2.0 tools used by the participants

they are blocked. A respondent corroborated this statement by writing, "I didn't check any of the Web 2.0 resources because they are blocked/filtered on our school network (student AND teacher computers)." Another participant stated, "Our school district BLOCKS all of the Web 2.0 except for the slideshow websites. So, even if I, or the Special Ed department wanted to use Web 2.0, we cannot go there with the filters—CIPA law is the excuse we're given."

11.5.2   Research Question 2

Is there a relationship between the frequency of Web 2.0 use among school librarians and the belief that a school librarian should provide assistance to students with ASD, the teachers of students with ASD, and the parents and guardians of students with ASD?

As Fig. 11.3 depicts, a majority of the respondents believed school librarians should provide assistance to students with ASD (95%), the teachers of students with ASD (94%), and the parents of students with ASD (71%). The relationships between the frequency of Web 2.0 use among the participants and their belief that school librarians should provide assistance were as follows:

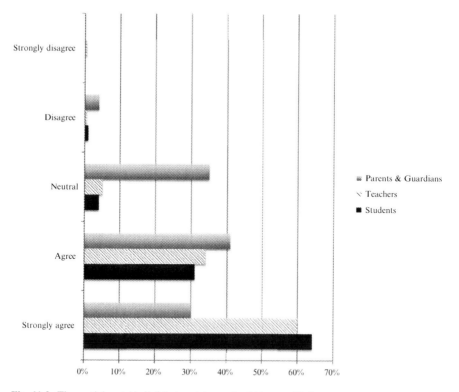

Fig. 11.3 The participants' belief that assistance should be provided

- The frequency of Web 2.0 use and the belief that school librarians should provide assistance to students with ASD had a positive correlation, $r_s=0.176$, $n=503$, $p=0.000$. The participants who used Web 2.0 tools more often were more likely to believe that school librarians should provide services to students with ASD.
- The frequency of Web 2.0 use and the belief that school librarians should provide assistance to the teachers of students with ASD had a positive correlation, $r_s=0.193$, $n=500$, $p=0.000$. The participants who used Web 2.0 tools more often were more likely to believe that school librarians should provide assistance to the teachers of students with ASD.
- The frequency of Web 2.0 use and the belief that school librarians should provide assistance to the parents and guardians of students with ASD had a positive correlation, $r_s=0.117$, $n=504$, $p=0.009$. The participants who used Web 2.0 tools more often were more likely to believe that school librarians should provide assistance to the parents and guardians of students with ASD.

These results may be explained by school librarians being overwhelmed with inhibitors like budget cuts and high student to educator ratios. The feeling that there was a need for additional resources in order to provide adequate assistance was a common thread among the responses. "To do a good job for all our students takes much more of a time investment than I think most people making educational budgeting decisions realize … and whether they want to state this or not, time=money. With 1 library media teacher to 900 students and 7 h student contact time per day (yes—all student contact time) I still only have a little over 2 min per student per week to get to know and serve these children—wish there were 2 or more of me!"

Because of these inhibitors, a few participants articulated the sentiment that school librarians should not be responsible for providing assistance. For example, one comment was, "I help the student, but it is not my job to educate the teacher." Another remark was, "I have 1,000+ students I currently work with. How can I also add parents/guardians to this workload?" Conversely these were counteracted by many more comments in favor of providing assistance such as, "Educating students on the spectrum is a challenge for everyone. All school staff members need to be sensitive to the individual needs and do all they can to help these students succeed."

11.5.3   Research Question 3

Is there a relationship between the frequency of Web 2.0 use among school librarians and their comfort level with providing assistance to students with ASD, the teachers of students with ASD, and the parents and guardians of students with ASD?

Figure 11.4 shows that a majority of the respondents were comfortable or very comfortable with providing assistance to students with ASD (78%), the teachers of students with ASD (87%), and the parents and guardians of students with ASD (66%). The relationships between the frequency of Web 2.0 use among the participants and their comfort levels with providing assistance were as follows:

- The frequency of Web 2.0 use and the participants' comfort level with providing assistance to students with ASD had a positive correlation, $r_s=0.116$, $n=504$, $p=0.009$. The participants who used Web 2.0 tools more often were more likely to be comfortable providing assistance to students with ASD.
- The frequency of Web 2.0 use and the participants' comfort level with providing assistance to teachers of students with ASD had a positive correlation, $r_s=0.152$, $n=503$, $p=0.001$. The participants who used Web 2.0 tools more often were more likely to be comfortable providing assistance to teachers of students with ASD.
- There was no significant correlation between the participants' use of Web 2.0 tools and their comfort levels in regards to assisting parents and guardians of students with ASD.

While a majority of the respondents are comfortable providing assistance, some of them are not confident in their skills to do so. A respondent commented, "Overall, I feel that my school library degree program prepared me for almost every situation except students with special needs. I do not feel familiar enough with how I can be of service to these students." Another said, "I have gone to the autistic teachers at

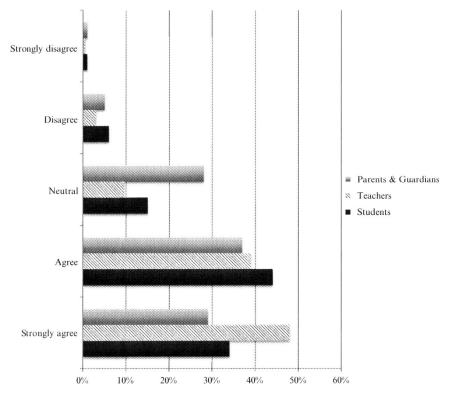

Fig. 11.4 The participants' comfort level with providing assistance

my school to learn the best way to present library lessons but was given very little feedback." Therefore, the following comment illustrates how school librarians understand technology more than the needs of students with ASD. "I have technology in my library but I am unsure as what the needs may be for the autistic student."

11.6 Discussion

11.6.1 Special Needs Students in School Libraries

Emam and Farrell (2009) observed that educators resist the inclusion of special needs students in regular education classrooms. Parallel sentiments were shared by a few of the survey participants. For instance, a participant said, "The behaviors that interrupt my type of programming lead me to think that sometimes having them in a small group instead of inclusion would be better for all of us. But that is not politically correct I know."

Some of the participants mentioned students with ASD should have the same services as the rest of the students. One participant wrote, "They are part of my student population and they all get individualized attention to some degree. So, no more, no less for these kids." These comments affirm Emam and Farrell's (2009) findings that educators do not feel the need to provide additional services to students with ASD.

In theory, providing the same service is a good practice. Still, one recommendation based on the results of this study is that school librarians begin to understand the needs of students that require more than average service. One participant shared this example, "We need to reach out to this audience and the teachers that teach the self contained special education students. I did this one year for one of my National Board Certification lessons and it was so popular and successful that we did a yearly project together after our first project. I called the parents to get information on the students and get their consent as well. The parents liked the attention and were grateful that their students were getting experience using a library." This participant demonstrates how a school librarian can bring school stakeholders together and improve the educational outcome for students. It is this type of work that will improve perceptions of school librarians and assert the significance of school librarian expertise in the educational system. This type of programming will help counteract the prevalent feeling that parents of students with ASD experience regarding the lack of services for their children (Lynch and Irvine 2009).

It is recommended that school librarians begin to make concentrated efforts to reach students with special needs regardless of their classroom setting. Many students with ASD need to learn social and information literacy skills and the library is a good place to practice such skills. "Nondisabled children, walking into the school library, see students with disabilities working with learning tools (a computer perhaps), and this creates a situation in which the two children may interact on an equal level, without the baggage that accompanies stereotypes" (Murray 1995, p. 113). While in the library, students with ASD can use Web 2.0 tools. These students can also benefit from periodic workshops offered to their teachers and parents in the school library about educational Web 2.0 tools.

11.6.2   The Educational Needs of School Librarians

School librarian guidelines such as those developed by the National Board for Professional Teaching Standards (2008) and the American Association of School Librarians (2007) advise school librarians to practice leadership in technology. The same standards recommend that school librarians be prepared to assist diverse stakeholders. These stakeholders include students, parents, and guardians (Martin and Zannier 2009).

It is understood that school librarians face multiple challenges such as perceptions, time constraints, and budgets (McCracken 2001). However, the results of this study suggest in order to assist diverse stakeholders such as students with ASD, their teachers, and their parents and guardians, school librarians will need to be educated during their degree programs and through ongoing professional development after graduation. This conclusion can be made because participants placed less of a priority on assisting parents and teachers.

The results of this study verify that school librarians are aware of technology trends. Yet they are unaware of how to use technology with ASD students. This is in alignment with Simpson et al.'s (2010) assertion that all educators need to be trained to support students with ASD. It concurs with Smith's (2010) results that specify school librarians need to be taught strategies for integrating technology through ongoing professional development.

11.6.3 The Incorporation of Web 2.0 Tools in School Libraries

This study corresponds with the findings of Baumbach (2009) and Farmer and Shontz (2009) who note school librarians are using Web 2.0 tools to enhance library programming. In addition, this study adds to the current knowledge base regarding the importance of using Web 2.0 tools in school libraries because of the relationship between the frequency of Web 2.0 use and the belief that school librarians should provide services to students with ASD, their teachers, and their parents and guardians. Moreover, the association between Web 2.0 use and the comfort levels with assisting students with ASD and their teachers provides an indication of how to help special needs students. These relationships are important because studies have provided evidence that technology is an effective component of educating students with ASD (Strickland et al. 1996; Wainer and Ingersoll 2011). Making a connection between Web 2.0 and services to help students with ASD is only a matter of school librarians sharing what they already understand about technology.

Furthermore, the results of this study coincide with other studies (Baumbach 2009; Farmer and Shontz 2009), which conveyed that some school librarians are not able to implement Web 2.0 tools because of filtering. The effects of filtering are unfortunate. It can be deduced that services to students with special needs such as ASD can be improved if school librarians were able to share Web 2.0 tools with their school communities. As such, the last recommendation based on the results of this study is that school librarians should rigorously advocate for unfiltered Internet or the ability to help select the websites that can be accessed.

11.7 Conclusion

Autism is an indiscriminate disease that strikes 1 out of every 110 children (Autism Speaks 2011). It is conceivable that each school librarian will encounter at least one student with an ASD during his or her career. However, the results of this study illustrate that many school librarians still need help conceptualizing their role in providing services to students with ASD without exceeding the boundaries of their time limits, skills, and budgeting resources. The results of this study signify that Web 2.0 tools can be instrumental in helping school librarians fulfill this role. Librarians can act as a consultant who is able to recommend Web 2.0 tools for students with ASD based on their needs. This role complements the skills of school librarians who already understand Web 2.0 tools and are able to interact with students, parents, and teachers.

There are several benefits associated with using Web 2.0 tools in the library to assist students with ASD, their teachers, and their parents. First, most Web 2.0 tools are free, easy to use, and can be accessed outside of school. This enhances the resources available to students without the consideration of time and budgetary constraints. Next, school librarians will be able to provide a needed service while feeling confident in the information they offer. When school librarians are confident and active in their school communities, the perceptions of the school librarians improve (Hartzell 2002). Additionally, the educational experience of students with ASD will improve as school librarians collaborate with parents and teachers to identify appropriate resources for improving information literacy and social skills. Finally, overall school environments have the potential to improve as school librarians set the example of educators and parents working together as a team.

Acknowledgement   Thank you to Jeanne Carter, Erin Keefe, Lesley Roane, and Kevin Thompson for their assistance with developing this chapter.

References

American Association of School Librarians. (2007). *Standards for the 21st-century learner.* Retrieved from http://www.ala.org/aasl/guidelinesandstandards/learningstandards/standards.

Autism Speaks. (2011). *What is autism?* Retrieved from http://www.autismspeaks.org/what-autism.

Barlow, T. (2008). Web 2.0: Creating a classroom without walls. *Teaching Science, 54*(1), 46–48.

Baumbach, D. J. (2009). Web 2.0 & you. *Knowledge Quest, 37*(4), 12–19.

Bolan, K., Canada, M., & Cullin, R. (2007). Web, library, and teen services 2.0. *Young Adult Library Services, 5*(2), 40–43.

Branch, J., & deGroot, J. (2011). The power of Web 2.0: Teacher-librarians become school technology leaders. *School Libraries Worldwide, 17*(2), 25–41.

Carnahan, C., Basham, J., & Musti-Rao, S. (2009). A low-technology strategy for increasing engagement of students with autism and significant learning needs. *Exceptionality: A Special Education Journal, 17*(2), 76–87.

Centers for Disease Control and Prevention. (2011). Autism spectrum disorders (ASDs). Retrieved from http://www.cdc.gov/ncbddd/autism/index.html.

D'Ateno, P., Mangiapanello, K., & Taylor, B. A. (2003). Using video modeling to teach complex play sequences to a preschooler with autism. *Journal of Positive Behavior Interventions, 5*(1), 5–11.

D'Auria, J. P. (2010). Autism on the web: Oh, the places you'll go! *Journal of Pediatric Health Care, 24*(6), e11–e15.

Emam, M. M., & Farrell, P. (2009). Tensions experienced by teachers and their views of support for pupils with autism spectrum disorders in mainstream schools. *European Journal of Special Needs Education, 24*(4), 407–422.

Farmer, L., & Shontz, M. (2009). School Library Journal's spending survey. *School Library Journal, 55*(4), 38–44.

Gooch, K., & Saine, P. (2011). Integration of the visual arts and Web 2.0 technologies in the classroom. *New England Reading Association Journal, 47*(1), 92–100.

Gooding, J., (2008). Web 2.0: A vehicle for transforming education. *International Journal of Information and Communication Technology Education, 4*(2), 44–54.

Grandin, T. (2010). *Thinking in pictures: My life with autism.* New York: Vintage Books.

Harris, C. (2006). School library 2.0. *School Library Journal, 52*(5), 50–53, 59.

Hartzell, G. (2002). The principal's perceptions of school libraries and teacher-librarians. *School Libraries Worldwide, 8*(1), 92–110.

Hetzroni, O., & Tannous, J. (2004). Effects of a computer-based intervention program on the communicative functions of children with autism. *Journal of Autism and Developmental Disorders, 34*(2), 95–113.

Hicks, A., & Graber, A. (2010). Shifting paradigms: Teaching, learning and Web 2.0. *Reference Services Review, 38*(4), 621–633.

Krebs, M., McDaniel, D., & Neeley, R. A. (2010). The effects of peer training on the social interactions of children with autism spectrum disorders. *Education, 131*(2), 393–403.

Lynch, S. L., & Irvine, A. N. (2009). Inclusive education and best practice for children with autism spectrum disorder: An integrated approach. *International Journal of Inclusive Education, 13*(8), 845–859.

MacDonald, R., Clark, M., Garrigan, E., & Vangala, M. (2005). Using video modeling to teach pretend play to children with autism. *Behavioral Interventions, 20*(4), 225–238.

Martin, B. S., & Zannier, M. (2009). *Fundamentals of school library media management: A how-to-do-it manual.* New York: Neal-Schuman.

McCracken, A. (2001). School library media specialists' perceptions of practice and importance of roles described in Information Power. *School Library Media Research, 4.* Retrieved from www.ala.org/ala/mgrps/divs/aasl/aaslpubsandjournals/slmrb/slmrcontents/volume42001/mccracken.cfm.

Moore, D. J., McGrath, P., & Thorpe, J. (2000). Computer aided learning for people with autism—A framework for research and development. *Innovations in Education and Training International, 37*(3), 218–228.

Murray, W. J. (1995). Accessibility of school library materials for special needs students. In C. L. Wesson & M. J. Keefe (Eds.), *Serving special needs students in the school library media center* (pp. 111–130). Westport, CT: Greenwood.

National Board for Professional Teaching Standards (2008). *NBPTS library media standards.* Retrieved from www.nbpts.org/userfiles/File/ecya_lm_standards.pdf.

National Institute of Mental Health. (2011). *Autism spectrum disorders (pervasive developmental disorders).* Retrieved from http://www.nimh.nih.gov/health/topics/autism-spectrum-disorders-pervasive-developmental-disorders/index.shtml.

Nikopoulos, C. K., & Keenan, M. (2007). Using video modeling to teach complex social sequences to children with autism. *Journal of Autism and Developmental Disorders, 37*(4), 678–693.

Norton, P., & Hathaway, D. (2008). On its way to K-12 classrooms, Web 2.0 goes to graduate school. *Computers in the Schools, 25*(3/4), 163–180.

Poon, K. (2011). Adaptive skills and maladaptive behavior of adolescents with autism spectrum disorders attending special schools in Singapore. *Journal of the International Association of Special Education, 12*(1), 65–70.

Simpson, R. L., Mundschenk, N. A., & Heflin, L. (2010). Issues, policies, and recommendations for improving the education of learners with autism spectrum disorders. *Journal of Disability Policy Studies, 22*(1), 3–17.

Smith, D. (2010). Making the case for the leadership role of school librarians in technology integration. *Library Hi Tech, 28*(4), 617–631.

Strain, P. S., Wilson, K., & Dunlap, G. (2011). Prevent-teach-reinforce: Addressing problem behaviors of students with autism in general education classrooms. *Behavioral Disorders, 36*(3), 160–171.

Strickland, D., Marcus, L. M., Mesibov, G. B., & Hogan, K. (1996). Brief report: Two case studies using virtual reality as a learning tool for autistic children. *Journal of Autism and Developmental Disorders, 26*(6), 651–659.

Tattersall, A., (2011). How the web was won…by some. *Health Information & Libraries Journal, 28*(3), 226–229.

U.S. Department of Education. (2004). *Building the legacy: IDEA 2004.* Retrieved from http://idea.ed.gov.

Wainer, A. L., & Ingersoll, B. R. (2011). The use of innovative computer technology for teaching social communication to individuals with autism spectrum disorders. *Research in Autism Spectrum Disorders, 5*(1), 96–107.

Williams, C., Wright, B., Callaghan, G., & Coughlan, B. (2002). Do children with autism learn to read more readily by computer assisted instruction or traditional book methods? A pilot study. *Autism, 6*(1), 71–91.

Part III
Organizations and Associations in North America

Chapter 12
Organizations and Associations

Michael Orey

12.1 Introduction

Part four includes annotated entries for associations and organizations, most of which are headquartered in North America, whose interests are in some manner significant to the fields of learning, design and technology or library and information science. For the most part, these organizations consist of professionals in the field or agencies that offer services to the educational media community. In an effort to only list active organizations, I deleted all organizations that had not updated their information since 2007. Any readers are encouraged to contact the editors with names of unlisted media-related organizations for investigation and possible inclusion in the 2013 edition.

Information for this section was obtained through e-mail directing each organization to an individual web form through which the updated information could be submitted electronically into a database created by Michael Orey. Although the section editor made every effort to contact and follow up with organization representatives, responding to the annual request for an update was the responsibility of the organization representatives. The editing team would like to thank those respondents who helped assure the currency and accuracy of this section by responding to the request for an update. Figures quoted as dues refer to annual amounts unless stated otherwise. Where dues, membership, and meeting information are not applicable, such information is omitted.

M. Orey (✉)
Learning, Design, and Technology Program, The University of Georgia,
Athens, GA, USA
e-mail: mikeorey@uga.edu

M. Orey et al. (eds.), *Educational Media and Technology Yearbook*, Educational
Media and Technology Yearbook 37, DOI 10.1007/978-1-4614-4430-5_12,
© Springer Science+Business Media New York 2013

Chapter 13
Educational Media and Technology Yearbook, 2012: Vol. 37

Organizations and Associations in the USA and Canada

Michael Orey

This information will be used solely to construct a directory of relevant organizations and associations within the 2012 Educational Media & Technology Yearbook. The data supplied here will not be intentionally shared or publicized in any other form. Thank you for your assistance.

Name of Organization or Association: Adaptech Research Network

Acronym: N/A.

Address: Dawson College, 3040 Sherbrooke Street West, Montreal, QC, Canada H3Z 1A4.

Phone Number: (514)931-8731 #1546; **Fax Number**: (514)931-3567 Attn: Catherine Fichten.

Email Contact: catherine.fichten@mcgill.ca; **URL**: http://www.adaptech.org.

Leaders: Catherine Fichten, Ph.D., Co-Director; Jennison V. Asuncion, M.A., Co-Director; Maria Barile, M.S.W., Co-Director.

Description: Based at Dawson College (Montreal), we are a Canada-wide, grant-funded team, conducting bilingual empirical research into the use of computer, learning, and adaptive technologies by postsecondary students with disabilities. One of our primary interests lies in issues around ensuring that newly emerging instructional technologies are accessible to learners with disabilities.

M. Orey (✉)
Learning, Design, and Technology Program, The University of Georgia, Athens, GA, USA
e-mail: mikeorey@uga.edu

M. Orey et al. (eds.), *Educational Media and Technology Yearbook*, Educational Media and Technology Yearbook 37, DOI 10.1007/978-1-4614-4430-5_13, © Springer Science+Business Media New York 2013

Membership: Our research team is composed of academics, practitioners, students, consumers, and others interested in the issues of access to technology by students with disabilities in higher education.

Dues: N/A.

Meetings: N/A.

Publications: Jorgensen, S., Fichten, C.S., & Havel, S. (2011). College satisfaction and academic success/Satisfaction et réussite académique au cégep. Final report presented to PAREA (206 pages). Montréal: Dawson College. Eric Document Reproduction Service (ED522996). Asuncion, J.V., Fichten, C.S., Ferraro, V., Barile, M., Chwojka, C., Nguyen, M.N., & Wolforth, J. (2010). Multiple perspectives on the accessibility of e-learning in Canadian colleges and universities. Assistive Technology Journal, 22(4), 187–199. DOI: 10.1080/10400430903519944. Fichten, C.S., Asuncion, J.V., Nguyen, M.N., Budd, J., & Amsel, R. (2010). The POSITIVES Scale: Development and validation of a measure of how well the ICT needs of students with disabilities are met. Journal of Postsecondary Education and Disability, 23(2), 137–154. Fichten, C.S., Nguyen, M.N., Asuncion, J.V., Barile, M., Budd, J., Amsel, R., & Libman, E. (2010). Information and communication technology for French and English speaking postsecondary students with disabilities: What are their needs and how well are these being met? Exceptionality Education International, 20(1), 2–17. Fichten, C.S., Asuncion, J.V., Nguyen, M.N., Budd, J., Barile, M., & Tibbs, A. (2010). The POSITIVES Scale: A method for assessing technology accessibility in postsecondary education. Proceedings of the CSUN (California State University, Northridge) Technology and Persons with Disabilities Conference, Los Angeles, California. Proceedings paper retrieved April 4, 2011, from http://www.letsgoexpo.com/utilities/File/viewfile.cfm?LCID=3861&eID=80000218. Asuncion, J.V., Fichten, C.S., Budd, J., Gaulin, C., Amsel, R., & Barile, M. (2010). Preliminary findings on social media use and accessibility: A Canadian perspective. Proceedings of the CSUN (California State University, Northridge) Technology and Persons with Disabilities Conference, Los Angeles, California. Proceedings paper retrieved April 4, 2011, from http://www.letsgoexpo.com/utilities/File/viewfile.cfm?LCID=4145&eID=80000218. Fichten, C.S., Ferraro, V., Asuncion, J.V., Chwojka, C., Barile, M., Nguyen, M.N., Klomp, R., & Wolforth, J. (2009). Disabilities and e-learning problems and solutions: An exploratory study. Educational Technology and Society, 12(4), 241–256. Fichten, C.S., Asuncion, J.V., Barile, M., Ferraro, & Wolforth, J. (2009). Accessibility of eLearning, computer and information technologies to students with visual impairments in postsecondary education. Journal of Visual Impairment and Blindness, 103(9), 543–557. Jorgensen, S., Fichten, C.S., & Havel, A. (2009). Academic success of graduates with and without disabilities—A comparative study of university entrance scores. Pédagogie Collégiale, 22(5) Special Issue, 26–29. Ferraro, V., Fichten, C.S., & Barile, M. (2009). Computer use by students with disabilities: Perceived advantages, problems and solutions. Pédagogie Collégiale, 22(5) Special Issue, 20–25. Nguyen, M.N., Fichten, C.S., & Barile, M. (2009). Les besoins technologiques des élèves handicapés du postsecondaire sont-ils satisfaits ? Résultats de l'utilisation de l'Échelle d'accessibilité des technologies informatiques adaptatives pour les élèves handicapés au postsecondaire (SAITAPSD): Version pour les élèves. Pédagogie Collégiale, 22(2), 6–11. Fichten, C.S., Asuncion, J.V., Nguyen, M.N., Wolforth, J., Budd, J., Barile, M., Gaulin, C., Martiniello, N., Tibbs, A., Ferraro, V., & Amsel, R. (2009). Development and validation of the Positives Scale (Postsecondary Information Technology Initiative Scale) (136 pages). Final report for the Canadian Council on Learning. ERIC (Education Resources Information Center) ED505763. Retrieved July 27, 2009, from http://www.eric.ed.gov/ERICWebPortal/contentdelivery/servlet/ERICServlet?accno=ED505763 and Retrieved August 29, 2010, from http://www.ccl-cca.ca/pdfs/OtherReports/Fichten-Report.pdf. Jorgensen, S., Fichten, C.S., & Havel, A. (2009). Prédire la situation de risque des étudiants au collège: Hommes et étudiants ayant des incapacités/Predicting the at risk status of college students: Males and students with disabilities. (257 pages). Final report to PAREA. ERIC (Education Resources Information Center) (ED505871). Retrieved July 30, 2009, from http://www.eric.ed.gov/ERICDocs/data/ericdocs2sql/content_storage_01/0000019b/80/44/a4/62.pdf. Jorgensen, S., Ferraro, V., Fichten, C.S., & Havel, A. (2009). Predicting college retention and dropout: Sex and disability (10 pages). ERIC (Education Resources Information Center) (ED505873). Retrieved July 30, 2009, from http://www.eric.ed.gov/ERICDocs/data/ericdocs2sql/content_storage_01/0000019b/80/44/a4/65.pdf.

Name of Organization or Association: Agency for Instructional Technology.

Acronym: AIT.

Address: Box A, Bloomington, IN 47402-0120, USA.

Phone Number: (812)339-2203; **Fax Number**: (812)333-4218.

Email Contact: info@ait.net; **URL**: http://www.ait.net.

Leaders: Charles E. Wilson, Executive Director.

Description: The Agency for Instructional Technology has been a leader in educational technology since 1962. A nonprofit organization, AIT, is one of the largest providers of instructional TV programs in North America. AIT is also a leading developer of other educational media, including online instruction, CDs, videodiscs, and instructional software. AIT learning resources are used on six continents and reach nearly 34 million students in North America each year. AIT products have received many national and international honors, including an Emmy and Peabody award. Since 1970, AIT has developed 39 major curriculum packages through the consortium process it pioneered. American state and Canadian provincial agencies have cooperatively funded and widely used these learning resources. Funding for other product development comes from state, provincial, and local departments of education; federal and private institutions; corporations and private sponsors; and AITs own resources.

Membership: None.

Dues: None.

Meetings: No regular public meetings.

Publications: None.

Name of Organization or Association: American Association of Colleges for Teacher Education.

Acronym: AACTE.

Address: 1307 New York Avenue, N.W., Suite 300, Washington, DC 20005-4701, USA.

Phone Number: (202)293-2450; **Fax Number**: (202)457-8095.

Email Contact: jmills@aacte.org; **URL**: http://www.aacte.org/.

Leaders: Sharon P. Robinson, President and Chief Executive Officer.

Description: The American Association of Colleges for Teacher Education is a national alliance of educator preparation programs dedicated to the highest quality professional development of teachers and school leaders in order to enhance PK-12 student learning. The 800 institutions holding AACTE membership represent public and private colleges and universities in every state, the District of Columbia, the Virgin Islands, Puerto Rico, and Guam. AACTE's reach and influence fuel its mission of serving learners by providing all school personnel with superior training and continuing education. AACTE employs three key strategies to achieve its goals: Advocacy: AACTE maintains a constant presence on Capitol Hill to expand its congressional network and provide members with up-to-the-minute analysis of education policy. Leadership: AACTE believes in consensus-building through open and free-flowing dialogue on education matters, consistent support for diverse learners, and serving as a principal authority on issues pertaining to teacher quality. Service: AACTE provides members with vital communication regarding policy issues and events, publications targeting various areas of interest, and unique professional development opportunities.

Membership: Membership in AACTE is institutional with over 5,500 institutional representatives. There are two categories of membership: Regular membership and affiliate membership. Regular membership is available to 4-year degree-granting colleges and universities with significant commitment to the preparation of education personnel and that meet all the criteria for regular membership. Affiliate membership is also available. For more information, please contact the membership department at membership@aacte.org or 202/293-2450.

Dues: –

Meetings: Annual Members Meeting, New Leadership Academy. State Leaders Institute, and more.

Publications: –

Name of Organization or Association: American Association of Community Colleges.

Acronym: AACC.

Address: One Dupont Circle, NW, Suite 410, Washington, DC 20036-1176, USA.

Phone Number: (202)728-0200; **Fax Number**: (202)833-9390.

Email Contact: twhissemore@aacc.nche.edu; **URL**: http://www.aacc.nche.edu.

Leaders: Walter G. Bumphus, President and CEO.

Description: AACC is a national organization representing the nations more than 1,195 community, junior, and technical colleges. Headquartered in Washington, DC, AACC serves as a national voice for the colleges and provides key services in the areas of advocacy, research, information, and leadership development. The nations community colleges serve more than 11 million students annually, almost half (46 %) of all US undergraduates.

Membership: 1,167 institutions, 31 corporations, 15 international associates, 79 educational associates, 4 foundations.

Dues: Vary by category.

Meetings: Annual Convention, April of each year; 2012: April 21–24 Orlando, FL.

Publications: Community College Journal (bi-monthly); Community College Times (bi-weekly online); Community College Press (books, research and program briefs, and monographs).

Name of Organization or Association: American Association of School Librarians.

Acronym: AASL.

Address: 50 East Huron Street, Chicago, IL 60611-2795, USA.

Phone Number: (312)280-4382 or (800) 545-2433, ext. 4382; **Fax Number**: (312)280-5276.

Email Contact: aasl@ala.org; **URL**: http://www.ala.org/aasl.

Leaders: Julie A. Walker, Executive Director.

Description: A division of the American Library Association, the mission of the American Association of School Librarians is to advocate excellence, facilitate change, and develop leaders in the school library media field.

Membership: 9,500.

Dues: Personal membership in ALA (beginning FY 2009, first year, $65; second year, $98; 3rd and subsequent years, $130) plus $50 for personal membership in AASL. Student, retired, organizational, and corporate memberships are available.

Meetings: National conference every 2 years; next national conference to be held in 2009.

Publications: School Library Media Research (electronic research journal at http://www.ala.org/aasl/SLMR) Knowledge Quest (print journal and online companion at http://www.ala.org/aasl/kqweb) AASL Hotlinks (e-mail newsletter) Non-serial publications (http://www.ala.org/ala/aasl/aaslpubsandjournals/aaslpublications.cfm).

Name of Organization or Association: American Educational Research Association.

Acronym: AERA.

Address: 1430K Street, NW, Suite 1200, Washington, DC 20005, USA.

Phone Number: (202)238-3200; **Fax Number**: (202)238-3250.

Email Contact: outreach@aera.net; **URL**: http://www.aera.net.

Leaders: Arnetha Ball, President of the Council, 2011–2012.

Description: The American Educational Research Association (AERA) is the national interdisciplinary research association for approximately 25,000 scholars who undertake research in education. Founded in 1916, AERA aims to advance knowledge about education, to encourage scholarly inquiry related to education, and to promote the use of research to improve education and serve the public good. AERA members include educators and administrators; directors of research, testing, or evaluation in federal, state, and local agencies; counselors; evaluators; graduate students; and behavioral scientists. The broad range of disciplines represented includes education, psychology, statistics, sociology, history, economics, philosophy, anthropology, and political science. AERA has more than 160 Special Interest Groups, including Advanced Technologies for Learning, NAEP Studies, Classroom Assessment, and Fiscal Issues, Policy, and Education Finance.

Membership: 25,000 Regular Members: Eligibility requires satisfactory evidence of active interest in educational research as well as professional training to at least the masters degree level or equivalent. Graduate Student Members: Any graduate student may be granted graduate student member status with the endorsement of a voting member who is a faculty members at the students university. Graduate Students who are employed full-time are not eligible. Graduate Student membership is limited to 5 years.

Dues: Vary by category, ranging from $40 for graduate students to $150 for voting members, for 1 year. See AERA website for complete details: www.aera.net.

Meetings: 2009 Annual Meeting, April 13–17, San Diego, CA.

Publications: Educational Researcher; American Educational Research Journal; Journal of Educational and Behavioral Statistics; Educational Evaluation and Policy Analysis; Review of Research in Education; Review of Educational Research. Books: Handbook of Research on Teaching, 2001 (revised, 4th edn) Ethical Standards of AERA, Cases and Commentary, 2002

Black Education: A Transformative Research and Action Agenda for the New Century, 2005 Studying Teacher Education: The Report of the AERA Panel on Research and Teacher Education, 2006 Handbook of Education Policy Research, 2009 Studying Diversity in Teacher Education, 2011 Standards for Educational and Psychological Testing (revised and expanded, 1999). Co-published by AERA, American Psychological Association, and the National Council on Measurement in Education.

Name of Organization or Association: American Foundation for the Blind.

Acronym: AFB.

Address: 11 Penn Plaza, Suite 300, New York, NY 10001, USA.

Phone Number: (212)502-7600, (800)AFB-LINE (232-5463); **Fax Number**: (212)502-7777.

Email Contact: afbinfo@afb.net; **URL**: http://www.afb.org.

Leaders: Carl R. Augusto, President; Kelly Parisi, Vice President of Communications.

Description: The American Foundation for the Blind (AFB) is a national nonprofit that expands possibilities for people with vision loss. AFB's priorities include broadening access to technology; elevating the quality of information and tools for the professionals who serve people with vision loss; and promoting independent and healthy living for people with vision loss by providing them and their families with relevant and timely resources. In addition, AFB's web site serves as a gateway to a wealth of vision loss information and services. AFB is also proud to house the Helen Keller Archives and honor the over 40 years that Helen Keller worked tirelessly with AFB. For more information visit us online at www.afb.org.

Membership: –

Dues: –

Meetings: –

Publications: AFB News (free); Journal of Visual Impairment & Blindness; AFB Press Catalog of Publications (free). AccessWorld™; Subscriptions Tel: (800)232-3044 or (412)741-1398.

Name of Organiza\tion or Association: American Library Association.

Acronym: ALA.

Address:50 E. Huron Street, Chicago, IL 60611 USA.

Phone Number: (800)545-2433; **Fax Number**: (312)440-9374.

Email Contact: library@ala.org; **URL**: http://www.ala.org.

Leaders: Keith Michael Fiels, Executive Director.

Description: The ALA is the oldest and largest national library association. Its 62,000 members represent all types of libraries: State, public, school, and academic, as well as special libraries serving persons in government, commerce, the armed services, hospitals, prisons, and other institutions. The ALA is the chief advocate of achievement and maintenance of high-quality library information services through protection of the right to read, educating librarians, improving services, and making information widely accessible. See separate entries for the following affiliated and subordinate organizations: American Association of School Librarians, Association of Library Trustees, Advocates, Friends and Foundations, Association for Library Collections and Technical Services, Association for Library Service to Children, Association of College and Research Libraries, Association of Specialized and Cooperative Library Agencies, Library Leadership and Management Association, Library and Information Technology Association, Public Library Association, Reference and User Services Association, Young Adult Library Services Association, and the Learning Round Table of ALA (formerly the Continuing Library Education Network and Exchange Round Table).

Membership: 62,000 members at present; everyone who cares about libraries is allowed to join the American Library Association.

Dues: Professional rate: $65, first year; $98, second year; third year and renewing: $130. Library Support Staff: $46. Student members: $33. Retirees: $46. International librarians: $78. Trustees: $59. Associate members (those not in the library field): $59.

Meetings: June 21–26, 2012—Anaheim, CA; June 27–July 2, 2013—Chicago, IL/ Midwinter Meeting: January 20–24, 2012—Dallas, TX; January 25–29, 2013—Seattle, WA.

Publications: American Libraries; Booklist; BooklistOnline.com; Choice; Choice Reviews Online; Guide to Reference; Library Technology Reports; Newsletter on Intellectual Freedom; RDA Toolkit; The Voice.

Name of Organization or Association: American Society for Training & Development.

Acronym: ASTD.

Address: 1640 King Street, Box 1443, Alexandria, VA 22313-2043, USA.

Phone Number: (703)683-8100; **Fax Number**: (703)683-8103.

Email Contact: customercare@astd.org; **URL**: http://www.astd.org.

Leaders: Tony Bingham, President and CEO.

Description: ASTD (American Society for Training & Development) is the world's largest professional association dedicated to the training and development field. In more than 100 countries, ASTD's members work in organizations of all sizes, in the private and public sectors, as independent consultants, and as suppliers. Members connect locally in 125 US chapters and with 20 international partners. ASTD started in 1943 and in recent years has widened the profession's focus to align learning and performance to organizational results, and is a sought-after voice on critical public policy issues. For more information, visit www.astd.org.

Membership: 37,000 members in 100 countries.

Dues: The Classic Membership ($199.00) is the foundation of ASTD member benefits. Publications, newsletters, research reports, discounts, services, and much more are all designed to help you do your job better. There are also student memberships, joint chapter memberships, and a special rate for international members. Here's what you have to look forward to when you join: T+D magazine: Monthly publication of ASTD. Stay informed on trends, successful practices, case studies, and more. ASTD LINKS: Bi-monthly newsletter for and about members. The Buzz: A weekly compilation of news about the training profession. Learning Circuits: Monthly Webzine features articles, departments, and columns that examine learning technologies and how they're being applied to workplace learning. Special Reports and Research: Research reports are published on topics that reflect important issues and trends in the industry. The State of the Industry report is published annually and analyzes spending, practices, and other important data related to learning and development. Do Your Own Research: Members can access the Online Library to research thousands of publications. Career Navigator Tool: Find out where you are in your career and what you need to do to develop professionally. Membership Directory: Online directory and searchable by a variety of criteria. Access to the Membership Directory is for members only. EXPO 365 Buyers Guide: A one stop resource for information on hundreds of training suppliers and consultants.

Meetings: TechKnowledge Conference: January 25–27, 2012, Las Vegas, NV; International Conference & Exposition, May 6–9, 2012, Denver, CO.

Publications: T+D (Training & Development) Magazine; Infoline; Learning Circuits; Training and Development Handbook; State of the Industry Report; ASTD Press books; Research reports.

Name of Organization or Association: Association for Childhood Education International.

Acronym: ACEI.

Address: 17904 Georgia Avenue, Suite 215, Olney, MD 20832, USA.

Phone Number: (301)570-2111; **Fax Number**: (301)570-2212.

Email Contact: headquarters@acei.org; **URL**: http://www.acei.org.

Leaders: Diane P. Whitehead, Acting Executive Director.

Description: ACEI publications reflect careful research, broad-based views, and consideration of a wide range of issues affecting children from infancy through early adolescence. Many are media-related in nature. The journal (Childhood Education) is essential for teachers, teachers-in-training, teacher educators, day care workers, administrators, and parents. Articles focus on child development and emphasize practical application. Regular departments include book reviews (child and adult); film reviews, pamphlets, software, research, and classroom idea-sparkers. Six issues are published yearly, including a theme issue devoted to critical concerns.

Membership: 10,000.

Dues: $45, professional; $29, student; $23, retired; $85, institutional.

Meetings: 2009 Annual Conference, March 18–21, Chicago, IL, USA.

Publications: Childhood Education (official journal) with ACEI Exchange (insert newsletter); Journal of Research in Childhood Education; professional focus newsletters (Focus on Infants and Toddlers, Focus on Pre-K and K, Focus on Elementary, Focus on Middle School, Focus on Teacher Education, and Focus on Inclusive Education); various books.

Name of Organization or Association: Association for Computers and the Humanities.

Acronym: ACH.

Address: [Address], [City], ON [Zip Code], [Country].

Phone Number: [phone number]; **Fax Number**: [fax number].

Email Contact: kretzsh@uga.edu; **URL**: http://www.ach.org/.

Leaders: Executive Secretary, ACH.

Description: The Association for Computers and the Humanities is an international professional organization. Since its establishment, it has been the major professional society for people working in computer-aided research in literature and language studies, history, philosophy, and other humanities disciplines, and especially research involving the manipulation and analysis of textual materials. The ACH is devoted to disseminating information among its members about work in the field of humanities computing, as well as encouraging the development and dissemination of significant textual and linguistic resources and software for scholarly research.

Membership: 300.

Dues: Individual regular member, US$65 Student or Emeritus Faculty member, US$55 Joint membership (for couples), Add US$7.

Meetings: Annual meetings held with the Association for Literary and Linguistic Computing.

Publications: ACH Publications: Literary & Linguistic Computing: Humanist.

Name of Organization or Association: Association for Continuing Higher Education.

Acronym: ACHE.

Address: OCCE Admin Building Room 233, 1700 Asp Avenue, Norman, OK 73072, USA.

Phone Number: (800)807-2243; **Fax Number**: (405)325-4888.

Email Contact: admin@acheinc.org; **URL**: http://www.acheinc.org/.

Leaders: James P. Pappas, Ph.D., Executive Vice President.

Description: ACHE is an institution-based organization of colleges, universities, and individuals dedicated to the promotion of lifelong learning and excellence in continuing higher education. ACHE encourages professional networks, research, and exchange of information for its members and advocates continuing higher education as a means of enhancing and improving society.

Membership: Approximately 1,600 individuals in approximately 650 institutions. Membership is open to institutions of higher learning, professionals and organizations whose major commitment is in the area of continuing education.

Dues: $85, professional; $510, institutional.

Meetings: For a list of Annual and Regional Meetings, see http://www.acheinc.org.

Publications: Journal of Continuing Higher Education (3/year); Five minutes with ACHE (newsletter, 9/year); Proceedings (annual).

Name of Organization or Association: Association for Educational Communications and Technology.

Acronym: AECT.

Address: 1800N Stonelake Dr., Suite 2 PO Box 2447, Bloomington, IN 47404-2447, USA.

Phone Number: (812)335-7675; **Fax Number**: (812)335-7678.

Email Contact: pharris@aect.org; **URL**: http://www.aect.org.

Leaders: Phillip Harris, Executive Director; Ana Donaldson, Board President.

Description: AECT is an international professional association concerned with the improvement of learning and instruction through media and technology. It serves as a central clearinghouse and communications center for its members, who include instructional technologists, library media specialists, religious educators, government media personnel, school administrators and specialists, and training media producers. AECT members also work in the armed forces, public libraries, museums, and other information agencies of many different kinds, including those related to the emerging fields of computer technology. Affiliated organizations include the International Visual Literacy Association (IVLA), Minorities in Media (MIM), New England Educational Media Association (NEEMA), SICET (the Society of International Chinese in Educational Technology), and KSET (the Korean Society for Educational Technology). The ECT Foundation is also related to AECT. Each of these affiliated organizations has its own listing in the Yearbook. AECT Divisions include: Instructional Design & Development, Information, & Training & Performance, Research & Theory, Systemic

Change, Distance Learning, Media & Technology, Teacher Education, International, and Multimedia Productions.

Membership: 2,500 members in good standing from K-12, college and university and private sector/government training. Anyone interested can join. There are different memberships available for students, retirees, corporations, and international parties. We also have a new option for electronic membership for international affiliates.

Dues: 125,00,00 standard membership discounts are available for students and retirees. Additional fees apply to corporate memberships or international memberships.

Meetings: Summer Leadership Institute held each July. In 2007 it will be in Chicago, IL. AECT holds an annual Conference each year in October. In 2007, it will be held in Anaheim, CA.

Publications: TechTrends (6/year, free with AECT membership; available by subscription through Springer at www.springeronline.com); Educational Technology Research and Development (6/year $46 members; available by subscription through Springer at www.springeronline.com); Quarterly Review of Distance Education (quarterly, $55 to AECT members); many books.

Name of Organization or Association: Association for Experiential Education.

Acronym: AEE.

Address: 3775 Iris Avenue, Suite 4, Boulder, CO 80301-2043, USA.

Phone Number: (303)440-8844; **Fax Number**: (303)440-9581

Email Contact: executive@aee.org; **URL**: http://www.aee.org.

Leaders: Paul Limoges, Executive Director.

Description: AEE is a nonprofit, international, professional organization committed to the development, practice, and evaluation of experiential education in all settings. AEE's vision is to be a leading international organization for the development and application of experiential education principles and methodologies with the intent to create a just and compassionate world by transforming education.

Membership: Nearly 1,500 members in over 30 countries including individuals and organizations with affiliations in education, recreation, outdoor adventure programming, mental health, youth service, physical education, management development training, corrections, programming for people with disabilities, and environmental education.

Dues: $55–115, individual; $145, family; $275–500, organizational.

Meetings: AEE Annual Conference in November. Regional Conferences in the Spring.

Publications: The Journal of Experiential Education (3/year); Experience and the Curriculum; Adventure Education; Adventure Therapy; Therapeutic Applications of Adventure Programming; Manual of Accreditation Standards for Adventure

Programs; The Theory of Experiential Education, Third Edition; Experiential Learning in Schools and Higher Education; Ethical Issues in Experiential Education, Second Edition; The K.E.Y (Keep Exploring Yourself) Group: An Experiential Personal Growth Group Manual; Book of Metaphors, Volume II; Women's Voices in Experiential Education; bibliographies, directories of programs, and membership directory. New publications since last year: Exploring the Boundaries of Adventure Therapy; A Guide to Women's Studies in the Outdoors; Administrative Practices of Accredited Adventure Programs; Fundamentals of Experience-Based Training; Wild Adventures: A Guidebook of Activities for Building Connections with Others and the Earth; Truth Zone: An Experimental Approach to Organizational Development; Exploring the Power of Solo, Silence, and Solitude.

Name of Organization or Association: Association for Library and Information Science Education.

Acronym: ALISE.

Address: 65 E. Wacker Place Suite 1900, Chicago, IL 60601, USA.

Phone Number: (312)795-0996; **Fax Number**: (312)419-8950.

Email Contact: contact@alise.org; **URL**: http://www.alise.org.

Leaders: Kathleen Combs, Executive Director.

Description: Seeks to advance education for library and information science and produces annual Library and Information Science Education Statistical Report. Open to professional schools offering graduate programs in library and information science; personal memberships open to educators employed in such institutions; other memberships available to interested individuals.

Membership: 201 individuals, 71 institutions.

Dues: Institutional, sliding scale, $350–2,500 International $145.00 Full-Time Personal, $125.00 Part-Time/Retired $75.00 Student $60.00.

Meetings: January 4–7, 2011, San Diego, CA.

Publications: Journal of Education for Library and Information Science; ALISE Directory; Library and Information Science Education Statistical Report.

Name of Organization or Association: Association for Library Collections & Technical Services.

Acronym: ALCTS.

Address: 50 E. Huron Street, Chicago, IL 60611, USA.

Phone Number: (312)280-5037; **Fax Number**: (312)280-5033.

Email Contact: alcts@ala.org; **URL**: www.ala.org/alcts.

Leaders: Charles Wilt, Executive Director.

Description: A division of the American Library Association, ALCTS is dedicated to acquisition, identification, cataloging, classification, and preservation of library materials; the development and coordination of the country's library resources; and aspects of selection and evaluation involved in acquiring and developing library materials and resources. Sections include Acquisitions, Cataloging and Classification, Collection Management and Development, Preservation and Reformatting, and Serials.

Membership: 4,300 membership is open to anyone who has an interest in areas covered by ALCTS.

Dues: $65 plus membership in ALA.

Meetings: Annual Conference; Anaheim, June 21–26, 2012, Chicago, June 27–July 2, 2013, Las Vegas, June 26–July 1, 2014, San Francisco June 25–30, 2015.

Publications: Library Resources & Technical Services (quarterly); ALCTS Newsletter Online (quarterly).

Name of Organization or Association: Association for Library Service to Children.

Acronym: ALSC.

Address: 50 E. Huron Street, Chicago, IL 60611, USA.

Phone Number: (312)280-2163; **Fax Number**: (312)944-7671.

Email Contact: alsc@ala.org; **URL**: http://www.ala.org/alsc.

Leaders: Diane Foote.

Description: Information about ALSC can be found at. Information on ALSCs various awards, including the nationally known Newbery Medal for authors and the Caldecott Medal for illustrators can be found at. The Association for Library Service to Children develops and supports the profession of children's librarianship by enabling and encouraging its practitioners to provide the best library service to our nation's children. The Association for Library Service to Children is interested in the improvement and extension of library services to children in all types of libraries. It is responsible for the evaluation and selection of book and nonbook library materials and for the improvement of techniques of library service to children from preschool through the eighth grade or junior high school age, when such materials and techniques are intended for use in more than one type of library. Committee membership is open to ALSC members. Full list of ALSC boards and committees can be found at.

Membership: Over 4,000 members.

Dues: $45 plus membership in ALA; $18 plus membership in ALA for library school students; $25 plus membership in ALA for retirees.

Meetings: National Institute, Fall.

Publications: Children and Libraries: The Journal of the Association for Library Service to Children (3x/year); ALSConnect (quarterly newsletter). ALSC Blog.

Name of Organization or Association: Association of American Publishers.

Acronym: AAP.

Address: 50F Street, NW, Suite 400, Washington, DC 20001, USA.

Phone Number: (202)347-3375; **Fax Number**: (202)347-3690.

Email Contact: aoconnor@publishers.org; **URL**: http://www.publishers.org.

Leaders: Tom Allen, President and CEO (DC); Judith Platt, Director of Communications/Public Affairs.

Description: The Association of American Publishers is the national trade association of the US book publishing industry. AAP was created in 1970 through the merger of the American Book Publishers Council, a trade publishing group, and the American Textbook Publishers Institute, a group of educational publishers. AAPs more than 300 members include most of the major commercial book publishers in the USA, as well as smaller and nonprofit publishers, university presses, and scholarly societies. AAP members publish hardcover and paperback books in every field and a range of educational materials for the elementary, secondary, postsecondary, and professional markets. Members of the Association also produce computer software and electronic products and services, such as online databases and CD-ROMs. AAP's primary concerns are the protection of intellectual property rights in all media, the defense of free expression and freedom to publish at home and abroad, the management of new technologies, development of education markets and funding for instructional materials, and the development of national and global markets for its member's products.

Membership: Regular Membership in the Association is open to all US companies actively engaged in the publication of books, journals, looseleaf services, computer software, audiovisual materials, databases, and other electronic products such as CD-ROM and CD-I, and similar products for educational, business, and personal use. This includes producers, packagers, and co-publishers who coordinate or manage most of the publishing process involved in creating copyrightable educational materials for distribution by another organization. "Actively engaged" means that the candidate must give evidence of conducting an ongoing publishing business with a significant investment in the business. Each Regular Member firm has one vote, which is cast by an official representative or alternate designated by the member company. Associate Membership (non-voting) is available to US not-for-profit organizations that otherwise meet the qualifications for regular membership. A special category of associate membership is open to nonprofit university presses. Affiliate Membership is a nonvoting membership open to paper manufacturers, suppliers, consultants, and other non-publishers directly involved in the industry.

Dues: Dues are assessed on the basis of annual sales revenue from the print and electronic products listed above (under Regular Membership), but not from services or equipment. To maintain confidentiality, data are reported to an independent agent.

Meetings: Annual Meeting (February), Small and Independent Publishers Meeting (February), School Division Annual Meeting (January), PSP Annual Meeting (February).

Publications: AAP Monthly Report.

Name of Organization or Association: Association of College and Research Libraries.

Acronym: ACRL.

Address: 50 E. Huron Street, Chicago, IL 60611-2795, USA.

Phone Number: (312)280-2523; **Fax Number**: (312)280-2520.

Email Contact: acrl@ala.org; **URL**: http://www.ala.org/acrl.

Leaders: Mary Ellen Davis, Executive Director.

Description: The Association of College and Research Libraries (ACRL), the largest division of the American Library Association, is a professional association of academic librarians and other interested individuals. It is dedicated to enhancing the ability of academic library and information professionals to serve the information needs of the higher education community and to improve learning, teaching, and research. ACRL is the only individual membership organization in North America that develops programs, products, and services to meet the unique needs of academic and research librarians Information on ACRLs various committees, task forces, discussion groups, and sections can be found at . Information on ACRLs various awards can be found at.

Membership: With over 13,000 members, is a national organization of academic and research libraries and librarians working with all types of academic libraries—community and junior college, college, and university—as well as comprehensive and specialized research libraries and their professional staffs.

Dues: $55 plus membership in ALA; $35 plus membership in ALA for library school students and for retirees SECTIONS (two at no charge, additional sections $5 each): African American Studies Librarians (AFAS); Anthropology and Sociology Section (ANSS); Arts Section; Asian, African, and Middle Eastern Section (AAMES); College Libraries Section (CLS); Community and Junior College Libraries Section (CJCLS); Distance Learning Section (DLS); Education and Behavioral Sciences Section (EBSS); Instruction Section (IS); Law and Political Science Section (LPSS); Literatures in English (LES); Rare Books and Manuscripts Section (RBMS); Science and Technology Section (STS); Slavic and East European Section (SEES); University Libraries Section (ULS); Western European Studies Section (WESS); Women's Studies Section (WSS).

Meetings: ACRL 14th National Conference: March 12–15, 2009, Seattle, WA, Theme: Pushing the Edge: Explore, Engage, Extend.

Publications: List of all print and electronic publications at ACRLog: Blogging for and by academic and research librarians: ACRL Insider: The mission of the ACRL Insider Weblog is to keep the world current and informed on the activities, services, and programs of the Association of College & Research Libraries, including publications, events, conferences, and eLearning opportunities. ACRL Podcasts: Academic Library Trends & Statistics (annually). Statistics data for all academic libraries reporting throughout the USA and Canada. Trends data examine a different subject each year. Available from ALA Order Fulfillment, PO Box 932501, Atlanta, GA 31193-2501 and from the ALA Online Store. Choice: Editor and Publisher, Irving E. Rockwood. ISSN 0009-4978. Published monthly. Only available by subscription: $315 per year for North America; $365 outside North America. CHOICE Reviews on Cards: $390 per year for North America—USA, Canada, and Mexico; $440 outside North America. ChoiceReviews.online: See pricing for site licenses at. College & Research Libraries (6 bimonthly journal issues). Sent to all ACRL members. Subscriptions, $70—US. $75—Canada and other PUAS countries. $80—Other foreign countries. College & Research Libraries News (11 monthly issues, July–August combined). Sent to all ACRL members. Subscriptions: $46—USA. $52—Canada and other PUAS countries. $57—Other foreign countries. RBM: A Journal of Rare Books, Manuscripts, and Cultural Heritage (2 issues). Subscriptions, $42—USA. $47—Canada and other PUAS countries. $58—Other foreign countries.

Name of Organization or Association: Association of Specialized and Cooperative Library Agencies.

Acronym: ASCLA.

Address:50 E. Huron Street, Chicago, IL 60611, USA.

Phone Number: (800)545-2433, ext. 4398.; **Fax Number**: (312)944-8085.

Email Contact: ascla@ala.org; **URL**: http://www.ala.org/ascla.

Leaders: Susan Hornung, Executive Director.

Description: A division of the American Library Association, the Association of Specialized and Cooperative Library Agencies (ASCLA) enhances the effectiveness of library service by providing networking, enrichment, and educational opportunities for its diverse members, who represent state library agencies, libraries serving special populations, library organizations, and independent librarians.

Membership: 800.

Dues: You must be a member of ALA to join ASCLA. See www.ala.org/membership for most current ALA dues rates. ASCLA individual membership: $50; organization membership: $50; State Library Agency dues: $500.

Meetings: ASCLA meets in conjunction with the American Library Association.

Publications: Interface, quarterly online newsletter; see web site http://www.ala.org/ascla for list of other publications.

Name of Organization or Association: Canadian Library Association/Association canadienne des bibliothèques.

Acronym: CLA/ACB.

Address: 1150 Morrison Drive, Suite 400, Ottawa, ON, Canada K2H 8S9.

Phone Number: (613)232-9625; **Fax Number**: (613)563-9895.

Email Contact: info@cla.ca; **URL**: http://www.cla.ca.

Leaders: Linda Sawden Harris, Manager of Financial Services; Judy Green, Manager, Marketing and Communications; Kelly Moore, Executive Director.

Description: Our Mission CLA/ACB is my advocate and public voice, educator, and network. We build the Canadian library and information community and advance its information professionals. *Our Values* We believe that libraries and the principles of intellectual freedom and free universal access to information are key components of an open and democratic society. Diversity is a major strength of our Association. An informed and knowledgeable membership is central in achieving library and information policy goals. Effective advocacy is based upon understanding the social, cultural, political, and historical contexts in which libraries and information services function. *Our Operating Principles* A large and active membership is crucial to our success. Our Association will have a governance structure that is reviewed regularly and ensures that all sectors of the membership are represented. Our Association will be efficiently run, fiscally responsible, and financially independent. Technology will be used in efficient and effective ways to further our goals. Our Association places a high value on each of our members. Our Association will ensure that its staff are provided with tools and training necessary for them to excel at their jobs. Our Association's strategic plan will be continually reviewed and updated.

Membership: The CLA/ACB membership consists of a diverse group of individuals and organizations involved or interested in library or information sciences. A large proportion of CLA/ACB Members work in college, university, public, special (corporate, nonprofit and government), and school libraries. Others sit on the boards of public libraries, work for companies that provide goods and services to libraries, or are students in graduate level or community college programs. Membership categories of the Canadian Library Association/Association canadienne des bibliothèques include: Personal, Institutional, Associate, and Trustee. Total membership at October 10, 2011 was 4,200:

Dues: $25–1,000.

Meetings: 2012—Ottawa, Ontario, Wednesday May 30—Saturday, June 2.

Publications: Feliciter (membership and subscription magazine, 6/year).

Name of Organization or Association: Canadian Museums Association/ Association des musées canadiens.

Acronym: CMA/AMC.

Address: 280 Metcalfe Street, Suite 400, Ottawa, ON, Canada K2P 1R7.

Phone Number: (613)567-0099; **Fax Number**: (613)233-5438.

Email Contact: info@museums.ca; **URL**: http://www.museums.ca.

Leaders: John G. McAvity, Executive Director.

Description: The Canadian Museum's Association is a nonprofit corporation and reg-istered charity dedicated to advancing public museums and museum works in Canada, promoting the welfare and better administration of museums, and fostering a continu-ing improvement in the qualifications and practices of museum professionals.

Membership: 2,000 museums and individuals, including art galleries, zoos, aquariums, historic parks, etc.

Dues: Voting Categories Individual: For those who are, or have been, associated with a recognized museum in Canada. A $10 discount applies if you are associated with a CMA institutional member or if you are a member of a provincial museum association. $85 a year. Senior: For those who are retired and have been associated with a recog-nized museum in Canada. $50 a year. Institutional Association: For all recognized Canadian museums that are nonprofit, have a collection, and are open to the public. The fee is 0.001 (one tenth of 1 %) of your operating budget (i.e. if your budget is $150,000, you would pay $150). The minimum fee payable is $100, and the maximum, $2,750. Non-voting Categories Affiliate: For those outside of the museum community who wish to support the aims and programs of the CMA. $100 a year. International: For individuals and institutions outside of Canada. $100 a year. Corporate: For corpora-tions wishing to support the aims and programs of the CMA while developing oppor-tunities within the museum community. $250 a year. Student: For students in Canada. Please enclose a photocopy of your student ID. $50 a year. *Membership fees may be tax deductible. Check with your financial advisor for details.

Meetings: CMA Annual Conference, Spring.

Publications: Muse (bi-monthly magazine, color, Canada's only national, bilingual, magazine devoted to museums, it contains museum-based photography, feature articles, commentary, and practical information); The Official Directory of Canadian Museums and Related Institutions (on-line directory) lists all museums in Canada plus information on government departments, agencies, and provincial and regional museum associations.

Name of Organization or Association: Centre for Educational Technology, University of Cape Town.

Acronym: CET.

Address: Hlanganani Building, Upper Campus University of Cape Town, Rondebosch, Cape Town, N/A 7700, South Africa.

Phone Number: 27(21)-650-3841; **Fax Number**: 27(21)-650-5045.

Email Contact: Laura.Czerniewicz@uct.ac.za; **URL**: http://www.cet.uct.ac.za.

Leaders: Directors Laura Czerniewicz.

Description: The Centre for Educational Technology (CET) enables and promotes and investigates the integration of learning technologies in teaching and learning at the University of Cape Town and in higher education. CET's areas of work are curriculum development, learning technologies, staff development, and research.

Membership: We employ educational technology researchers, developers, staff developers, and learning designers with strong educational interests in diversity, redress, and access.

Dues: None.

Meetings: None.

Publications: See our web site at http://www.cet.uct.ac.za. Recent research publications are listed at http://www.cet.uct.ac.za/ResearchOut.

Name of Organization or Association: Close Up Foundation.

Acronym: CUF.

Address: 44 Canal Center Plaza, Alexandria, VA 22314, USA.

Phone Number: (703)706-3300; **Fax Number**: (703)706-3329.

Email Contact: cutv@closeup.org; **URL**: http://www.closeup.org.

Leaders: Timothy S. Davis, President and CEO.

Description: A nonprofit, nonpartisan civic engagement organization dedicated to providing individuals of all backgrounds with the knowledge, skills, and confidence to actively participate in democracy. Each year, Close Up brings 15,000 secondary and middle school students and teachers to Washington, DC for week-long government study programs. In addition, Close Up produces an array of multimedia civic education resources for use in classrooms and households nationwide, including Close Up at the Newseum, a weekly youth-focused current affairs program C-SPAN.

Membership: Any motivated middle or high school student who wants to learn about government and American history is eligible to come on our programs. No dues or membership fees.

Dues: Tuition is required to participate on Close Up educational travel programs. A limited amount of tuition assistance is available to qualified students through the Close Up Fellowship program. With a designated number of students, teachers receive a fellowship that covers the adult tuition and transportation price. Please contact 1-800-CLOSE UP for more information.

Meetings: Meetings take place during weeklong educational programs in Washington, DC.

Publications: Current Issues (new edition produced annually); The Bill of Rights: A Users Guide; Perspectives; International Relations; The American Economy; Face the Music: Copyright, Art & the Digital Age; documentaries on domestic and foreign policy issues.

Name of Organization or Association: Computer Assisted Language Instruction Consortium.

Acronym: CALICO.

Address: 214 Centennial Hall, Texas State University, 601 University Dr., San Marcos, TX 78666, USA.

Phone Number: (512)245-1417; **Fax Number**: (512)245-9089.

Email Contact: info@calico.org; **URL**: http://calico.org.

Leaders: Esther Horn, Manager.

Description: CALICO is devoted to the dissemination of information on the application of technology to language teaching and language learning.

Membership: 1,000 members from USA and 20 foreign countries. Anyone interested in the development and use of technology in the teaching/learning of foreign languages is invited to join.

Dues: $65 annual/individual.

Meetings: 2012, University of Notre Dame; 2013, University of Hawaii; 2014, University of Ohio; 2015, University of Colorado; 2016, Michigan State University.

Publications: CALICO Journal Online (3 issues/year), CALICO Monograph Series (Monograph IX, 2010: Web 2.0 topics; Monograph V, second edition 2011: Teaching languages with technology topics; Monograph X, 2012: Teaching writing with technology topics).

Name of Organization or Association: Consortium of College and University Media Centers.

Acronym: CCUMC.

Address: 601 E. Kirkwood Avenue, Franklin Hall 0009, Bloomington, IN 47405, USA.

Phone Number: (812)855-6049; **Fax Number**: (812)855-2103.

Email Contact: ccumc@ccumc.org; **URL**: www.ccumc.org.

Leaders: Aileen Scales, Executive Director.

Description: CCUMC is a professional group whose mission is to provide leadership and a forum for information exchange to the providers of media content, academic technology, and support for quality teaching and learning at institutions of higher education. Foster's cooperative media/instructional technology-related support in higher education institutions and companies providing related products. Gathers and disseminates information on improved procedures and new developments in instructional technology and media center management.

Membership: 750 individuals at 325 institutions/corporations: Institutional Memberships—Individuals within an institution of higher education who are associated with the support to instruction and presentation technologies in a media center and/or technology support service. Corporate Memberships—Individuals within a corporation, firm, foundation, or other commercial or philanthropic enterprise whose business or activity is in support of the purposes and objectives of CCUMC. Associate Memberships—Individuals not eligible for an Institutional or Corporate membership; from a public library, religious, governmental, or other organizations not otherwise eligible for other categories of membership. Student Memberships—Any student in an institution of higher education who is not eligible for an institutional membership.

Dues: Institutional or Corporate Membership: $325 for 1–2 persons, $545 for 3–4 persons, $795 for 5–6 persons, $130 each additional person beyond six Associate Membership: $325 per person Student Membership: $55 per person.

Meetings: 2010 Conference, Buffalo New York (October 6–10, 2010); 2011 Conference South Padre Island Texas (October 5–9, 2011).

Publications: College & University Media Review (journal: Annual) Leader (newsletter: 3 issues annually).

Name of Organization or Association: Council for Exceptional Children.

Acronym: CEC.

Address: 1110 N. Glebe Road, #300 Arlington, VA 22201, USA.

Phone Number: (703)620-3660. TTY: (703)264-9446; **Fax Number**: (703)264-9494.

Email Contact: cec@cec.sped.org.; **URL**: http://www.cec.sped.org.

Leaders: Bruce Ramirez, Executive Director.

Description: CEC is the largest international organization dedicated to improving the educational success of students with disabilities and/or gifts and talents. CEC advocates for governmental policies supporting special education, sets professional standards, provides professional development, and helps professionals obtain conditions and resources necessary for high quality educational services for their students.

Membership: Teachers, administrators, professors, related service providers (occupational therapists, school psychologists, etc.), and parents. CEC has approximately 50,000 members.

Dues: $111 a year.

Meetings: Annual Convention & Expo attracting approximately 6,000 special educators.

Publications: Journals, newsletters books, and videos with information on new research findings, classroom practices that work, and special education publications (See also the ERIC Clearinghouse on Disabilities and Gifted Education.).

Name of Organization or Association: National Association of State Textbook Administrators.

Acronym: NASTA.

Address: 120 S. Federal Place, Room 206, Santa Fe, NM 87501, USA.

Phone Number: (505)827-1801; **Fax Number**: (505)827-1826.

Email Contact: webmaster@nasta.org; **URL**: http://www.nasta.org.

Leaders: David P. Martinez, President.

Description: NASTAs purposes are to (1) foster a spirit of mutual helpfulness in adoption, purchase, and distribution of instructional materials; (2) arrange for study and review of textbook specifications; (3) authorize special surveys, tests, and studies; and (4) initiate action leading to better quality instructional materials. Services provided include a working knowledge of text construction, monitoring lowest prices, sharing adoption information, identifying trouble spots, and discussions in the industry. The members of NASTA meet to discuss the textbook adoption process and to improve the quality of the instructional materials used in the elementary, middle, and high schools. NASTA is not affiliated with any parent organization and has no permanent address.

Membership: Textbook administrators from each of the 21 states that adopt instructional material at the state level on an annual basis.

Dues: $25 annually per individual.

Meetings: NASTA meets annually during the month of July.

Publications: Manufacturing Standards and Specifications for Textbooks (MSST).

Name of Organization or Association: East–west Center.

Acronym: None.

Address: 1601 East–West Road, Honolulu, HI 96848-1601, USA.

Phone Number: (808)944-7111; **Fax Number**: (808)944-7376.

Email Contact: ewcinfo@EastWestCenter.org; **URL**: http://www.eastwestcenter.org/.

Leaders: Dr Charles E. Morrison, President.

Description: The US Congress established the East–west Center in 1960 with a mandate to foster mutual understanding and cooperation among the governments and peoples of Asia, the Pacific, and the USA. Officially known as the Center for Cultural and Technical Interchange Between East and West, it is a public, nonprofit institution with an international board of governors. Funding for the center comes from the US government, with additional support provided by private agencies, individuals, and corporations, and several Asian and Pacific governments. The Center, through research, education, dialog, and outreach, provides a neutral meeting ground where people with a wide range of perspectives exchange views on topics of regional concern. Scholars, government and business leaders, educators, journalists, and other professionals from throughout the region annually work with Center staff to address issues of contemporary significance in such areas as international economics and politics, the environment, population, energy, the media, and Pacific islands development.

Membership: The East–West Center is not a membership-based institution. However, our alumni organization, The East–west Center Association (EWCA), is an international network of professionals who have a past affiliation with the East–west Center. Regardless of length of stay or type of participation, all are automatically members (associates) of the EWCA. There are no membership fees or other requirements to participate in the EWCA.

Dues: None.

Meetings: Events are listed on our Web site, visit: eastwestcenter.org/events.

Publications: East–West Center expertise and research findings are published by the East–West Center and by presses and collaborating organizations throughout the region and the world. Publications address a range of critical issues in the Asia Pacific region. The East–West Center sponsors or publishes several series, from short papers to books (see below). For more information about EWC publications, visit: http://www.eastwestcenter.org/publications/ The Asia Pacific Bulletin (APB), produced by the East–West Center in Washington, publishes summaries of Congressional Study Groups, conferences, seminars, and visitor roundtables, as well as short articles and opinion pieces. APB summaries are always two pages or less, designed for the busy professional or policymaker to capture the essence of dialogue and debate on issues of concern in US–Asia relations. East–West Dialogue, an online publication, is an interactive forum for discussion and debate of key issues in Asia–US economic relations. The East–West Dialogue seeks to develop and promote innovative policy, business, and civic initiatives to enhance this critical partnership. Contemporary Issues in Asia and the Pacific is a book series that focuses on issues of contemporary significance in the Asia Pacific region, most notably political, social, cultural, and economic change. The series seeks books that focus on topics of regional importance, on problems that cross disciplinary boundaries, and that have the capacity to reach academic and other interested audiences. The Contemporary Issues in Asia and the Pacific book series is published by Stanford University Press. The Studies in Asian Security book series, published by Stanford University Press and sponsored by the East–West Center, promotes analysis, understanding, and explanation of the dynamics of domestic, transnational, and international security challenges in Asia.

The peer-reviewed publications in the Series analyze contemporary security issues and problems to clarify debates in the scholarly community, provide new insights and perspectives, and identify new research and policy directions. With a Series committee comprising individuals from diverse theoretical persuasions who have undertaken extensive work on Asian security, books in the Studies in Asian Security series are designed to encourage original and rigorous scholarship, and seek to engage scholars, educators, and practitioners. Policy Studies presents scholarly analysis of key contemporary domestic and international political, economic, and strategic issues affecting Asia in a policy relevant manner. Written for the policy community, academics, journalists, and the informed public, the peer-reviewed publications in this series provide new policy insights and perspectives based on extensive fieldwork and rigorous scholarship. Pacific Islands Policy examines critical issues, problems, and opportunities that are relevant to the Pacific Islands region. The series is intended to influence the policy process, affect how people understand a range of contemporary Pacific issues, and help fashion solutions. A central aim of the series is to encourage scholarly analysis of economic, political, social, and cultural issues in a manner that will advance common understanding of current challenges and policy responses. East–West Center Special Reports present in-depth analysis and exposition that offer insights to specialists yet are accessible to readers outside the author's discipline. These peer-reviewed publications address diverse topics relevant to current and emerging policy debates in the Asia Pacific region and the USA. Papers in the AsiaPacific Issues series address topics of broad interest and significant impact relevant to current and emerging policy debates. These eight-page, peer-reviewed papers are accessible to readers outside the author's discipline.

Name of Organization or Association: Education Development Center, Inc.

Acronym: EDC.

Address: 55 Chapel Street, Newton, MA 02458-1060, USA.

Phone Number: (617)969-7100; **Fax Number**: (617)969-5979.

Email Contact: emarshall@edc.org; **URL**: http://www.edc.org.

Leaders: Dr Luther S. Luedtke, President and CEO.

Description: EDC is a global nonprofit organization that designs, delivers, and evaluates innovative programs to address some of the world's most urgent challenges in education, health, and economic opportunity. Working with public-sector and private partners, we harness the power of people and systems to improve education, health promotion and care, workforce preparation, communications technologies, and civic engagement. EDC conducts 350 projects in 35 countries around the world.

Membership: Not applicable.

Dues: Not applicable.

Meetings: Not applicable.

Publications: (1) Annual Report; (2) EDC Update, quarterly magazine; (3) EDC Online Report, quarterly enewsletter; (4) Detailed Web site with vast archive of publications, technical reports, and evaluation studies.

Name of Organization or Association: Education Northwest (formerly Northwest Regional Educational Laboratory).

Acronym: N/A.

Address: 101 SW Main Street, Suite 500, Portland, OR 97204, USA.

Phone Number: (503)275-9500; **Fax Number**: (503)275-0448.

Email Contact: info@educationnorthwest.org; **URL**: http://educationnorthwest.org.

Leaders: Dr Carol Thomas, Executive Director.

Description: Chartered in the Pacific Northwest in 1966 as Northwest Regional Educational Laboratory, Education Northwest now conducts more than 200 projects annually, working with schools, districts, and communities across the country on comprehensive, research-based solutions to the challenges they face. At Education Northwest, we are dedicated to and passionate about learning. Through our work, we strive to create vibrant learning environments where all youth and adults can succeed. Everything we do is evidence-based, giving us a solid foundation upon which we stand with confidence. We work with teachers, administrators, policymakers, and communities to identify needs, evaluate programs, and develop new solutions. The breadth of our work—ranging from training teachers, to developing curriculum, to restructuring schools, to evaluating programs—allows us to take a comprehensive look at education and to bring wide-ranging expertise and creativity to our clients' challenges. Our approach is highly customized to meet the needs of our clients, and our staff members take great pride in working closely with customers in the field to design the right approach for each situation. We are proud of our 40-year track record, but we don't rest on our laurels—instead, we strive constantly to identify and address emerging needs and trends in teaching and learning.

Membership: 856 organizations.

Dues: None.

Meetings: None.

Publications: Education Northwest Magazine (quarterly journal).

Name of Organization or Association: Educational Communications, Inc., Environmental and Media Projects of.

Acronym: –

Address: PO Box 351419, Los Angeles, CA 90035, USA.

Phone Number: (310)559-9160; **Fax Number**: (310)559-9160.

Email Contact: ECNP@aol.com; **URL**: www.ecoprojects.org.

Leaders: Nancy Pearlman, Executive Director and Executive Producer.

Description: Educational Communications is dedicated to enhancing the quality of life on this planet and provides radio and television programs about the environment and cultural documentaries. Serves as a clearinghouse on ecological issues through the Ecology Center of Southern California. Programming is available on 50 stations in 25 states and the Internet. These include: ECONEWS television series and Environmental Directions Radio Series. Provides ethnic folk dance performances through Earth Cultures. Assists groups in third-world countries through Humanity and the Planet, especially "Wells for Burkina Faso" and "Environmental Education in Kenya." Services provided include a speakers bureau, award-winning public service announcements, radio and television documentaries, volunteer and intern opportunities, and input into the decision-making process. Its mission is to educate the public about both the problems and the solutions in the environment. Other projects include Project Ecotourism, Environmental Resources Library, and more.

Membership: $20.00 for yearly subscription to the Compendium Newsletter.

Dues: $20 for regular. All donations accepted.

Meetings: As needed.

Publications: Compendium Newsletter (bi-monthly newsletter) Environmental Direction's radio audio cassettes (1,750 produced to date) ECONEWS and ECO-TRAVEL television series (over 550 shows in the catalog available on 3/4", VHS, and DVD).

Name of Organization or Association: Edvantia, Inc. (formerly AEL, Inc.).

Acronym: Edvantia.

Address: PO Box 1348, Charleston, WV 25325-1348, USA.

Phone Number: (304)347-0400, (800)624-9120; **Fax Number**: (304)347-0487.

Email Contact: carla.mcclure@edvantia.org; **URL**: http://www.edvantia.org.

Leaders: Dr Doris L. Redfield, President and CEO.

Description: Edvantia is a nonprofit education research and development corporation, founded in 1966, that partners with practitioners, education agencies, publishers, and service providers to improve learning and advance student success. Edvantia provides clients with a range of services, including research, evaluation, professional development, and consulting.

Membership: –

Dues: –

Meetings: –

Publications: The Edvantia Electronic Library contains links to free online tools and information created by staff on a wide array of education-related topics. Visitors to the Edvantia Web site can also access archived webcasts and webinars and sign up for a free monthly newsletter.

Name of Organization or Association: ENC Learning Inc.

Acronym: ENC.

Address: 1275 Kinnear Road, Columbus, OH 43212, USA.

Phone Number: 800-471-1045; **Fax Number**: 877-656-0315.

Email Contact: info@goenc.com; **URL**: www.goenc.com.

Leaders: Dr Len Simutis, Director.

Description: ENC provides K-12 teachers and other educators with a central source of information on mathematics and science curriculum materials, particularly those that support education reform. Among ENCs, products and services is ENC Focus, a free online magazine on topics of interest to math and science educators. Users include K-12 teachers, other educators, policymakers, and parents.

Membership: ENC is a subscription-based online resource for K-12 educators. Subscriptions are available for schools, school districts, college and universities, and individuals. Information for subscribers is available at www.goenc.com/subscribe.

Dues: None.

Meetings: None.

Publications: ENC Focus is available as an online publication in two formats: ENC Focus on K-12 Mathematics, and ENC Focus on K-12 Science. Each are accessible via www.goenc.com/focus.

Name of Organization or Association: Film Arts Foundation.

Acronym: Film Arts.

Address: 145 9th Street #101, San Francisco, CA 94103, USA.

Phone Number: (415)552-8760; **Fax Number**: (415)552-0882.

Email Contact: info@filmarts.org; **URL**: http://www.filmarts.org.

Leaders: K.C. Price, Interim Executive Director.

Description: Service organization that supports the success of independent film and video makers. Some services are for members only and some open to the public. These include low-cost classes in all aspects of filmmaking; affordable equipment rental (including digital video, 16 mm, Super-8, Final Cut Pro editing, ProTools mix room, optical printer, etc.); Resource Library; free legal consultation; bi-monthly magazine Release Print; grants program; year-round events and exhibitions;

nonprofit sponsorship; regional and national advocacy on media issues, and significant discounts on film- and video-related products and services.

Membership: Nearly 3,000.

Dues: $45 for "Subscriber" level benefits including bi-monthly magazine, discounts, and access to libraries and online databases. $65 for full "Filmmaker" benefits including above plus: Significant discounts on classes and equipment rentals, eligibility for nonprofit fiscal sponsorship, free legal consultation, and filmmaking consultation.

Meetings: Annual membership meeting and regular networking events.

Publications: The award-winning bimonthly magazine Release Print.

Name of Organization or Association: Great Plains National ITV Library.

Acronym: GPN.

Address: PO Box 80669, Lincoln, NE 68501-0669, USA.

Phone Number: (402)472-2007, (800)228-4630; **Fax Number**: (800)306-2330.

Email Contact: npba@umd.edu; **URL**: http://shopgpn.com/.

Leaders: Stephen C. Lenzen, Executive Director.

Description: Produces and distributes educational media, video, CD-ROMs and DVDs, prints, and Internet courses. Available for purchase for audiovisual or lease for broadcast use.

Membership: Membership not required.

Dues: There are no dues required.

Meetings: There are no meetings. We do attend subject specific conventions to promote our products.

Publications: GPN Educational Video Catalogs by curriculum areas; periodic brochures. Complete listing of GPN's product line is available via the Internet along with online purchasing. Free previews available.

Name of Organization or Association: Health Sciences Communications Association

Acronym: HeSCA.

Address: One Wedgewood Dr., Suite 27, Jewett City, CT 06351-2428, USA.

Phone Number: (203)376-5915; **Fax Number**: (203)376-6621.

Email Contact: hesca@hesca.org; **URL**: http://www.hesca.org/.

Leaders: Ronald Sokolowski, Executive Director.

Description: An affiliate of AECT, HeSCA is a nonprofit organization dedicated to the sharing of ideas, skills, resources, and techniques to enhance communications and educational technology in the health sciences. It seeks to nurture the professional growth of its members; serve as a professional focal point for those engaged in health sciences communications; and convey the concerns, issues, and concepts of health science communications to other organizations which influence and are affected by the profession. International in scope and diverse in membership, HeSCA is supported by medical and veterinary schools, hospitals, medical associations, and businesses where media are used to create and disseminate health information.

Membership: 150.

Dues: $150, individual.; $195, institutional ($150 additional institutional dues); $60, retiree; $75, student; $1,000, sustaining. All include subscriptions to the journal and newsletter.

Meetings: Annual meetings, May–June.

Publications: Journal of Biocommunications; Feedback (newsletter).

Name of Organization or Association: Institute for the Future.

Acronym: IFTF.

Address: 124 University Avenue, 2nd Floor, Palo Alto, CA 94301, USA.

Phone Number: (650)854-6322; **Fax Number**: (650)854-7850.

Email Contact: info@iftf.org; **URL**: http://www.iftf.org.

Leaders: Dale Eldredge, COO.

Description: The Institute for the Future (IFTF) is an independent nonprofit research group. We work with organizations of all kinds to help them make better, more informed decisions about the future. We provide the foresight to create insights that lead to action. We bring a combination of tools, methodologies, and a deep understanding of emerging trends and discontinuities to our work with companies, foundations, and government agencies. We take an explicitly global approach to strategic planning, linking macro trends to local issues in such areas as: *Work and daily life, *Technology and society, *Health and health care, *Global business trends, *Changing consumer society The Institute is based in California's Silicon Valley, in a community at the crossroads of technological innovation, social experimentation, and global interchange. Founded in 1968 by a group of former RAND Corporation researchers with a grant from the Ford Foundation to take leading-edge research methodologies into the public and business sectors, the IFTF is committed to building the future by understanding it deeply.

Membership: *Become a Member* To become a member of IFTF, companies and organizations can join one or more of our membership programs or contract with us for private work. Each membership program offers a distinct set of deliverables at different membership prices and enrollment terms. Please visit the individual program sites for more detailed information on a particular program. For more information on membership, contact Sean Ness at sness@iftf.org or 650-854-6322. *Ten-Year Forecast Program *Technology Horizons Program *Health Horizons Program *Custom Private Work.

Dues: Corporate-wide memberships are for 1 year periods: *Ten-Year Forecast: $15,000/year, *Technology Horizons: $65,000/year, *Health Horizons: $65,000/year At present, we do not have university, individual, or small-company programs set up. For those companies that support our research programs, we will often conduct custom research.

Meetings: Several a year, for supporting members.

Publications: IFTF blogs *Future Now: http://future.iftf.org: Emerging technologies and their social implications *Virtual China: http://www.virtual-china.org: An exploration of virtual experiences and environments in and about China *Future of Marketing: http://fom.iftf.org: Emerging technology, global change, and the future of consumers and marketing *Ten-Year Forecast (members only): http://blogger.iftf.org/tyf: A broad scan of the leading edge of change in business, government, and the global community *Technology Horizons (members only): http://blogger.iftf.org/tech: Emerging technologies and their implications for business, society, and family life.

Name of Organization or Association: Instructional Technology Council.

Acronym: ITC.

Address: One Dupont Circle, NW, Suite 360, Washington, DC 20036-1130, USA.

Phone Number: (202)293-3110; **Fax Number**: (202)822-5014.

Email Contact: cmullins@itcnetwork.org; **URL**: http://www.itcnetwork.org.

Leaders: Christine Mullins, Executive Director.

Description: An affiliated council of the American Association of Community Colleges established in 1977, the Instructional Technology Council (ITC) provides leadership, information, and resources to expand access to, and enhance learning through, the effective use of technology. ITC represents higher education institutions in the USA and Canada that use distance learning technologies. ITC members receive a subscription to the ITC News and ITC list serve with information on what's happening in distance education, participation in ITCs professional development audioconference series, distance learning grants information, updates on distance learning legislation, discounts to attend the annual e-Learning Conference which features more than 80 workshops and seminars.

Membership: Members include single institutions and multi-campus districts; regional and statewide systems of community, technical, and 2-year colleges; for-profit organizations; 4-year institutions; and, nonprofit organizations that are interested or involved in instructional telecommunications. Members use a vast array of ever-changing technologies for distance learning. They often combine different systems according to students needs. The technologies they use and methods of teaching include: Audio and video conferences, cable television, compressed and full-motion video, computer networks, fiber optics, interactive videodisc, ITFS, microwave, multimedia, public television, satellites, teleclasses, and telecourses.

Dues: $450, Institutional; $750, Corporate.

Meetings: Annual e-Learning Conference.

Publications: ITC Newsletter: Quarterly Quality Enhancing Practices in Distance Education: Vol. 2 Student Services; Quality Enhancing Practices in Distance Education: Vol. 1 Teaching and Learning; New Connections: A Guide to Distance Education (2nd ed.); New Connections: A College President's Guide to Distance Education; Digital Video: A Handbook for Educators; Faculty Compensation and Support Issues in Distance Education; ITC News (monthly publication/newsletter); ITC Listserv.

Name of Organization or Association: International Association for Language Learning Technology.

Acronym: IALLT.

Address: Information Technology Services, Concordia College, Moorhead, MN 56562, USA.

Phone Number: (218)299-3464; **Fax Number**: (218)299-3246.

Email Contact: business@iallt.org; **URL**: http://iallt.org.

Leaders: Mikle Ledgerwood, President; Ron Balko, Treasurer.

Description: IALLT is a professional organization whose members provide leadership in the development, integration, evaluation, and management of instructional technology for the teaching and learning of language, literature, and culture.

Membership: 400 members Membership/Subscription Categories *Educational Member: For people working in an academic setting such as a school, college, or university. These members have voting rights. *Full-time Student Member: For full-time students interested in membership. Requires a signature of a voting member to verify student status. These members have voting rights. *Commercial Member: For those working for corporations interested in language learning and technology. This category includes for example language laboratory vendors, software, and textbook companies. *Library Subscriber: Receive our journals for placement in libraries.

Dues: 1 year: $50, voting member; $25, student; $200, commercial. 2 year: $90, voting member; $380, commercial.

Meetings: Biennial IALLT conferences treat the entire range of topics related to technology in language learning as well as management and planning. IALLT also sponsors sessions at conferences of organizations with related interests, including CALICO and ACTFL

Publications: IALLT Journal of Language Learning Technologies (2 times annually); materials for language lab management and design, language teaching, and technology. Visit our website for details. http://iallt.org.

Name of Organization or Association: International Association of School Librarianship.

Acronym: IASL.

Address: PO Box 83, Zillmere, QLD 4034, Australia.

Phone Number: 61-7-3216-5785; **Fax Number**: 61-7-3633-0570.

Email Contact: iasl@kb.com.au; **URL**: www.iasl-slo.org/.

Leaders: Peter Genco, President; Karen Bonanno, Executive Secretary.

Description: Seeks to encourage development of school libraries and library programs throughout the world; promote professional preparation and continuing education of school librarians; achieve collaboration among school libraries of the world; foster relationships between school librarians and other professionals connected with children and youth and to coordinate activities, conferences, and other projects in the field of school librarianship.

Membership: 550 plus.

Dues: $50 Zone A (e.g., USA, Canada, Western Europe, Japan), $35 Zone B (e.g., Eastern Europe, Latin America, Middle East), $20 Zone C (e.g., Angola, India, Bulgaria, China) based on GNP.

Meetings: Annual Conference, Lisbon, Portugal, July 2006.

Publications: IASL Newsletter (3/year); School Libraries Worldwide (semi-annual); Conference Professionals and Research Papers (annual).

Name of Organization or Association: International Center of Photography.

Acronym: ICP.

Address: 1114 Avenue of the Americas at 43rd Street, New York, NY 10036, USA.

Phone Number: (212)857-0045; **Fax Number**: (212)857-0090.

Email Contact: info@icp.org; **URL**: http://www.icp.org.

Leaders: Willis Hartshorn, Director; Phil Block, Deputy Director for Programs and Director of Education; Kelly Heisler, Director of Marketing Communications.

Description: The International Center of Photography (ICP) was founded in 1974 by Cornell Capa (1918–2008) as an institution dedicated to photography that occupies a vital and central place in contemporary culture as it reflects and influences social change. Through our museum, school, and community programs, we embrace photography's ability to open new opportunities for personal and aesthetic expression, transform popular culture, and continually evolve to incorporate new technologies. ICP has presented more than 500 exhibitions, bringing the work of more than 3,000 photographers and other artists to the public in one-person and group exhibitions and provided thousands of classes and workshops that have enriched tens of thousands of students. Visit www.icp.org for more information.

Membership: 4,000.

Dues: Current levels available on request.

Meetings: xxxx.

Publications: Hiroshima: Ground Zero 1945; The Mexican Suitcase; Jasper, Texas: The Community Photographs of Alonzo Jordan; Miroslav Tichý; Dress Codes: The Third ICP Triennial of Photography and Video; Martin Munkacsi; Ecotopia; Atta Kim: ON-AIR; Snap Judgments: New Positions in Contemporary African Photography; African American Vernacular Photography: Selections from the Daniel Cowin Collection; Modernist Photography: Selections from the Daniel Cowin Collection; Young America: The Daguerreotypes of Southworth and Hawes; and others!

Name of Organization or Association: International Council for Educational Media.

Acronym: ICEM.

Address: Postfach 114, Vienna, N/A, A-1011, Austria.

Phone Number: 43-660-5113241; **Fax Number**: N/A.

Email Contact: lylt@a1.net; **URL**: www.icem-cime.org.

Leaders: John Hedberg, President; Ray Laverty, Secretary General.

Description: *Welcome to ICEM* Our purposes are: *To provide a channel for the international exchange and evaluation of information, experience, and materials in the field of educational media as they apply to pre-school, primary and secondary education, to technical and vocational, industrial, and commercial training, teacher training, continuing, and distance education. *To foster international liaison among individuals and organizations with professional responsibility in the field of educational media. *To cooperate with other international organizations in the development and application of educational technology for practice, research, production, and distribution in this field.

Membership: What are the main advantages of ICEM membership? IICEM membership enables those professionally involved in the production, distribution, and use of media in teaching and learning to establish a broad network of contacts with educators, researchers, managers, producers, and distributors of educational media from around the world. It also provides opportunities to discuss topics of mutual concern in an atmosphere of friendship and trust, to plan and carry out co-productions, to compare and exchange ideas and experiences, to keep abreast of the latest developments, and to work together towards the improvement of education on an international level. Membership in ICEM includes a subscription to the ICEM quarterly journal, Educational Media International, an entry in the Who's who on the ICEM Webpage, registration at ICEM events and activities either free of charge or at reduced rates, eligibility to engage in working groups or become a member of the Executive Committee, participate at the General Assembly and numerous other advantages. Our purposes are: *To provide a channel for the international exchange and evaluation of information, experience, and materials in the field of educational media as they apply to pre-school, primary, and secondary education, to technical and vocational, industrial and commercial training, teacher training, continuing, and distance education. *To foster international liaison among individuals and organizations with professional responsibility in the field of educational media. *To cooperate with other international organizations in the development and application of educational technology for practice, research, production, and distribution in this field. Who can be a member of ICEM? Members are organizations and individuals who are involved in educational technology in any one of a variety of ways. There are several different types and categories of ICEM members, Individual Members, National Representatives, Deputy Representatives, and Coordinators. Individual Members may join ICEM by paying individual membership fees. National Representatives are appointed by their Ministry of Education. National Coordinators are elected by other ICEM members in their country. Regional Representatives and Coordinators represent a group of several countries. ICEM Secretariat, c/o Ray Laverty SG Pf 114 1011 Wien, Austria, E-mail: lylt-at-a1.net.

Dues: N/A.

Meetings: Annual General Assembly in Autumn; Executive Committee meeting in Spring; Locations vary.

Publications: Educational Media International (quarterly journal) http://www.icem-cime.org/emi/issues.asp Aims & Scope Educational media has made a considerable impact on schools, colleges, and providers of open and distance education. This journal provides an international forum for the exchange of information and views on new developments in educational and mass media. Contributions are drawn from academics and professionals whose ideas and experiences come from a number of countries and contexts. Abstracting & Indexing Educational Media International is covered by the British Education Index; Contents Pages in Education; Educational Research Abstracts online (ERA); Research into Higher Education Abstracts; ERIC; EBSCOhost; and Proquest Information and Learning.

Name of Organization or Association: International Recording Media Association.

Acronym: IRMA.

Address: 182 Nassau Street, Suite 204, Princeton, NJ 08542-7005, USA.

Phone Number: (609)279-1700; **Fax Number**: (609)279-1999.

Email Contact: info@recordingmedia.org; **URL**: http://www.recordingmedia.org.

Leaders: Charles Van Horn, President; Guy Finley, Associate Executive Director.

Description: IRMA, the content delivery and storage association, is the worldwide forum on trends and innovation for the delivery and storage of entertainment and information. Founded in 1970, this global trade association encompasses organizations involved in every facet of content delivery. Beginning with the introduction of the audiocassette, through the home video revolution, and right up to today's digital delivery era, IRMA has always been the organization companies have turned to for news, networking, market research, information services, and leadership.

Membership: Over 400 corporations, IRMA's membership includes raw material providers, manufacturers, replicators, duplicators, packagers, copyright holders, logistics providers, and companies from many other related industries. Corporate membership includes benefits to all employees.

Dues: Corporate membership dues based on gross dollar volume in our industry.

Meetings: Annual Recording Media Forum (Palm Springs, CA); December Summit (New York, NY).

Publications: 9X annual Mediaware Magazine; Annual International Source Directory, Quarterly Market Intelligence.

Name of Organization or Association: International Society for Performance Improvement.

Acronym: ISPI.

Address: 1400 Spring Street, Suite 260, Silver Spring, MD 20910, USA.

Phone Number: (301)587-8570; **Fax Number**: (301)587-8573.

Email Contact: emember@ispi.org; **URL**: http://www.ispi.org.

Leaders: Richard D. Battaglia, Executive Director.

Description: The International Society for Performance Improvement (ISPI) is dedicated to improving individual, organizational, and societal performance. Founded in 1962, ISPI is the leading international association dedicated to improving productivity and performance in the workplace. ISPI represents more than 10,000 international and chapter members throughout the USA, Canada, and 40 other countries. ISPI's mission is to develop and recognize the proficiency of our members and advocate the use of Human Performance Technology. This systematic approach to improving productivity and competence uses a set of methods and procedures and a strategy for solving problems for realizing opportunities related to the performance of people. It is a systematic combination of performance analysis, cause analysis, intervention design and development, implementation, and evaluation that can be applied to individuals, small groups, and large organizations.

Membership: 10,000 performance technologists, training directors, human resources managers, instructional technologists, human factors practitioners, and organizational consultants are members of ISPI. They work in a variety of settings including business, academia, government, health services, banking, and the armed forces.

Dues: Membership Categories Active Membership ($145 annually). This is an individual membership receiving full benefits and voting rights in the Society. Student Membership ($60 annually). This is a discounted individual full membership for full-time students. Proof of full-time enrollment must accompany the application. Retired Membership ($60 annually). This is a discounted individual full membership for individuals who are retired from full-time employment. Special Organizational Membership Categories: These groups support the Society at the top level. Sustaining Membership ($950 annually). This is an organizational membership and includes five active memberships and several additional value-added services and discounts. Details available upon request. Patron Membership ($1,400 annually). This is an organizational membership and includes five active memberships and several additional value-added services and discounts. Details available upon request.

Meetings: Annual International Performance Improvement Conference, Fall Symposiums, Professional Series Workshops, Human Performance Technology Institutes.

Publications: Performance Improvement Journal (10/year): The common theme is performance improvement practice or technique that is supported by research or germane theory. PerformanceXpress (12/year): Monthly newsletter published online. Performance Improvement Quarterly, PIQ, is a peer-reviewed journal created to stimulate professional discussion in the field and to advance the discipline of HPT through publishing scholarly works. ISPI Bookstore: The ISPI online bookstore is hosted in partnership with John Wiley & Sons.

Name of Organization or Association: International Visual Literacy Association.

Acronym: IVLA.

Address: Dr Karen Kaminski, IVLA Treasurer, Colorado State University, School of Education: 1588, Fort Collins, CO 80523, USA.

Phone Number: (970)491-3713; **Fax Number**: (970)491-1317.

Email Contact: IVLA_Treasurer@netzero.com; **URL**: www.ivla.org.

Leaders: IVLA Treasurer, Karen Kaminski.

Description: IVLA provides a multidisciplinary forum for the exploration, presentation, and discussion of all aspects of visual learning, thinking, communication, and expression. It also serves as a communication link bonding professionals from many disciplines who are creating and sustaining the study of the nature of visual experiences and literacy. It promotes and evaluates research, programs, and projects intended to increase effective use of visual communication in education, business, the arts, and commerce. IVLA was founded in 1968 to promote the concept of visual literacy and is an affiliate of AECT.

Membership: Membership of 500 people, mostly from academia and from many disciplines. We are an international organization and have conferences abroad once every third year. Anyone interested in any visual-verbal area should try our organization: Architecture, engineering, dance, the arts, computers, video, design, graphics, photography, visual languages, mathematics, acoustics, physics, chemistry, optometry, sciences, literature, library, training, education, etc.

Dues: $60 regular; $30 student and retired; $60 outside USA; $500 lifetime membership.

Meetings: Yearly conference usually Oct./Nov. in selected locations.

Publications: The Journal of Visual Literacy (bi-annual: Juried research papers) and Selected Readings from the Annual Conference.

Name of Organization or Association: Knowledge Alliance.

Acronym: N/A.

Address: 815 Connecticut Avenue, NW, Suite 220, Washington, DC 20006, USA.

Phone Number: (202)518-0847; **Fax Number**: N/A.

Email Contact: waters@KnowledgeAll.net; **URL**: http://www.knowledgeall.net.

Leaders: James W. Kohlmoos, President.

Description: Knowledge Alliance (formerly known as NEKIA) was founded in 1997 as a nonprofit, nonpartisan strategic alliance to address the increasingly urgent need to apply rigorous research to persistent educational challenges facing our country's schools. Composed of leading education organizations, Alliance members are involved in high-quality education research, development, dissemination, technical assistance and evaluation at the federal, regional, state, tribal, and local levels. The Alliance works closely with the US Congress, US Department of Education, and other federal agencies in advocating knowledge-based policy for innovation and improvement in education. Our Mission Knowledge Alliance's mission is to improve K-12 education by widely expanding the development and use of research-based knowledge in policy and practice. We believe that the effective use of research-based knowledge is essential to increasing student achievement and closing achievement gaps and should be a central organizing concept for the education reform efforts at all levels. We envision a new knowledge era in education policy and practice that focuses on the effective use of research-based knowledge to achieve successful and sustainable school improvement.

Membership: 28.

Dues: Not available.

Meetings: Board Meetings and Retreats; Invitational R&D Summit (2009); Hill Days; Communicators Institute.

Publications: None.

Name of Organization or Association: Learning Point Associates.

Acronym: (none).

Address: 1120 E. Diehl Road Suite 200, Naperville, IL 60563-1486, USA.

Phone Number: (630)649-6500, (800)356-2735; **Fax Number**: (630)649-6700.

Email Contact: info@learningpt.org; **URL**: www.learningpt.org.

Leaders: Gina Burkhardt, Chief Executive Officer.

Description: Learning Point Associates, with offices in Naperville, Illinois; Chicago; New York; and Washington, D.C., is a nonprofit educational organization with more than 20 years of direct experience working with and for educators and policymakers to transform educational systems and student learning. The national and international reputation of Learning Point Associates is built on a solid foundation of conducting rigorous and relevant education research and evaluation; analyzing and synthesizing education policy trends and practices; designing and conducting client-centered evaluations; delivering high-quality professional services; and developing and delivering tools, services, and resources targeted at pressing education issues. Learning Point Associates manages a diversified portfolio of work ranging from direct consulting assignments to major federal contracts and grants, including REL Midwest, the National Comprehensive Center for Teacher Quality, Great Lakes East Comprehensive Assistance Center, Great Lakes West Comprehensive Assistance Center, The Center for Comprehensive School Reform and Improvement, and the NCLB Implementation Center.

Membership: Not applicable.

Dues: None.

Meetings: None.

Publications: Visit the Publications section of our website.

Name of Organization or Association: Library Administration and Management Association.

Acronym: LAMA.

Address: 50 E. Huron Street, Chicago, IL 60611, USA.

Phone Number: (312)280-5032; **Fax Number**: (312)280-5033.

Email Contact: lama@ala.org; **URL**: http://www.ala.org/lama.

Leaders: Lorraine Olley, Executive Director; Catherine Murray-Rust, President

Description: MISSION: The Library Administration and Management Association encourage and nurture current and future library leaders, and develop and promote outstanding leadership and management practices. VISION: LAMA will be the foremost organization developing present and future leaders in library and information services. IMAGE: LAMA is a welcoming community where aspiring and experienced leaders from all types of libraries, as well as those who support libraries, come together to gain skills in a quest for excellence in library management, administration, and leadership. Sections include: Buildings and Equipment Section (BES); Fundraising & Financial Development Section (FRFDS); Library Organization & Management Section (LOMS); Human Resources Section (HRS); Public Relation and Marketing Section (PRMS); Systems & Services Section (SASS); and Measurement, Assessment and Evaluation Section (MAES).

Membership: 4,800.

Dues: $50, regular (in addition to ALA membership); $65, organizations and corporations; $15, library school students.

Meetings: ALA Annual Conference 2006, New Orleans, June 22–27; Midwinter Meeting 2007, San Diego, January 9–14.

Publications: Library Administration & Management (quarterly); LEADS from LAMA (electronic newsletter, irregular).

Name of Organization or Association: Library and Information Technology Association.

Acronym: LITA.

Address: 50 E. Huron Street, Chicago, IL 60611, USA.

Phone Number: (312)280-4270, (800)545-2433, ext. 4270; **Fax Number**: (312)280-3257.

Email Contact: lita@ala.org; **URL**: http://www.lita.org.

Leaders: Mary C. Taylor, Executive Director (mtaylor@ala.org).

Description: A division of the American Library Association, LITA is concerned with library automation; the information sciences; and the design, development, and implementation of automated systems in those fields, including systems development, electronic data processing, mechanized information retrieval, operations research, standards development, telecommunications, video communications, networks and collaborative efforts, management techniques, information technology, optical technology, artificial intelligence and expert systems, and other related aspects of audiovisual activities and hardware applications.

Membership: LITA members come from all types of libraries and institutions focusing on information technology in libraries. They include library decision-makers, practitioners, information professionals, and vendors. Approximately 4,300 members.

Dues: $60 plus membership in ALA; $25 plus membership in ALA for library school students.

Meetings: National Forum, fall.

Publications: LITA Blog, Information Technology and Libraries (ITAL): Contains the table of contents, abstracts, and some full-text of ITAL, a refereed journal published quarterly by the Library and Information Technology Association. Technology Electronic Reviews (TER): TER is an irregular electronic serial publication that provides reviews and pointers to a variety of print and electronic resources about information technology. LITA Publications List: Check for information on LITA Guides and Monographs.

Name of Organization or Association: Lister Hill National Center for Biomedical Communications.

Acronym: LHNCBC.

Address: US National Library of Medicine, 8600 Rockville Pike, Bethesda, MD 20894, USA.

Phone Number: (301)496-4441; **Fax Number**: (301)402-0118.

Email Contact: lhcques@lhc.nlm.nih.gov; **URL**: http://lhncbc.nlm.nih.gov/.

Leaders: Clement J. McDonald, MD, Director (ClemMcDonald@mail.nih.gov).

Description: The Lister Hill National Center for Biomedical Communications is an intramural research and development division of the US National Library of Medicine (NLM). The Center conducts and supports research and development in the dissemination of high quality imagery, medical language processing, high-speed access to biomedical information, intelligent database systems development, multimedia visualization, knowledge management, data mining, and machine-assisted indexing. The Center also conducts and supports research and development projects focusing on educational applications of state-of-the-art technologies including the use of microcomputer technology incorporating stereoscopic imagery and haptics, the Internet, and videoconferencing technologies for training health care professionals and disseminating consumer health information. The Centers Collaboratory for High Performance Computing and Communication serves as a focus for collaborative research and development in those areas, cooperating with faculties and staff of health science's educational institutions. Health profession educators are assisted in the use and application of these technologies through periodic training, demonstrations, and consultations. High Definition (HD) video is a technology area that has been explored and developed within the Center, and is now used as the NLM standard for all motion imaging projects considered to be of archival value. Advanced 3D animation and photorealistic rendering techniques have also become required tools for use in visual projects within the Center.

Membership: None.

Dues: None.

Meetings: None.

Publications: Fact sheet (and helpful links to other publications) at: http://www. nlm.nih.gov/pubs/factsheets/lister_hill.html Fellowship and PostDoctoral opportunities are ongoing: http://lhncbc.nlm.nih.gov/lhc/servlet/Turbine/template/ training%2CTrainingoppor.vm.

Name of Organization or Association: Media Communications Association: International.

Acronym: MCA-I.

Address: PO Box 5135, Madison, WI 53705-0135, USA.

Phone Number: Use Contact Form; **Fax Number**: Please Ask.

Email Contact: info@mca-i.org; **URL**: http://www.mca-i.org.

Leaders: Lois Weiland and Connie Terwilliger, Co-Executive Director.

Description: Formerly the International Television Association. Founded in 1968, MCA-I's mission is to provide media communications professionals opportunities for networking, forums for education, and resources for information. MCA-I also offers business services, such as low-cost insurance, buying programs, etc., to reduce operating costs. MCA-I also confers the highly acclaimed MCA-I Media Festival awarding the Golden Reel. Visit MCA-Is Web site for full details.

Membership: Individual, student, and corporate members. Membership programs also are available to vendors for relationship and business development.

Dues: $80, individual. See Web site for complete dues schedule.

Meetings: Various Partnerships with Association Conferences.

Publications: MCA-I eNews (Monthly), LeaderLinks (Monthly), CONNECT (quarterly), Find a Pro Directory (online).

Name of Organization or Association: Medical Library Association.

Acronym: MLA.

Address: 65 E. Wacker Place, Suite 1900, Chicago, IL 60601-7246, USA.

Phone Number: (312)419-9094; **Fax Number**: (312)419-8950.

Email Contact: info@mlahq.org; **URL**: http://www.mlanet.org.

Leaders: Carla J. Funk, MLS, MBA, CAE, Executive Director.

Description: MLA, a nonprofit, educational organization, comprises health science's information professionals with more than 4,500 members worldwide. Through its programs and services, MLA provides lifelong educational opportunities,

supports a knowledgebase of health information research, and works with a global network of partners to promote the importance of quality information for improved health to the health care community and the public.

Membership: MLA, a nonprofit, educational organization, comprises health sciences information professionals with more than 4,500 members worldwide. Through its programs and services, MLA provides lifelong educational opportunities, supports a knowledgebase of health information research, and works with a global network of partners to promote the importance of quality information for improved health to the health care community and the public. Membership categories: Regular Membership, Institutional Membership, International Membership, Affiliate Membership, Student Membership

Dues: $165, regular; $110, introductory; $255–600, institutional, based on total library expenditures, including salaries, but excluding grants and contracts; $110, international; $100, affiliate; $40, student.

Meetings: National annual meeting held every May; most chapter meetings are held in the fall.

Publications: MLA News (newsletter, 10/year); Journal of the Medical Library Association (quarterly scholarly publication.); MLA DocKit series, collections of representative, unedited library documents from a variety of institutions that illustrate the range of approaches to health sciences library management topics; MLA BibKits, selective, annotated bibliographies of discrete subject areas in the health sciences literature; standards; surveys; and copublished monographs.

Name of Organization or Association: Mid-continent Research for Education and Learning.

Acronym: McREL.

Address: 4601 DTC Boulevard, Suite 500, Denver, CO 80237, USA.

Phone Number: (303)337-0990; **Fax Number**: (303)337-3005.

Email Contact: info@mcrel.org; **URL**: http://www.mcrel.org.

Leaders: J. Timothy Waters, Executive Director.

Description: McREL is a private, nonprofit organization whose purpose is to improve education through applied research and development. McREL provides products and services, primarily for K-12 educators, to promote the best instructional practices in the classroom. McREL houses 1 of 10 regional educational laboratories funded by the US Department of Education, Institute for Educational Science. The regional laboratory helps educators and policymakers work toward excellence in education for all students. It also serves at the North Central Comprehensive Center, providing school improvement support to the states of Iowa, Minnesota, Nebraska, North Dakota, and South Dakota. McREL has particular expertise in standard-based education systems, leadership for school improvement, effective instructional practices, teacher quality, mathematics and science education improvement, early literacy development, and education outreach programs.

Membership: Not a membership organization.

Dues: No dues.

Meetings: NA.

Publications: Changing Schools (quarterly newsletter); Noteworthy (irregular monograph on topics of current interest in education reform). Numerous technical reports and other publications. Check website for current listings.

Name of Organization or Association: Minorities in Media (an affiliate of the Association for Educational Communications & Technology).

Acronym: MIM.

Address: PO Box 439147, Chicago, IL 60643-9147, USA.

Phone Number: (773)841-3732; **Fax Number**: (773)409-8583.

Email Contact: pyoung@umbc.edu; **URL**: http://aectmim.ning.com/.

Leaders: Patricia A. Young, President (2009–2011); Brandon C. Taylor, President Elect (2011–2013).

Description: Mission Statement—Minorities in Media's purpose is to encourage the effective utilization of educational media in the teaching learning process; provide leadership opportunities in advancing the use of technology as an integral part of the learning process; provide a vehicle through which minorities might influence the utilization of media in institutions; develop an information exchange network common to minorities in media; study, evaluate, and refine the educational technology process as it relates to the education of minorities and to encourage and improve the production of effective materials for the education of minorities.

Membership: Dr Wesley Joseph McJulien founded Minorities In Media (MIM) around the late 1970s. In the April 1987 issue of Tech Trends, the article Black Contributors to Educational Technology chronicles the history of MIM. John W. Green and Wesley J. McJulien write: "In 1975, a group of Black technologists met in Dallas in an effort to band together and provide more opportunities for Blacks in the Association for Educational Communications and Technology. One of the assignments was to find the Black person who was the outstanding author in the field of educational technology and invite him to speak at the 1977 meeting of BUDDIES (an organization now called Minorities In Media). Dr. Greene was selected and his presentation, "The Role of Blacks in Instructional Technology," stressed that Black must participate in all areas of AECT and especially in research (p. 18)" This history is the foundation of who we are today as an organization. We celebrate our past and continue to spearhead our future. Membership is open to professionals and academics whose interests align with MIM's mission.

Dues: $10, student; $30, professional.

Meetings: Annual meetings held during the Association for Educational Communications & Technology conference—www.aect.org.

Publications: MIM NING is free to sign up—http://aectmim.ning.com/

Name of Organization or Association: National Aeronautics and Space Administration.

Acronym: NASA.

Address: NASA Headquarters, 300 E Street SW, Washington, DC 20546, USA.

Phone Number: (202)358-0103; **Fax Number**: (202)358-3032.

Email Contact: education@nasa.gov; **URL**: http://education.nasa.gov.

Leaders: Angela Phillips Diaz, Assistant Administrator for Education.

Description: From elementary through postgraduate school, NASA's educational programs are designed to inspire the next generation of explorers by capturing students interest in science, mathematics, and technology at an early age; to channel more students into science, engineering, and technology career paths; and to enhance the knowledge, skills, and experiences of teachers and university faculty. NASA's educational programs include NASA Spacelink (an electronic information system); videoconferences (60-min interactive staff development videoconferences to be delivered to schools via satellite); and NASA Television (informational and educational television programming). Additional information is available from the Office of Education at NASA Headquarters and counterpart offices at the nine NASA field centers. Further information may be obtained from the NASA Education Homepage and also accessible from the NASA Public Portal at See learning in a whole new light!

Membership: N/A.

Dues: N/A.

Meetings: N/A.

Publications: Publications and Products can be searched and downloaded from the following URL—http://www.nasa.gov/audience/foreducators/5-8/learning/index.html.

Name of Organization or Association: National Alliance for Media Arts and Culture.

Acronym: NAMAC.

Address: 145 Ninth Street, Suite 250, San Francisco, CA 94103, USA.

Phone Number: (415)431-1391; **Fax Number**: (415)431-1392.

Email Contact: namac@namac.org; **URL**: http://www.namac.org.

Leaders: Helen DeMichel, Co-Director.

Description: NAMAC is a nonprofit organization dedicated to increasing public understanding of and support for the field of media arts in the USA. Members include media centers, cable access centers, universities, and media artists, as well as other individuals and organizations providing services for production, education, exhibition, distribution, and preservation of video, film, audio, and intermedia. NAMAC's information services are available to the general public, arts and non-arts organizations, businesses, corporations, foundations, government agencies, schools, and universities.

Membership: 300 organizations, 75 individuals.

Dues: $75–450, institutional (depending on annual budget); $75, individual.

Meetings: Biennial Conference.

Publications: Media Arts Information Network; The National Media Education Directory, annual anthology of case-studies "A Closer Look," periodic White Paper reports, Digital Directions: Convergence Planning for the Media Arts.

Name of Organization or Association: National Association for Visually Handicapped.

Acronym: NAVH.

Address: 22 West 21st Street, 6th Floor, New York, NY 10010, USA.

Phone Number: (212)889-3141; **Fax Number**: (212)727-2931.

Email Contact: navh@navh.org; **URL**: http://www.navh.org.

Leaders: Dr Lorraine H. Marchi, Founder/CEO; Cesar Gomez, Executive Director.

Description: NAVH ensures that those with limited vision do not lead limited lives. We offer emotional support; training in the use of visual aids and special lighting; access to a wide variety of optical aids, electronic equipment, and lighting; a large print, nationwide, free-by-mail loan library; large print educational materials; free quarterly newsletter; referrals to eye care specialists and local low vision resources; self-help groups for seniors and working adults; and educational outreach to the public and professionals.

Membership: It is not mandatory to become a member in order to receive our services. However, your membership helps others retain their independence by allowing NAVH to provide low vision services to those who cannot afford to make a donation. In addition, members receive discounts on visual aids, educational materials, and our catalogs. Corporations and publishers may also join to help sponsor our services. Please contact us for more information.

Dues: Membership is $50 a year for individuals. Publishers and corporations interested in membership should contact NAVH.

Meetings: Seniors support group two times at month; Seminar on low vision for ophthalmology residents; yearly showcase of the latest in low vision technology, literature, and services.

Publications: Free quarterly newsletter distributed free throughout the English-speaking world; Visual Aids Catalog; Large Print Loan Library Catalog; informational pamphlets on vision, common eye diseases, and living with limited vision; booklets for professionals who work with adults and children with limited vision.

Name of Organization or Association: National Association of Media and Technology Centers.

Acronym: NAMTC.

Address: NAMTC, 7105 First Avenue, SW Cedar Rapids, IA 52405, USA.

Phone Number: (319)654-0608; **Fax Number**: (319)654-0609.

Email Contact: bettyge@mchsi.com; **URL**: www.namtc.org.

Leaders: Betty Gorsegner Ehlinger, Executive Director.

Description: NAMTC is committed to promoting leadership among its membership through networking, advocacy, and support activities that will enhance the equitable access to media, technology, and information services to educational communities. Membership is open to regional, K-12, and higher education media centers which serve K-12 students as well as commercial media and technology centers.

Membership: Institutional and corporate members numbering approximately 200.

Dues: $125 institutions; $335 corporations.

Meetings: A national Leadership Summit is held in the winter.

Publications: Electronic NAMTC Newsletter is published five times per academic year.

Name of Organization or Association: National Commission on Libraries and Information Science.

Acronym: NCLIS.

Address: 1800 M Street, NW; Suite 350 North Tower, Washington, DC 20036-5841, USA.

Phone Number: (202)606-9200; **Fax Number**: (202)606-9203.

Email Contact: info@nclis.gov.; **URL**: http://www.nclis.gov.

Leaders: C. Beth Fitzsimmons, Chairman.

Description: A permanent independent agency of the US government charged with advising the executive and legislative branches on national library and information policies and plans. The Commission reports directly to the president and Congress on the implementation of national policy; conducts studies, surveys, and analyses of the nations library and information needs; appraises the inadequacies of current resources and services; promotes research and development activities; conducts hearings and issues publications as appropriate; and develops overall plans for meeting national library and information needs and for the coordination of activities at the federal, state, and local levels. The Commission provides general policy advice to the Institute of Museum and Library Services (IMLS) director relating to library services included in the Library Services and Technology Act (LSTA).

Membership: 16 commissioners (14 appointed by the president and confirmed by the Senate, the Librarian of Congress, and the Director of the IMLS).

Dues: None.

Meetings: Average 2–3 meetings a year.

Publications: N/A.

Name of Organization or Association: National Communication Association.

Acronym: NCA.

Address: 1765 N Street, NW, Washington, DC 22003, USA.

Phone Number: (202)464-4622; **Fax Number**: (202)464-4600.

Email Contact: dwallick@natcom.org; **URL**: http://www.natcom.org.

Leaders: Roger Smitter, Executive Director.

Description: A voluntary society organized to promote study, criticism, research, teaching, and application of principles of communication, particularly of speech communication. Founded in 1914, NCA is a nonprofit organization of researchers, educators, students, and practitioners, whose academic interests span all forms of human communication. NCA is the oldest and largest national organization serving the academic discipline of Communication. Through its services, scholarly publications, resources, conferences, and conventions, NCA works with its members to strengthen the profession and contribute to the greater good of the educational enterprise and society. Research and instruction in the discipline focus on the study of how messages in various media are produced, used, and interpreted within and across different contexts, channels, and cultures.

Membership: 7,700.

Dues: From $60 (Student) to $300 (Patron). Life membership also available.

Meetings: Four regional conferences (ECA, ESCA SSCA, WSCA) and one Annual National Conference.

Publications: Spectra Newsletter (mo.); Quarterly Journal of Speech; Communication Monographs; Communication Education; Critical Studies in Mass Communication; Journal of Applied Communication Research; Text and Performance Quarterly;

Communication Teacher; Index to Journals in Communication Studies through 1995; National Communication Directory of NCA and the Regional Speech Communication Organizations (CSSA, ECA, SSCA, WSCA). For additional publications, request brochure.

Name of Organization or Association: National Council of Teachers of English.

Acronym: NCTE.

Address: 1111 W. Kenyon Road, Urbana, IL 61801-1096, USA.

Phone Number: (217)328-3870; **Fax Number**: (217)328-0977.

Email Contact: public_info@ncte.org; **URL**: http://www.ncte.org.

Leaders: Kent Williamson, NCTE Executive Director.

Description: The National Council of Teachers of English, with 35,000 individual and institutional members worldwide, is dedicated to improving the teaching and learning of English and the language arts at all levels of education. Among its position statements and publications related to educational media and technology are "Code of Best Practices in Fair Use for Media Literacy Education," "The NCTE Definition of 21st Century Literacies," and "Position Statement on Teaching, Learning, and Assessing Writing in Digital Environments."

Membership: NCTE members include elementary, middle, and high school teachers; supervisors of English programs; college and university faculty; teacher educators; local and state agency English specialists; and professionals in related fields.

Dues: Membership in NCTE is $50 a year; subscriptions to its journals are in addition to the membership fee.

Meetings: http://www.ncte.org/annual/ 101st NCTE Annual Convention, Nov. 17–20, 2011, Chicago, IL; 102nd NCTE Annual Convention, Nov. 15–20, 2012, Las Vegas, NV; 103rd NCTE Annual Convention, Nov. 21–26, 2013, Boston, MA.

Publications: NCTE publishes about 10 books a year. Visit http://www.ncte.org/books and http://www.ncte.org/store. NCTE's journals include Language Arts Voices from the Middle English Journal College English College Composition and Communication English Education Research in the Teaching of English Teaching English in the Two-Year College Talking Points; English Leadership Quarterly; The Council Chronicle (included in NCTE membership). Journal information is available at http://www.ncte.org/journals/.

Name of Organization or Association: National EBS Association.

Acronym: NEBSA.

Address: PO Box 121475, Clermont, FL 34712-1475, USA.

Phone Number: (407) 401-4630; **Fax Number**: (321) 406-0520.

Email Contact: execdirector@nebsa.org; **URL**: http://nebsa.org.

Leaders: Lynn Rejniak, Chair, Board of Directors; Don MacCullough, Executive Director.

Description: Established in 1978, NEBSA is a nonprofit, professional organization of Educational Broadband Service (EBS) licensees, applicants, and others interested in EBS broadcasting. EBS is a very high frequency television broadcast service that is used to broadcast distance learning classes, two way internet service, wireless and data services to schools and other locations where education can take place. The goals of the association are to gather and exchange information about EBS, gather data on utilization of EBS, act as a conduit for those seeking EBS information, and assist migration from video broadcast to wireless, broadband Internet services using EBS channels. The NEBSA represents EBS interests to the FCC, technical consultants, and equipment manufacturers. The association uses its Web site and Listserv list to provide information to its members in areas such as technology, programming content, FCC regulations, excess capacity leasing, and license and application data.

Membership: The current membership consists of Educational Institutions and nonprofit organizations that hold licenses issued by the Federal Communications Commission for Educational Broadband Service (EBS). We also have members that have an interest in EBS and members such as manufacturers of EBS related equipment and Law firms that represent Licensees.

Dues: We have two main types of memberships: Voting memberships for EBS licensees only, and nonvoting memberships for other educational institutions and sponsors. See the Web site http://www.nebsa.org for details.

Meetings: Annual Member Conference, February 20–23, 2012 Newport Beach Marriott, Newoirt Beach, CA.

Publications: http://www.nebsa.org.

Name of Organization or Association: National Endowment for the Humanities.

Acronym: NEH.

Address: Division of Public Programs, Americas Media Makers Program, 1100 Pennsylvania Avenue, NW, Room 426, Washington, DC 20506, USA.

Phone Number: (202)606-8269; **Fax Number**: (202)606-8557.

Email Contact: publicpgms@neh.gov; **URL**: http://www.neh.gov.

Leaders: Karen Mittelman, Deputy Director, Division of Public Programs.

Description: The NEH is an independent federal grant-making agency that supports research, educational, and public programs grounded in the disciplines of the humanities. The Division of Public Programs Media Program supports film and radio programs in the humanities for public audiences, including children and adults. All programs in the Division of Public Program support various technologies, specifically

Web sites both as standalone projects and as extensions of larger projects such as museum exhibitions.

Membership: Nonprofit institutions and organizations including public television and radio stations.

Dues: Not applicable.

Meetings: Not applicable.

Publications: Visit the web site (http://www.neh.gov) for application forms and guidelines as well as the Media Log, a cumulative listing of projects funded through the Media Program.

Name of Organization or Association: National Federation of Community Broadcasters.

Acronym: NFCB.

Address: 1970 Broadway, Suite 1000, Oakland, CA 94612, USA.

Phone Number: (510)451-8200; **Fax Number**: (510)451-8208.

Email Contact: ginnyz@nfcb.org; **URL**: http://www.nfcb.org.

Leaders: Maxie C Jackson III, President and CEO.

Description: NFCB represents non-commercial, community-based radio stations in public policy development at the national level and provides a wide range of practical services, including technical assistance.

Membership: 250. Noncommercial community radio stations, related organizations, and individuals.

Dues: Range from $200 to 4,000 for participant and associate members.

Meetings: Annual Community Radio Conference; 2010 St. Paul; 2011 San Francisco; 2012 Houston.

Publications: Public Radio Legal Handbook; Digital AudioCraft; Guide to Underwriting.

Name of Organization or Association: National Film Board of Canada.

Acronym: NFBC.

Address: 1123 Broadway, STE 307, New York, NY 10010, USA.

Phone Number: (212)629-8890; **Fax Number**: (212)629-8502.

Email Contact: NewYork@nfb.ca; **URL**: www.nfb.ca.

Leaders: Dylan McGinty, US Sales Manager; Laure Parsons, US Sales and Marketing Associate.

Description: Established in 1939, the NFBC's main objective is to produce and distribute high-quality audiovisual materials for educational, cultural, and social purposes.

Membership: None.

Dues: None.

Meetings: N/A.

Publications: N/A.

Name of Organization or Association: National Freedom of Information Coalition.

Acronym: NFOIC.

Address: 133 Neff Annex, University of Missouri, Columbia, MO 65211-0012, USA.

Phone Number: (573)882-4856; **Fax Number**: (573)884-6204

Email Contact: daviscn@missouri.edu; **URL**: http://www.nfoic.org.

Leaders: Dr Charles N. Davis, Executive Director.

Description: The National Freedom of Information Coalition is a national membership organization devoted to protecting the public's right to oversee its government. NFOIC's goals include helping start-up FOI organizations; strengthening existing FOI organizations; and developing FOI programs and publications appropriate to the membership.

Membership: The NFOIC offers active memberships to freestanding nonprofit state or regional Freedom of Information Coalitions, academic centers and First Amendment Centers, and associated memberships to individuals and entities supporting NFOIC's mission. Membership information is available on the NFOIC Web page. Achieving and maintaining active membership in all 50 states is the primary goal of NFOIC.

Dues: Membership categories and levels of support are described on the NFOIC Web site.

Meetings: The National Freedom of Information Coalition hosts an annual meeting and a spring conference.

Publications: The FOI Advocate, an electronic newsletter available for free through email subscription. The FOI Report, a periodic White Paper, published electronically.

Name of Organization or Association: National Gallery of Art.

Acronym: NGA.

Address: Department of Education Resources, 2000B South Club Drive, Landover, MD 20785, USA.

Phone Number: (202)842-6269; **Fax Number**: (202)842-6935.

Email Contact: EdResources@nga.gov; **URL**: http://www.nga.gov/education/classroom/loanfinder/.

Leaders: Leo J. Kasun, Head, Department of Education Resources.

Description: This department of NGA is responsible for the production and distribution of 120+ educational audiovisual programs, including interactive technologies. Materials available (all loaned free to individuals, schools, colleges and universities, community organizations, and non-commercial television stations) range from DVDs, CD-ROMs, videocassettes, and teaching packets with either image CD-ROMs or color slides. All DVD and videocassette programs are closed captioned. A free catalog describing all programs is available upon request. Many of these programs are available for long-term loan.

Membership: Our free-loan lending program resembles that of a library and because we are a federally funded institution we do not have a membership system. Last year we lent programs directly to over one million borrowers. Our programs are available to anyone who requests them which ranges from individuals to institutions.

Dues: None.

Meetings: None.

Publications: Extension Programs Catalogue.

Name of Organization or Association: National PTA.

Acronym: National PTA.

Address: 541 North Fairbanks Ct, Suite 1300, Chicago, IL 60611, USA.

Phone Number: (312)670-6782; **Fax Number**: (312)670-6783.

Email Contact: info@pta.org; **URL**: http://www.pta.org.

Leaders: Warlene Gary, Chief Executive Officer.

Description: Advocates the education, health, safety, and well-being of children and teens. Provides parenting education and leadership training to PTA volunteers. National PTA partners with the National Cable & Telecommunications Association on the "Taking Charge of Your TV" project by training PTA and cable representatives to present media literacy workshops. The workshops teach parents and educators how to evaluate programming so they can make informed decisions about what to allow their children to see. The National PTA in 1997 convinced the television industry to add content information to the TV rating system.

Membership: 6.2 million Membership open to all interested in the health, welfare, and education of children and support the PTA mission: http://www.pta.org/aboutpta/mission_en.asp.

Dues: Vary by local unit: National dues portion is $1.75 per member annually.

Meetings: National convention, held annually in June in different regions of the country, is open to PTA members; convention information available on the Web site.

Publications: Our Children (magazine) plus electronic newsletters and other web-based information for members and general public.

Name of Organization or Association: National Public Broadcasting Archives.

Acronym: NPBA.

Address: Hornbake Library, University of Maryland, College Park, MD 20742, USA.

Phone Number: (301)405-9160; **Fax Number**: (301)314-2634.

Email Contact: npba@umd.edu; **URL**: http://www.lib.umd.edu/NPBA.

Leaders: Karen King, Acting Curator.

Description: NPBA brings together the archival record of the major entities of noncommercial broadcasting in the USA. NPBA's collections include the archives of the Corporation for Public Broadcasting (CPB), the Public Broadcasting Service (PBS), and National Public Radio (NPR). Other organizations represented include the Midwest Program for Airborne Television Instruction (MPATI), the Public Service Satellite Consortium (PSSC), Americas Public Television Stations (APTS), Children's Television Workshop (CTW), and the Joint Council for Educational Telecommunications (JCET). NPBA also makes available the personal papers of many individuals who have made significant contributions to public broadcasting, and its reference library contains basic studies of the broadcasting industry, rare pamphlets, and journals on relevant topics. NPBA also collects and maintains a selected audio and video program record of public broadcasting's national production and support centers and of local stations. Oral history tapes and transcripts from the NPR Oral History Project and the Televisionaries Nal History Project are also available at the archives. The archives are open to the public from 9 A.M. to 5 P.M., Monday through Friday. Research in NPBA collections should be arranged by prior appointment. For further information, call (301)405-9988.

Membership: NA.

Dues: NA.

Meetings: NA.

Publications: NA.

Name of Organization or Association: National Telemedia Council Inc.

Acronym: NTC.

Address: 1922 University Avenue, Madison, WI 53726, USA.

Phone Number: (608)218-1182; **Fax Number**: None.

Email Contact: NTelemedia@aol.com; **URL**: http://www.nationaltelemedia-council.org and www.journalofmedialiteracy.org.

Leaders: Karen Ambrosh, President; Marieli Rowe, Executive Director.

Description: The National Telemedia Council is a national, nonprofit professional organization that has been promoting a media wise society for nearly six decades. Embracing a positive, non-judgmental philosophy that values education, evaluation, and reflective judgment, NTC has a long history of a broad array of initiatives that have included annual conferences, workshops, major and innovative interactive forums, local, national, and international events for diverse participants (including children); and its major ongoing award, the "Jessie McCanse Award for Individual, Long-Term Contribution to the Field of Media Literacy". NTC's ongoing current activities continue to include its major publication, The Journal of Media Literacy, published up to three times per year (and a part of the organization since its inception in 1953 and earlier); the development of its archival website; and interactive collaborations to advance the field such as the "media literacy cafes" in connection with issues of the Journal of Media Literacy.

Membership: Member/subscribers to the Journal of Media Literacy, currently over 500, including individuals, organizations, schools, and university libraries across the Globe including Asia, Australia, Europe, North and South America. Our membership is open to all those interested in media literacy.

Dues: Individuals: $35, basic; $50, contributing; $100, patron. Organizations/Library: $60. Corporate sponsorship: $500 (Additional Postage for Overseas: Canada or Mexico, add $18.00. All other outside North America, add $23.00).

Meetings: No major meetings scheduled this year.

Publications: The Journal of Media Literacy.

Name of Organization or Association: Native American Public Telecommunications, Inc.

Acronym: NAPT.

Address: 1800 North 33rd Street, Lincoln, NE 68503, USA.

Phone Number: (402)472-3522; **Fax Number**: (402)472-8675.

Email Contact: native@unl.edu; **URL**: http://www.nativetelecom.org.

Leaders: Shirley K. Sneve, Executive Director.

Description: Native American Public Telecommunications, Inc. (NAPT), a nonprofit 501(c)(3) which receives major funding from the Corporation for Public Broadcasting, shares Native stories with the world through support of the creation, promotion, and distribution of Native media. Founded in 1977, through various media—Public

Television, Public Radio, and the Internet—NAPT brings awareness of Indian and Alaska Native issues. NAPT operates AIROS Audio, offering downloadable podcasts with Native filmmakers, musicians, and Tribal leaders. VisionMaker is the premier source for quality Native American educational and home videos. All aspects of our programs encourage the involvement of young people to learn more about careers in the media—to be the next generation of storytellers. NAPT is located at the University of Nebraska, Lincoln. NAPT offers student employment, internships, and fellowships. Reaching the general public and the global market is the ultimate goal for the dissemination of Native-produced media.

Membership: No Membership.

Dues: None.

Meetings: None.

Publications: VisionMaker E-Newsletter, NAPT General E-Newsletter, Producer E-Newsletter, AIROS E-Newsletter, Educational Catalog, Annual Report Post Viewer Discussion Guides Educational Guides.

Name of Organization or Association: Natural Science Collections Alliance.

Acronym: NSC Alliance.

Address: PO Box 44095, Washington, DC 20026-4095, USA.

Phone Number: (202)633-2772; **Fax Number**: (202)633-2821.

Email Contact: ddrupa@burkine.com; **URL**: http://www.nscalliance.org.

Leaders: Executive Director.

Description: Fosters the care, management, and improvement of biological collections and promotes their utilization. Institutional members include free-standing museums, botanical gardens, college and university museums, and public institutions, including state biological surveys and agricultural research centers. The NSC Alliance also represents affiliate societies, and keeps members informed about funding and legislative issues.

Membership: 80 institutions, 30 affiliates, 120 individual and patron members.

Dues: Depend on the size of collections.

Meetings: Annual Meeting (May or June).

Publications: Guidelines for Institutional Policies and Planning in Natural History Collections; Global Genetic Resources; A Guide to Museum Pest Control.

Name of Organization or Association: New England School Library Association (formerly New England Educational Media Association).

Acronym: NESLA (formerly NEEMA).

Address: c/o Merlyn Miller, President Burr & Burton Academy, 57 Seminary Avenue, Manchester, VT 05254, USA.

Phone Number: (802)362-1775; **Fax Number**: (802)362-0574.

Email Contact: mmiller@burrburton.org; **URL**: www.neschoollibraries.org.

Leaders: Merlyn Miller, President.

Description: An affiliate of AECT, NESLA is a regional professional association dedicated to the improvement of instruction through the effective utilization of school library media services, media, and technology applications. For over 90 years, it has represented school library media professionals through activities and networking efforts to develop and polish the leadership skills, professional representation, and informational awareness of the membership. The Board of Directors consists of representatives from local affiliates within all six of the New England states, as well as professional leaders of the region. An annual leadership conference is offered.

Membership: NESLA focuses on school library media issues among the six New England states; consequently, membership is encouraged for school library media specialists in this region.

Dues: Regular membership $30. Student/retired membership $15.

Meetings: Annual Leadership Conference and Business Meeting.

Publications: NESLA Views.

Name of Organization or Association: New York Festivals.

Acronym: NYF.

Address: 260 West 39th Street, 10th Floor, New York, NY 10018, USA.

Phone Number: (212)643-4800; **Fax Number**: (212)643-0170.

Email Contact: info@newyorkfestivals.com; **URL**: http://www.newyorkfestivals.com.

Leaders: Rose Anderson, Executive Director.

Description: The New York Festivals® Worlds Best Television & Films™ recognize the "Worlds Best Work™" in news, sports, documentary, information, and entertainment program as well as in music videos, infomercials, promotion spots, openings, and IDs. Now entering its 55th year, the total number of entries continues to grow, now representing over 35 different countries, making the NYF™ Television & Film Awards one of the most well known and widely respected competitions on the globe. In 2010, NYF™ combined both the Television Program Awards and the Film & Video Awards, thus creating one of the world's largest international competitions dedicated to both the TV and film industries. New categories mirror today's trends in worldwide program and encourage the next generation of story-tellers. The 2012 TV & Film Awards ceremony for The Worlds Best TV & Films will be held in conjunction with The NAB Show in Las Vegas in April. The ceremony will be held on Tuesday April 17th. The Grand Award winners will be screened in the Content Theater on April 18th. Deadline Extended to: November 7th, 2011. For more information and fees, plus a full list of categories and the rules & regulations, please visit www.newyorkfestivals.com.

Membership: No membership feature. The competition is open to any broadcast and nonbroadcast including online media production.

Dues: N/A.

Meetings: N/A.

Publications: Winners are posted on our web site at www.newyorkfestivals.com.

Name of Organization or Association: Northwest College and University Council for the Management of Educational Technology.

Acronym: NW/MET.

Address: c/o WITS, Willamette University, 900 State Street, Salem, OR 97301, USA.

Phone Number: (503)370-6650; **Fax Number**: (503)375-5456.

Email Contact: mmorandi@willamette.edu; **URL**: http://www.nwmet.org.

Leaders: Doug McCartney, Director (effective April 14, 2007); Marti Morandi, Membership Chair.

Description: NW/MET is a group of media professionals responsible for campus-wide media services. Founded in 1976, NW/MET is comprised of members from two provinces of Canada and 4 northwestern states.

Membership: The membership of NW/MET is composed of individuals who participate by giving time, energy, and resources to the support and advancement of the organization. Full Membership may be awarded to individuals whose primary professional role involves the facilitation of educational technology, who are employed by an institution of higher education located in the NW/MET membership region, and who submit a membership application in which they list their professional qualifications and responsibilities.

Dues: $35.

Meetings: An annual conference and business meeting are held each year, rotating through the region.

Publications: An annual Directory and website.

Name of Organization or Association: OCLC Online Computer Library Center, Inc.

Acronym: OCLC.

Address: 6565 Kilgour Place, Dublin, OH 43017-3395, USA.

Phone Number: (614)764-6000; **Fax Number**: (614)764-6096.

Email Contact: oclc@oclc.org; **URL**: http://www.oclc.org.

Leaders: Jay Jordan, President and CEO.

Description: Founded in 1967, OCLC is a nonprofit, membership, computer library service and research organization dedicated to the public purposes of furthering access to the world's information and reducing information costs. More than 60,000 libraries in 112 countries and territories around the world use OCLC services to locate, acquire, catalog, lend, and preserve library materials. Researchers, students, faculty, scholars, professional librarians, and other information seekers use OCLC services to obtain bibliographic, abstract, and full-text information. OCLC and its member libraries cooperatively produce and maintain WorldCat, the world's largest database for discovery of library materials. OCLC publishes the Dewey Decimal Classification. OCLC Digital Collection and Preservation Services provide digitization and archiving services worldwide. OCLC's NetLibrary provides libraries with eContent solutions that support Web-based research, reference, and learning.

Membership: OCLC welcomes information organizations around the world to be a part of our unique cooperative. A variety of participation levels are available to libraries, museums, archives, historical societies, other cultural heritage organizations, and professional associations. OCLC membership represents more than 60,000 libraries in 112 countries and territories around the world.

Dues: N/A.

Meetings: OCLC Members Council (3/year) Held in Dublin, OH.

Publications: Annual Report (1/year; print and electronic); OCLC Newsletter (4/year; print and electronic); OCLC Abstracts (1/week, electronic only).

Name of Organization or Association: Online Audiovisual Catalogers.

Acronym: OLAC.

Address: N/A, USA.

Phone Number: N/A; **Fax Number**: N/A.

Email Contact: treasurer@olac.org; **URL**: http://www.olacinc.org/.

Leaders: N/A.

Description: In 1980, OLAC was founded to establish and maintain a group that could speak for catalogers of audiovisual materials. OLAC provides a means for exchange of information, continuing education, and communication among catalogers of audiovisual materials and with the Library of Congress. While maintaining a voice with the bibliographic utilities that speak for catalogers of audiovisual materials, OLAC works toward common understanding of AV cataloging practices and standards.

Membership: 1,388.

Dues: United States and Canada Personal Memberships: 1 year $20.00, 2 years $38.00, 3 years $55.00. Institutional Memberships: 1 year $25.00, 2 years $48.00, 3 years $70.00. Other Countries: All Memberships: 1 year $25.00, 2 years $48.00, 3 years $70.00

Meetings: Bi-annual.

Publications: OLAC Newsletter.

Name of Organization or Association: Ontario Film Association, Inc. (also known as the Association for the Advancement of Visual Media/L'association pour lavancement des médias visuels).

Acronym: OLA.

Address: 50 Wellington Street, East Suite 201, Toronto, ON, Canada M5E 1C8.

Phone Number: (416)363-3388; **Fax Number**: 1-800-387-1181.

Email Contact: info@accessola.com; **URL**: www.accessola.com.

Leaders: Lawrence A. Moore, Executive Director.

Description: A membership organization of buyers, and users of media whose objectives are to promote the sharing of ideas and information about visual media through education, publications, and advocacy.

Membership: 112.

Dues: $120, personal membership; $215, associate membership.

Meetings: OFA Media Showcase, Spring.

Publications: Access.

Name of Organization or Association: Pacific Film Archive.

Acronym: PFA.

Address: University of California, Berkeley Art Museum, 2625 Durant Avenue, Berkeley, CA 94720-2250, USA.

Phone Number: (510)642-1437 (library); (510)642-1412 (general); **Fax Number**: (510)642-4889.

Email Contact: NLG@berkeley.edu; **URL**: http://www.bampfa.berkeley.edu.

Leaders: Susan Oxtoby, Senior Curator of Film; Nancy Goldman, Head, PFA Library and Film Study Center.

Description: Sponsors the exhibition, study, and preservation of classic, international, documentary, animated, and avant-garde films. Provides on-site research screenings of films in its collection of over 10,000 titles. Provides access to its collections of books, periodicals, stills, and posters (all materials are non-circulating). Offers BAM/PFA members and University of California, Berkeley, affiliates reference and research services to locate film and video distributors, credits, stock footage, etc. Library hours are 1–5 P.M. Monday–Thursday. Research screenings are by appointment only and must be scheduled at least 2 weeks in advance; other collections are available for consultation on a drop-in basis during Library hours.

Dues: $50 individuals and nonprofit departments of institutions.

Meetings: None.

Publications: BAM/PFA Calendar (6/year).

Name of Organization or Association: Pacific Resources for Education and Learning.

Acronym: PREL.

Address: 900 Fort Street Mall, Suite 1300, Honolulu, HI 96813, USA.

Phone Number: (808)441-1300; **Fax Number**: (808)441-1385.

Email Contact: askprel@prel.org; **URL**: http://www.prel.org/.

Leaders: Thomas W. Barlow, Ed.D., President and Chief Executive Officer.

Description: Pacific Resources for Education and Learning (PREL) is an independent, nonprofit 501(c)(3) corporation that serves the educational community in the US-affiliated Pacific islands, the continental USA, and countries throughout the world. PREL bridges the gap between research, theory, and practice in education and works collaboratively to provide services that range from curriculum development to assessment and evaluation. PREL serves the Pacific educational community with quality programs and products developed to promote educational excellence. We work throughout school systems, from classroom to administration, and collaborate routinely with governments, communities, and businesses. Above all, we specialize in multicultural and multilingual environments. From direct instruction to professional development to creation of quality educational materials, PREL is committed to ensuring that all students, regardless of circumstance or geographic location, have an equal opportunity to develop a strong academic foundation. PREL brings together in the Center for Information, Communications, and Technology (CICT) an experienced cadre of specialists in Web site development and design, educational technology, distance and online learning, multimedia production, interactive software development, writing and editing, graphics, and print production. By combining tested pedagogy with leading edge technology, PREL can create learning materials encompassing a wide variety of subject matter and delivery methods. PREL partners with researchers, schools, evaluators, publishers, and leaders in the learning technology industry to develop state-of-the-art learning tools and technology solutions. There are vast disparities across the Pacific when it comes to school resources, technology access, and bandwidth. PREL's goal is to work effectively in any type of setting in which an application is needed. With routine travel and a staff presence throughout the northern Pacific, PREL has resolved to reach underserved communities, determine their needs, and meet their requirements with the appropriate delivery and dissemination methods. Multimedia, Software, and Website conception, design, and delivery have become critical components of many learning programs. Our projects include development of teacher and student resources and resource kits, learning games, software solutions, and complex inter-active database design. Distance Learning Content and Delivery extend educational resources to audiences and individuals outside the classroom setting. Distance options both enhance and exponentially increase learning opportunities. The CICT is a premier provider of distance education, integrating curriculum and technology. High-Quality Publications are a PREL hallmark. PREL produces and distributes numerous high-quality publications for educators, including its research compen-dium, Research into Practice; Pacific Educator magazine; educational books and videos; and briefs and reports on research findings and current topics of interest.

Membership: PREL serves teachers and departments and ministries of education in American Samoa, Commonwealth of the Northern Mariana Islands, Federated States of Micronesia (Chuuk, Kosrae, Pohnpei, and Yap) Guam, Hawaii, the Republic of the Marshall Islands, and the Republic of Palau. In addition we work with the educational community on the continental USA and countries throughout the world. We are not a membership organization. We are grant funded with grants from the US Departments of Education, Labor, Health and Human Services, and other federal funding agencies such as the Institute of Museum and Library Services and the National Endowment for the Arts. In addition we have projects in partner-ship with regional educational institutions. Internationally we have worked with the International Labor Organization and the World Health Organization and are cur-rently working with Save the Children on a US AID project in the Philippines.

Dues: N/A.

Meetings: PREL supports the annual Pacific Educational Conference (PEC), held each July.

Publications: Publications are listed on the PREL Web site at http://ppo.prel.org/. Most are available in both PDF and HTML format. Some recent publications are described below: Focus on Professional Development, A (Research Based Practices in Early Reading Series). A Focus on Professional Development is the fourth in the Research-Based Practices in Early Reading Series published by the Regional Educational Laboratory (REL) at Pacific Resources for Education and Learning (PREL). Because reading proficiency is fundamental to student achievement across all subjects and grades, the preparation of the teachers and administrators who are responsible for providing early reading instruction is of special importance. This booklet examines what research tells us about professional development and about the role that effective professional development plays in improving both teacher performance and student achievement. http://www.prel.org/products/re_/prodevel opment.pdf (902K) Look and See: Using the Visual Environment as Access to

Literacy (Research Brief): This paper describes how the visual environment—what we see when we look—can be used to develop both visual and verbal literacy, including aesthetic appreciation, comprehension, and vocabulary. http://www.prel. org/products/re_/look_see.pdf (1M) Measuring the Effectiveness of Professional Development in Early Literacy: Lessons Learned (Research Brief): This Research Brief focuses on the methodology used to measure professional development (PD) effectiveness. It examines the needs that generated this research, what PREL did to meet those needs, and lessons that have been learned as a result. In particular, it discusses the development of a new instrument designed to measure the quality of PD as it is being delivered. http://www.prel.org/products/re_/effect_of_pd.pdf (730K) Pacific Early Literacy Resource Kit CD-ROM (Early Literacy Learning Resources): The Pacific Early Literacy Resource Kit was developed from PREL's research-based work performed with early literacy teachers in US-affiliated Pacific islands. The contents of the Resource Kit represent information, products, and pro-cesses we found beneficial as we worked to support literacy teachers in their efforts to improve student literacy achievement. http://www.prel.org/toolkit/index.htm Research Into Practice 2006 (PREL Compendium: This 86-page volume of PREL's annual research compendium brings together articles detailing research conducted during 2005 by PREL. The six articles in this issue focus on putting research findings to work to improve education. http://www.prel.org/products/pr_/compendium06/tableofcontents.asp.

Name of Organization or Association: Reference and User Services Association, a division of the American Library Association.

Acronym: RUSA.

Address: 50 E. Huron Street, Chicago, IL 60611, USA.

Phone Number: (800)545-2433, ext. 4398.; **Fax Number**: Fax (312)280-5273.

Email Contact: rusa@ala.org; **URL**: http://rusa.ala.org.

Leaders: Susan Hornung, Executive Director.

Description: A division of the American Library Association, the Reference and User Services Division (RUSA) is responsible for stimulating and supporting in the delivery of general library services and materials, and the provision of reference and information services, collection development, readers advisory, and resource shar-ing for all ages, in every type of library.

Membership: 4,200.

Dues: Join ALA and RUSA $120; RUSA membership $60 (added to ALA member-ship); student member $55 ($30 for ALA and $25 for RUSA); retired, support staff or nonsalaried $72 ($42 for ALA and $30 for RUSA).

Meetings: Meetings are held in conjunction with the American Library Association.

Publications: RUSQ (quarterly), information provided on RUSA Web site at www.
ala.org/rusa; RUSA Update, online membership newsletter, select publications.

Name of Organization or Association: Research for Better Schools, Inc.

Acronym: RBS.

Address: 112 North Broad Street, Philadelphia, PA 19102-1510, USA.

Phone Number: (215)568-6150; **Fax Number**: (215)568-7260.

Email Contact: info@rbs.org; **URL**: http://www.rbs.org/.

Leaders: Keith M. Kershner, Executive Director.

Description: Research for Better Schools is a nonprofit education organization that
has been providing services to teachers, administrators, and policy makers since 1966.
Our mission is to help students achieve high learning standards by supporting improvement efforts in schools and other education environments. The staff are dedicated to
and well experienced in providing the array of services that schools, districts, and
states need to help their students reach proficient or higher learning standards: (1)
technical assistance in improvement efforts; (2) professional development that is
required for the successful implementation of more effective curricula, technologies,
or instruction; (3) application of research in the design of specific improvement efforts;
(4) evaluation of improvement efforts; (5) curriculum implementation and assessment; and (6) effective communication with all members of the school community.
RBS has worked with a wide range of clients over the years, representing all levels of
the education system, as well as business and community groups.

Membership: There is no membership in Research for Better Schools.

Dues: N/A.

Meetings: N/A.

Publications: RBS publishes a variety of books and other products designed for
educators to use for schools improvement. The catalog for RBS Publications is
online (visit our homepage at http://www.rbs.org).

Name of Organization or Association: SERVE Center at UNCG.

Acronym: We no longer use the acronym.

Address: 5900 Summit Avenue, Dixon Building, Browns Summit, FL 27214,
USA.

Phone Number: (800)755-3277, 336-315-7457; **Fax Number**: (336)315-7457.

Email Contact: info@serve.org; **URL**: http://www.serve.org/.

Leaders: Ludy van Broekhuizen, Executive Director.

Description: The SERVE Center at the University of North Carolina at Greensboro,
under the leadership of Dr Ludwig David van Broekhuizen, is a university-based

education organization with the mission to promote and support the continuous improvement of educational opportunities for all learners in the Southeast. The organization's commitment to continuous improvement is manifest in an applied research-to-practice model that drives all of its work. Building on research, professional wisdom, and craft knowledge, SERVE staff members develop tools, processes, and interventions designed to assist practitioners and policymakers with their work. SERVE's ultimate goal is to raise the level of student achievement in the region. Evaluation of the impact of these activities combined with input from stakeholders expands SERVE's knowledge base and informs future research. This rigorous and practical approach to research and development is supported by an experienced staff strategically located throughout the region. This staff is highly skilled in providing needs assessment services, conducting applied research in schools, and developing processes, products, and programs that support educational improvement and increase student achievement. In the last 3 years, in addition to its basic research and development work with over 170 southeastern schools, SERVE staff provided technical assistance and training to more than 18,000 teachers and administrators across the region. The SERVE Center is governed by a board of directors that includes the governors, chief state school officers, educators, legislators, and private sector leaders from Alabama, Florida, Georgia, Mississippi, North Carolina, and South Carolina. SERVE's operational core is the Regional Educational Laboratory. Funded by the US Department of Educations Institute of Education Sciences, the Regional Educational Laboratory for the Southeast is one of ten Laboratories providing research-based information and services to all 50 states and territories. These Laboratories form a nationwide education knowledge network, building a bank of information and resources shared and disseminated nationally and regionally to improve student achievement. SERVE's National Leadership Area, Expanded Learning Opportunities, focuses on improving student outcomes through the use of exemplary pre–K and extended-day programs.

Membership: None.

Dues: None.

Meetings: None.

Publications: Three titles available in the highlighted products area of Web site: A Review Of Methods and Instruments Used In State and Local School Readiness Evaluations Abstract: This report provides detailed information about the methods and instruments used to evaluate school readiness initiatives, discusses important considerations in selecting instruments, and provides resources and recommendations that may be helpful to those who are designing and implementing school readiness evaluations. Levers for Change: Southeast Region State Initiatives To Improve High Schools Abstract: This descriptive report aims to stimulate discussion about high school reform among Southeast Region states. The report groups recent state activities in high school reform into six "levers for change." To encourage critical reflection, the report places the reform discussion in the context of an evidence-based decisionmaking process and provides sample research on reform activities.

Evidence-Based Decision making: Assessing Reading Across the Curriculum Intervention Abstract: When selecting reading across the curriculum interventions, educators should consider the extent of the evidence base on intervention effectiveness and the fit with the school or district context, whether they are purchasing a product from vendors or developing it internally. This report provides guidance in the decision making.

Name of Organization or Association: Society for Photographic Education.

Acronym: SPE.

Address: 126 Peabody Hall, The School of Interdisciplinary Studies, Miami University, Oxford, OH 45056, USA.

Phone Number: (513)529-8328; **Fax Number**: (513)529-9301.

Email Contact: speoffice@spenational.org; **URL**: www.spenational.org.

Leaders: Richard Gray, Chairperson of SPE Board of Directors.

Description: An association of college and university teachers of photography, museum photographic curators, writers, publishers and students. Promotes discourse in photography education, culture, and art.

Membership: 1,800 membership dues are for the calendar year, January through December.

Dues: Membership Dues: $90—Regular Membership; $50—Student Membership; $600—Corporate Member; $380—Collector Member (with print); $150—Sustaining Member; $65—Senior Member.

Meetings: Denver, CO, March 13–16, 2008.

Publications: Exposure (Photographic Journal)—biannual—Quarterly Newsletter—Membership Directory—Conference Program Guide.

Name of Organization or Association: Society of Cable Telecommunications Engineers.

Acronym: SCTE.

Address: 140 Philips Road, Exton, PA 19341-1318, USA.

Phone Number: (610)363-6888; **Fax Number**: (610)363-5898.

Email Contact: scte@scte.org; **URL**: http://www.scte.org.

Leaders: Mark L, Dzuban, President and CEO.

Description: The Society of Cable Telecommunications Engineers (SCTE) is a nonprofit professional association that provides technical leadership for the telecommunications industry and serves its members through professional development, standards, certification, and information. SCTE currently has more than 14,000 members from the USA and 70 countries worldwide and offers a variety of programs and services for the industry's educational benefit. SCTE has 68 chapters and meeting groups and more than 3,000 employees of the cable telecommunications industry hold SCTE technical certifications. SCTE is an ANSI-accredited standards development organization. Visit SCTE online at www.scte.org.

Membership: SCTE is comprised of a global network of more than 14,000 Broadband engineers, technology experts, industry analysts, technicians, corporate managers, and CEOs who work within the Cable Telecommunications industry. SCTE offers industry professionals a multitude of learning opportunities on the latest technological advances, industry news, and targeted resources to help keep members better informed, outperform their peers, and advance in their careers at a pace that works best for them.

Dues: $68 Individual $350 Expo Partner $34 Full-time Student, Unemployed or Retired (1-year).

Meetings: SCTE Cable-Tec Expo®, Denver, CO, Oct. 28–30, 2009; SCTE Conference on Broadband Learning & Development, Denver, CO, Oct. 27, 2009; SCTE Conference on Emerging Technologies®.

Publications: SCTE Interval SCTE Monthly SCTE NewsBreak Credentials Standards Bulletin.

Name of Organization or Association: Society of Photo Technologists.

Acronym: SPT.

Address: 11112 S. Spotted Road, Cheney, WA 99004, USA.

Phone Number: (800)624-9621 or (509)624-9621; **Fax Number**: (509)624-5320.

Email Contact: cc5@earthlink.net; **URL**: http://www.spt.info/.

Leaders: Chuck Bertone, Executive Director.

Description: An organization of photographic equipment repair technicians, which improves and maintains communications between manufacturers and repair shops and technicians. We publish Repair Journals, Newsletters, Parts & Service Directory, and Industry Newsletters. We also sponsor SPTNET (a technical email group), Remanufactured parts, and residence workshops.

Membership: 1,000 shops and manufactures worldwide, eligible people or businesses are any who are involved full or part time in the camera repair field.

Dues: $125.00–370. Membership depends on the size/volume of the business. Most one man shops are Class A/$195 dues. Those not involved full time in the field is $125.00/Associate Class.

Meetings: SPT Journal; SPT Parts and Services Directory; SPT Newsletter; SPT Manuals—Training and Manufacturer's Tours.

Publications: Journals and Newsletters.

Name of Organization or Association: Southwest Educational Development Laboratory.

Acronym: SEDL.

Address: 211 East Seventh Street, Austin, TX 78701, USA.

Phone Number: (512)476-6861; **Fax Number**: (512)476-2286.

Email Contact: info@sedl.org; **URL**: http://www.sedl.org.

Leaders: Dr Wesley A. Hoover, President and CEO.

Description: The Southwest Educational Development Laboratory (SEDL) is a private, not-for-profit education research and development corporation based in Austin, Texas. SEDL has worked in schools to investigate the conditions under which teachers can provide student-centered instruction supported by technology, particularly computers alone with other software. From that field-based research with teachers, SEDL has developed a professional development model and modules, which resulted in the production of Active Learning with Technology (ALT) portfolio. ALT is a multimedia training program for teachers to learn how to apply student-centered, problem-based learning theory to their instructional strategies that are supported by technologies. Copies of Active Learning with Technology Portfolio and other products used to integrate technology in the classroom can be viewed and ordered online at http://www.sedl.org/pubs/category_technology.html from SEDL's Office of Institutional Communications. SEDL operates the Southeast Comprehensive Center (SECC), funded by the US Department of Education, which provides high-quality technical assistance in the states of Alabama, Georgia, Louisiana, Mississippi, and South Carolina. The goals of the SECC are to build the capacities of states in its region to implement the programs and goals of the No Child Left Behind Act of 2001 (NCLB) and to build states capacity to provide sustained support of high-needs districts and schools. SECC works closely with each state in its region to provide access and use of information, models, and materials that facilitate implementation of and compliance with NCLB. SEDL's Texas Comprehensive Center provides technical assistance and support to the Texas Education Agency to assure Texas has an education system with the capacity and commitment to eliminate achievement gaps and enable all students to achieve at high levels.

Membership: Not applicable.

Dues: Not applicable.

Meetings: Not applicable.

Publications: SEDL Letter and other newsletters and documents are available for free general distribution in print and online. Topic-specific publications related to educational change, education policy, mathematics, language arts, science, and disability research and a publications catalog are available at http://www.sedl.org/pubs on the SEDL Web site.

Name of Organization or Association: Special Libraries Association.

Acronym: SLA.

Address: 331 South Patrick Street, Alexandria, VA 22314, USA.

Phone Number: (703)647-4900; **Fax Number**: (703)647-4901.

Email Contact: sla@sla.org; **URL**: http://www.sla.org.

Leaders: The Honorable Janice R. Lachance, CEO.

Description: The Special Libraries Association (SLA) is a nonprofit global organization for innovative information professionals and their strategic partners. SLA serves more than 11,000 members in 75 countries in the information profession, including corporate, academic, and government information specialists. SLA promotes and strengthens its members through learning, advocacy, and networking initiatives. For more information, visit us on the Web at www.sla.org.

Membership: 11,500.

Dues: Full Membership: US$160.00 (members earning greater than US$35,000 in annual salary); US$99.00 (members earning US$35,000 or less in annual salary). Student/Retired Membership: US$35.00

Meetings: 2006 Annual Conference and Exposition: 11–14 June, Baltimore; 2007 Annual Conference and Exposition: 3–6 June, Denver.

Publications: Information Outlook (monthly glossy magazine that accepts advertising). SLA Connections (monthly electronic newsletter for members and stakeholders).

Name of Organization or Association: Teachers and Writers Collaborative.

Acronym: T&W.

Address: 520 Eighth Avenue, Suite 2020, New York, NY 10018, USA.

Phone Number: (212)691-6590, Toll-free (888)266-5789; **Fax Number**: (212)675-0171.

Email Contact: bmorrow@twc.org; **URL**: http://www.twc.org and http://www.writenet.org.

Leaders: Amy Swauger, Director.

Description: T&W brings the joys and pleasures of reading and writing directly to children. As an advocate for the literary arts and arts education, we support writers and teachers in developing and implementing new teaching strategies; disseminate models for literary arts education to local, national, and international audiences; and showcase both new and established writers via publications and literary events held in our Center for Imaginative Writing. T&W was founded in 1967 by a group of writers and educators who believed that professional writers could make a unique contribution to the teaching of writing and literature. Over the past 40 years, 1,500 T&W writers have taught writing workshops in New York City's public schools. Approximately 700,000 New York City students have participated in our workshops, and we have worked with more than 25,000 teachers. Our wealth of experience, which is reflected in T&W's 80 books about teaching writing, led the National Endowment for the Arts to single out T&W as the arts-in-education group "most familiar with creative writing/literature in primary and secondary schools." The American Book Review has written that T&W "has created a whole new pedagogy in the teaching of English."

Membership: T&W has over 1,000 members across the country. The basic membership is $35; patron membership is $75; and benefactor membership is $150 or more. Members receive a free book or T-shirt; discounts on publications; and a free 1-year subscription to Teachers & Writers magazine (Please see http://www.twc.org/member.htm.).

Dues: T&W is seeking general operating support for all of our programs and program support for specific projects, including: (1) T&W writing residencies in New York City area schools; (2) T&W publications, books and a quarterly magazine, which we distribute across the country; (3) T&W events, including readings for emerging writers and small presses; and (4) T&Ws Internet programs for teachers, writers, and students. Grants to T&Ws Endowment support the stability of the organization and help guarantee the continuation of specific programs.

Meetings: T&W offers year-round public events in our Center for Imaginative Writing in New York City. For a list of events, please see http://www.twc.org/events.htm.

Publications: T&W has published over 80 books on the teaching of imaginative writing, including The T&W Handbook of Poetic Forms; The Dictionary of Wordplay; The Story in History; Personal Fiction Writing; Luna, Luna: Creative Writing from Spanish and Latino Literature; The Nearness of You: Students and Teachers Writing On-Line. To request a free publications catalog, please send email to info@twc.org or call 888-BOOKS-TW (Please see http://www.twc.org/pubs).

Name of Organization or Association: The George Lucas Educational Foundation.

Acronym: GLEF.

Address: PO Box 3494, San Rafael, CA 94912, USA.

Phone Number: (415)662-1600; **Fax Number**: (415)662-1619.

Email Contact: edutopia@glef.org; **URL**: http://edutopia.org.

Leaders: Milton Chen, PhD., Executive Director.

Description: Mission: The George Lucas Educational Foundation (GLEF) is a nonprofit operating foundation that documents and disseminates models of the most innovative practices in our nation's K-12 schools. We serve this mission through the creation of media—from films, books, and magazine to CD-ROMS and DVDs.

GLEF works to provide its products as tools for discussion and action in conferences, workshops, and professional development settings. Audience: A successful educational system requires the collaborative efforts of many different stakeholders. Our audience includes teachers, administrators, school board members, parents, researchers, and business and community leaders who are actively working to improve teaching and learning. Vision: The Edutopian vision is thriving today in our country's best schools: Places where students are engaged and achieving at the highest levels, where skillful educators are energized by the excitement of teaching, where technology brings outside resources and expertise into the classroom, and where parents and community members are partners in educating our youth.

Membership: All online content and the Edutopia magazine are offered free of charge to educators.

Dues: Free subscription to Edutopia magazine for those working in education.

Meetings: No public meetings; advisory council meets annually; board of directors meets quarterly.

Publications: Edutopia Online: The Foundation's Web site, Edutopia (www.edutopia. org) celebrates the unsung heroes who are making Edutopia a reality. All of GLEF's multimedia content dating back to 1997 is available on its Web site. A special feature, the Video Gallery, is an archive of short documentaries and expert interviews that allow visitors to see these innovations in action and hear about them from teachers and students. Detailed articles, research summaries, and links to hundreds of relevant Web sites, books, organizations, and publications are also available to help schools and communities build on successes in education. Edutopia: Success Stories for Learning in the Digital Age: This book and CD-ROM include numerous stories of innovative educators who are using technology to connect with students, colleagues, the local community, and the world beyond. The CD-ROM contains more than an hour of video footage. Published by Jossey-Bass. Teaching in the Digital Age (TDA) Videocassettes. This video series explores elements of successful teaching in the Digital Age. The project grows out of GLEF's belief that an expanded view is needed of all our roles in educating children and supporting teachers. The series explores School Leadership, Emotional Intelligence, Teacher Preparation, and Project-Based Learning and Assessment. Learn & Live. This documentary film and 300-page companion resource book showcases innovative schools across the country. The film, hosted by Robin Williams, aired on public television stations nationwide in 1999 and 2000. The Learn & Live CD-ROM includes digital versions of the film and book in a portable, easy-to-use format. Edutopia Magazine: A free magazine which shares powerful examples of innovative and exemplary learning and teaching. Edutopia Newsletter: This free, semiannual print newsletter includes school profiles, summaries of recent research, and resources and tips for getting involved in public education. Instructional Modules: Free teaching modules developed by education faculty and professional developers. They can be used as extension units in existing courses, or can be used independently in workshops. Includes presenter notes, video segments, and discussion questions. Topics include project-based learning, technology integration, and multiple intelligences.

Name of Organization or Association: The NETWORK, Inc.

Acronym: NETWORK.

Address: 136 Fenno Drive, Rowley, MA 01969-1004, USA.

Phone Number: (800)877-5400, (978)948-7764; **Fax Number**: (978)948-7836.

Email Contact: davidc@thenetworkinc.org; **URL**: www.thenetworkinc.org.

Leaders: David Crandall, President.

Description: A nonprofit research and service organization providing training, research and evaluation, technical assistance, and materials for a fee to schools, educational organizations, and private sector firms with educational interests. The NETWORK has been helping professionals manage and learn about change since 1969. Our Leadership Skills series of computer-based simulations extends the widely used board game versions of Making Change (tm) and Systems Thinking/Systems Changing(tm) with the addition of Improving Student Success: Teachers, Schools, and Parents to offer educators a range of proven professional development tools. Now available, Networking for Learning, originally developed for the British Department for Education and Skills, offers a contemporary leadership development resource for educators exploring the challenges of complex collaborations involving multiple organizations.

Membership: None required.

Dues: No dues, fee for service.

Meetings: Call.

Publications: Making Change: A Simulation Game [board and computer versions]; Systems Thinking/Systems Changing: A Simulation Game [board and computer versions]; Improving Student Success: Teachers, Schools, and Parents [computer based simulation]; Systemic Thinking: Solving Complex Problems; Benchmarking: A Guide for Educators; Networking for Learning; Check Yourself into College: A quick and easy guide for high school students.

Name of Organization or Association: University Continuing Education Association.

Acronym: UCEA.

Address: One Dupont Circle, NW, Suite 615, Washington, DC 20036, USA.

Phone Number: (202)659-3130; **Fax Number**: (202)785-0374.

Email Contact: kjkohl@ucea.edu; **URL**: http://www.ucea.edu/.

Leaders: Kay J. Kohl, Executive Director (kjkohl@ucea.edu).

Description: UCEA is an association of public and private higher education institutions concerned with making continuing education available to all population segments and to promoting excellence in continuing higher education. Many institutional members offer university and college courses via electronic instruction.

Membership: 425 institutions, 2,000 professionals.

Dues: Vary according to membership category; see: http://www.ucea.edu/membership.htm.

Meetings: UCEA has an annual national conference and several professional development seminars throughout the year. See: http://www.ucea.edu/page02.htm.

Publications: Monthly newsletter; quarterly; occasional papers; scholarly journal, Continuing Higher Education Review; Independent Study Catalog. With Peterson's, The Guide to Distance Learning; Guide to Certificate Programs at American Colleges and Universities; UCEA-ACE/Oryx Continuing Higher Education book series; Lifelong Learning Trends (a statistical factbook on continuing higher education); organizational issues series; membership directory.

Name of Organization or Association: Young Adult Library Services Association.

Acronym: YALSA.

Address: 50 E. Huron Street, Chicago, IL 60611, USA.

Phone Number: (312)280-4390; **Fax Number**: (312)280-5276.

Email Contact: yalsa@ala.org; **URL**: http://www.ala.org/yalsa.

Leaders: Beth Yoke, Executive Director; Judy T. Nelson, President.

Description: A division of the American Library Association (ALA), the Young Adult Library Services Association (YALSA) seeks to advocate, promote, and strengthen service to young adults as part of the continuum of total library services. Is responsible within the ALA to evaluate and select books and media and to interpret and make recommendations regarding their use with young adults. Selected List Committees include Best Books for Young Adults, Popular Paperbacks for Young Adults, Quick Picks for Reluctant Young Adult Readers, Outstanding Books for the College Bound, Selected Audiobooks for Young Adults, Great Graphic Novels for Teens, and Selected Films for Young Adults. To learn more about our literary awards, such as the Odyssey Award for best audiobook production, and recommended reading, listening and viewing lists go to www.ala.org/yalsa/booklists. YALSA celebrates Teen Tech Week the first full week of March each year. To learn more go to www.ala.org/teentechweek.

Membership: 5,500. YALSA members may be young adult librarians, school librarians, library directors, graduate students, educators, publishers, or anyone for whom library service to young adults is important.

Dues: $50; $20 students; $20 retirees (in addition to ALA membership).

Meetings: 2 ALA conferences yearly, Midwinter (January) and Annual (June); one biennial Young Adult Literature Symposium (beginning in 2008).

Publications: Young Adult Library Services, a quarterly print journal YAttitudes, a quarterly electronic newsletter for members only.

Part IV
Graduate Programs

Chapter 14
Graduate Programs

Michael Orey

14.1   Introduction

Part five includes annotated entries for graduate programs that offer degrees in the fields of learning, design and technology or library, and information science. In an effort to only list active organizations, I deleted all programs that had not updated their information since 2007. All readers are encouraged to contact the institutions that are not listed for investigation and possible inclusion in the 2013 edition.

Information for this section was obtained through e-mail directing each program to an individual web form through which the updated information could be submitted electronically into a database created by Michael Orey. Although the section editor made every effort to contact and follow up with program representatives, responding to the annual request for an update was the responsibility of the program representatives. The editing team would like to thank those respondents who helped assure the currency and accuracy of this section by responding to the request for an update. In this year's edition, I asked for some data on numbers of graduates, number of faculty, and amount of grants and contracts. These data were used as self-report top 20 lists in the preface to this book. Readers should be aware that these data are only as accurate as the person who filled the form for their program.

M. Orey (✉)
Learning, Design, and Technology Program, The University of Georgia,
Athens, GA, USA
e-mail: mikeorey@uga.edu

M. Orey et al. (eds.), *Educational Media and Technology Yearbook*, Educational
Media and Technology Yearbook 37, DOI 10.1007/978-1-4614-4430-5_14,
© Springer Science+Business Media New York 2013

Chapter 15
Educational Media & Technology Yearbook, 2012, Vol. 37

Organizations and Associations in the USA and Canada

Michael Orey

This information will be used solely to construct a directory of relevant organizations and associations within the *2012 Educational Media & Technology Yearbook*. The data supplied here will **not** be intentionally shared or publicized in any other form. Thank you for your assistance.

Name of Institution: Athabasca University

Name of Department or Program: Centre for Distance Education.

Address: 1 University Drive, Athabasca, AB, Canada T9S 3A3.

Phone Number: 1-780-675-6406; **Fax Number**: 1-780-675-6170.

Email Contact: mohameda@athabascau.ca; **URL**: http://cde.athabascau.ca

Contact Person: Mohamed Ally.

Specializations: Doctor of Education in Distance Education, Master of Distance Education, Graduate Diploma in Distance Education, Technology Graduate Diploma in Instructional Design, Graduate Certificate in Instructional Design

Features: Doctor of Education in Distance Education, Master of Distance Education, Graduate Diploma in Distance Education, Technology Graduate Diploma in Instructional Design, Graduate Certificate in Instructional Design

Admission Requirements: Doctorate of Education in Distance Education Admission requirements for the doctoral program include both academic and experiential elements. *Completion of a masters degree, preferably with a thesis or research project, in a relevant field or area of study (e.g., education or distance education, psychology or educational psychology, instructional technology, adult education, curriculum

M. Orey (✉)
Learning, Design, and Technology Program, The University of Georgia,
Athens, GA, USA
e-mail: mikeorey@uga.edu

M. Orey et al. (eds.), *Educational Media and Technology Yearbook*, Educational
Media and Technology Yearbook 37, DOI 10.1007/978-1-4614-4430-5_15,
© Springer Science+Business Media New York 2013

and instruction, and the like) from a recognized university, normally with a GPA of at least 3.7 or 85% (Graduate Grading Policy); *Significant experience in open or distance learning, which demonstrates that the student is capable of study at a distance, and of completing high quality original research with distance supervision only. Master of Distance Education Applicants to the MDE program must hold a baccalaureate degree from a recognized post-secondary education institution. If the potential applicant does not have a degree, but believes his or her education and experience is equivalent to an undergraduate degree, then it is the responsibility of the applicant to put forward this position in writing as part of the application process. Graduate Diploma in Distance Education Technology Applicants to the GDDET program must hold a baccalaureate degree from a recognized post-secondary education institution. If the potential applicant does not have a degree, but believes that his or her education and experience is equivalent to an undergraduate degree, then it is the responsibility of the applicant to put forward this position in writing as part of the application process. Graduate Diploma in Instructional Design Applicants to the GDID program must hold a baccalaureate degree from a recognized post-secondary education institution. If the potential applicant does not have a degree, but believes that his or her education and experience is equivalent to an undergraduate degree, then it is the responsibility of the applicant to put forward this position in writing as part of the application process. Graduate Certificate in Instructional Design Applicants to the GCID program must hold a baccalaureate degree from a recognized post-secondary education institution. If the potential applicant does not have a degree, but believes that his or her education and experience is equivalent to an undergraduate degree, then it is the responsibility of the applicant to put forward this position in writing as part of the application process.

Degree Requirements: Doctor of Education in Distance Education: The Doctor of Education in Distance Education program will address the needs of a wide range of practitioners, scholars, and researchers who operate in the distance education arena. The doctorate will provide critical direction as distance education evolves and expands. The primary goal of the doctoral program is to provide students with a complete and rigorous preparation to assume senior responsibilities for planning, teaching, directing, designing, implementing, evaluating, researching, and managing distance education programs. Master of Distance Education: Athabasca University's Master of Distance Eduation (MDE) program is designed to provide a common base of skills, knowledge, and values regarding distance education and training, independent of any special area of interest. Graduate Diploma in Distance Education Technology: Athabasca University's Graduate Diploma in Distance Education Technology GDDET is a focused, 18-credit (six courses) program designed to provide a solid grounding in the current principles and practices of technology use in distance education and training. The program structure and course content emphasize the concepts and skills required of practitioners who are employed as instructors, teachers, trainers, decision makers, planners, managers, and administrators in distance education or "virtual" programs. The emphasis of the GDDET is on the user of technology for the preparation, delivery, and management of instruction. Graduate Diploma in

Instructional Design: The Graduate Diploma in Instructional Design is an 18-credit program comprised of six (6) courses. For those who wish to pursue instructional design as a profession, this Diploma program provides more depth and breadth than the certificate. Graduate Certificate in Instructional Design: The Graduate Certificate in Instructional Design is a 9-credit program, comprised of three (3) courses. For those wanting to enhance their instructional design expertise, the Certificate program is an expedient way to obtain the appropriate skills and knowledge.

Number of Full Time Faculty: 11; **Number of Other Faculty**: 15.

Degrees awarded in 2010–2011 Academic Year—Masters: 52; **Ph.D.**: 0; **Other**: 12.

Grant Monies awarded in 2010–2011 Academic Year: 0.

Name of Institution: University of Calgary.

Name of Department or Program: Office of Graduate Programs, Faculty of Education.

Address: Education Tower 940, 2500 University Drive NW, University of Calgary, Calgary, AB, Canada T2N 1N4.

Phone Number: (403)-220-5675; **Fax Number**: (403)-282-3005.

Email Contact: dmjacobs@ucalgary.ca; **URL**: http://ucalgary.ca/gpe/

Contact Person: Dr. Michele Jacobsen.

Specializations: In a knowledge-based economy, the Ph.D., Ed.D., M.A., and M. Ed. programs in the Educational Technology specialization in Educational Research at the University of Calgary have proven valuable to public and private sector researchers, post-secondary faculty, school teachers and school leaders, military/industrial trainers, health educators, instructional designers, managers, and leaders. A spectrum of entrepreneurs and educational experts have successfully completed our graduate programs in educational technology and are using their research, knowledge, and competencies in schools, in higher education, and a range of corporate and private workplaces today. Our graduates have careers as practitioners and scholars in the top government, industry, K-12, and higher education institutions as professors, education and training leaders, teachers, and instructors—worldwide. Your academic and professional career growth is possible through our innovative, student-centered programs and supervision processes in this growing, vibrant area. Degree programs can be completed on campus, in blended formats or completely online.

Features: The Educational Technology Specialization is interdisciplinary and is addressed to at least two audiences: (a) Post-secondary teachers and leaders, and school leaders and classroom teachers who are interested in the study and practice of educational technology to facilitate learning or who are interested in technology leadership positions or who are interested in academic careers in higher education; (b) Those who are interested in instructional design and development in settings both within and outside elementary/secondary/tertiary schools, e.g., instructional developers and faculty developers in colleges, institutes of technology and universities, military/industrial trainers, health educators, and private training consultants. Graduate students in the educational technology specialization have the opportunity to investigate a broad spectrum of knowledge building, participatory cultures, instructional design, and development theories and practices as they apply to current and emergent technologies and to explore new directions in instructional design and development and evaluation as they emerge in the literature and in practice.

Admission Requirements: The Master of Education (M.Ed.) is a course-based professional degree. The M.Ed. program is available in online formats. Admission requirements normally include a completed 4-year bachelor's degree and a 3.0 GPA. The Master of Arts (M.A.) is a thesis-based degree with a residency requirement that is intended to prepare students for further research. Admission requirements normally include a completed 4-year bachelor's degree and a 3.3 GPA. The Doctor of Education (Ed.D.) is a thesis-based degree intended to prepare scholars of the profession for careers in leadership and teaching. The Ed.D. program is available in the online format. Admission requirements normally include a completed Masters Degree and a 3.5 GPA. The Doctor of Philosophy (Ph.D.) is a thesis-based degree with a residency requirement intended to prepare scholars of the discipline for careers in research and teaching. The Ph.D. program is available for full-time, on-campus engagement in apprenticeship. Admission requirements normally include a completed Masters Thesis and a 3.5 GPA.

Degree Requirements: Program requirements for the Master of Education (M.Ed.) program are completion of a minimum of six full-course equivalents (12 half-courses). In Educational Technology, master of education students complete 7 half-courses in the specialization of educational technology and 5 half-courses in educational research methodology and action research. The Master of Education cohort-based degree consists of a total of 36 credits (12 half-courses). Graduate students are required to complete their courses in a prescribed sequence. Students are expected to complete all program requirements within 2 years. Program requirements for the Master of Arts (M.A.) thesis program include: (a) One full-course equivalent (two half-courses) in research methods; (b) A minimum of one full-course equivalent (two half-courses) in the students area of specialization; (c) Additional graduate courses or seminars are determined by the supervisor in consultation with the student; (d) A Masters thesis and an oral examination on the thesis. The Education Doctorate (Ed.D.) in Educational Technology is a 3-year cohort-based program consisting of: (a) Course work, (b) Candidacy examination, (c) Dissertation Year 1: is designed primarily to develop students' competencies as "critical consumers of educational research" and skills to conduct practitioner-inquiry. As outlined within the program to which the student has applied, first year students must complete: (a) two half-courses in research: EDER 701.06, and either EDER 701.07 or EDER 701.08, (b) two half-courses in the students specialization area Year 2 is designed to engage students in an in-depth analysis of an identified problem of practice through diverse academic disciplines (e.g., leadership, adult learning, etc.). Specialization coursework exposes students to context specific best practices and cutting edge research and emphasizes the application of theory and research to practice within collaboratories of practice. As outlined within the program to which the student has applied, students must complete: (a) two half-courses in the students specialization area, (b) two specialization collaboratories of practice half-courses, (c) comprehensive candidacy examination Year 3 is designed to support students in synthesizing their Year 2 inquiry projects into a dissertation. Students work collaboratively with faculty and practitioners from their field to complete a dissertation that addresses a contemporary issue in education. As outlined within the program to which the student has applied, students must complete: (a) Dissertation Seminar I, (b) Dissertation Seminar II, (c) Doctoral Dissertation Program requirements for the on campus Doctor of Philosophy (Ph.D.) program include: (a) Three 600- or 700-level half-courses in research methods. (b) In addition, Ph.D. students in the Educational Technology specialization are required to complete EDER 771 and two half-courses at the 700 level in technology. (c) Candidacy examination (d) Dissertation.

Number of Full Time Faculty: 8; **Number of Other Faculty**: 72.

Degrees awarded in 2010–2011 Academic Year—Masters: 250; **Ph.D.**: 15; **Other**: 15.

Grant Monies awarded in 2010–2011 Academic Year: 20,000,000

Name of Institution: University of British Columbia

Name of Department or Program: Master of Educational Technology degree program.

Address: 1304-2125 Main Mall, Vancouver, BC, Canada V6T 1Z4.

Phone Number: 1-888-492-1122; **Fax Number**: 1-604-822-2015.

Email Contact: info@met.ubc.ca; **URL**: http://met.ubc.ca.

Contact Person: David Roy.

Specializations: This innovative online program provides an excellent environment to learn the techniques of instructional design including the development and management of programs for international and intercultural populations. Attracting students from more than 30 countries, the program provides a unique opportunity to learn and collaborate with professionals and colleagues from around the world. The MET curriculum is designed for K-12 teachers, college and university faculty, course designers, adult, and industry educators.

Features: MET fully online graduate degree. MET Graduate Certificate in Technology-Based Distributed Learning. MET Graduate Certificate in Technology-Based Learning for Schools.

Admission Requirements: Please see website.

Degree Requirements: Masters Program: 10 courses; Graduate Certificates: 5 courses.

Number of Full Time Faculty: 9; **Number of Other Faculty**: 8.

Degrees awarded in 2010–2011 Academic Year — **Masters**: 36; **Ph.D.**: 0; **Other**: 0.

Grant Monies awarded in 2010–2011 Academic Year: 0.

Name of Institution: University of New Brunswick.

Name of Department or Program: Faculty of Education.

Address: PO Box 4400, Fredericton, NB, Canada E3B 5A3.

Phone Number: (506)-452-6125; **Fax Number**: (506)-453-3569.

Email Contact: erose@unb.ca; **URL**: http://www.unbf.ca/education/

Contact Person: Dr. Ellen Rose

Specializations: Courses are offered in instructional design theories and processes, cultural studies in instructional design, instructional design processes, needs assessment, designing constructivist learning environments, instructional message design, and instructional design for online learning. In addition, students are allowed to take other courses in the Faculty of Education or other applicable areas.

Features: Students can choose the course, project, or thesis stream. UNB's M.Ed. in Instructional Design is very flexible, allowing students to customize their own learning experiences in order to meet their particular learning outcomes. While this is not an online program, several of the Instructional Design courses, and many other relevant courses in the Faculty of Education, are available online.

Admission Requirements: Applicants must have an undergraduate degree in Education or a relevant field, a grade point average of at least 3.0 (B, or its equivalent), and at least 1 year of teaching or related professional experience. Applicants whose first language is not English must submit evidence of their proficiency in the use of the English language. The minimum proficiency levels accepted by the Faculty of Education are scores of 650 on the TOEFL (280 computer-based) and 5.5 on the TWE.

Degree Requirements: Course route: ten 3-credit hour courses Project route: eight 3-credit hour courses and one project/report Thesis route: five 3-credit hour courses and one thesis Required courses: ED 6221 Instructional Design Theories and ED 6902 Introduction to Research in Education.

Number of Full Time Faculty: 1; **Number of Other Faculty**: 2.

Degrees awarded in 2010–2011 Academic Year—Masters: 10; **Ph.D.**: 0; **Other**: 0.

Grant Monies awarded in 2010–2011 Academic Year: 0.

Name of Institution: Concordia University

Name of Department or Program: Education — M.A. in Educational Technology, Diploma in Instructional Technology and Ph.D. (Education), Specialization, Educational Technology.

Address: 1455 de Maisonneuve Boulevard, West, Montreal, QC, Canada H3G 1M8.

Phone Number: (514)848-2424-x2030; **Fax Number**: (514)848-4520.

Email Contact: anne@education.concordia.ca; **URL**: education.concordia.ca.

Contact Person: Ms. Anne Brown-MacDougall, Programs Coordinator.

Specializations: Concordias Department of Education offers a 30-credit graduate Diploma in Instructional Technology, an M.A. in Educational Technology and our Ph.D. in Education has a specialization in the area of Educational Technology as well. Main areas within the programs: Human Performance Technology, Distance Education, Interactive Multi-Media Applications, -Cybernetics, Administration and Project Management plus many other areas.

Features: Only graduate program in Quebec in this area.

Admission Requirements: For the M.A. program: Applicants must have a GPA or 3.0 or higher from a variety of undergraduate disciplines. References, official transcripts, CV, and statement of purpose also required. For the Diploma program: Applicants must have a GPA of 2.7 or higher from a variety of undergraduate disciplines. References, official transcripts, CV, and statement of purpose also required. For students, for the Ph.D. (Education): Applicants must have a GPA of 3.0 in a master's degree, preferably in the field of educational technology, but related disciplines are also acceptable. References, official transcripts, CV, and statement of purpose.

Degree Requirements: The Ph.D. (Education) is 90-credit program, which includes required courses, tutorials, plus comprehensive examination, dissertation proposal, and dissertation. The M.A. program is 60 credits which includes required courses, electives plus either an internship experience and a report or a small internship, thesis proposal, and thesis. The Diploma consists of 30 credits of course work only.

Number of Full Time Faculty: 9; **Number of Other Faculty**: 40.

Degrees awarded in 2010–2011 Academic Year—Masters: 25; **Ph.D.**: 5; **Other**: 5.

Grant Monies awarded in 2010–2011 Academic Year: 100,000.

Name of Institution: University of Saskatchewan.

Name of Department or Program: Educational Technology and Design.

Address: 28 Campus Drive, College of Education, Saskatoon, SK, Canada S7N 0X1.

Phone Number: (306)-966-7558; **Fax Number**: (306)-966-7658.

Email Contact: richard.schwier@usask.ca; **URL**: http://www.edct.ca.

Contact Person: Richard A. Schwier.

Specializations: We offer a general educational technology degree, but with a particular emphasis on instructional design in all coursework.

Features: Almost all of our courses are delivered in flexible formats. Courses can be taken completely online or blended with classroom experiences. A few courses are only offered face-to-face, but an entire program can be taken online. Many of our courses emphasize authentic learning options, where students work on projects with clients.

Admission Requirements: A professional Bachelors degree or the equivalent of a 4-year Bachelor of Arts. Normally, we require a minimum of 1 year of practical experience in education or a related field. An average of 70% in your most recent 60 credit units of university coursework.

Degree Requirements: M.Ed. (course-based) students need to complete 30 credit units of graduate level coursework for the degree. M.Ed. (project) students require 24 credit units of graduate level coursework and the project seminar (ETAD 992.6) supervised by a faculty member in the program. M.Ed. (thesis) students need to complete 21 units of graduate level coursework and a thesis supervised by a faculty member in the program and a committee.

Number of Full Time Faculty: 4; **Number of Other Faculty**: 2.

Degrees awarded in 2010–2011 Academic Year—Masters: 20; **Ph.D.**: 0; **Other**: 0.

Grant Monies awarded in 2010–2011 Academic Year: 225,000.

Name of Institution: The University of Hong Kong.

Name of Department or Program: Faculty of Education.

Address: Pokfulam Road, Hong Kong, China.

Phone Number: (852)-2241-5856; **Fax Number**: (852)-2517-0075.

Email Contact: mite@cite.hku.hk; **URL**: http://web.edu.hku.hk/programme/mite/

Contact Person: Dr. Mark King.

Specializations: The Master of Science in Information Technology in Education [MSc(ITE)] program offers the following four specialist strands: E-leadership, E-learning, and Learning technology design.

Features: The program aims to provide: an investigation into Web2.0, mobile learning and other emerging learning and teaching technology applications—an opportunity to apply technology in learning and teaching—an opportunity to work in technology-rich learning environment—an exploration of the cultural, administrative theoretical, and practical implications of technology in education—an introduction to research in technology for education—an opportunity for those wishing to develop leadership capabilities in the use of technology in education.

Admission Requirements: Applicants should normally hold a recognized Bachelor's Degree or qualifications of equivalent standard. Applicants may be required to sit for a qualifying examination.

Degree Requirements: To complete the following modules in 1 year full-time study or no more than 4 years of part-time studies: 3 core modules, 2 modules from a specialist strand plus either of the following: 1 Independent project and 2 elective modules; or 1 Dissertation.

Number of Full Time Faculty: 20; **Number of Other Faculty**: 90.

Degrees awarded in 2010–2011 Academic Year—Masters: 0; **Ph.D.**: 0; **Other**: 0.

Grant Monies awarded in 2010–2011 Academic Year: 0.

Name of Institution: Université de Poitiers.

Name of Department or Program: Ingénierie des médias pour léducation.

Address: UFR Lettres et Langues, Bâtiment A3, 1 rue Raymond Cantel, Poitiers, PC 86000, France.

Phone Number: +33 5 49 36 62 06; **Fax Number**: /

Email Contact: cerisier@univ-poitiers.fr; **URL**: http://ll.univ-poitiers.fr/dime/

Contact Person: Jean-François Cerisier.

Specializations: EUROMIME: European Master in Media Engineering for Education (Erasmus Mundus master). It trains project managers in the field of design, development, and implementation of educational and training programs resorting to computer mediated environments. It also trains researchers specializing the study of the use of these technologies. The master, which gives right to continuing to doctoral studies, prepares students to work in various settings such as business firms, government agencies as well as universities. Many of the graduate students work in public or private settings involved in projects related to distance education. MIME: national Master in Media Engineering for Education.

Features: The Euromime consortium is composed of seven universities, three in south-west Europe (Université de Poitiers—France; Universidad Nacional de Educación a Distancia, Madrid—España; Universidade Técnica de Lisboa—Portugal), and four in Latin America (Universidad de Los Lagos, Osorno—Chile; Pontificia Universidad Católica del Perú, Lima; Universidade de Brasilia—Brasil; Universidad Nacional Autónoma de México—México). More information: http://www.euromime.org/en/home.

Admission Requirements: application and interview.

Degree Requirements: Bachelors degree.

Number of Full Time Faculty: 25; **Number of Other Faculty**: 25.

Degrees Awarded in 2010–2011 Academic Year—Masters: 30; **Ph.D.**: 0; **Other**: 0.

Grant Monies awarded in 2010–2011 Academic Year: 1,000,000.

Name of Institution: Ewha Womans University.

Name of Department or Program: Educational Technology Department.

Address: 11-1 Daehyun-dong, Seodaemun-ku, Seoul, KO 120-750, Korea.

Phone Number: 82-2-3277-2671; **Fax Number**: 82-2-3277-2728.

Email Contact: et2670@hanmail.net; **URL**: http://home.ewha.ac.kr/~et.

Contact Person: Department Chair, Myunghee Kang.

Specializations: Theory & Practice of Instructional Technology e-Leaning Design and Development, Quality Assurance HRD/HPT Program development.

Features: Undergraduate Masters Program, Ph.D. Program Special Masters, Program for In-Service Teachers.

Admission Requirements: Portfolio Interview English Competency.

Degree Requirements: 24 credit hours of coursework for Masters; 60 credit hours of coursework for Ph.D and Qualifying Exam Dissertation.

Number of Full Time Faculty: 8; **Number of Other Faculty**: 2.

Degrees awarded in 2010–2011 Academic Year—Masters: 6; **Ph.D.**: 4; **Other**: 0.

Grant Monies awarded in 2010–2011 Academic Year: 2,000,000.

Name of Institution: Andong National University.

Name of Department or Program: Department of Educational Technology, College of Education.

Address: 388 Songchun-dong, Andong, Kyungbuk 760-749, Korea.

Phone Number: +82-54-820-5580, 5585; **Fax Number**: +82-54-820-7653.

Email Contact: ycyang@andong.ac.kr; **URL**: http://edutech.andong.ac.kr/~try/2009-10/main1.html.

Contact Person: Dr. Yong-Chil Yang.

Specializations: Instruction Systems Design and e-HRD major for Master Degree Educational Technology major for Ph.D.

Features: *Only Department supported by Ministry of Education in Korea, *B.A., M.A., and Ph.D. programs are offered, *Established in 1996, *Inexpensive tuition and living expenses, *Small class size.

Admission Requirements: Fluent commanding English or Korean language.

Degree Requirements: B.A. degree for Master M.A. degree in Education for Ph.D.

Number of Full Time Faculty: 5; **Number of Other Faculty**: 9.

Degrees awarded in 2010–2011 Academic Year—Masters: 8; **Ph.D.**: 2; **Other**: 11.

Grant Monies awarded in 2010–2011 Academic Year: 35,000.

Name of Institution: Universiti Sains Malaysia.

Name of Department or Program: Centre for Instructional Technology and Multimedia.

Address: Centre for Instructional Tech and Multimedia, Universiti Sains Malaysia, 11800 Minden, Penang, Malaysia.

Phone Number: 604-6533222; **Fax Number**: 604-6576749.

Email Contact: Fauzy@usm.my; **URL**: http://www.ptpm.usm.my.

Contact Person: Associate Professor Wan Mohd. Fauzy Wan Ismail, Director.

Specializations: Instructional Design Web/Internet Instruction and Learning Educational Training/Resource Management Instructional Training Technology/ Evaluation Instructional System Development Design and Development of Multimeida/Video/Training materials Instructional and Training Technology Constructivism in Instructional Technology E-Learning Systems, Learning Management Systems.

Features: Masters in Instructional Technology: entering its third academic year 2004–2005: Full-time: 1–2 years, Part-time: 2–4 years. Teaching Programs: Post Graduate programs and research Consultancy: services on the application of Educational/Instructional Design technology in teaching and learning Training and Diffusion, Continuing Education in support of Life Long Learning Academic Support Services: services to support research, teaching, and learning activities and centers within the University.

Admission Requirements: Bachelors and Masters degree from accredited institution or relevant work experience.

Degree Requirements: Part-time, Full-time.

Number of Full Time Faculty: –; **Number of Other Faculty**: –.

Degrees awarded in 2010–2011 Academic Year—Masters: –; **Ph.D.**: –; **Other**: –

Grant Monies awarded in 2010–2011 Academic Year: –.

Name of Institution: Taganrog State Pedagogical Institute.

Name of Department or Program: Media Education (Social Pedagogic Faculty).

Address: Iniciativnaya, 48 Taganrog, 347936 Russia.

Phone Number: (8634)601753; **Fax Number**: (8634)605397.

Email Contact: tgpi@mail.ru; **URL**: http://www.tgpi.ru.

Contact Person: Professor Dr. Alexander Fedorov.

Specializations: Media Education, Media Literacy, and Media Competence.

Admission Requirements: Varies per year, please see http://www.tgpi.ru.

Degree Requirements: admission after high school.

Number of Full Time Faculty: 10; **Number of Other Faculty**: 20.

Degrees awarded in 2010–2011 Academic Year—Masters: 0; **Ph.D.**: 1; **Other**: 25.

Grant Monies awarded in 2010–2011 Academic Year: 150,000.

Name of Institution: Keimyung University.

Name of Department or Program: Department of Education.

Address: 2800 Dalgubeldaro, Dalseogu, Daegu 704-701, South Korea.

Phone Number: 82-53-580-5962.

Email Contact: weom@kmu.ac.kr.

Contact Person: Wooyong Eom.

Number of Full Time Faculty: 9; **Number of Other Faculty**: 0.

Degrees awarded in 2010–2011 Academic Year—Masters: 2; **Ph.D.**: 1; **Other**: 0.

Grant Monies awarded in 2010–2011 Academic Year: 0.

Name of Institution: University of Balearic Islands.

Name of Department or Program: Sciences of Education.

Address: Ctra. Valldemossa km 7, 5 Palma de Mallorca, IB 07010, Spain.

Phone Number: 34 071173000; **Fax Number**: 34 971173190.

Email Contact: jesus.salinas@uib.es; **URL**: http://www.uib.es.

Contact Person: Dr. Jesus Salinas.

Specializations: Doctorado Interuniversitario de Tecnología Educativa [Interuniversity Doctorate of Educational Technology]. University of Sevilla, University of Murcia, University of Balearic Islands and Rovira i Virgili Universitity: Master en Tecnología Educativa. E-learning y gestión del conocimiento. [Master in Educational Technology. E-learning and knowledge management]. University of Balearic Islands and Universitat Rovira i Virgili—Especialista Universitario en Tecnología Educativa. Diseño y elaboración de medios didácticos multimedia. [Specialist in Educational Technology. Design and development of didactic multimedia environments]. "Curso de Dirección y gestión pedagógica de entornos virtuales". [Course of direction and pedagogical management of virtual environments]. University of Balearic Islands, Rovira I Virgili University, University of Sevilla, University Central of Venezuela, University of Panamá, Higher Institute Polytechnic Jose Antonio Echevarria.

Number of Full Time Faculty: 6; **Number of Other Faculty**: 9.

Degrees awarded in 2010–2011 Academic Year—Masters: 12; **Ph.D.**: 6; **Other**: 28.

Grant Monies awarded in 2010–2011 Academic Year: 0.

Name of Institution: University of Geneva.

Name of Department or Program: TECFA–Master of Science in Learning and Teaching Technologies.

Address: Bat. Pignon, 40 bd du Pont dArve, Geneva, GE 1205, Switzerland.

Phone Number: 41-22-379-93-75; **Fax Number**: 41-22-379-93-79.

Email Contact: Daniel.Peraya@unige.ch; **URL**: http://tecfa.unige.ch http://tecfa-sun7.unige.ch/maltt/

Contact Person: Professor Dr. Daniel Peraya.

Specializations: Basics in information and communication technologies. Design of computer-supported learning technology Mediated Communication and e-learning User-centered design and ergonomics. Research methods in educational technologies. Blended education (face-to-face sessions alternately with tutored distance periods): 120 ECTS, 2-year program. Learning approach: mostly project-based, with authentic project design and collaborative work French language.

Features: http://edutechwiki.unige.ch/en/Main_Page.

Admission Requirements: Applicants should qualify to be admitted in master program at the University of Geneva. For more information, see http://tecfaetu.unige.ch/maltt/staf.php3?id_article=27.

Degree Requirements: Bachelor degree Training or experience in training, education or psychology.

Number of Full Time Faculty: 4; **Number of Other Faculty**: 1.

Degrees awarded in 2010–2011 Academic Year—Masters: 10; **Ph.D.**: 2; **Other**: 5.

Grant Monies awarded in 2010–2011 Academic Year: 500,000.

Name of Institution: Università della Svizzera italiana.

Name of Department or Program: New Media in Education Laboratory & RED-INK doctoral school.

Address: via Buffi 13, Lugano, TI 6900, Switzerland.

Phone Number: +41586664674; **Fax Number**: +41586664647.

Email Contact: luca.botturi@lu.unisi.ch; **URL**: www.newmine.org.

Contact Person: Lorenzo Cantoni, Professor and Luca Botturi, Ph.D.

Specializations: –.

Features: RED-INK is a doctoral school whose name stands for "Rethinking Education in the Knowledge Society." It strives to understand the complex issues related to the introduction, management, and impact of educational technologies and eLearning in the perspective of the new context of the knowledge society. To this purpose, RED-INK federates three Swiss universities in order to establish an outstanding multidisciplinary research team at National level, with expected international visibility and impact. The RED-INK doctoral school is funded by the pro*doc program of the Swiss National Research Fund, started in 2008 and will award its first doctoral degrees in 2010.

Admission Requirements: Completed master's degree in educational technology or related field.

Degree Requirements: x.

Number of Full Time Faculty: 3; **Number of Other Faculty**: 0.

Degrees awarded in 2010–2011 Academic Year—Masters: 0; **Ph.D.**: 0; **Other**: 0.

Grant Monies awarded in 2010–2011 Academic Year: 0.

Name of Institution: Utrecht University.

Name of Department or Program: Educational Sciences.

Address: Heidelberglaan 1, Utrecht, 3581RW, The Netherlands.

Phone Number: +31302534786; **Fax Number**: +31302534300.

Email Contact: m.brekelmans@uu.nl; **URL**: http://www.uu.nl/NL/Informatie/master/edsci/Pages/study.aspx.

Contact Person: Mieke Brekelmans, Ph.D.

Specializations: The 2-year (120 EC) program concentrates on the theory, use, and effects of innovative teaching and learning arrangements aimed at meaningful, enjoyable learning through the application of different theories, paradigms, and media. Research projects use both experimental design-based, and longitudinal approaches and combine qualitative and quantitative analyses of interaction processes and learning products in different teaching and/or learning environments.

Features: The program combines high-level coursework with hands-on research skill and competence development. Students take courses on various theories of learning, instruction, and teaching, and are trained in advanced research techniques and statistical methods to study the design and effectiveness of innovative teaching and learning arrangements. Research seminars help students develop their academic skills. Participation in a senior faculty member's research project introduces each student to "hands-on" research. Throughout the program, various electronic learning environments are used to support students in their collaborative study assignments, and to allow them to experiment with these innovative learning and instruction tools. The program offers a systematic theoretical and empirical analysis of educational phenomena and problems. It emphasizes three goals. Helping students develop: (1) A strong foundation in research and in theories of learning, instruction, and teaching.

(2) Competence in conducting high-quality educational research. (3) Capacities and skills to apply basic knowledge and specific research methods from various domains to the study of learning in interaction in education. The program concludes with writing a Master's thesis in the form of a draft research article for international publication.

Admission Requirements: Applicants should hold a B.A. or B.Sc. in one of the relevant social or behavioral sciences (such as education, psychology, cognitive science, informatics, artificial intelligence) or in a domain relevant to teaching in schools (e.g., math, science, linguistics, history). It is required of applicants to have successfully completed several undergraduate courses on statistics in order to have a basic knowledge of multivariate analysis at the beginning of their first semester. There is a summer school for students who do not meet this requirement. Students meeting the above criteria who have a GPA of at least 2.85 (Dutch equivalent: 7.0) are encouraged to apply for admission. Students will be selected on the basis of their Grade Point Average (GPA), an essay on their motivation and their recommendations; in some cases, an intake interview will also be conducted. All courses are taught in English; therefore, all students are required to provide proof of their English language proficiency. Examples of accepted minimum English language test scores: TOEFL paper: 580 TOEFL, computer: 237 TOEFL, Internet: 93.

Degree Requirements: Completion of all courses and thesis.

Number of Full Time Faculty: 12; **Number of Other Faculty**: 7.

Degrees awarded in 2010–2011 Academic Year—Masters: 100; **Ph.D.**: 5; **Other**: 0.

Grant Monies awarded in 2010–2011 Academic Year: 150,000.

Name of Institution: Middle East Technical University.

Name of Department or Program: Computer Education & Instructional Technology.

Address: Inonu Bulvari, Ankara, Cankaya 06800, Turkey.

Phone Number: +90-3122104193; **Fax Number**: +90-3122107986.

Email Contact: myozden@metu.edu.tr; **URL**: http://www.ceit.metu.edu.tr.

Contact Person: M. Yasar Ozden.

Specializations: Computer education, instructional technology.

Features: x.

Admission Requirements: x.

Degree Requirements: x.

Number of Full Time Faculty: 20; **Number of Other Faculty**: 40.

Degrees awarded in 2010–2011 Academic Year—Masters: 5; **Ph.D.**: 10; **Other**: 0.

Grant Monies awarded in 2010–2011 Academic Year: 0.

Name of Institution: Hacettepe University.

Name of Department or Program: Computer Education and Instructional Technology.

Address: Faculty of Education, Hacettepe University, Beytepe, Ankara 06800, Turkey.

Phone Number: +90-312-2977176; **Fax Number**: +90-312-2977176.

Email Contact: altunar@hacettepe.edu.tr; **URL**: http://www.ebit.hacettepe.edu.tr/

Contact Person: Arif Altun.

Specializations: The CEIT department has been established in 1998. Innovations and improvements in technology have changed so many things in people's life. There have been huge improvements in terms of diffusion of information. Computers continue to make an ever increasing impact on all aspects of education from primary school to university and in the growing areas of open and distance learning. In addition, the knowledge and skills related to computers have become essential for everybody in the information age. However, at all levels in society, there is a huge need for qualified personnel equipped with the skills that help them to be successful in their personal and professional life. The department aims to train students (prospective teachers) who would teach computer courses in K-12 institutions. It also provides individuals with professional skills in the development, organization, and application of resources for the solution of instructional problems within schools.

Features: The department has MS and Ph.D. programs. The research areas are: Learning objects and ontologies, diffusion of innovation, computerized testing, e-learning environments, design, development, and assessment.

Admission Requirements: B.S. in education or computer related fields.

Degree Requirements: B.S.

Number of Full Time Faculty: 10; **Number of Other Faculty**: 12.

Degrees awarded in 2010–2011 Academic Year—Masters: 16; **Ph.D.**: 4; **Other**: 0.

Grant Monies awarded in 2010–2011 Academic Year: 0.

Name of Institution: Anadolu University.

Name of Department or Program: Computer Education and Instructional Technology.

Address: Faculty of Education, Eskisehir, 26470 Turkey.

Phone Number: 00902223350580/3519; **Fax Number**: 00902223350579.

Email Contact: fodabasi@anadolu.edu.tr; **URL**: http://www.anadolu.edu.tr/akademik/fak_egt/bilgveogrttekegt/eindex.htm.

Contact Person: Professor Dr. H. Ferhan Odabasi.

Specializations: The basic aim of the department is to equip students, with up-to-date knowledge about computer and other information technologies, required for K-12 computer teachers. Graduated students of the department can be employed in public or private schools of The Ministry of National Education, as teachers, instructional technologists, or academicians in the universities. The department offers Bachelor, Master, and Doctorate programs. Both department staff and students collaborate with international schools in terms of teaching and research through exchange programs. Some of the themes, having been studied by academic staff of the department, are: computer assisted instruction, computer assisted language instruction, educational technology, computer use in education and school systems, effects of technology on individuals, computer anxiety, industrial design, using Internet in education, instructional design, instructional software design, statistics, professional development, ICT action competence, technology integration into education, technology integration into special education, safe internet use, cyber-bullying and digital story telling, and mobile learning.

Features: Computer Education and Instructional Technologies Department has two computer labs. Technical properties of the computers in both of the labs are up to date. In addition, students can use the main library which is around 100 m to department building. Students may reach many books and journals about computers and instructional technologies, and have access to various data bases and electronic journals. There is a nonsmoking cafeteria for students in the faculty building where they can find snacks, sandwiches, hot and cold drinks. There is also a small room for the smokers. There is a main student cafeteria for students on the campus. There are also fast food restaurants on the campus.

Admission Requirements: High School Diploma plus required scores from the Student Selection Examination administered by Student Selection and Placement Centre and successful completion of qualification examinations. For foreign students, High School Diploma plus required scores from the Foreign Student Examination and successful completion of qualification examinations. Associate Degree plus placement by Student Selection and Placement Centre according to the score obtained in the Student Selection Examination and the students preferences. In addition, may apply to masters or doctorate programs in any field or proficiency in fine art programs. May apply to bachelor's degree completion programs in related fields of study in Distance Education System.

Degree Requirements: For bachelor degree, students are selected by Student Selection and Placement Center according to the students' scores in the Student Selection Exam. About 50 students are admitted to the department each year. The duration of the program is 4 years. Students must pass all courses and obtain a minimum GPA (Grade Point Average) of 2.00 before they can graduate. The official language of instruction is Turkish. Students who want to learn English can attend a 1-year English preparatory school before taking the department courses. The students are required to take courses and prepare and defend a thesis based on their research. It takes approximately 2 years to complete the Master degree.

The doctorate degree requires course work and research. The students will conduct original research and prepare a dissertation, and then make an oral defense of their completed research. Students require about 4 years beyond the Masters degree to complete a doctorate program.

Number of Full Time Faculty: 12; **Number of Other Faculty**: 9.

Degrees awarded in 2010–2011 Academic Year—Masters: 0; **Ph.D.**: 5; **Other**: 0.

Grant Monies awarded in 2010–2011 Academic Year: 157,592.

Name of Institution: University of Manchester.

Name of Department or Program: M.A.: Digital Technologies, Communication and Education.

Address: LTA, School of Education, Ellen Wilkinson Building, Oxford Road, Manchester M13 9PL, UK.

Phone Number: +44-161-275-7843; **Fax Number**: +44-161-275-3484.

Email Contact: andrew.whitworth@manchester.ac.uk; **URL**: http://www.MAdigitaltechnologies.com.

Contact Person: Dr. Andrew Whitworth.

Specializations: Educators from any sector are catered for by the program: that is, primary, secondary (K-12), tertiary/higher education, adult education, corporate training, home educators, private tutors, and so on.

Features: The goals of this program are to promote the use of digital technologies, the broadcast media, and/or interpersonal, group or organizational communication techniques to enhance practice, and the professional and academic development of educators in technology-rich environments. There is, therefore, a particular focus on professional development techniques, enquiry-based and problem-based learning, and transformations of practice as well as work with practical EMT techniques (such as web design, Flash, and video production). Students will study the history of educational media and technology, and its impact on the organization and management of education as well as on pedagogy. The course is available to study in both face-to-face and distance modes.

Admission Requirements: A first degree to at least a 2:2 (UK degree classification) or equivalent. IELTS score of at least 6.5 and preferably 7.0, or 600 in TOEFL. Teaching experience is desirable, though not mandatory.

Degree Requirements: x.

Number of Full Time Faculty: 2; **Number of Other Faculty**: 3.

Degrees awarded in 2010–2011 Academic Year—Masters: 20; **Ph.D.**: 0; **Other**: 0.

Grant Monies awarded in 2010–2011 Academic Year: 0.

Name of Institution: The Ohio State University.

Name of Department or Program: Cultural Foundations, Technology, & Qualitative Inquiry.

Address: 29 W Woodruff Drive, Columbus, OH 43210, USA.

Phone Number: (614)688-4007.

Email Contact: voithofer.2@osu.edu; **URL**: http://ehe.osu.edu/epl/academics/ cftqi/technology.cfm.

Contact Person: Rick Voithofer.

Specializations: The Technology area in CFTQI offers both M.A. and Ph.D. degrees. This interdisciplinary educational technology program focuses on intersections of learning, technology, and culture in formal and informal education and in society at large. Some of the settings addressed in the program include K-12 environments, distance education, e-learning, online education, higher education, urban education, private and non-profit organizations, museums, and community-based organizations and programs. Students in the program are exposed to a variety of technologies and media including educational multimedia, computer-based instruction, pod/video casts, blogs and wikis, educational games, web-based instruction, video, and electronic portfolios. Recent areas of focus studied by faculty and students include: Educational technology, digital divides, and diverse populations; Implications of Web 2.0 technologies for education; Education and globalization; Online educational research; Education Policy and Technology; Visual Culture and Visual Media; Multiliteracies, learning, and technology; Games and Simulations Technology, virtuality, and student identities; Students in this area integrate theoretical and practical studies of technologies and media through pedagogical, social, cultural, economic, historical, and political inquiry and critique, in addition to the production of educational media and cultural artifacts.

Features: http://www.facebook.com/pages/Ohio-State-University-Educational-Technology-Program/138548946182406.

Admission Requirements: Please see: http://ehe.osu.edu/epl/academics/cftqi/ downloads/cftqi-checklist.pdf.

Degree Requirements: Please see: http://ehe.osu.edu/epl/academics/cftqi/degree-req.cfm.

Number of Full Time Faculty: 3; **Number of Other Faculty**: 2.

Degrees awarded in 2010–2011 Academic Year—Masters: 10; **Ph.D.**: 5; **Other**: 5.

Grant Monies awarded in 2010–2011 Academic Year: 1,200,000.

Name of Institution: Widener University.

Name of Department or Program: Instructional Technology.

Address: One University Place, Media, PA 19013, USA.

Phone Number: (610)-499-4256.

Email Contact: kabowes@Widener.Edu; **URL**: www.educator.widener.edu.

Contact Person: Dr. Kathleen A. Bowes.

Specializations: Instructional Technology, Educational Leadership.

Features: Widener's Instructional Technology program has three branches: (1) Masters of Education in Instructional Technology, (2) Instructional Technology Specialist Certification (PA non-teaching certificate), and (3) Doctor of School Administration with an Instructional Technology Tract Most courses are hybrids.

Admission Requirements: 3.0 undergraduate, MAT's three letters of recommendation, writing sample.

Degree Requirements: undergraduate degree.

Number of Full Time Faculty: 1; **Number of Other Faculty**: 4.

Degrees awarded in 2010–2011 Academic Year—Masters: 0; **Ph.D.**: 0; **Other**: 2.

Grant Monies awarded in 2010–2011 Academic Year: 150,000.

Name of Institution: University of Alabama.

Name of Department or Program: School of Library and Information Studies.

Address: Box 870252, Tuscaloosa, AL 35487-0252, USA.

Phone Number: (205)348-4610; **Fax Number**: (205)348-3746.

Email Contact: vwright@bamaed.ua.edu; **URL**: http://www.slis.ua.edu.

Contact Person: Joan Atkinson, Director; Gordy Coleman, Coordinator of School Media Program.

Specializations: M.L.I.S. degrees in a varied program including school, public, academic, and special libraries. Ph.D. in the larger College of Communication and Information Sciences; flexibility in creating individual programs of study. Also a Master of Fine Arts Program in Book Arts (including history of the book).

Features: M.L.I.S. is one of 56 accredited programs in the USA and Canada.

Admission Requirements: M.L.I.S.: 3.0 GPA; 50 MAT or 1,000 GRE and an acceptable score on Analytical Writing. Doctoral: 3.0 GPA; 60 MAT or 1200 GRE, and an acceptable score on Analytical Writing.

Degree Requirements: Master's: 36 semester hours. Doctoral: 48–60 semester hours plus 24 hours dissertation research.

Number of Full Time Faculty: 0; **Number of Other Faculty**: 0.

Degrees awarded in 2010–2011 Academic Year—Masters: 0; **Ph.D.**: 0; **Other**: 0.

Grant Monies awarded in 2010–2011 Academic Year: 0.

Name of Institution: University of Central Arkansas.

Name of Department or Program: Leadership Studies.

Address: 201 Donaghey, Conway, AR 72035, USA.

Phone Number: (501)450-5430; **Fax Number**: (501)852-2826.

Email Contact: steph@uca.edu; **URL**: http://www.coe.uca.edu/

Contact Person: Stephanie Huffman, Program Director of the Library Media and Information Technologies Program.

Specializations: M.S. in Library Media and Information Technologies is School Library Media program.

Features: Facebook page.

Admission Requirements: transcripts, GRE scores, and a copy of the candidates teaching certificate.

Degree Requirements: 36 semester hours, practicum (for School Library Media), and a professional portfolio.

Number of Full Time Faculty: 4; **Number of Other Faculty**: 2.

Degrees awarded in 2010–2011 Academic Year—Masters: 40; **Ph.D.**: 0; **Other**: 20.

Grant Monies awarded in 2010–2011 Academic Year: 0.

Name of Institution: Arizona State University; Educational Technology Program.

Name of Department or Program: Division of Psychology in Education.

Address: Box 870611, Tempe, AZ 85287-0611, USA.

Phone Number: (480)965-3384; **Fax Number**: (480)965-0300.

Email Contact: dpe@asu.edu; **URL**: http://coe.asu.edu/psyched.

Contact Person: Dr. Willi Savenye, Associate Professor; Nancy Archer, Admissions Secretary.

Specializations: The Educational Technology program at Arizona State University offers an M.Ed. degree and a Ph.D. degree which focus on the design, development, and evaluation of instructional systems and educational technology applications to support learning.

Features: The program offers courses in a variety of areas such as instructional design technology, media development, technology integration, performance improvement, evaluation, and distance education. The doctoral program emphasizes research using educational technology in applied settings.

Admission Requirements: Requirements for admission to the M.Ed. program include a 4-year undergraduate GPA of 3.0 or above and a score of either 500 or above on verbal section of the GRE or a scaled score of 400 on the MAT. A score of 550 or above on the paper-based TOEFL (or 213 on the computer-based test or 80

Internet-based test) is also required for students who do not speak English as their first language. Requirements for admission to the Ph.D. program include a 4-year undergraduate GPA of 3.20 or above and a combined score of 1,200 or above on the verbal and quantitative sections of the GRE. A score of 600 or above on the paper-based TOEFL (or 250 on the computer-based test or 100 Internet-based test) is also required for students who do not speak English as their first language.

Degree Requirements: The M.Ed. degree requires completion of a minimum of 30 credit hours including 18 credit hours of required course work and a minimum of 12 credit hours of electives. M.Ed. students also must complete an internship and a comprehensive examination. The Ph.D. degree requires a minimum of 84 semester hours beyond the bachelor's degree. At least 54 of these hours must be taken at ASU after admission to the program. Ph.D. students must fulfill a residence requirement and are required to be continuously enrolled in the program. Students also take a comprehensive examination and must satisfy a publication requirement prior to beginning work on their dissertation.

Number of Full Time Faculty: 5; **Number of Other Faculty**: 5.

Degrees awarded in 2010–2011 Academic Year—Masters: 10; **Ph.D.**: 5; **Other**: 0.

Grant Monies awarded in 2010–2011 Academic Year: 2,000,000.

Name of Institution: California State University at East Bay.

Name of Department or Program: Educational Technology Leadership.

Address: 25800 Carlos Bee Boulevard, Hayward, CA 94542, USA.

Phone Number: (510)-885-2509; **Fax Number**: (510)-8854632.

Email Contact: bijan.gillani@csueastbay.edu; **URL**: http://edtech.csueastbay.edu.

Contact Person: Dr. Bijan Gillani.

Specializations: Advances in the field of technology and the explosive growth of the Internet in recent years have revolutionized the way instruction is delivered to students. In parallel with these technological advances, the field of Learning Sciences has made phenomenal contributions to how people learn. For the most part, the advances in these two fields (technology and learning sciences) have gone their separate ways. A synergy of these two fields would enable educators and instructional designers to design and develop more effective educational materials to be transmitted over the Internet. To provide a solution for this synergy, we the Institute of Learning Sciences and Technology focuses on providing a systematic and more intelligent approach to the design of e-learning environments by applying the research findings in the field of Learning Sciences to the design and development of technological environments.

Features: How do people learn? What are learning theories? What are the instructional principles that we can derive from learning theories? How can we apply these instructional principles to the design of meaningful learning with existing and emerging technology? How do we make these principles accessible to faculty who wish to use technology more effectively? How do we develop pedagogically sound learning environments that prepare students to pursue meaningful lifework that has local and global contribution?

Admission Requirements: A completed University Graduate Application (Online Only); Two official copies of each transcript (Mail to the Enrollment Office); Statement of residency (Mail to the Department); A Department Application Form (Mail to the Department); Two letters of recommendations (Mail to the Department. GPA 3.0).

Degree Requirements: (1) Completion of required 24 units of Core Courses. (2) Completion of 16 units of Elective Courses. (3) Completion of Master Degree Project or Thesis Project. (4) Completion of graduate checklist (Online and Forms).

Number of Full Time Faculty: 3; **Number of Other Faculty**: 3.

Degrees awarded in 2010–2011 Academic Year—Masters: 20; **Ph.D.**: 0; **Other**: 20.

Grant Monies awarded in 2010–2011 Academic Year: 90.

Name of Institution: California State University-San Bernardino.

Name of Department or Program: Department of Science, Mathematics, and Technology Education.

Address: 5500 University Parkway, San Bernardino, CA 92407, USA.

Phone Number: (909)537-5692; **Fax Number**: (909)537-7040.

Email Contact: aleh@csusb.edu; **URL**: http://www.csusb.edu/coe/programs/inst_tech/index.htm.

Contact Person: Dr. Amy Leh.

Specializations: Technology integration, online instruction, instructional design, STEM education.

Features: Preparing educators in K-12, corporate, and higher education.

Admission Requirements: Bachelors degree, 3.0 GPA, completion of university writing requirement.

Degree Requirements: 48 units including a Master's project (33 units completed in residence); 3.0 GPA; grades of "C" or better in all courses.

Number of Full Time Faculty: 4; **Number of Other Faculty**: 2.

Degrees awarded in 2010–2011 Academic Year—Masters: 9; **Ph.D.**: 0; **Other**: 0.

Grant Monies awarded in 2010–2011 Academic Year: 100,000.

Name of Institution: San Diego State University.

Name of Department or Program: Educational Technology.

Address: 5500 Campanile Drive, San Diego, CA 92182-1182, USA.

Phone Number: (619)594-6718; **Fax Number**: (619)594-6376.

Email Contact: bober@mail.sdsu.edu; **URL**: http://edtec.sdsu.edu/

Contact Person: Dr. Marcie Bober, Associate Professor, Chair.

Specializations: Certificate in Instructional Technology. Advanced Certificate in Distance Learning, and Software Design. Masters degree in Education with an emphasis in Educational Technology. Doctorate in Education with an emphasis in Educational Technology (a joint program with the University of San Diego).

Features: Focus in design of intervention to improve human performance via strategies that combine theory and practice in relevant, real-world experiences. Offer both campus and online programs.

Admission Requirements: Please refer to SDSU Graduate bulletin at http://libweb. sdsu.edu/bulletin/. Requirements include a minimum score of 950 on the GRE (verbal+quantitative), and 4.5 on the analytical. See our website at http://edtec.sdsu. edu for more information.

Degree Requirements: 36 semester hours for the masters (including 6 prerequisite hours). 15–18 semester hours for the certificates.

Number of Full Time Faculty: –; **Number of Other Faculty**: –.

Degrees awarded in 2010–2011 Academic Year—Masters: 40; **Ph.D.**: –; **Other**: –.

Grant Monies awarded in 2010–2011 Academic Year: –.

Name of Institution: San Jose State University.

Name of Department or Program: Instructional Technology.

Address: One Washington Square, San Jose, CA 95192-0076, USA.

Phone Number: (408)924-3620; **Fax Number**: (408)924-3713.

Email Contact: rbarba@email.sjsu.edu; **URL**: http://sweeneyhall.sjsu.edu/depts/it.

Contact Person: Dr. Robertta Barba, Program Chair.

Specializations: Master's degree.

Features: M.A. in Education with an emphasis on Instructional Technology.

Admission Requirements: Baccalaureate degree from approved university, appropriate work experience, minimum GPA of 2.5, and minimum score of 550 on TOEFL (Test of English as a Foreign Language). 36 semester hours (which includes 6 prerequisite hours).

Degree Requirements: 30 units of approved graduate studies.

Number of Full Time Faculty: –; **Number of Other Faculty**: –.

Degrees awarded in 2010–2011 Academic Year—Masters: 42; **Ph.D.**: –; **Other**: –.

Grant Monies awarded in 2010–2011 Academic Year: –.

Name of Institution: University of Southern California, Rossier School of Education.

Name of Department or Program: Educational Psychology & Instructional Technology.

Address: 3470 Trousdale Parkway, Los Angeles, CA 90089-4036, USA.

Phone Number: (213)740-3465; **Fax Number**: (213)740-2367.

Email Contact: rsoemast@usc.edu; **URL**: http://www.usc.edu/dept/education/academic/masters/index.htm.

Contact Person: For Admissions Info (soeinfo@usc.edu), For general program info (rsoemast@usc.edu), For specific program info (rueda@usc.edu).

Specializations: The Educational Psychology/Instructional Technology program focuses on learning and motivation, emphasizing the study of new information and performance technologies used to improve instruction among diverse student populations. To understand human learning, educational psychologists study areas such as: motivation; developmental and individual differences; social, cultural, and group processes; instructional technology; and the evaluation of instruction. Students will be prepared to apply a wide range of computer and telecommunications technologies in achieving educational goals within school, community, corporate, and public settings.

Features: Distinctive Features: Focus on learning and motivation with a strong emphasis on technology and a major concern with urban education settings.—Major objective is to learn how to diagnose and solve learning and motivation problems, especially those characteristic of urban learning settings. —Faculties are well-known in the field and are active researchers. Special emphasis upon instructional design, human performance at work, systems analysis, and computer-based training.

Admission Requirements: Bachelor's degree, 1,000 GRE.

Degree Requirements: Program of Study: 28 units 7 core courses and 2 elective courses. Core Courses: EDPT 576 Technology in Contemporary Education and Training; EDPT 550 Statistical Inference; EDPT 502 Learning and Individual Differences; EDPT 510 Human Learning; EDPT 540 Introduction to Educational Measurement and Evaluation; EDPT 571 Instructional Design. CTSE 593A & B Master's Seminar Electives (2 classes): EDPT 511 Human Motivation in Education; EDPT 520 Human Lifespan Development; EDPT 570 Language and Cultural Diversity in Learning. CTSE 573 Management of Instructional Resources: EDPA 671 The Computer and Data Processing Education.

Number of Full Time Faculty: –; **Number of Other Faculty**: –.

Degrees awarded in 2010–2011 Academic Year—Masters: 15; **Ph.D.**: –; **Other**: –.

Grant Monies awarded in 2010–2011 Academic Year: –.

Name of Institution: Azusa Pacific University.

Name of Department or Program: EDUCABS—Advanced Studies.

Address: 901 E Alosta, Azusa, CA 91702, USA.

Phone Number: (626)815-5355; **Fax Number**: (626)815-5416.

Email Contact: kbacer@apu.edu; **URL**: http://www.apu.edu.

Contact Person: Kathleen Bacer, Online Master of Arts in Educational Technology.

Specializations: Educational Technology, online learning, Infusing technology in teaching/learning environments, digital learning for the twenty-first century learner.

Features: 100% Online Master of Arts in Educational Technology program designed for the K-12 educator.

Admission Requirements: Undergraduate degree from accredited institution with at least 12 units in education, 3.0 GPA.

Degree Requirements: 36 unit program.

Number of Full Time Faculty: 2; **Number of Other Faculty**: 8.

Degrees awarded in 2010–2011 Academic Year—Masters: 90; **Ph.D.**: 0; **Other**: 0.

Grant Monies awarded in 2010–2011 Academic Year: 10,000.

Name of Institution: San Francisco State University.

Name of Department or Program: College of Education, Department of Instructional Technology.

Address: 1600 Holloway Avenue, San Francisco, CA 94132, USA.

Phone Number: (415)338-1509; **Fax Number**: (415)338-0510.

Email Contact: kforeman@sfsu.edu; **URL**: www.itec.sfsu.edu.

Contact Person: Dr. Kim Foreman, Chair; Anna Kozubek, Office Coordinator.

Specializations: Masters degree with emphasis on Instructional Multimedia Design, Training and Designing Development, and Instructional Computing. The school also offers an 18-unit Graduate Certificate in Training Systems Development, which can be incorporated into the Master's degree.

Features: This program emphasizes the instructional systems approach to train teachers, trainers, and e-learning professionals by providing practical design experience in the field. Most of our courses are delivered both face-to-face and online.

Admission Requirements: Bachelors degree, appropriate work experience, 2.5 GPA, purpose statement, 2 letters of recommendation, interview with the department chair.

Degree Requirements: 30 semester hours, field study project, or thesis. Three to nine units of prerequisites, assessed at entrance to the program.

Number of Full Time Faculty: 3; **Number of Other Faculty**: 9.

Degrees awarded in 2010–2011 Academic Year—Masters: 50; **Ph.D.**: 0; **Other**: 0.

Grant Monies awarded in 2010–2011 Academic Year: 0.

Name of Institution: University of Colorado Denver.

Name of Department or Program: School of Education and Human Development.

Address: Campus Box 106, PO Box 173364, Denver, CO 80217-3364, USA.

Phone Number: (303)315-4963; **Fax Number**: (303)315-6311.

Email Contact: brent.wilson@cudenver.edu; **URL**: http://www.ucdenver.edu/academics/colleges/SchoolOfEducation/Academics/MASTERS/ILT/Pages/eLearning.aspx.

Contact Person: Brent Wilson, Program Coordinator, Information and Learning Technologies.

Specializations: M.A. in Information & Learning Technologies (ILT)—includes options for eLearning, K12 Teaching, Instructional Design/Adult Learning, and School Librarianship. Graduate Certificates are available in eLearning Design and Implementation (15 graduate credits), and Digital Storytelling (9 graduate credits). The Ed.D. in Educational Equity is available with concentration in adult education and professional learning, where students can focus on learning technologies. A Ph.D. program option is also available for those choosing careers in higher education and research.

Features: The ILT program focuses on design and use of digital learning resources and social support for online learning. Masters students prepare a professional portfolio, published online, that showcases their skills and accomplishments. The doctoral program is cross-disciplinary, drawing on expertise in technology, adult learning, professional development, social justice, systemic change, research methods, reflective practice, and cultural studies.

Admission Requirements: M.A. and Ph.D.: satisfactory GPA, GRE, writing sample, letters of recommendation, transcripts. See website for more detail.

Degree Requirements: M.A.: 30 semester hours including 27 hours of core coursework; professional portfolio; field experience. Ed.D.: 50 semester hours of coursework and labs, plus 20 dissertation hours; dissertation.

Number of Full Time Faculty: 3; **Number of Other Faculty**: 8.

Degrees awarded in 2010–2011 Academic Year—Masters: 84; **Ph.D.**: 1; **Other**: 0.

Grant Monies awarded in 2010–2011 Academic Year: 5,600.

Name of Institution: University of Northern Colorado.

Name of Department or Program: Educational Technology.

Address: College of Education and Behavioral Sciences, Greeley, CO 80639, USA.

Phone Number: (970)351-2807; **Fax Number**: (970)351-1622.

Email Contact: james.gall@unco.edu; **URL**: http://www.unco.edu/cebs/edtech.

Contact Person: James Gall, Department Chair, Educational Technology.

Specializations: M.A. in Educational Technology; Ph.D. in Educational Technology; M.A. in School Library Education; Non-Degree Endorsement for School Library Education.

Features: The Educational Technology programs are designed to develop knowledge and skills in instructional design and technologies for a variety of learning contexts (K-12, higher education, military training, business/organizational, and international settings). The School Library program is tailored to K-12 professionals who would like to obtain employment in Colorados K-12 libraries and learning resource/media centers.

Admission Requirements: Masters Criteria: Bachelors degree from a regionally accredited college or university and a GPA of 3.00 or better (on a 4.00 scale) on the most recent 60 semester hours of work. Applicants must submit academic transcripts, three letters of recommendations, and a statement of purpose. Applications are reviewed continuously. Doctoral Criteria: Bachelor's degree from a regionally accredited college or university, a minimal level of achievement combining GPA and GRE scores (GRE scores must be less than 5 years old). Applicants must submit academic transcripts, current GRE scores, three letters of recommendations, and a statement of purpose. They must also participate in an interview with the faculty. The deadline for applications for programs beginning in the Fall is March 1. The deadline for applications for programs beginning in the Spring is November 1. Applicants with no or limited English ability can apply for the University's Intensive English Program. Under this option, a conditional admission is made to the academic program, but the student first attends English language courses until skilled enough to being the regular course work.

Degree Requirements: M.A. in Educational Technology: 33 credit hours of coursework followed by a comprehensive exam. Ph.D. in Educational Technology: 67 credit hours of coursework followed by a comprehensive exam and an oral defense. An original piece of research must be conducted with both a proposal and dissertation defense. M.A. in School Library Education: 32 credit hours of coursework followed by a comprehensive exam. School Librarian Endorsement: 26 credit hours.

Number of Full Time Faculty: 5; **Number of Other Faculty**: 0.

Degrees awarded in 2010–2011 Academic Year—Masters: 16; **Ph.D.**: 4; **Other**: 0.

Grant Monies awarded in 2010–2011 Academic Year: 0.

Name of Institution: Fairfield University.

Name of Department or Program: Educational Technology.

Address: N. Benson Road, Fairfield, CT 06824, USA.

Phone Number: (203)254-4000; **Fax Number**: (203)254-4047.

Email Contact: graded@mail.fairfield.edu; **URL**: http://www.fairfield.edu.

Contact Person: Dr. Elizabeth Langran, Director, Educational Technology Program; Dr. Gayle Bogel, Assistant Professor of Educational Technology.

Specializations: M.A. in Educational Technology; certification (initial and cross-endorsement) in School Library Media.

Features: emphasis on theory, practice, and new instructional developments in computers in education, multimedia, school/media, and applied technology in education.

Admission Requirements: See http://fairfield.edu/gseap/gseap_policies.html.

Degree Requirements: 33 credits. Additional coursework for certification.

Number of Full Time Faculty: 2; **Number of Other Faculty**: 5.

Degrees awarded in 2010–2011 Academic Year—Masters: 12; **Ph.D.**: 0; **Other**: 0.

Grant Monies awarded in 2010–2011 Academic Year: 0.

Name of Institution: University of Connecticut.

Name of Department or Program: Educational Psychology.

Address: 249 Glenbrook Road, Unit-2064, Storrs, CT 06269-2064, USA.

Phone Number: (860)486-0182; **Fax Number**: (860)486-0180.

Email Contact: myoung@UConn.edu; **URL**: http://www.epsy.uconn.edu/

Contact Person: Michael Young, Program Coordinator.

Specializations: M.A. in Educational Technology (portfolio or thesis options), 1-year partially online Masters (summer, fall, spring, summer), 6th year certificate in Educational Technology and Ph.D. in Learning Technology.

Features: M.A. can be on-campus or 2 Summers (on campus) and Fall-Spring (Online) that can be completed in a year. The Ph.D.. emphasis in Learning Technology is a unique program at UConn. It strongly emphasizes Cognitive Science and how technology can be used to enhance the way people think and learn. The Program seeks to provide students with knowledge of theory and applications regarding the use of advanced technology to enhance learning and thinking. Campus facilities include $2 billion twenty-first century UConn enhancement to campus infrastructure, including a new wing to the Neag School of Education. Faculty research interests include interactive video for anchored instruction and situated learning, telecommunications for cognitive apprenticeship, technology-mediated interactivity for learning by design activities, and in cooperation with the National

Research Center for Gifted and Talented, research on the use of technology to enhance cooperative learning, and the development of gifted performance in all students.

Admission Requirements: admission to the graduate school at UConn, GRE scores (or other evidence of success at the graduate level). Previous experience in a related area of technology, education, or experience in education or training.

Degree Requirements: completion of plan of study coursework, comprehensive exam (portfolio-based with multiple requirements), and completion of an approved dissertation.

Number of Full Time Faculty: 0; **Number of Other Faculty**: 0.

Degrees awarded in 2010–2011 Academic Year—Masters: 0; **Ph.D.**: 0; **Other**: 0.

Grant Monies awarded in 2010–2011 Academic Year: 0.

Name of Institution: George Washington University.

Name of Department or Program: School of Education and Human Development.

Address: 2134 G Street, NW Suite 103, Washington, DC 20052, USA.

Phone Number: (202)994-1701; **Fax Number**: (202)994-2145.

Email Contact: nmilman@gwu.edu; **URL**: http://www.gwu.edu/~etl.

Contact Person: Dr. Natalie Milman, Educational Technology Leadership Program Coordinator.

Specializations: The Educational Technology Leadership program began in 1988. It was one of the first online degree programs in the field. The program uses the over 20 years of experience to be able to offer a high quality, flexible program rich in knowledge of the field and distance education delivery. The result is an outstanding experience for our students. M.A. in Education and Human Development with a major in Educational Technology Leadership as well as the following Graduate Certificates: Instructional Design, Multimedia Development, Leadership in Educational Technology, E-Learning, Training and Educational Technology, Integrating Technology into Education.

Features: 0.

Admission Requirements: Application fee, transcripts, GRE or MAT scores (50th percentile), two letters of recommendation from academic professionals, computer access, undergraduate degree with 2.75 GPA. No GRE or MAT is required for entry into the Graduate Certificate programs.

Degree Requirements: Masters Program: 36 credit hours (including 27 required hours and 9 elective credit hours). Required courses include computer application management, media and technology application, software implementation and design, public education policy, and quantitative research methods.

Graduate Certificate Programs: 18 credit hours.

Number of Full Time Faculty: 0; **Number of Other Faculty**: 0.

Degrees awarded in 2010–2011 Academic Year—Masters: 0; **Ph.D.**: 0; **Other**: 0.

Grant Monies awarded in 2010–2011 Academic Year: 0.

Name of Institution: Florida Institute of Technology.

Name of Department or Program: Science and Mathematics Education Department.

Address: 150 University Boulevard, Melbourne, FL 32901-6975, USA.

Phone Number: (321)674-8126; **Fax Number**: (321)674-7598.

Email Contact: dcook@fit.edu; **URL**: http://www.fit.edu/catalog/sci-lib/comp-edu.html#master-info.

Contact Person: Dr. David Cook, Head of Department.

Specializations: Master's degree in Computer Education, Ph.D. degree in Science Education with options for research and major technical area concentrations in Computer Science, Computer Education and Instructional Technology.

Features: Flexible program depending on student experience.

Admission Requirements: Masters: 3.0 GPA for regular admission Ph.D.: Masters degree and 3.2 GPA.

Degree Requirements: Masters: 33 semester hours (15 in computer and/or technology education, 9 in education, 9 electives); practicum; no thesis or internship required or 30 semester hrs for thesis option. Ph.D.: 42 semester hours (Includes dissertation and research. Also requires 21 graduate hours in computer science/computer information systems 6 of which may be applicable to the required 42 hours).

Number of Full Time Faculty: 2; **Number of Other Faculty**: 4.

Degrees awarded in 2010–2011 Academic Year—Masters: 0; **Ph.D.**: 0; **Other**: 0.

Grant Monies awarded in 2010–2011 Academic Year: 0.

Name of Institution: Nova Southeastern University—Fischler Graduate School of Education and Human Services.

Name of Department or Program: Programs in Instructional Technology and Distance Education (ITDE).

Address: 1750 NE 167th Street, North Miami Beach, FL 33162, USA.

Phone Number: (954)-262-8572. (800)986-3223, ext. 8572; **Fax Number**: (954)262-3905.

Email Contact: itdeinfo@nova.edu;scisinfo@nova.edu; **URL**: http://itde.nova.edu.

Contact Person: Marsha L. Burmeister, Recruitment Coordinator & Program Professor ITDE.

Specializations: M.S. and Ed.D. in Instructional Technology and Distance Education.

Features: M.S. 21 months (M.S. ITDE program graduates may continue with the Ed.D. program as second year students), Ed.D. 36 months, M.S. and Ed.D. combined: 4+ years Blended/hybrid delivery model with limited face-to-face and via instruction at-a-distance using Web-based technologies.

Admission Requirements:

Active employment in the field of instructional technology/distance education.

Completion of bachelor's degree for M.S. program (2.5 minimum GPA); master's degree required for admission to Ed.D. program (3.0 minimum GPA).

Miller Analogies Test (MAT) score (test taken within last 5 years).

Submission of application/supplementary materials.

Approval of Skills Checklist (application).

Three letters of recommendation.

Official copies of transcripts for all graduate work.

Resume.

Oral interview (via telephone).

Demonstrated potential for successful completion of the program via acceptance of application.

Internet Service Provider; Laptop computer.

Degree Requirements: 21 months and 30 semester credits. Ed.D. 3 years and 65 semester credits. M.S. program: 3 "extended weekends:" One extended weekend in the fall (5 days), one extended weekend in the spring (4 days), one summer instructional session (4–5 days; July), final term online delivery. Ed.D. program: same as above, continues throughout the 3 years (3 sessions in first year, 2 sessions in the second year, and one instructional session in the third year for a total of six (6) face-to-face sessions).

Number of Full Time Faculty: 0; **Number of Other Faculty**: 0.

Degrees awarded in 2010–2011 Academic Year—Masters: 100; **Ph.D.**: 0; **Other**: 0.

Grant Monies awarded in 2010–2011 Academic Year: 0.

Name of Institution: Barry University.

Name of Department or Program: Department of Educational Computing and Technology, School of Education.

Address: 11300 NE Second Avenue, Miami Shores, FL 33161, USA.

Phone Number: (305)899-3608; **Fax Number**: (305)899-3718.

Email Contact: dlenaghan@bu4090.barry.edu; **URL**: http://www.barry.edu/ed/programs/masters/ect/default.htm.

Contact Person: Donna Lenaghan, Dir.

Specializations: M.S. and Ed.S. in Educational Technology Applications and Ph.D. degree in Educational Technology Leadership.

Features: These programs and courses prepare educators to integrate computer/technologies in their disciplines and/or train individuals to use computers/technologies. The focus is on improving the teaching and learning process thought integration of technologies into curricula and learning activities.

Admission Requirements: GRE scores, letters of recommendation, GPA, interview, achievements.

Degree Requirements: M.S. or Ed.S.: 36 semester credit hours. Ph.D.: 54 credits beyond the Masters including dissertation credits.

Number of Full Time Faculty: 0; **Number of Other Faculty**: 0.

Degrees awarded in 2010–2011 Academic Year—Masters: 75; **Ph.D.**: 0; **Other**: 0.

Grant Monies awarded in 2010–2011 Academic Year: 0.

Name of Institution: Florida State University.

Name of Department or Program: Educational Psychology and Learning Systems.

Address: 3210 Stone Building, Tallahassee, FL 32306-4453, USA.

Phone Number: (850)644-4592; **Fax Number**: (850)644-8776.

Email Contact: mmckee@oddl.fsu.edu; **URL**: http://insys.fsu.edu.

Contact Person: Mary Kate McKee, Program Coordinator.

Specializations: M.S. and Ph.D. in Instructional Systems with specializations for persons planning to work in academia, business, industry, government, or military, both in the USA and in International settings.

Features: Core courses include systems and materials development, performance improvement, online learning, development of multimedia, project management, psychological foundations, current trends in instructional design, and research and statistics. Internships are recommended. Strong alumni network. M.S. courses available both on campus and online.

Admission Requirements: M.S.: 3.0 GPA in last 2 years of undergraduate program, 1,000 GRE (verbal plus quantitative), 550 TOEFL (for international applicants). Ph.D.: 1,100 GRE (V+Q), 3.5 GPA in last 2 years; international students, 550 TOEFL.

Degree Requirements: M.S.: 36 semester hours, 2–4 hours internship, comprehensive exam preparation of professional portfolio.

Number of Full Time Faculty: 4; **Number of Other Faculty**: 4.

Degrees awarded in 2010–2011 Academic Year—Masters: 25; **Ph.D.**: 6; **Other**: 0.

Grant Monies awarded in 2010–2011 Academic Year: 0.

Name of Institution: University of Central Florida.

Name of Department or Program: College of Education: ERTL.

Address: 4000 Central Florida Boulevard, Orlando, FL 32816-1250, USA.

Phone Number: (407)823-4835; **Fax Number**: (407)823-4880.

Email Contact: atsusi.hirumi@ucf.edu; **URL**: http://www.education.ucf.edu/insttech/

Contact Person: Dr. Atsusi Hirumi, Dr. Glenda Gunter.

Specializations: Graduate Certificates in (a) Instructional Design of Simulations, (b) Educational Technology, and (c) e-Learning Professional Development. M.A. in Instructional Design and Technology with professional tracks in Instructional Systems, Educational Technology and e-Learning; Ph.D. in Education with Instructional Design and Technology track; Ed.D. in Education with Instructional Design & Technology concentration. There are approximately 120 students in M.A. program, 5 in Ed.D., and 30 in Ph.D. programs.

Features: All programs rely heavily on understanding of fundamental competencies as reflected by NCATE, ASTD, AECT, AASL, and ISTE. There is an emphasis on the practical application of theory through intensive hands-on experiences. Orlando and the surrounding area are home to a plethora of high-tech companies, military training and simulation organizations, and tourist attractions. UCF, established in 1963, now has in excess of 36,000 students, representing more than 90 countries. It has been ranked as one of the leading "most-wired" universities in North America.

Admission Requirements: GRE score of 1,000 for consideration for doctoral program. No GRE required for M.A. or graduate certificate programs. GPA of 3.0 of greater in last 60 hours of undergraduate degree for M.A. program; TOEFL of 550 (270 computer-based version) if English is not first language; three letters of recommendation; resume, statement of goals; residency statement and health record. Financial statement if coming from overseas.

Degree Requirements: M.A. in Instructional Technology/Instructional Systems, 39 semester hours; M.A. in Instructional Technology/Educational Technology, 39 semester hours, M.A. in Instructional Technology/eLearning, 39 semester hours. Practicum required in all three programs; thesis, research project, or substitute additional course work. Ph.D. and Ed.D. require between 58 and 69 hours beyond the masters for completion.

Number of Full Time Faculty: 3; **Number of Other Faculty**: 5.

Degrees awarded in 2010–2011 Academic Year—Masters: 75; **Ph.D.**: 7; **Other**: 2.

Grant Monies awarded in 2010–2011 Academic Year: 100,000.

Name of Institution: University of South Florida.

Name of Department or Program: Instructional Technology Program, Secondary Education Department, College of Education.

Address: 4202 E Fowler Avenue, EDU162, Tampa, FL 33620-5650, USA.

Phone Number: (813)974-3533; **Fax Number**: (813)974-3837.

Email Contact: IT@coedu.usf.edu; **URL**: http://www.coedu.usf.edu/it.

Contact Person: Dr. William Kealy, Graduate Certificates; Dr. Frank Breit, Master's program; Dr. Ann Barron, Education Specialist program; Dr. James White, Doctoral program.

Specializations: Graduate Certificates in Web Design, Instructional Design, Multimedia Design, School Networks, and Distance Education M.Ed., Ed.S., and Ph.D. in Curriculum and Instruction with emphasis in Instructional Technology.

Features: Many student gain practical experience in the Florida Center for Instructional Technology (FCIT), which provides services to the Department of Education and other grants and contracts; the Virtual Instructional Team for the Advancement of Learning (VITAL), which provides USF faculty with course development services; and Educational Outreach. The College of Education is one of the largest in the USA in terms of enrollment and facilities. As of Fall 1997, a new, technically state-of-the-art building was put into service. The University of South Florida has been classified by the Carnegie Foundation as a Doctoral/Research University: Extensive.

Admission Requirements: See http://www.coedu.usf.edu/it.

Degree Requirements: See http://www.coedu.usf.edu/it.

Number of Full Time Faculty: 0; **Number of Other Faculty**: 0.

Degrees awarded in 2010–2011 Academic Year—Masters: 60; **Ph.D.**: 0; **Other**: 0.

Grant Monies awarded in 2010–2011 Academic Year: 0.

Name of Institution: Georgia Southern University.

Name of Department or Program: College of Education.

Address: Box 8131, Statesboro, GA 30460-8131, USA.

Phone Number: (912)478-5307; **Fax Number**: (912)478-7104.

Email Contact: JRepman@georgiasouthern.edu; **URL**: http://coe.georgiasouthern.edu/eltr/tech/inst_tech/index.htm.

Contact Person: Judi Repman, Professor, Department of Leadership, Technology, and Human Development.

Specializations: Online M.Ed. and GA certification for School Library Media and Instructional Technology Specialists. An online Ed.S. is available in both concentrations as well. The Online Teaching and Learning Endorsement is offered at both levels.

Features: Completely online program. Strong emphasis on technology and use of Web 2.0 tools Online portfolios as culminating program requirement for M.Ed. students. http://www.facebook.com/itec.georgiasouthern.

Admission Requirements: B.S. (teacher certification NOT required), GRE or MAT not required for applicants who are certified teachers with a 2.5 undergraduate grade point average M.Ed. required for admission to the Ed.S. program.

Degree Requirements: 36 semester hours for the M.Ed. 30 semester hours for the Ed.S. 9 semester hour Online Teaching and Learning Endorsement.

Number of Full Time Faculty: 8; **Number of Other Faculty**: 1.

Degrees awarded in 2010–2011 Academic Year—Masters: 50; **Ph.D.**: 0; **Other**: 0.

Grant Monies awarded in 2010–2011 Academic Year: 0.

Name of Institution: Georgia State University.

Name of Department or Program: Middle-Secondary Education and Instructional Technology.

Address: Box 3976, Atlanta, GA, 30302-3976, USA.

Phone Number: (404)413-8060; **Fax Number**: (404)413-8063.

Email Contact: swharmon@gsu.edu.; **URL**: http://edtech.gsu.edu.

Contact Person: Dr. Stephen W. Harmon

Specializations: M.S. and Ph.D. in Instructional Design and Technology. Endorsement in Online Teaching and Learning.

Features: Focus on research and practical application of instructional technology in educational and corporate settings. Online MS in Instructional Design and Technology available.

Admission Requirements: M.S.: Bachelors degree, 2.5 undergraduate GPA, 800 GRE, 550 TOEFL. Ph.D.: Master's degree, 3.30 graduate GPA, 500 verbal plus 500 quantitative GRE or 500 analytical GRE.

Degree Requirements: M.S.: 36 semester hours, internship, portfolio, comprehensive examination. Ph.D.: 66 semester hours, internship, comprehensive examination, dissertation.

Number of Full Time Faculty: 5; **Number of Other Faculty**: 2.

Degrees awarded in 2010–2011 Academic Year—Masters: 15; **Ph.D.**: 6; **Other**: 1.

Grant Monies awarded in 2010–2011 Academic Year: 1,250,000.

Name of Institution: University of Georgia.

Name of Department or Program: Department of Educational Psychology and Instructional Technology, College of Education.

Address: 604 Aderhold Hall, Athens, GA 30602-7144, USA.

Phone Number: (706)542-3810; **Fax Number**: (706)542-4032.

Email Contact: mikeorey@uga.edu; **URL**: http://www.coe.uga.edu/epit/

Contact Person: Dr. Michael Orey, LDT Program Chair.

Specializations: M.Ed. and Ed.S. in Learning, Design, and Technology with two emphasis areas: Instructional Design & Development and School Library Media; Ph.D. for leadership positions as specialists in instructional design and development and university faculty. The program offers advanced study for individuals with previous preparation in instructional media and technology, as well as a preparation for personnel in other professional fields requiring a specialty in instructional systems or instructional technology. Representative career fields for graduates include designing new courses, educational multimedia (especially web-based), tutorial programs, and instructional materials in state and local school systems, higher education, business and industry, research and non-profit settings, and in instructional products development.

Features: Minor areas of study available in a variety of other departments. Personalized programs are planned around a common core of courses and include practical, internships, or clinical experiences. Research activities include grant-related activities and applied projects, as well as dissertation studies.

Admission Requirements: All degrees: application to graduate school, satisfactory GRE score, other criteria as outlined in Graduate School Bulletin and on the program Web site.

Degree Requirements: M.Ed.: 36 semester hours with 3.0 GPA, portfolio with oral exam. Ed.S.: 30 semester hours with 3.0 GPA and project exam. Ph.D.: 3 full years of study beyond the Master's degree, two consecutive semester's full-time residency, comprehensive exam with oral defense, internship, dissertation with oral defense.

Number of Full Time Faculty: 11; **Number of Other Faculty**: 0.

Degrees awarded in 2010–2011 Academic Year—Masters: 40; **Ph.D.**: 11; **Other**: 10.

Grant Monies awarded in 2010–2011 Academic Year: 600,000.

Name of Institution: University of West Georgia.

Name of Department or Program: Department of Media and Instructional Technology.

Address: 138 Education Annex, Carrollton, GA 30118, USA.

Phone Number: (678)-839-6558; **Fax Number**: (678)-839-6153.

Email Contact: ebennett@westga.edu; **URL**: http://coe.westga.edu/mit.

Contact Person: Dr. Elizabeth Bennett, Professor and Chair.

Specializations: M.Ed. with specializations in School Library Media or Instructional Technology and Add-On certification in School Library Media for students with Master's degrees in other disciplines. The Department also offers an Ed.S. program in Media with two options, Media Specialist or Instructional Technology. The program strongly emphasizes technology integration in the schools and online and blended learning environments in P-12 school settings.

Features: School library media and certification students complete field experiences as part of each school library media course they take. All courses range from 85 to 100% online.

Admission Requirements: M.Ed.: 800 GRE, 396 MAT, 2.7 undergraduate GPA. Ed.S.: 900 GRE, 400 MAT, and 3.00 graduate GPA.

Degree Requirements: 36 semester hours for M.Ed. 27 semester hours for Ed.S.

Number of Full Time Faculty: 10; **Number of Other Faculty**: 4.

Degrees awarded in 2010–2011 Academic Year—Masters: 40; **Ph.D.**: 0; **Other**: 45.

Grant Monies awarded in 2010–2011 Academic Year: 50,000.

Name of Institution: Valdosta State University.

Name of Department or Program: Curriculum, Leadership, & Technology.

Address: 1500 N Patterson Street, Valdosta, GA 31698, USA.

Phone Number: (229)333-5633; **Fax Number**: (229)259-5094.

Email Contact: ewiley@valdosta.edu; **URL**: http://www.valdosta.edu/coe/clt/

Contact Person: Ellen Wiley.

Specializations: M.Ed. in Instructional Technology with two tracks: Library/Media or Technology Applications; Online Ed.S. in Instructional Technology with two tracks: Library/Media or Technology Applications; Ed.D. in Curriculum and Instruction.

Features: The program has a strong emphasis on systematic design and technology in M.Ed., Ed.S., and Ed.D. Strong emphasis on change leadership, reflective practice, applied research in Ed.S and Ed.D.

Admission Requirements: M.Ed.: 2.5 GPA, 800 GRE. Ed.S.: Master's degree, 3 years of experience, 3.0 GPA, 850 GRE, MAT 390 and less than 5 years old. Ed.D.: Master's degree, 3 years of experience, 3.50 GPA, 1,000 GRE.

Degree Requirements: M.Ed.: 33 semester hours. Ed.S.: 27 semester hours. Ed.D.: 54 semester hours.

Number of Full Time Faculty: 12; **Number of Other Faculty**: 4.

Degrees awarded in 2010–2011 Academic Year—Masters: 8; **Ph.D.**: 0; **Other**: 34.

Grant Monies awarded in 2010–2011 Academic Year: 0.

Name of Institution: University of Hawaii-Manoa.

Name of Department or Program: Department of Educational Technology.

Address: 1776 University Avenue, Honolulu, HI 96822-2463, USA.

Phone Number: (808)956-7671; **Fax Number**: (808)956-3905.

Email Contact: edtech-dept@hawaii.edu; **URL**: http://etec.hawaii.edu.

Contact Person: Catherine P. Fulford, Ph.D., Chair.

Specializations: M.Ed. in Educational Technology.

Features: This nationally accredited program prepares students to create resources for teaching and learning through diverse media as well as integrate technology into educational environments. Educational Technology (ETEC) provides theoretical knowledge and scientific principles that can be applied to problems that arise in a social context; prepares individuals to devise effective messages, teams, materials, devices, techniques, and settings; and, involves the study of theory and practice of design, development, utilization, management, and evaluation of processes and resources for learning. Practitioners in educational technology, whether they are teachers, trainers, developers, administrators, or support personnel, seek innovative and effective ways of organizing the teaching and learning process through the best possible application of technological developments. The program places emphasis on applications of technology in educational settings rather than simple technical skills. Individuals from diverse backgrounds can immediately apply what they learn to their particular context. Upon graduation, these new professionals will have a clearer vision of how they can prepare learners for the future. ETEC graduates are found in many learning environments including K-12 and higher education, government, business, industry, and health occupations.

Admission Requirements: A baccalaureate degree from an accredited institution in any field of study is acceptable to the Department, provided the student's undergraduate scholastic record is acceptable to the Graduate Division. A "B" average (i.e., 3.0 on a 4-point scale) in the last 60 semester hours of the undergraduate program is required for regular admission. Students from foreign countries must submit the results of the Test of English as a Foreign Language (TOEFL). The minimum score is 600, representing approximately the 77th percentile rank. Students must submit: an "Intent to Apply for Admission Form," a "Graduate Program Supplemental Information Form," and a "Statement of Objectives Form." These are available on the ETEC website. Three letters of recommendation, to be submitted with the application for admission, should evaluate the applicant's potential in the field of educational technology, not only his or her academic abilities to do graduate work. All applicants should submit a resume, and additional materials, documentation, or samples of work relevant to the evaluation and selection process.

Degree Requirements: The ETEC M.Ed. program requires a minimum of 36 semester credit hours, with seven required and five elective ETEC courses. All required and most elective courses are three credits each. Full-time students usually complete their coursework in two academic years. Students attending part-time may take three or more years to finish program requirements. Of the seven (7) required courses, four comprise the core of the Educational Technology program. Students are required to complete the core courses in sequence during the first year. The program is designed as a cohort system in which students admitted at the same time take initial courses together to build a sense of support and professional community. In the final year of the program, the students will complete an electronic portfolio and final master's project.

Number of Full Time Faculty: 7; **Number of Other Faculty**: 7.

Degrees awarded in 2010–2011 Academic Year—Masters: 21; **Ph.D.**: 0; **Other**: 0.

Grant Monies awarded in 2010–2011 Academic Year: 1,097,246.

Name of Institution: University of Northern Iowa.

Name of Department or Program: Instructional Technology Program.

Address: 618 Schinder Education Center, Cedar Falls, IA 50614-0606, USA.

Phone Number: (319)273-3249; **Fax Number**: (319)273-5886.

Email Contact: leigh.zeitz@uni.edu; **URL**: http://www.uni.edu/itech.

Contact Person: Leigh E. Zeitz, Ph.D.

Specializations: M.A. in Curriculum & Instruction: Instructional Technology.

Features: The Instructional Technology master's program is designed to prepare educators for a variety of professional positions in K-12 and adult learning/corporate educational settings. This is a hands-on program that requires students to apply the theoretical foundations presented in the courses. The UNI Instructional Technology Master's program is available both on-line and on-campus. A 2-year cohort is initiated during the summer in even numbered years. The program's practical perspective prepares professionals for fulfilling technology leadership roles. On a PK-12 level, these roles include technology coordinators, master teachers, special education media specialists, and county educational specialists. On an adult and corporate level, the roles include instructors at vocational-technical schools, community colleges, and universities. They can work as trainers in the corporate world as well as higher education. Many of our graduates have also become successful instructional designers throughout the country. The master's degree is aligned with the AECT/ECIT standards and is focused on addressing specific career choices.

Admission Requirements: Bachelors degree, 3.0 undergraduate GPA, 500 TOEFL Licensure as a teacher is not required for admission to the master's program. The bachelor's degree may be in any field.

Degree Requirements: 35 semester credits. Research paper (literature review, project report, journal article, or research report on original research) is required. A thesis option is available. An online digital portfolio will be created by each student to share and reflect upon the student's learning experiences in the program.

Number of Full Time Faculty: 2; **Number of Other Faculty**: 3.

Degrees awarded in 2010–2011 Academic Year—Masters: 20; **Ph.D.**: 1; **Other**: 0.

Grant Monies awarded in 2010–2011 Academic Year: 0.

Name of Institution: Boise State University.

Name of Department or Program: Instructional & Performance Technology.

Address: 1910 University Drive, ENGR-327, Boise, ID 83725, USA.

Phone Number: (208)426-2489; (800)824-7017 ext. 61312; **Fax Number**: (208)426-1970.

Email Contact: jfenner@boisestate.edu; **URL**: http://ipt.boisestate.edu/

Contact Person: Dr. Don Stepich, IPT Program Chair.; Jo Ann Fenner, IPT Program Developer and distance program contact person.

Specializations: The Master of Science in Instructional & Performance Technology (IPT) degree is intended to prepare students for careers in the areas of instructional technology, performance technology, instructional design, performance improvement, training, education and training management, e-learning, human resources, organizational development, and human performance consulting. The department also offers three graduate certificate programs in; Human Performance Technology (HPT), Workplace E-Learning and Performance Support (WELPS), and Workplace Instructional Design. The graduate certificates can be earned enroute to the MS with the credits eligible for application to the degree.

Features: The IPT students write a monthly column called Tales from the Field in the International Society for Performance Improvements free e-newsletter performance express; http://ipt.boisestate.edu/AboutProgram/performanceXpress. htm. We have a group on LinkedIn called the Instructional & Performance Technology—Network (IPT-N) that individuals are invited to join; http://ipt. boisestate.edu/Resources/IPT-N.htm.

Admission Requirements: undergraduate degree with 3.0 GPA, one-to-two page essay describing why you want to pursue this program and how it will contribute to your personal and professional development, and a resume of personal qualifications and work experience. For more information, visit: http://ipt.boisestate.edu/applica tion_admission.htm.

Degree Requirements: 36 semester hours in instructional and performance technology and related course work; and two options for a culminating activity; thesis or portfolio defense (included in 36 credit hours).

Number of Full Time Faculty: 6; **Number of Other Faculty**: 8.

Degrees awarded in 2010–2011 Academic Year—Masters: 45; **Ph.D.**: 0; **Other**: 0.

Grant Monies awarded in 2010–2011 Academic Year: 0.

Name of Institution: Governors State University.

Name of Department or Program: College of Arts and Sciences.

Address: 1 University Parkway, University Park, IL 60466, USA.

Phone Number: (708)534-4051; **Fax Number**: (708)534-7895.

Email Contact: mlanigan@govst.edu; **URL**: http://www.govst.edu/hpt.

Contact Person: Mary Lanigan, Associate Professor, Human Performance and Training.

Specializations: M.A. in Communication and Training with HP&T major—Program concentrates on building instructional design skills. Most classes are delivered in a hybrid format of online and face to face. Some classes are almost all online.

Features: Instructional Design overview; front-end analysis including both needs and task; design and delivery using various platforms; evaluation skills and how to predict behavior transfer; various technologies; consulting; project management; systems thinking; principles of message design; and more.

Admission Requirements: Undergraduate degree in any field; 2.75 GPA and a statement of purpose.

Degree Requirements: 36 credit hours. All in instructional and performance technology; internship or advanced field project required. Metropolitan Chicago area based.

Number of Full Time Faculty: 1; **Number of Other Faculty**: 3.

Degrees awarded in 2010–2011 Academic Year—Masters: 10; **Ph.D.**: 0; **Other**: 0.

Grant Monies awarded in 2010–2011 Academic Year: 0.

Name of Institution: Southern Illinois University at Carbondale.

Name of Department or Program: Department of Curriculum and Instruction.

Address: 625 Wham Drive, Mailcode 4610, Carbondale, IL 62901, USA.

Phone Number: (618)4534218; **Fax Number**: (618)4534244.

Email Contact: sashrock@siu.edu.; **URL**: http://idt.siu.edu/

Contact Person: Sharon Shrock, Coordinator, Instructional Design/Instructional Technology.

Specializations:

M.S.Ed. in Curriculum & Instruction (with specializations in Instructional Design and Instructional Technology).

Ph.D. in Education (with concentration in Instructional Technology).

Features:

All specializations are oriented to multiple education settings.

The ID program emphasizes non-school (primarily corporate) learning environments, human performance technology, and criterion-referenced performance assessment.

The IT program covers many essential skills and tools leading to the production of e-Learning and performance assessment using digital games and other virtual learning environments.

Admission Requirements:

M.S.: Bachelor's degree, 2.7 undergraduate GPA, transcripts.

Ph.D.: Master's degree, 3.25 GPA, GRE scores, three letters of recommendation, transcripts, writing sample.

International students without a degree from a US institution must submit TOEFL score.

Degree Requirements:

M.S., 32 credit hours with thesis; 36 credit hours without thesis.

Ph.D., 40 credit hours beyond the master's degree in courses, 24 credit hours for the dissertation.

Number of Full Time Faculty: 3; **Number of Other Faculty**: 1.

Degrees awarded in 2010–2011 Academic Year—Masters: 5; **Ph.D.**: 0; **Other**: 0.

Grant Monies awarded in 2010–2011 Academic Year: 71,000.

Name of Institution: University of Illinois at Urbana-Champaign.

Name of Department or Program: Curriculum, Technology, and Education Reform (CTER) Program, Department of Educational Psychology.

Address: 226 Education Building, 1310 S 6th Street, Champaign, IL 61820, USA.

Phone Number: (217)244-3315; **Fax Number**: (217)244-7620.

Email Contact: cter-info-L@listserv.illinois.edu; **URL**: http://cter.ed.uiuc.edu.

Contact Person: Doe-Hyung Kim, Visiting Project Coordinator, Department of Educational Psychology.

Specializations: Ed.M. in Educational Psychology with emphasis in Curriculum, Technology, and Education Reform.

Features: This Master of Education program is geared toward teachers and trainers interested in learning more about the integration of computer-based technology in the classroom. This online set of project-based courses offers an opportunity to earn a coherent, high-quality master's degree online, with most interactions through personal computers and Internet connections at home or workplace.

Admission Requirements: Application to the Graduate College, three letters of recommendation, personal statement. For more information go to: http://cterport. ed.uiuc.edu/admissions_folder/application_procedures_html.

Degree Requirements: Eight courses (5 requirements + 3 electives) required for Ed.M.

Number of Full Time Faculty: 4; **Number of Other Faculty**: 2.

Degrees awarded in 2010–2011 Academic Year—Masters: 28; **Ph.D.**: 0; **Other**: 0.

Grant Monies awarded in 2010–2011 Academic Year: 0.

Name of Institution: Northern Illinois University.

Name of Department or Program: Educational Technology, Research and Assessment.

Address: 208 Gabel Hall, DeKalb, IL 60115, USA.

Phone Number: (815)753-9339; **Fax Number**: (815)753-9388.

Email Contact: edtech@niu.edu; **URL**: http://www.cedu.niu.edu/etra.

Contact Person: Dr. Jeffrey B. Hecht, Department Chair.

Specializations: M.S.Ed. in Instructional Technology with concentrations in Instructional Design, Distance Education, Educational Computing, and Media Administration; Ed.D. in Instructional Technology, emphasizing instructional design and development, computer education, media administration, and preparation for careers in business, industry, and higher education. In addition, Illinois state certification in school library media is offered in conjunction with either degree or alone.

Features: Program is highly individualized. All facilities remodeled and modernized in 2002–2003 featuring five smart classrooms and over 110 student use desktop and laptop computers. Specialized equipment for digital audio and video editing, web site and CD creation, and presentations. All students are encouraged to create portfolios highlighting personal accomplishments and works (required at Masters). Master's program started in 1968, doctorate in 1970.

Admission Requirements: M.S.Ed.: 2.75 undergraduate GPA, GRE verbal and quantitative scores, two references. Ed.D.: 3.25 M.S. GPA, writing sample, three references, interview.

Degree Requirements: M.S.Ed.: 39 hours, including 30 in instructional technology; portfolio. Ed.D.: 63 hours beyond Master's, including 15 hours for dissertation.

Number of Full Time Faculty: 0; **Number of Other Faculty**: 0.

Degrees awarded in 2010–2011 Academic Year—Masters: 0; **Ph.D.**: 0; **Other**: 0.

Grant Monies awarded in 2010–2011 Academic Year: 0.

Name of Institution: Southern Illinois University Edwardsville.

Name of Department or Program: Instructional Technology Program.

Address: School of Education, Edwardsville, IL 62026-1125, USA.

Phone Number: (618)650-3277; **Fax Number**: (618)650-3808.

Email Contact: mthomec@siue.edu; **URL**: http://www.siue.edu/education/edld/it/index.shtml.

Contact Person: Dr. Melissa Thomeczek, Program Director, Department of Educational Leadership.

Specializations: The Educational Technologies option enables teachers and other school personnel to learn how to plan, implement, and evaluate technology-based instruction and learning activities in p-12 settings. Students pursuing this option will become knowledgeable users of technology as well as designers of curriculum and instruction that effectively utilize and integrate technology to improve student learning. Students interested in leadership roles in educational technology, such as those wishing to become technology coordinators in schools or school districts, can work toward meeting the standards for the Illinois State Board of Education's (ISBE) Technology Specialist endorsement through this program. The Library Information Specialist option enables teachers and other school personnel to learn how to plan, implement, and evaluate library information-based activities in P-12 settings. Students pursuing this option will become knowledgeable users of library information as well as designers of curriculum and instruction that effectively utilize and integrate library information to improve student learning. Students interested in Library Information Specialist endorsement can work towards meeting the standards for the Illinois State Board of Education's Library Information Specialist endorsement through this program. The Instructional Design & Performance Improvement option focuses on skills necessary for careers in the areas of instructional technology, performance technology, instructional design, training, and performance consulting. Emphasis is placed on systematic instructional design and on the use of various media and technologies for learning and instruction. Students in this option may also focus on the design and development of online learning and other performance improvement strategies. The Interactive Multimedia Technologies option is appropriate for people wishing to pursue the design and development of various interactive multimedia and web-based learning experiences. This option prepares students for careers with publishing and production companies, consulting firms, and other businesses that produce engaging multimedia applications for learning and other opportunities. Course work focuses on theories and methods for designing compelling user experiences, developing skills with tools for web and other delivery media, and project management strategies.

Features: Several unique features of the program provide students with opportunities for important practical experiences that complement course work. Juried presentations provide students with an opportunity to share their work with a jury of professors and peers, and defend their work in light of their own goals and the content of their degree program. Design Studios provide students with opportunities to work on real-world projects for a variety of real clients in order to develop skills in collaboration, design, development tools and techniques, and project management.

Admission Requirements: The requirements for admission are a bachelor's degree and a GPA of 3.0 or above during their last 2 years of undergraduate work.

Degree Requirements: 36 semester hours; Thesis or Final Project options.

Number of Full Time Faculty: 4; **Number of Other Faculty**: 1.

Degrees awarded in 2010–2011 Academic Year—Masters: 6; **Ph.D.**: 0; **Other**: 0.

Grant Monies awarded in 2010–2011 Academic Year: 0.

Name of Institution: Western Illinois University.

Name of Department or Program: Instructional Technology and Telecommunications.

Address: 47 Harrabin Hall, Macomb, IL 61455, USA.

Phone Number: (309)298-1952; **Fax Number**: (309)298-2978.

Email Contact: hh-hemphill@wiu.edu; **URL**: http://www.wiu.edu/idt.

Contact Person: Hoyet H. Hemphill, Ph.D., Chair. Ph.D. in Instructional Technology.

Specializations: Undergraduate programs B.S. options in: Instructional Multimedia and Web-Based Development, Instructional Simulation and Games, Instructional Methods and Training Undergraduate Minors in: Web Design, Digital Media, Photographic Media Graduate Program; M.S. in Instructional Design and Technology (available online); Six Post-Baccalaureate Certificates (PBC)—two completely online (K-12 Technology Specialist option for M.S. or PBC).

Features: M.S. program approved by Illinois Board of Higher Education in January 1996 with emphases in Instructional Design and Technology, Web-Design, Interactive Multimedia, and Distance Education. M.S. can be completed entirely online. M.S. and Post-Baccalaureate Certificate in P-12 Technology Specialist. B.S. in Instructional Design and Technology approved in 1997. Three options for B.S. Courses are lab-based, hands-on. Undergraduate Minors in: Web Design, Digital Media, Photographic Media.

Admission Requirements: M.S.: Bachelor's degree with minimum 2.75 GPA overall or 3.0 for last 2 years. Otherwise, 12 semester hours of graduate work with GPA of 3.2 or higher. English proficiency (TOEFL) for international students.

Degree Requirements: M.S.: 32 semester hours, thesis or applied project, or 35 semester hours with portfolio. Certificate Program in Instructional Technology Specialization. Graphic applications, training development, video production. Each track option is made of 5 courses or a total of 15 semester hours, except for Technology Specialist, which is 24 semester hours. B.S.: 120 hours program.

Number of Full Time Faculty: 8; **Number of Other Faculty**: 3.

Degrees awarded in 2010–2011 Academic Year—Masters: 24; **Ph.D.**: 0; **Other**: 11.

Grant Monies awarded in 2010–2011 Academic Year: 0.

Name of Institution: Indiana State University.

Name of Department or Program: Department of Curriculum, Instruction, and Media Technology.

Address: N/A, Terre Haute, IN 47809, USA.

Phone Number: (812)237-2937; **Fax Number**: (812)237-4348.

Email Contact: espowers@isugw.indstate.edu; **URL**: 0.

Contact Person: Dr. James E. Thompson, Program Coordinator.

Specializations: Master's degree in Instructional Technology with education focus or with non-education focus; Specialist Degree program in Instructional Technology; Ph.D. in Curriculum, Instruction with specialization in Media Technology.

Features: 0.

Admission Requirements: 0.

Degree Requirements: Master's: 32 semester hours, including 18 in media; thesis optional; Ed.S.: 60 semester hours beyond bachelor's degree; Ph.D., approximately 100 hours beyond bachelor's degree.

Number of Full Time Faculty: 0; **Number of Other Faculty**: 0.

Degrees awarded in 2010–2011 Academic Year—Masters: 0; **Ph.D.**: 0; **Other**: 0.

Grant Monies awarded in 2010–2011 Academic Year: 0.

Name of Institution: Clarke College.

Name of Department or Program: Graduate Studies.

Address: 1550 Clarke Drive, Dubuque, IA 52001, USA.

Phone Number: (563)588-8180; **Fax Number**: (563)584-8604.

Email Contact: llester@clarke.edu; **URL**: http://www.clarke.edu.

Contact Person: Margaret Lynn Lester.

Specializations: M.A.E. (Two tracks: Instructional Leadership & Literacy).

Features: The "Instructional Leadership" track of this program offers hybrid courses in educational technology. Courses are offered through WEB-ST and face to face. Outcomes are aligned with the National Educational Technology Standards for Educators.

Admission Requirements: Completed graduate application, official transcripts, photocopy of all teaching certificates and licenses, 2.75 GPA (4-point scale), two letters of reference, interview, statement of goals, and $25 application fee. (Minimum TOEFL score of 550 if English is not first language.)

Degree Requirements: 9 hours in Research Core; 9 hours in Instructional Core; and 18 hours in Instructional Leadership Track.

Number of Full Time Faculty: –; **Number of Other Faculty**: –.

Degrees awarded in 2010–2011 Academic Year—Masters: –; **Ph.D.**: –; **Other**: –.

Grant Monies awarded in 2010–2011 Academic Year: –.

Name of Institution: Iowa State University.

Name of Department or Program: College of Education.

Address: E262 Lagomarcino Hall, Ames, IA 50011, USA.

Phone Number: (515)294-7021; **Fax Number**: (515)294-6260.

Email Contact: pkendall@iastate.edu; **URL**: http://www.educ.iastate.edu/

Contact Person: Niki Davis, Director, Center for Technology in Learning and Teaching.

Specializations: M.Ed., M.S., and Ph.D. in Curriculum and Instructional Technology. Features: Prepares candidates as practitioners and researchers in the field of curriculum and instructional technology. All areas of specialization emphasize appropriate and effective applications of technology in teacher education. M.Ed. program also offered at a distance (online and face-to-face learning experiences).

Features: practicum experiences related to professional objectives, supervised study, and research projects tied to long-term studies within the program, development, and implementation of new techniques, teaching strategies, and operational procedures in instructional resources centers and computer labs, program emphasis on technologies for teachers.

Admission Requirements: Admission Requirements: M.Ed. and M.S.: Bachelor's degree, top half of undergraduate class, official transcripts, three letters, autobiography. Ph.D.: top half of undergraduate class, official transcripts, three letters, autobiography, GRE scores, scholarly writing sample.

Degree Requirements: Degree Requirements: M.Ed. 32 credit hours (7 research, 12 foundations, 13 applications, and leadership in instructional technology); and action research project. M.S. 36 credit hours (16 research, 12 foundations, 8 applications, and leadership in instructional technology); and thesis. Ph.D. 78 credit hours (minimum of 12 research, minimum of 15 foundations, additional core credits in conceptual, technical and advanced specialization areas, minimum of 12 dissertation); portfolio and dissertation.

Number of Full Time Faculty: 0; **Number of Other Faculty**: 0.

Degrees awarded in 2010–2011 Academic Year—Masters: 0; **Ph.D.**: 0; **Other**: 0.

Grant Monies awarded in 2010–2011 Academic Year: 0.

Name of Institution: Emporia State University.

Name of Department or Program: School of Library and Information Management.

Address: 1200 Commercial, PO Box 4025, Emporia, KS 66801, USA.

Phone Number: (800)552-4770; **Fax Number**: (620)341-5233.

Email Contact: idt@emporia.edu; **URL**: http://slim.emporia.edu.

Contact Person: Daniel Roland, Director of Communications.

Specializations: Masters of Library Science (ALA accredited program); Masters in Legal Information Management—in partnership with the University of Kansas School of Law—50 semester hours or 15 hours certificate. School Library Certification program, which includes 27 hours of the M.L.S. program; Ph.D. in Library and Information Management B.S. in Information Resource Studies Information Management Certificate—18 hours of MLS curriculum Library Services Certificates—6 separate 12-hour programs of undergraduate work available for credit or noncredit. Areas include Information Sources and Services; Collection Management; Technology; Administration; Youth Services; and Generalist.

Features: The Master of Library Science program is also delivered to satellite campus sites in Denver, Salt Lake City, Portland, Oregon. New programs tend to start every 3 years in each location. New programs include Denver—Summer 2004, Portland—Spring 2005, Salt Lake City—Fall 2005.

Admission Requirements: Undergrad GPA of 3.0 or better for master's degrees, 3.5 or better for Ph.D.. GRE score of 1,000 points combined in Verbal and Analytical sections for master's degrees, 1,100 for Ph.D.. GRE can be waived for students already holding a graduate degree in which they earned a 3.75 GPA or better. Admission interview.

Degree Requirements: M.L.S.: 42 semester hours. Ph.D.: total of 55–59 semester hours beyond the masters.

Number of Full Time Faculty: 0; **Number of Other Faculty**: 0.

Degrees awarded in 2010–2011 Academic Year—Masters: 0; **Ph.D.**: 0; **Other**: 0.

Grant Monies awarded in 2010–2011 Academic Year: 0.

Name of Institution: Kansas State University.

Name of Department or Program: Curriculum & Instruction.

Address: 261 Bluemont Hall, Manhattan, KS 66506, USA.

Phone Number: (785)-532-5716; **Fax Number**: (785)-532-7304.

Email Contact: talab@ksu.edu; **URL**: http://coe.ksu.edu/ecdol.

Contact Person: Dr. Rosemary Talab.

Specializations: The Educational Computing, Design, and Online Learning Program has these specializations: (I) M.S. in Curriculum & Instruction with specialties in (1) Educational Computing, Design, and Online Learning (online option), (2) Digital Teaching and Learning (online). (II) Ph.D. in Curriculum & Instruction with specialty in Educational Computing, Design, and Online Learning (online). (III) KSU Graduate School Certificate in Digital Teaching and Learning Masters program started in 1982; doctoral in 1987; Certificate in 1999.

Features: All coursework for the Certificate, M.A., and Ph.D. can be taken online. ECDOL is an online program that focuses on research, theory, practice, ethics, and the design of learning environments, with an emphasis on emerging technologies. Coursework includes instructional design, virtual learning environments, game-based learning, the design and evaluation of online courses, etc. Classes are offered regularly on a rotating basis. A cohort group is begun each fall for the Professional Seminar 1 and 2 academic year via videoconferencing, in which major areas of the field (change and ID models, distance education and online learning, etc.) are explored, as well as various delivery methods and technologies. E-portfolios are required at the Certificate and Master's degree levels. The Ph.D. program allows the student to tailor the classes to individual needs. At the Certificate and Master's degree levels, the DTL program offers classroom teachers leadership opportunities as technology facilitators and lead teachers, with coursework available in integrating emerging technologies into instruction to improve student achievement through a blend of practical technology skills with research and theory. The Master's degree level ECDOL program is offered to those who have B.A.s in other fields who wish to pursue a specialty in instructional design or prepare for the Ph.D. in ECDOL or who wish to design instructional environments in online and virtual learning environments. The KSU Graduate School Certificate in Digital Teaching and Learning is a 15-hour completely online program for the classroom teacher with uniform exit outcomes and an e-portfolio requirement. The emphasis is on the application of technological and pedagogical theory, knowledge, and practical application skills that can be directly translated into the classroom. The ECDOL program, as a whole, is on Twitter (#Proseminar1) and on Facebook (KSUECDOL), http://www.facebook.com/group.php?gid=113228718719613, though the group is private.

Admission Requirements: M.S. in ECDOL: B average in undergraduate work, mid-range scores on TOEFL. M.S./Certificate in DTL: B average in undergraduate work and teaching experience. Ph.D.: B average in undergraduate and graduate work, GRE, three letters of recommendation, experience or basic courses in educational computing.

Degree Requirements: Certificate is 15 hours and requires an e-portfolio and technology project DTL is a 15-hour KSU Graduate School Certificate program; e-portfolio and project are required M.S.: 31 semester hours (minimum of 15 in specialty); thesis, internship, or practicum not required, but all three are possible; e-portfolio and project are required. The Ph.D. degree is 36–42 hours, with 30 hours of research, for a total of 60 hours, minimum. Certificate: 15 hours M.S. 31 hours Ph.D.: 60 hours semester hours are required and 30 hours are taken from the students' master's program. There is a minimum of 21 hours in Educational Computing, Design, and Online Learning or related area approved by committee and 30 hours for dissertation research.

Number of Full Time Faculty: 1; **Number of Other Faculty**: 5.

Degrees awarded in 2010–2011 Academic Year: –; **Masters**: 7; **Ph.D.**: 3; **Other**: 1.

Grant Monies awarded in 2010–2011 Academic Year: 0.

Name of Institution: University of Louisville.

Name of Department or Program: Workforce and Human Resource Education Program.

Address: 1905 South 1st Street, Louisville, KY 40292, USA.

Phone Number: (502)852-6667; **Fax Number**: (502)852-4563.

Email Contact: rod.githens@louisville.edu; **URL**: http://louisville.edu/education/departments/elfh/whre.

Contact Person: Rod Githens.

Specializations: B.S. in Workforce Leadership (specialization in Training and Development) (100% online or face-to-face), M.S. in Human Resource Education (100% online or face-to-face), M.Ed. in Instructional Technology (please note: this program is offered for educators in P-12 settings through the Department of Teaching and Learning), Ph.D. in Educational Leadership and Organizational Development (specialization in Human Resource Development).

Features: Our program is Relevant, Rigorous, and Research-based: Relevant. The program has a strong emphasis on hands-on, applied projects that provide direct application to the field. Our instructors have practitioner experience in the field and many currently work in HR-related positions in Louisville and around the country: Rigorous. Expect to work hard and complete challenging assignments. Our goal is to help you develop the skills to think unconventionally about conventional problems: Research-based. The program is designed around research-based competencies from the American Society for Training and Development, International Society for Performance Improvement, and the Society for Human Resource Management. Faculty members have strong theoretical and conceptual backgrounds that guide both their teaching and their practical approach to the field.

Admission Requirements: Masters Degree: 3.0 GPA, 800 GRE, two letters of recommendation, goal statement, resume Ph.D.: 3.5 GPA, 1,000 GRE, letters of recommendation, goal statement, resume.

Degree Requirements: See program websites:

B.S. in Workforce Leadership: http://louisville.edu/education/degrees/files/bs-wl-tdc-curriculum.pdf

M.S. in Human Resource Education: http://louisville.edu/education/degrees/ms-hre.html

M.Ed. in Instructional Technology: http://louisville.edu/education/degrees/med-it.html

Ph.D. in Educational Leadership and Organization Development (HRD Specialty): http://louisville.edu/education/degrees/files/phd-elod-hr.pdf.

Number of Full Time Faculty: 11; **Number of Other Faculty**: 14.

Degrees awarded in 2010–2011 Academic Year—Masters: 25; **Ph.D.**: 5; **Other**: 0.

Grant Monies awarded in 2010–2011 Academic Year: 4,500,000.

Name of Institution: Louisiana State University.

Name of Department or Program: School of Library and Information Science.

Address: 267 Coates Hall, Baton Rouge, LA 70803, USA.

Phone Number: (225)578-3158; **Fax Number**: (225)578-4581.

Email Contact: bpaskoff@lsu.edu; **URL**: http://slis.lsu.edu.

Contact Person: Beth Paskoff, Dean, School of Library and Information Science.

Specializations: Archives, academic libraries, information technology, medical libraries, public libraries, special libraries, youth services, Louisiana School Library Certification. Dual degrees are available in Systems Science and in History.

Features: Distance education courses available at seven locations in Louisiana.

Admission Requirements: Bachelors degree, prefer 3.00 GPA GRE scores: prefer 500+ on verbal.

Degree Requirements: M.L.I.S.: 40 hours, comprehensive exam, completion of degree program in 5 years.

Number of Full Time Faculty: 11; **Number of Other Faculty**: 0.

Degrees awarded in 2010–2011 Academic Year—Masters: 60; **Ph.D.**: 0; **Other**: 2.

Grant Monies awarded in 2010–2011 Academic Year: 111,841.

Name of Institution: Boston University.

Name of Department or Program: School of Education.

Address: Two Silber Way, Boston, MA 02215-1605, USA.

Phone Number: (617)353-3181; **Fax Number**: (617)353-3924.

Email Contact: whittier@bu.edu; **URL**: http://www.bu.edu/sed; http://www.bu.edu/emt.

Contact Person: David B. Whittier, Clinical Associate Professor and Coordinator, Program in Educational Media and Technology.

Specializations: Ed.M., CAGS (Certificate of Advanced Graduate Study) in Educational Media and Technology; Ed.D. in Curriculum and Teaching, Specializing in Educational Media and Technology; preparation for Massachusetts public school License as Instructional Technology Specialist.

Features: The Master's Program prepares graduates for professional careers as educators, instructional designers, developers of educational materials, and managers of the human and technology-based resources necessary to support education and training with technology. Graduates are employed in pK-12 schools, higher education, industry, medicine, public health, government, publishing, and a range of services such as finance and insurance. Students come to the program from many different backgrounds and with a wide range of professional goals. The doctoral program sets the study of Educational Media & Technology within the context of education and educational research in general, and curriculum and teaching in particular. In addition to advanced work in the field of Educational Media and Technology, students examine and conduct research and study the history of educational thought and practice. Graduates make careers in education as professors and researchers, technology directors and managers, and as developers of technology-based materials and systems. Graduates who work in both educational and non-educational organizations are often responsible for managing the human and technological resources required to create learning experiences that include the development and delivery of technology-based resources and distance education.

Admission Requirements: All degree programs require either the GRE or MAT test score completed within past 5 years and recommendations. Specific programs also include: Ed.M.: undergraduate degree and GPA. For CAGS, in addition to above, an earned Ed.M. is required. For Ed.D., three letters of recommendation, test scores, transcripts, earned masters degree, and two writing samples: a statement of goals and qualifications and an analytical essay are required. Contact Graduate Admissions office at.

Degree Requirements: Ed.M.: 36 credit hours (including 26 hours from required core curriculum, 10 from electives). CAGs: 32 credits beyond Ed.M., one of which must be a curriculum and teaching course and a comprehensive exam. Ed.D.: 60 credit hours of courses selected from Educational Media and Technology, curriculum and teaching, and educational thought and practice with comprehensive exams; course work and apprenticeship in research; dissertation.

Number of Full Time Faculty: 1; **Number of Other Faculty**: 10.

Degrees awarded in 2010–2011 Academic Year—Masters: 12; **Ph.D.**: 4; **Other**: 0.

Grant Monies awarded in 2010–2011 Academic Year: 20,000.

Name of Institution: Fitchburg State University.

Name of Department or Program: Division of Graduate and Continuing Education.

Address: 160 Pearl Street, Fitchburg, MA 01420, USA.

Phone Number: (978)665-3544; **Fax Number**: (978)665-3055.

Email Contact: rhowe@fitchburgstate.edu; **URL**: www.fitchburgstate.edu.

Contact Person: Dr. Randy Howe, Chair.

Specializations: M.Ed. in Educational Leadership and Management with specialization in Technology Leadership.

Features: Collaborating with professionals working in the field both for organizations and as independent producers, Fitchburg offers a unique M.Ed. program. The objectives are to develop in candidates the knowledge and skills for the effective implementation of technology within business, industry, government, not-for-profit agencies, health services, and education.

Admission Requirements: MAT or GRE scores, official transcript(s) of a baccalaureate degree, 2 or more years of experience in communications or media or education, three letters of recommendation.

Degree Requirements: 39 semester credit hours.

Number of Full Time Faculty: 5; **Number of Other Faculty**: 7.

Degrees awarded in 2010–2011 Academic Year—Masters: 4; **Ph.D.**: 0; **Other**: 0.

Grant Monies awarded in 2010–2011 Academic Year: 0.

Name of Institution: Lesley University.

Name of Department or Program: Technology in Education.

Address: 29 Everett Street, Cambridge, MA 02138-2790, USA.

Phone Number: (617)349-8419; **Fax Number**: (617)349-8169.

Email Contact: gblakesl@lesley.edu; **URL**: http://www.lesley.edu/soe/111tech.html.

Contact Person: Dr. George Blakeslee, Division Director.

Specializations: M.Ed. in Technology in Education CAGS/Ed.S. in Technology in Education Ph.D. in Educational Studies with specialization in Technology in Education.

Features: M.Ed. program is offered off-campus at 70+ sites in 21 states; contact 617-349-8311 for information. The degree is also offered completely online. Contact Maureen Yoder, myoder@lesley.edu, or (617)348-8421 for information. Or check our website: URL above.

Admission Requirements: Completed bachelor's Teaching certificate.

Degree Requirements: M.Ed.: 33 semester hours in technology, integrative final project in lieu of thesis, no internship or practicum. C.A.G.S.: 36 semester hours. Ph.D. requirements available on request.

Number of Full Time Faculty: –; **Number of Other Faculty**: –.

Degrees awarded in 2010–2011 Academic Year—Masters: –; **Ph.D.**: –; **Other**: –.

Grant Monies awarded in 2010–2011 Academic Year: –

Name of Institution: Harvard University.

Name of Department or Program: Graduate School of Education.

Address: Appian Way, Cambridge, MA 02138, USA.

Phone Number: (617)495-3543; **Fax Number**: (617)495-9268.

Email Contact: pakir@gse.harvard.edu; **URL**: http://www.gse.harvard.edu/tie.

Contact Person: Joseph Blatt, Director, Technology, Innovation, and Education Program; Irene Pak, program coordinator, Technology, Innovation, and Education Program.

Specializations: The Technology, Innovation, and Education Program (TIE) at Harvard prepares students to contribute to the thoughtful design, implementation, and assessment of educational media and technology initiatives. Graduates of the program fill leadership positions in a wide range of fields, including design and production, policy development and analysis, technology integration and administration, research and evaluation, and teaching with new technologies. Some distinctive features of studying educational technology in TIE include: *Focus on learning and teaching: Our approach puts learning and teaching at the center, with technology as the means, not the mission. Our courses examine cutting-edge technologies that bridge distance and time, the research behind them, and the design that goes into them—but we always center on the cognitive, affective, and social dimensions of learning, not on hardware or fashion. *A world-class faculty: Our faculty combines internationally recognized researchers with leading professionals in design and evaluation. We are all committed teachers and learners, dedicated to supporting you as a student and helping you craft a course of study that meets your goals. *A curriculum that builds leaders: Our curriculum bridges three broad strands of design, implementation, and research. Design courses apply learning principles to creating software, networks, digital video and television, handheld applications, and multi-user virtual environments. Implementation courses focus on using new technologies to bring about transformative changes in educational practice. Courses on research emphasize formulating evaluation designs that are both rigorous and practical. To deepen connections between theory and practice, TIE students often undertake an internship in one of the many research projects, educational technology firms, or media production organizations in the Boston area. *A diverse community of learners: Our community includes students of all ages, from all parts of the globe, with varied professional backgrounds and experience in technology. The upshot is that students have endless opportunities to learn from one another, exchanging insights about the potential role for learning technologies in different settings and cultures. More information about the program, our faculty, and the student experience is available on our Web site, http://www.gse.harvard.edu/tie.

Features: Courses in design, technology policy and leadership, research and evaluation, leading to the Ed.M. degree in Technology, Innovation, and Education. The program offers access to other courses throughout Harvard University, and at MIT, as well as many internship opportunities in the Greater Boston media and technology community.

Admission Requirements: GRE scores, 600 TOEFL, academic transcripts, three letters of recommendation, and a statement of purpose. Students interested in further information about the TIE Program should visit our Web site, http://www.gse.harvard.edu/tie, which includes a link to the Harvard Graduate School of Education online application.

Degree Requirements: 32 semester credits.

Number of Full Time Faculty: 5; **Number of Other Faculty**: 6.

Degrees awarded in 2010–2011 Academic Year—Masters: 40; **Ph.D.**: 0; **Other**: 0.

Grant Monies awarded in 2010–2011 Academic Year: 3,000,000.

Name of Institution: McDaniel College (formerly Western Maryland College).

Name of Department or Program: Graduate and Professional Studies.

Address: 2 College Hill, Westminster, MD 21157, USA.

Phone Number: (410)857-2507; **Fax Number**: (410)857-2515.

Email Contact: rkerby@mcdaniel.edu; **URL**: http://www.mcdaniel.edu.

Contact Person: Dr. Ramona N.Kerby, Coordinator, School Library Media Program, Graduate Studies.

Specializations: M.S. in Education with an emphasis in School Librarianship.

Features: School librarianship.

Admission Requirements: 3.0 Undergraduate GPA, three reference checklist forms from principal and other school personnel, acceptable application essay, acceptable Praxis test scores.

Degree Requirements: 37 credit hours, including professional digital portfolio.

Number of Full Time Faculty: 1; **Number of Other Faculty**: 5.

Degrees awarded in 2010–2011 Academic Year—Masters: 15; **Ph.D.**: 0; **Other**: 0.

Grant Monies awarded in 2010–2011 Academic Year: 0.

Name of Institution: Towson University.

Name of Department or Program: College of Education.

Address: Hawkins Hall, Towson, MD 21252, USA.

Phone Number: (410)704-4226; **Fax Number**: (410)704-4227.

Email Contact: jkenton@towson.edu; **URL**: http://grad.towson.edu/program/master/istc-ms/

Contact Person: Dr. Jeffrey M. Kenton, Assistant Dean: College of Education.

Specializations: M.S. degrees in Instructional Development, and Educational Technology (Contact Liyan Song: lsong@towson.edu); M.S. degree in School Library Media (Contact, David Robinson: derobins@towson.edu); Ed.D. degree in Instructional Technology (Contact, William Sadera, bsadera@towson.edu) (http://grad.towson.edu/program/doctoral/istc-edd/).

Features: Excellent labs. Strong practical hands-on classes. Focus of MS program—Students produce useful multimedia projects for use in their teaching and training. Many group activities within courses. School library media degree confers with Maryland State Department of Education certification as a Prek-12 Library Media Specialist. Innovative Ed.D. program with online hybrid courses and strong mix of theory and practical discussions.

Admission Requirements: Bachelor's degree from accredited institution with 3.0 GPA. (Conditional admission granted for many applicants with a GPA over 2.75). Doctoral requirements are listed: http://grad.towson.edu/program/doctoral/istc-edd/ar-istc-edd.asp.

Degree Requirements: MS degree is 36 graduate semester hours without thesis. Ed.D. is 63 hours beyond the MS degree.

Number of Full Time Faculty: 17; **Number of Other Faculty**: 5.

Degrees awarded in 2010–2011 Academic Year—Masters: 180; **Ph.D.**: 0; **Other**: 2.

Grant Monies awarded in 2010–2011 Academic Year: 0.

Name of Institution: Eastern Michigan University.

Name of Department or Program: Teacher Education.

Address: 313 John W Porter Building, Ypsilanti, MI 48197, USA.

Phone Number: (734)487-3260; **Fax Number**: (734)487-2101.

Email Contact: ncopeland@emich.edu; **URL**: http://www.emich.edu.

Contact Person: Nancy L. Copeland, Ed.D.—Associate Professor/Graduate Coordinator.

Specializations: M.A. and Graduate Certificate in Educational Media and Technology. The mission of this program is to prepare professionals who are capable of facilitating student learning in a variety of settings. The program is designed to provide students with both the knowledge base and the application skills that are required to use technology effectively in education. Focusing on the design, development, utilization, management, and evaluation of instructional systems moves us toward achieving this mission. Students who complete the educational technology concentration will be able to: (a) provide a rationale for using technology in the educational process; (b) identify contributions of major leaders in the field of educational media technology and instructional theory, and the impact that each leader has had on the field; (c) assess current trends in the area of educational media technology and relate the trends to past events and future implications; (d) integrate technology into instructional programs; (e) teach the operation and various uses of educational technology in instruction; (f) act as consultants/facilitators in educational media technology; (g) design and develop instructional products to meet specified needs; and (h) evaluate the effectiveness of instructional materials and systems.

Features: Courses in our 30 credit hour Educational Media & Technology (EDMT) program include technology and the reflective teacher, technology and student-centered learning, technology enhanced learning environments, issues and emerging technologies, instructional design, development of online materials, psychology of the adult learner, principles of classroom learning, curriculum foundations, research seminar, and seminar in educational technology. Since Spring 2003, all of the EDMT courses have been taught online. The program can be completed online. Students who do not want to receive a master's degree can apply for admission to our 20 credit hour Educational Media and Technology certificate. The EDMT courses for the certificate are also offered online.

Admission Requirements: Individuals seeking admission to this program must: (1) Comply with the Graduate School admission requirements. (2) Score 550 or better on the TOEFL, and 5 or better on TWE, if a non-native speaker of English. (3) Have a 2.75 undergraduate grade point average, or a 3.30 grade point average in 12 hours or more of work in a masters program. (4) Solicit two letters of reference. (5) Submit a statement of professional goals.

Degree Requirements: In order to graduate, each student is expected to: (1) Complete all work on an approved program of study (30 semester hours). (2) Maintain a "B" (3.0 GPA) average or better on course work taken within the program. (3) Get a recommendation from the faculty adviser. (4) Fill out an application for graduation and obtain the adviser's recommendation. (5) Meet all other requirements for a master's degree adopted by the Graduate School of Eastern Michigan University. (5) Complete a culminating experience (research, instructional development, or evaluation project) as determined by the student and faculty adviser.

Number of Full Time Faculty: 5; **Number of Other Faculty**: 0.

Degrees awarded in 2010–2011 Academic Year—Masters: 10; **Ph.D.**: 0; **Other**: 1.

Grant Monies awarded in 2010–2011 Academic Year: 0.

Name of Institution: Michigan State University.

Name of Department or Program: College of Education.

Address: 509D Erickson Hall, East Lansing, MI 48824, USA.

Phone Number: (517)-432-7195; **Fax Number**: (517)-353-6393.

Email Contact: edutech@msu.edu; **URL**: http://edutech.msu.edu.

Contact Person: Leigh Wolf.

Specializations: M.A. in Educational Technology with Learning, Design and Technology specialization.

Features: Extensive opportunities to work with faculty in designing online courses and online learning environments.

Admission Requirements: Please visit: http://edutech.msu.edu/apply_masters.html.

Degree Requirements: 30 semester hours, Web-based portfolio.

Number of Full Time Faculty: 6; **Number of Other Faculty**: 6.

Degrees awarded in 2010–2011 Academic Year—Masters: 60; **Ph.D.**: 0; **Other**: 0.

Grant Monies awarded in 2010–2011 Academic Year: 0.

Name of Institution: Wayne State University.

Name of Department or Program: Instructional Technology.

Address: 381 Education, Detroit, MI 48202, USA.

Phone Number: (313)577-1728; **Fax Number**: (313)577-1693.

Email Contact: tspannaus@wayne.edu; **URL**: http://coe.wayne.edu/aos/it/

Contact Person: Timothy W. Spannaus, Ph.D., Program Coordinator, Instructional Technology Programs, Div. of Administrative and Organizational Studies, College of Education.

Specializations: M.Ed. degrees in Instructional Design, Performance Improvement and Training, K-12 Technology Integration, and Interactive Technologies. Ed.D. and Ph.D. programs to prepare individuals for leadership in academic, business, industry, health care, and the K-12 school setting as professor, researcher, instructional design, and development specialists; media or learning resources managers or consultants; specialists in instructional video; and web-based instruction and multimedia specialists. The school also offers a 6-year specialist degree program in Instructional Technology. The IT program offers certificates in Online Learning, Educational Technology, and University Teaching.

Features: Guided experiences in instructional design and development activities in business and industry are available. Specific classes use a variety of technologies, including blogs, wikis, Twitter, Facebook, Google docs, and many others. M.Ed. programs are available face-to-face and online.

Admission Requirements: Ph.D.: Master's degree, 3.5 GPA, GRE, strong academic recommendations, interview.

Degree Requirements: Ph.D. 113 credit hours, including IT core and electives, research courses, graduate seminars, 30 credit dissertation. M.Ed.: 36 semester hours, including required project; internship recommended.

Number of Full Time Faculty: 6; **Number of Other Faculty**: 10.

Degrees awarded in 2010–2011 Academic Year—Masters: 48; **Ph.D.**: 11; **Other**: 8.

Grant Monies awarded in 2010–2011 Academic Year: 110,000.

Name of Institution: Northwest Missouri State University.

Name of Department or Program: Department of Computer Science/Information Systems.

Address: 800 University Avenue, Maryville, MO 64468, USA.

Phone Number: (660)562-1600.; **Fax Number**: (660)-562-1963.

Email Contact: nzeliff@nwmissouri.edu; **URL**: http://www.nwmissouri.edu/csis.

Contact Person: Dr. Nancy Zeliff.

Specializations: M.S.Ed. in Instructional Technology. Certificate Program in Instructional Technology.

Features: These degrees are designed for industry trainers and computer educators at the elementary, middle school, high school, and junior college level.

Admission Requirements: 3.0 undergraduate GPA, 700 GRE (V+Q).

Degree Requirements: 32 semester hours of graduate courses in computer science, education, and instructional technology courses. Fifteen hours of computer education and instructional technology courses for the Certificate.

Number of Full Time Faculty: 5; **Number of Other Faculty**: 7.

Degrees awarded in 2010–2011 Academic Year—Masters: 10; **Ph.D.**: 0; **Other**: 0.

Grant Monies awarded in 2010–2011 Academic Year: 0.

Name of Institution: St. Cloud State University.

Name of Department or Program: College of Education.

Address: 720 Fourth Avenue South, St. Cloud, MN 56301-4498, USA.

Phone Number: (308)255-2062; **Fax Number**: (308)255-4778.

Email Contact: cim@stcloudstate.edu; **URL**: http://www.stcloudstate.edu/cim.

Contact Person: Merton E. Thompson Coordinator, Center for Information Media.

Specializations: Undergraduate major and minor in Information Media. Undergraduate certificate in Instructional Technology. Masters degrees in Information Technologies, Educational Media, and Instructional Design & Training. Graduate certificates in Instructional Technology, Design for E-learning, and School Library Media.

Features: Most courses are available online as well as face to face.

Admission Requirements: Acceptance to Graduate School, written and oral preliminary examination.

Degree Requirements: Master's: 42 semester credits with thesis; 39 semester credits with starred paper or portfolio; 200-hour practicum is required for library media licensure. Course work for licensure may be applied to Educational Media Master's program.

Number of Full Time Faculty: 5; **Number of Other Faculty**: 21.

Degrees awarded in 2010–2011 Academic Year—Masters: 15; **Ph.D.**: 0; **Other**: 0.

Grant Monies awarded in 2010–2011 Academic Year: 0.

Name of Institution: University of Missouri-Columbia.

Name of Department or Program: School of Information Science & Learning Technologies.

Address: 303 Townsend Hall, Columbia, MO 65211, USA.

Phone Number: (573)884-2670; **Fax Number**: (573)884-2917.

Email Contact: caplowj@missouri.edu; **URL**: http://sislt.missouri.edu.

Contact Person: Julie Caplow.

Specializations: The Educational Technology program takes a theory-based approach to designing, developing, implementing, and researching computer-mediated environments to support human activity. We seek individuals who are committed to life-long learning and who aspire to use advanced technology to improve human learning and performance. Graduates of the program will find opportunities to use their knowledge and competencies as classroom teachers, media specialists, district technology specialists and coordinators, designers and developers of technology-based learning and information systems, training specialists for businesses, medical settings, and public institutions, as well as other creative positions. The curriculum at the Masters and Specialist levels has two focus areas: Technology in Schools and Learning Systems Design and Development; with coursework tailored to each focus area. For information regarding our Ph.D., see http://education.missouri.edu/SISLT/Ph.D./index.php.

Features: Both focus areas are available online via the Internet or on the MU campus. The Technology in Schools focus area is based on the ISTE competencies and culminates in an online portfolio based on these competencies. Several courses are augmented by technical resources developed at MU, including a technology integration knowledge repository and online collaboration tools. The Learning Systems Design and Development focus area links to business, military, and government contexts. This focus area offers a challenging balance of design and development coursework, in addition to coursework dealing with needs assessment and evaluation. For information regarding our Ph.D., see http://sislt.missouri.edu/phd.

Admission Requirements: Master: Bachelor's degree, GRE (V> 500; A >500; W >3.5); Ed.S.: Masters degree, GRE (V >500; A >500; W >3.5); Ph.D.: 3.5 graduate GPA, GRE (V >500; A >500; W >3.5); See website for details.

Degree Requirements: Masters and Ed.S.: Minimum of 30 graduate credit hours required for the degree; 15 hours of upper division coursework. Maximum of 6 hours of transfer credit. Ph.D. See website for details.

Number of Full Time Faculty: 10; **Number of Other Faculty**: 8.

Degrees awarded in 2010–2011 Academic Year—Masters: 59; **Ph.D.**: 10; **Other**: 18.

Grant Monies awarded in 2010–2011 Academic Year: 1,585,885.

Name of Institution: The University of Southern Mississippi.

Name of Department or Program: Instructional Technology and Design.

Address: 118 College Drive #5036 Hattiesburg, MS 39406-0001, USA.

Phone Number: (601)-266-4446; **Fax Number**: (601)-266-5957.

Email Contact: Taralynn.Hartsell@usm.edu; **URL**: http://dragon.ep.usm.edu/~it.

Contact Person: Dr. Taralynn Hartsell.

Specializations: The Department of Technology Education at the University of Southern Mississippi has two graduate programs relating to Instructional Technology and Design. The Masters of Science in Instructional Technology is a 33–36 hours program, and the Ph.D. of Instructional Technology and Design is a 60–75 hours program.

Features: The Masters of Science concentrates more on the technology application and integration aspect that helps students learn both hands-on application of technology, as well as theoretical and historical aspects related to the field of study. A majority of the coursework in the program can be completed online (about 70%), and the remaining coursework are hybrid or blended in nature (about 60% online and 40% traditional). The Ph.D. program is a new advanced study program for those wishing to pursue their education in the application of technology and design, research, and leadership (begins in Fall 2009). The Ph.D. program also has two emphasis areas that meet students' needs: instructional technology or instructional design. A majority of the coursework in the program can be completed online (between 60 and 80% depending upon emphasis area selected), and the remaining coursework are hybrid or blended in form (about 60% online and 40% traditional).

Admission Requirements: Please review the IT Web site for more information on the application procedures for each program: http://dragon.ep.usm.edu/~it. The GRE is mandatory for graduate programs.

Degree Requirements: Please review the IT Web site for more information on degree requirements for each program: http://dragon.ep.usm.edu/~it.

Number of Full Time Faculty: 4; **Number of Other Faculty**: 2.

Degrees awarded in 2010–2011 Academic Year—Masters: 7; **Ph.D.**: 0; **Other**: 0.

Grant Monies awarded in 2010–2011 Academic Year: 0.

Name of Institution: University of Montana.

Name of Department or Program: School of Education.

Address: 32 Campus Drive, Missoula, MT 59812, USA.

Phone Number: (406)243-2563; **Fax Number**: (406)243-4908.

Email Contact: sally.brewer@mso.umt.edu; **URL**: http://www.umt.edu.

Contact Person: Dr. Sally Brewer, Associate Professor of Library/Media.

Specializations: M.Ed. and Specialist degrees; K-12 School Library Media specialization with Library Media endorsement. Not represented in the rest of this is that we also have a Masters in Curricular Studies with an option in Instructional Design for Technology. Dr. Martin Horejsi is the coordinator of this program. His phone is (406)243-5785. His email is martin.horejsi@umontana.edu. This program is 37 credits and can be taken totally online. There are three full time faculty members in this program.

Features: Combined online program with University of Montana-Western in Dillon, MT. 25 credits.

Admission Requirements: (both degrees): GRE, letters of recommendation, 2.75 GPA.

Degree Requirements: M.Ed.: 37 semester credit hours (18 overlap with library media endorsement). Specialist: 28 semester hours (18 overlap).

Number of Full Time Faculty: 3; **Number of Other Faculty**: 1.

Degrees awarded in 2010–2011 Academic Year—Masters: 2; **Ph.D.**: 0; **Other**: 19.

Grant Monies awarded in 2010–2011 Academic Year: 0.

Name of Institution: East Carolina University.

Name of Department or Program: Department of Mathematics, Science, and Instructional Technology Education.

Address: MSITE Department, Mail Stop 566 East Carolina University, Greenville, NC 27858-4353, USA.

Phone Number: (252)328-9353; **Fax Number**: (252)328-4368.

Email Contact: browncar@mail.ecu.edu; **URL**: http://www.ecu.edu/educ/msite/it/maed/index.cfm.

Contact Person: Dr. Carol Brown, M.A.E.d. Program Coordinator.

Specializations: Master of Arts in Education (North Carolina Instructional Technology Specialist licensure); Master of Science in Instructional Technology; Certificate in Distance Education; Certificate in Virtual Reality in Education and Training; Certificate in Performance Improvement; Certificate for Special Endorsement in Computer Education.

Features: M.A.Ed. graduates are eligible for North Carolina Instructional Technology certification; Cert. for Special Endorsement in Computer Education for North Carolina Licensure as Technology Facilitator. ALL programs available 100% online. The program is housed in the Department of Mathematics, Science, and Instructional Technology Education. An important mission for this program is the emphasis on STEM in K12 schools including support of math and science teachers who are teacher leaders in their school systems.

Admission Requirements: Bachelor's degree; Admission to East Carolina University Graduate School. GRE [or Millers Analogy Test], references, and writing sample.

Degree Requirements: M.A.Ed.: 39 semester hours.

Number of Full Time Faculty: 7; **Number of Other Faculty**: 2.

Degrees awarded in 2010–2011 Academic Year—Masters: 48; **Ph.D.**: 0; **Other**: 0.

Grant Monies awarded in 2010–2011 Academic Year: 0.

Name of Institution: North Carolina State University.

Name of Department or Program: Department of Curriculum and Instruction, Instructional Technology Program.

Address: 602 Poe Hall, Campus Box 7801, Raleigh, NC 27695-7801, USA.

Phone Number: (919)515-6229; **Fax Number**: (919)515-6978.

Email Contact: kevin_oliver@ncsu.edu; **URL**: http://ced.ncsu.edu/cice/it/index.php.

Contact Person: Dr. Kevin Oliver, Associate Professor.

Specializations: Certificate in E-Learning. M.Ed. and M.S. in Instructional Technology. Ph.D. in Curriculum and Instruction with a concentration in Instructional Technology.

Features: Fully online E-Learning Certificate and Master's programs with flexibility for residents near the Raleigh-Durham area to take some on-campus courses if they wish. Doctoral program is not online. A limited number of assistantships are available for students who live near Raleigh, go to school full-time (9 hours/semester), and can work on campus 20 hours per week. Pays $15–20 k per semester with health benefits and tuition remission.

Admission Requirements: Master's: undergraduate degree from an accredited institution, 3.0 GPA in major or in latest graduate degree program; transcripts; GRE or MAT scores; three references; goal statement. Ph.D.: undergraduate degree from accredited institution, 3.0 GPA in major or latest graduate program; transcripts; recent GRE scores, writing sample, three references, vita, research and professional goals statement (see http://ced.ncsu.edu/cice/admissions.php).

Degree Requirements: Master's: 30 semester hours (M.Ed.), 36 semester hours (M.S.), thesis required for M.S. program. Ph.D.: 60 hours. Up to 12 hours of graduate-level transfer credits may be applied to any Masters program if the transfer credits are from Instructional Technology courses similar to those in the program. Transfer credits not accepted for doctoral program—60 new hours required at NC State.

Number of Full Time Faculty: 3; **Number of Other Faculty**: 3.

Degrees awarded in 2010–2011 Academic Year—Masters: 10; **Ph.D.**: 1; **Other**: 0.

Grant Monies awarded in 2010–2011 Academic Year: 0.

Name of Institution: University of North Carolina.

Name of Department or Program: School of Information and Library Science.

Address: 100 Manning Hall, CB#3360, Chapel Hill, NC 27599-3360, USA.

Phone Number: (919)843-5276; **Fax Number**: (919)962-8071.

Email Contact: smhughes@email.unc.edu; **URL**: http://www.ils.unc.edu/

Contact Person: Sandra Hughes-Hassell, Associate Professor, Coordinator, School Media Program.

Specializations: Master of Science Degree in Library Science (M.S.L.S.) with specialization in school library media. Post-Master's certification program.

Features: Rigorous academic program plus field experience requirement; excellent placement record.

Admission Requirements: Competitive admission based on all three GRE components (quantitative, qualitative, analytical), undergraduate GPA (plus graduate work if any), letters of recommendation, and student statement of career interest and school choice.

Degree Requirements: 48 semester hours, field experience, comprehensive exam, Master's paper.

Number of Full Time Faculty: 31; **Number of Other Faculty**: 1.

Degrees awarded in 2010–2011 Academic Year—Masters: 111; **Ph.D.**: 3; **Other**: 22.

Grant Monies awarded in 2010–2011 Academic Year: 6,843,136.

Name of Institution: University of Nebraska at Kearney.

Name of Department or Program: Teacher Education.

Address: 905 West 25th Street, Kearney, NE 68849-5540, USA.

Phone Number: (308)865-8833; **Fax Number**: (308)865-8097.

Email Contact: fredricksons@unk.edu; **URL**: http://www.unk.edu/academics/ecampus.aspx?id=6217.

Contact Person: Dr. Scott Fredrickson, Professor and Chair of the Instructional Technology Graduate Program.

Specializations: M.S.Ed. in Instructional Technology, M.S.Ed. in Library Media.

Features: Two main emphasis areas—Instructional Technology and School Library Media; The Instructional Technology track has an Information Technology endorsement module, and the School Library track has a module to obtain a School Library endorsement. To obtain either endorsement requires a current teaching certificate, however the degree itself does not.

Admission Requirements: Graduate Record Examination or completion of an electronic portfolio meeting department requirements, acceptance into graduate school, and approval of Instructional Technology Committee.

Degree Requirements: 36 credit hours—18 of which are required and 18 are elective. (30 hours are required for either endorsement with 6 hours of electives), and a capstone Instructional Technology project.

Number of Full Time Faculty: 5; **Number of Other Faculty**: 24.

Degrees awarded in 2010–2011 Academic Year—Masters: 44; **Ph.D.**: 0; **Other**: 0.

Grant Monies awarded in 2010–2011 Academic Year: 0.

Name of Institution: University of Nebraska-Omaha.

Name of Department or Program: College of Education Department of Teacher Education.

Address: Roskens Hall 308, Omaha, NE 68182, USA.

Phone Number: (402)554-2119; **Fax Number**: (402)554-2125.

Email Contact: rpasco@unomaha.edu; **URL**: http://www.unomaha.edu/libraryed/

Contact Person: Dr. Rebecca J. Pasco.

Specializations: Undergraduate Library Science Program (public, academic, and special libraries); School Library Endorsement (Undergraduate and Graduate); M.S. in Secondary Education with School Library concentration; M.S. in Elementary Education with School Library concentration; M.S. in Reading with School Library concentration; Master's in Library Science Program (Cooperative program with University of Missouri).

Features: Web-assisted format (combination of online and on-campus) for both undergraduate and graduate programs. School Library programs nationally recognized by American Association of School Librarians (AASL); Public, Academic and Special Libraries programs; Cooperative UNO/University of Missouri MLS program is ALA accredited.

Admission Requirements: As per University of Nebraska at Omaha undergraduate and graduate admissions requirements.

Degree Requirements: School Library Endorsement (Undergraduate and Graduate): 30 hours M.S. in Secondary and Elementary Education with School Library endorsement: 36 hours M.S. in Reading with School Library endorsement: 36 hours Masters in Library Science Program (Cooperative program with University of Missouri at Columbia): 42 hours.

Number of Full Time Faculty: 2; **Number of Other Faculty**: 10.

Degrees awarded in 2010–2011 Academic Year—Masters: 34; **Ph.D.**: 0; **Other**: 9.

Grant Monies awarded in 2010–2011 Academic Year: 2,500.

Name of Institution: Rutgers-The State University of New Jersey.

Name of Department or Program: School of Communication and Information.

Address: 4 Huntington Street, New Brunswick, NJ 08901-1071, USA.

Phone Number: (732)932-7500 Ext 8264; **Fax Number**: (732)932-2644.

Email Contact: kcassell@rutgers.edu; **URL**: http://www.comminfo.rutgers.edu/

Contact Person: Dr. Kay Cassell, Director, Master of Library and Information Science, Department of Library and Information Studies, School of Communication, Information and Library Studies. (732)932-7500 Ext 8955. Fax (732)932-2644. Dr. Michael Lesk, Chair.

Specializations: The Master of Library and Information Science (M.L.I.S.) program provides professional education for a wide variety of service and management careers in libraries, information agencies, the information industry, and in business, industry, government, research, and similar environments where information is a vital resource. Specializations include: school library media; services for children and youth; digital libraries; information retrieval/information systems; knowledge management (http://comminfo.rutgers.edu/master-of-library-and-information-science/curriculum-overview.html).

Features: The M.L.I.S. program, available both on campus and online, is organized around six themes in the field of library and information science: human–information interaction; information access; information and society; information systems; management; and organization of information. Six lead courses, one in each area, form the foundation of the curriculum and offer general knowledge of the major principles and issues of the field. Two or more central courses in each theme offer basic understanding and competencies in important components of the field. Specialization courses in each theme allow students to develop expertise in preparation for specific career objectives. The specialization in School Librarianship is certified with the NJ Department of Education. All students in the New Brunswick M.L.I.S. program work with an advisor to plan a course of study appropriate for their interests and career objectives.

Admission Requirements: A bachelor's degree or its equivalent from a recognized institution of higher education with a B average or better; GRE scores; Personal statement which presents a view of the library and information science profession and applicant's aspirations and goals in the library and information science professions; three letters of recommendation which focus on the applicants academic capacity to undertake a rigorous program of graduate study.

Degree Requirements: A minimum of 36 credits, or 12 courses, is required to earn the M.L.I.S. degree. All students are required to enroll in two non-credit classes, 501—Introduction to Library and Information Professions in their first semester, and 502—Colloquium in a later semester. There are no language requirements for the M.L.I.S. degree, and there is no thesis or comprehensive examination.

Number of Full Time Faculty: 22; **Number of Other Faculty**: 15.

Degrees awarded in 2010–2011 Academic Year—Masters: 161; **Ph.D.**: 10; **Other**: 0.

Grant Monies awarded in 2010–2011 Academic Year: 500,000.

Name of Institution: Appalachian State University.

Name of Department or Program: Department of Curriculum and Instruction.

Address: College of Education, Boone, NC 28608, USA.

Phone Number: (828)-262-2277; **Fax Number**: (828)-262-2686.

Email Contact: muffoletto@appstate.edu;riedlre@appstate.edu; **URL**: http:// edtech.ced.appstate.edu.

Contact Person: Robert Muffoletto.

Specializations: M.A. in Educational Media and Technology with three areas of concentration: Computers, Media Literacy, and Media Production. A plan of study in Internet distance teaching is offered online. Two certificate programs: (1) Distance Learning—Internet delivered; (2) Media Literacy.

Features: Business, university, community college, and public school partnership offer unusual opportunities for learning. The programs are focused on developing learning environments over instructional environments.

Admission Requirements: Undergraduate degree.

Degree Requirements: 36 graduate semester hours. We also have certificates in (1) Distance Learning and (2) Media Literacy.

Number of Full Time Faculty: 0; **Number of Other Faculty**: 0.

Degrees awarded in 2010–2011 Academic Year—Masters: 5; **Ph.D.**: 0; **Other**: 0.

Grant Monies awarded in 2010–2011 Academic Year: 0.

Name of Institution: Buffalo State College.

Name of Department or Program: Computer Information Systems Department.

Address: 1300 Elmwood Avenue, Chase Hall 201, Buffalo, NY 14222-1095, USA.

Phone Number: (716)878-5528; **Fax Number**: (716)878-6677.

Email Contact: gareause@buffalostate.edu; **URL**: http://www.buffalostate.edu/cis/x471.xml.

Contact Person: Dr. Stephen E. Gareau, Program Coordinator.

Specializations: M.S. in Education in Educational Technology.

Features: This program is designed for K-12 and higher education educators, as well as trainers from business and industry, who wish to develop and expand their knowledge and skills in the development and application of various educational technologies. A wide range of media and tools are covered in the program, including text, graphics, audio, video, animation, models, simulations, games, and Web tools.

Admission Requirements: Bachelor's degree from accredited institution, undergraduate 3.0 GPA, three letters of recommendation, one letter from applicant.

Degree Requirements: 36 semester hours. See http://www.buffalostate.edu/cis/x471.xml for full details.

Number of Full Time Faculty: 3; **Number of Other Faculty**: 2.

Degrees awarded in 2010–2011 Academic Year—Masters: 50; **Ph.D.**: 0; **Other**: 0.

Grant Monies awarded in 2010–2011 Academic Year: 25,000.

Name of Institution: Fordham University.

Name of Department or Program: M.A. Program in Public Communications in the Department of Communication and Media Studies.

Address: Rose Hill Campus, 441 E Fordham Road, Bronx, NY 10458, USA.

Phone Number: (718)817-4860; **Fax Number**: (718)817-4868.

Email Contact: andersen@fordham.edu; **URL**: http://www.fordham.edu.

Contact Person: Fred Wertz, Department Chair, Tom McCourt, Director of Graduate Studies.

Specializations: The M.A. in Public Communications has three concentrations, (1) Media Analysis and Criticism, (2) Industries, Publics and Policy, (3) Screen Arts and Culture.

Features: Extensive Internship program: full-time students can complete program in 12 months, but many students take 8 months to complete the program.

Admission Requirements: 3.0 undergraduate GPA. Fellowship Applicants must take the GREs.

Degree Requirements: 10 courses (30) credits and either a media project, or a research paper or an M.A. Thesis to complete the degree.

Number of Full Time Faculty: 12; **Number of Other Faculty**: 4.

Degrees awarded in 2010–2011 Academic Year—Masters: 20; **Ph.D.**: 0; **Other**: 0.

Grant Monies awarded in 2010–2011 Academic Year: 150,000.

Name of Institution: Ithaca College.

Name of Department or Program: School of Communications.

Address: Park Hall, Ithaca, NY 14850, USA.

Phone Number: (607)274-1025; **Fax Number**: (607)274-7076.

Email Contact: hkalman@ithaca.edu; **URL**: http://www.ithaca.edu/gps/grad programs/comm/

Contact Person: Howard K. Kalman, Associate Professor, Chair, Graduate Program in Communications; Roy H. Park, School of Communications.

Specializations: M.S. in Communications. Students in this program find employment in such areas as instructional design/training, web development, corporate/community/public relations and marketing, and employee communication. The program can be tailored to individual career goals.

Features: Program is interdisciplinary, incorporating organizational communication, instructional design, management, and technology.

Admission Requirements: 3.0 GPA, recommendations, statement of purpose, resume, application forms and transcripts, TOEFL 550 (or 213 computer-scored; 80 on the iBT version) where applicable.

Degree Requirements: 36 semester hours including capstone seminar.

Number of Full Time Faculty: 6; **Number of Other Faculty**: 0.

Degrees awarded in 2010–2011 Academic Year—Masters: 15; **Ph.D.**: 0; **Other**: 0.

Grant Monies awarded in 2010–2011 Academic Year: 0.

Name of Institution: State University College of Arts and Science at Potsdam.

Name of Department or Program: Organizational Leadership and Technology.

Address: 392 Dunn Hall, Potsdam, NY 13676, USA.

Phone Number: (315)267-2670; **Fax Number**: (315)267-3189.

Email Contact: betrusak@potsdam.edu; **URL**: http://www.potsdam.edu/olt.

Contact Person: Dr. Anthony Betrus, Program Coordinator.

Specializations: M.S. in Education in Instructional Technology with concentrations in: Educational Technology Specialist, K-12 Track Educational Technology Specialist, Non-K-12 Track Organizational Performance, Leadership, and Technology.

Features: Live instruction Evening courses 12-week courses Group Work Internships.

Admission Requirements: (1) Submission of an official transcript of an earned baccalaureate degree from an accredited institution. (2) A minimum GPA of 2.75 (4.0 scale) in the most recent 60 credit hours of coursework. (3) Submission of the Application for Graduate Study (w/$50 non-refundable fee). (4) For students seeking the Educational Technology Specialist Certification, a valid NYS Teaching Certificate is required.

Degree Requirements: 36 semester hours, including internship or practicum; culminating project required.

Number of Full Time Faculty: 3; **Number of Other Faculty**: 3.

Degrees awarded in 2010–2011 Academic Year—Masters: 32; **Ph.D.**: 0; **Other**: 0.

Grant Monies awarded in 2010–2011 Academic Year: 0.

Name of Institution: Wright State University.

Name of Department or Program: College of Education and Human Services, Department of Educational Leadership.

Address: 421 Allyn Hall, 3640 Colonel Glenn Highway, Dayton, OH 45435, USA.

Phone Number: (937)775-2509 or (937)775-4148; **Fax Number**: (937)775-2405.

Email Contact: susan.berg@wright.edu; **URL**: http://www.cehs.wright.edu/academic/educational_leadership/lib-media/index.php.

Contact Person: Dr. Susan Berg, Library Media Program Advisor.

Specializations: M.Ed. or M.A. in Computer/Technology or Library Media.

Features: Ohio licensure available in Multi-age library media (ages 3–21); Computer/technology endorsement; Above licensure only available on a graduate basis. Multi-age library media licensure available in two tracks: initial (no previous teaching license) and advanced (with current teaching license in another field). The computer/technology endorsement must be added to a current teaching license.

Admission Requirements: Completed application with nonrefundable application fee, Bachelor's degree from accredited institution, official transcripts, 2.7 overall GPA for regular status (conditional acceptance possible), statement of purpose, satisfactory scores on MAT or GRE.

Degree Requirements: M.Ed. requires a comprehensive portfolio; M.A. requires a 6-hour thesis.

Number of Full Time Faculty: 3; **Number of Other Faculty**: 5.

Degrees awarded in 2010–2011 Academic Year—Masters: 10; **Ph.D.**: 0; **Other**: 0.

Grant Monies awarded in 2010–2011 Academic Year: 0.

Name of Institution: Kent State University.

Name of Department or Program: Instructional Technology.

Address: 405 White Hall, Kent, OH 44242, USA.

Phone Number: (330)672-0607; **Fax Number**: (330)672-2512.

Email Contact: dtiene@kent.edu; **URL**: http://www.kent.edu/ehhs/itec/index.cfm.

Contact Person: Dr. Drew Tiene, Coordinator: Instructional Technology Program.

Specializations: M.Ed. in Instructional Technology, and licensure programs in Computing/Technology and Library/Media; Ph.D. in Educational Psychology with concentration in Instructional Technology.

Features: Programs are planned with advisors to prepare students for careers in elementary, secondary, or higher education, business, industry, government agencies, or health facilities. Students may take advantage of independent research, individual study, and internships. Most courses and programs can be taken online.

Admission Requirements: Master's: Bachelors degree with 3.00 undergraduate GPA.

Degree Requirements: Master's: 34–39 semester hours, portfolio, practicum for licensure Doctoral: minimum of 45 post-masters semester hours, comprehensive exam, dissertation.

Number of Full Time Faculty: 5; **Number of Other Faculty**: 5.

Degrees awarded in 2010–2011 Academic Year—Masters: 30; **Ph.D.**: 5; **Other**: 0.

Grant Monies awarded in 2010–2011 Academic Year: 0.

Name of Institution: Ohio University.

Name of Department or Program: Instructional Technology.

Address: McCracken Hall, Athens, OH 45701-2979, USA.

Phone Number: (740)597-1322; **Fax Number**: (740)593-0477.

Email Contact: moored3@ohio.edu; **URL**: http://www.cehs.ohio.edu/academics/es/it/index.htm.

Contact Person: David Richard Moore, Instructional Technology Program Coordinator.

Specializations: M.Ed. in Computer Education and Technology. Ph.D. in Curriculum and Instruction with a specialization in Instructional Technology also available; call for details (740-593-4561) or visit the website: http://www.ohio.edu/education/dept/es/it/index.cfm.

Features: Master's program is a blended online delivery.

Admission Requirements: Bachelor's degree, 3.0 undergraduate GPA, 35 MAT, 500 GRE (verbal), 500 GRE (quantitative), 550 TOEFL, three letters of recommendation, Paper describing future goals and career expectations from completing a degree in our program.

Degree Requirements: Master's: 36 semester credits, electronic portfolio or optional thesis worth 2–10 credits or alternative seminar research paper. Students may earn two graduate degrees simultaneously in education and in any other field. Ph.D.: 66 hours with 15 hours being dissertation work.

Number of Full Time Faculty: 4; **Number of Other Faculty**: 0.

Degrees awarded in 2010–2011 Academic Year—Masters: 18; **Ph.D.**: 10; **Other**: 0.

Grant Monies awarded in 2010–2011 Academic Year: 500,000.

Name of Institution: University of Cincinnati.

Name of Department or Program: College of Education.

Address: 401 Teachers College, ML002, Cincinnati, OH 45221-0002, USA.

Phone Number: (513)556-3579; **Fax Number**: (513)556-1001.

Email Contact: richard.kretschmer@uc.edu; **URL**: http://www.uc.edu/

Contact Person: Richard Kretschmer.

Specializations: M.Ed. or Ed.D. in Curriculum and Instruction with an emphasis on Instructional Design and Technology; Educational Technology degree programs for current professional, technical, critical, and personal knowledge.

Features: Contact division for features.

Admission Requirements: Bachelor's degree from accredited institution, 2.8 undergraduate GPA; GRE 1500 or better.

Degree Requirements: 54 quarter hours, written exam, thesis, or research project. (12–15 credit hours college core; 12–15 C&I; 18–27 credit hours specialization; 3–6 credit hours thesis or project).

Number of Full Time Faculty: -; **Number of Other Faculty**: –.

Degrees awarded in 2010–2011 Academic Year—Masters: –; **Ph.D.**: –; **Other**: –.

Grant Monies awarded in 2010–2011 Academic Year: –

Name of Institution: University of Toledo.

Name of Department or Program: Curriculum & Instruction.

Address: 2801 W Bancroft Street, Mail Stop 924, Toledo, OH 43606, USA.

Phone Number: (419)530-7979; **Fax Number**: (419)530-2466.

Email Contact: Berhane.Teclehaimanot@utoledo.edu; **URL**: http://tipt3.utoledo.edu.

Contact Person: Berhane Teclehaimanot, Ph.D.

Specializations: Technology Using Educator/Technology Coordinator and Instructional Designer.

Features: Graduate students may concentrate in one of the two primary "roles," or may choose a blended program of study. Program was completely redesigned in 2004.

Admission Requirements: Master's: 3.0 undergrad. GPA, GRE (if undergrad. GPA <2.7), recommendations; Doctorate: Master's degree, GRE, TOEFL (as necessary), recommendations, entrance writing samples, and interview.

Degree Requirements: Master's: 30 semester hours, culminating project; Doctorate: 60 semester hours (after Ms), major exams, dissertation.

Number of Full Time Faculty: 3; **Number of Other Faculty**: 4.

Degrees awarded in 2010–2011 Academic Year—Masters: 16; **Ph.D.**: 3; **Other**: 1.

Grant Monies awarded in 2010–2011 Academic Year: 0.

Name of Institution: The University of Oklahoma.

Name of Department or Program: Instructional Psychology and Technology, Department of Educational Psychology.

Address: 321 Collings Hall, Norman, OK 73019, USA.

Phone Number: (405)325-5974; **Fax Number**: (405)325-6655.

Email Contact: mcrowson@ou.edu; **URL**: http://education.ou.edu/ipt/

Contact Person: Dr. H. Michael Crowson, Program Area Coordinator.

Specializations: Master's degree with emphases in Instructional Design & Technology (includes tracks: Instructional Design; and Interactive Learning Technologies), and Instructional Psychology & Technology (includes tracks: Instructional Psychology & Technology; Teaching & Assessment; Teaching & Learning; and Integrating Technology in Teaching). Doctoral degree in Instructional Psychology and Technology.

Features: Strong interweaving of principles of instructional psychology with instructional design and development. Application of IP&T in K-12, vocational education, higher education, business and industry, and governmental agencies.

Admission Requirements: Master's: acceptance by IPT program and Graduate College based on minimum 3.00 GPA for last 60 hours of undergraduate work or last 12 hours of graduate work; written statement that indicates goals and interests compatible with program goals. Doctoral: minimum 3.25 GPA, GRE scores, written statement that indicates goals and interests compatible with program goals, writing sample, and letters of recommendation.

Degree Requirements: Master's: 36 hours course work with 3.0 GPA; successful completion of thesis or comprehensive exam. Doctorate: see program description from institution or http://education.ou.edu/ipt/

Number of Full Time Faculty: 11; **Number of Other Faculty**: 0.

Degrees awarded in 2010–2011 Academic Year—Masters: 9; **Ph.D.**: 2; **Other**: 0.

Grant Monies awarded in 2010–2011 Academic Year: 0.

Name of Institution: Bloomsburg University.

Name of Department or Program: Instructional Technology & Institute for Interactive Technologies.

Address: 2221 McCormick Building, Bloomsburg, PA 17815, USA.

Phone Number: (717)389-4875; **Fax Number**: (717)389-4943.

Email Contact: tphillip@bloomu.edu; **URL**: http://iit.bloomu.edu.

Contact Person: Dr. Timothy L. Phillips.

Specializations: M.S. in Instructional Technology: Corporate Concentration; M.S. in Instructional Technology: Instructional Technology Specialist Concentration (education). M.S. Instructional Technology: Instructional Game and Interactive Environments Concentration (currently under development) eLearning Developer Certificate.

Features: M.S. in Instructional Technology with emphasis on preparing for careers as Instructional Technologist in corporate, government, healthcare, higher education, and K-12 educational settings. The program is highly applied and provides opportunities for students to work on real world projects as part of their coursework. Our program offers a corporate concentration and an Instructional Technology Specialist Concentration for educators. The program offers a complete master's degree online as well as on campus. Graduate assistantships are available for full-time students. The program is closely associated with the nationally known Institute for Interactive Technologies.

Admission Requirements: Bachelors degree.

Degree Requirements: 33 semester credits (27 credits + 6 credit thesis, or 30 credits + three credit internship).

Number of Full Time Faculty: 4; **Number of Other Faculty**: 3.

Degrees awarded in 2010–2011 Academic Year—Masters: 60; **Ph.D.**: 0; **Other**: 5.

Grant Monies awarded in 2010–2011 Academic Year: 350,000.

Name of Institution: Drexel University.

Name of Department or Program: The iSchool at Drexel, College of Information Science and Technology.

Address: 3141 Chestnut Street, Philadelphia, PA 19104-2875, USA.

Phone Number: (215)895-2474; **Fax Number**: (215)895-2494.

Email Contact: info@ischool.drexel.edu; **URL**: http://www.ischool.drexel.edu.

Contact Person: Dr. David E. Fenske, Dean.

Specializations: The ALA-accredited Master of Science (MS) in Library and Information Science curriculum prepares professionals for information-providing organizations. In April 2009, the MS was ranked 9th among library science programs in the nation, according to U.S. News & World Report's "America's Best Graduate Schools." The MS degree qualifies students for a wide variety of positions, including school library media specialist. Students may formally declare a concentration in School Library Media, Youth Services, Competitive Intelligence and Knowledge Management, Digital Libraries, or Information and Library Services. The School Library Media concentration is for students who wish to work in K-12 school library programs in both public and private schools. Designed to prepare graduates to be eligible for certification as school librarians by the Pennsylvania Department of Education (PDE), the program meets the requirements of the State of Pennsylvania and provides a strong basis for seeking certification in other states as well. Three course sequences are available within the concentration: one for students who have no prior teaching certification from PDE; one for students who have prior teaching certification from PDE and who wish to add school librarian certification to their credentials; and one for students with ALA-accredited master's degrees who wish to seek school librarian certification from PDE. In addition to the concentrations outlined above, students may choose to specialize in Healthcare Informatics or Archival Management. In keeping with the flexibility and personal planning emphasis of the College's MS, students may also select a "no concentration" option. The College also offers a Master of Science in Information Systems (MSIS), a Master of Science in Software Engineering (MSSE), and a Ph.D. There is an Advanced Certificate in Information Studies and Technology which is a non-degree program providing specialized training beyond the master's degree, and an online Certificate in Healthcare Informatics providing knowledge and skills in the application of information technology (IT) in the provision of healthcare.

Features: The M.S. degree (as well as the MSIS and MSSE) is offered on campus and online. Students may take the degree completely on campus, completely online, or as a mixture of the two. Currently, all courses in the School Library Media Concentration except the Field Study (INFO 891) are offered online. INFO 891 must be completed in approved sites and is augmented with an online seminar.

Admission Requirements: Admission Requirements for the masters program: Official Graduate Record Exam (GRE) Scores (may be waived with a 3.2 GPA

CUM or in the last half (credits) of a completed undergraduate or graduate degree; department decision). For a full list of admission requirements, visit the website at www.ischool.drexel.edu.

Degree Requirements: 15 courses. Additional coursework is required for those seeking teaching certification in Pennsylvania.

Number of Full Time Faculty: 38; **Number of Other Faculty**: 73.

Degrees awarded in 2010–2011 Academic Year—Masters: 332; **Ph.D.**: 9; **Other**: 91.

Grant Monies awarded in 2010–2011 Academic Year: 2,000,000.

Name of Institution: Lehigh University.

Name of Department or Program: Teaching, Learning, and Technology.

Address: 111 Research Drive, Bethlehem, PA 18015, USA.

Phone Number: (610)758-3249; **Fax Number**: (610)758-6223.

Email Contact: TLTProgram@Lehigh.edu; **URL**: http://www.lehigh.edu/education/tlt/

Contact Person: MJ Bishop, Associate Professor and Teaching, Learning, and Technology Program Director.

Specializations: M.S. in Instructional Technology: Emphasizes design, development, implementation, integration, and evaluation of technology for teaching and learning. The degree is well suited to both designers (producers) and implementers (consumers) of instructional technologies. Graduate certificate in Technology Use in the Schools: This 12-credit grad certificate focuses on integrating technology into daily practice in the schools. Ph.D. in Teaching and Learning, concentration in Instructional Design and Technology: Emphasizes cognitive processes and their implications for the design, development, and evaluation of technology-based teaching and learning products in a variety of settings.

Features: High level of integration with teacher education and certification, leading to a practical and quickly applicable program of study. Our Integrated Professional Development School approach offers further opportunities to get into the schools and work on solving meaningful teaching and learning problems, not just "tech support." Both masters and doctoral students collaborate with faculty on projects and studies (including national presentation and publication).

Admission Requirements: M.S. (competitive): 3.0 undergraduate GPA or 3.0 graduate GPA, GREs recommended, transcripts, at least two letters of recommendation, statement of personal and professional goals, application fee. Application deadlines: July 15 for fall admission, Dec 1 for spring admission, Apr 30 for summer admission. Ph.D. (highly competitive): 3.5 graduate GPA, GREs required. Copy of two extended pieces of writing (or publications); statement of future professional goals; statement of why Lehigh best place to meet those goals; identification of which presentations, publications, or research by Lehigh faculty attracted applicant to Lehigh. Application deadline: February 1 (admission only once per year from competitive pool).

Degree Requirements: M.S.: 30 credits; thesis option. Ph.D.: 48 credits past masters (including dissertation). Qualifying Exam (written and oral)+General Examination Research Project (publication quality)+dissertation.

Number of Full Time Faculty: 5; **Number of Other Faculty**: 1.

Degrees awarded in 2010–2011 Academic Year—Masters: 40; **Ph.D.**: 2; **Other**: 0.

Grant Monies awarded in 2010–2011 Academic Year: 1,000,000.

Name of Institution: Pennsylvania State University.

Name of Department or Program: Instructional Systems.

Address: 314 Keller Building, University Park, PA 16802, USA.

Phone Number: (814)865-0473; **Fax Number**: (814)865-0128.

Email Contact: nxc1@psu.edu; **URL**: http://www.ed.psu.edu/insys/

Contact Person: Priya Sharma, Associate Professor of Education, Professor in Charge of Instructional Systems.

Specializations: M.Ed., M.S., D.Ed., and Ph.D. in Instructional Systems. Current teaching emphases are on Learning Technology Design, Educational Systems Design, Learning Sciences, and Corporate Training. Research interests include multimedia, visual learning, educational reform, emerging technologies, constructivist learning, open-ended learning environments, scaffolding, technology integration in classrooms, technology in higher education, change and diffusion of innovations.

Features: A common thread throughout all programs is that candidates have basic competencies in the understanding of human learning; instructional design, development, and evaluation; and research procedures. Practical experience is available in mediated independent learning, research, instructional development, computer-based education, and dissemination projects. Exceptional opportunities for collaboration with faculty (30%+ of publications and presentations are collaborative between faculty and students).

Admission Requirements: D.Ed., Ph.D.: GRE (including written GRE), TOEFL, transcript, three letters of recommendation, writing sample, vita or resume, and letter of application detailing rationale for interest in the degree, match with interests of faculty.

Degree Requirements: M.Ed.: 33 semester hours; M.S.: 36 hours, including either a thesis or project paper; doctoral: candidacy exam, courses, residency, comprehensives, dissertation.

Number of Full Time Faculty: 7; **Number of Other Faculty**: 5.

Degrees awarded in 2010–2011 Academic Year—Masters: 28; **Ph.D.**: 10; **Other**: 0.

Grant Monies awarded in 2010–2011 Academic Year: 373,028.

Name of Institution: The University of Rhode Island.

Name of Department or Program: Graduate School of Library and Information Studies.

Address: Rodman Hall, 94 W Alumni Ave., Kingston, RI 02881-0815, USA.

Phone Number: (401)874-2947; **Fax Number**: (401)874-4964.

Email Contact: geaton@mail.uri.edu; **URL**: http://www.uri.edu/artsci/lsc.

Contact Person: E. Gale Eaton, Director.

Specializations: M.L.I.S. degree with specialties in School Library Media Services, Information Literacy Instruction, Youth Services Librarianship, Public Librarianship, Academic Librarianship, and Special Library Services.

Features: 15-credit Post-Baccalaureate Certificate in Information Literacy Instruction.

Admission Requirements: undergraduate GPA of 3.0, score in 50th percentile or higher on SAT or MAT, statement of purpose, current resume, letters of reference.

Degree Requirements: 42 semester-credit program offered in Rhode Island and regionally in Worcester, MA and Durham, NH.

Number of Full Time Faculty: 7; **Number of Other Faculty**: 36.

Degrees awarded in 2010–2011 Academic Year—Masters: 80; **Ph.D.**: 0; **Other**: 0.

Grant Monies awarded in 2010–2011 Academic Year: 0.

Name of Institution: University of South Carolina Aiken and University of South Carolina Columbia.

Name of Department or Program: Aiken: School of Education; Columbia: Department of Educational Psychology.

Address: 471 University Parkway, Aiken, SC 29801, USA.

Phone Number: (803)-641-3489; **Fax Number**: (803)-641-3720.

Email Contact: smyth@usca.edu; **URL**: http://edtech.usca.edu.

Contact Person: Dr. Thomas Smyth, Professor, Program Director.

Specializations: Master of Education in Educational Technology (A Joint Program of The University of South Carolina Aiken and Columbia).

Features: The Master's Degree in Educational Technology is designed to provide advanced professional studies in graduate level coursework to develop capabilities essential to the effective design, evaluation, and delivery of technology-based instruction and training (e.g., software development, multimedia development, assistive technology modifications, web-based development, and distance learning).

The program is intended (1) to prepare educators to assume leadership roles in the integration of educational technology into the school curriculum, and (2) to provide graduate-level instructional opportunities for several populations (e.g., classroom teachers, corporate trainers, educational software developers) that need to acquire both technological competencies and understanding of sound instructional design principles and techniques. The program is offered entirely online as high-quality, interactive, web-based courses. There are occasional synchronous online meetings, but the vast majority of the program is asynchronous. Candidates present a program portfolio for review by the faculty at the end of the program.

Admission Requirements: Application to the Educational Technology Program can be made after completion of at least the bachelor's degree from a college or university accredited by a regional accrediting agency. The standard for admission will be based on a total profile for the applicant. The successful applicant should have an undergraduate grade point average of at least 3.0, a score of 45 on the Miller's Analogies Test or scores of 450 on both the verbal and quantitative portions of the Graduate Record Exam, a well-written letter of intent that matches the objectives of the program and includes a description of previous technology experience, and positive letters of recommendation from individuals who know the professional characteristics of the applicant. Any exceptions for students failing to meet these standards shall be referred to the Admissions Committee for review and final decision.

Degree Requirements: 36 semester hours, including instructional theory, computer design, and integrated media.

Number of Full Time Faculty: 3; **Number of Other Faculty**: 3.

Degrees awarded in 2010–2011 Academic Year—Masters: 18; **Ph.D.**: 0; **Other**: 0.

Grant Monies awarded in 2010–2011 Academic Year: 0.

Name of Institution: Dakota State University.

Name of Department or Program: Educational Technology.

Address: 820 North Washington Avenue, Madison, SD 57042, USA.

Phone Number: 1-888-DSU-9988; **Fax Number**: (605)256-5093.

Email Contact: mark.hawkes@dsu.edu; **URL**: http://www.dsu.edu/mset/index.aspx.

Contact Person: Mark Hawkes.

Specializations: The MSET program offers two specializations: Distance Education and Technology Systems. These specializations are indicated on the official transcript. Students who wish to choose one of these specializations or the technology endorsement must take designated electives as follows: Distance Education: CET 747 Web & ITV Based Applications of Dist Ed (3 credit hours); CET 749 Policy and Management of Distance Education (3 credit hours); CET 769 Adult Learning for Distance Education (3 credit hours) Technology Systems; CET 747 Web & ITV Based Applications of Dist Ed (3 credit hours); CET 750 Multimedia II (2 credit hours); CET 753 Network Management in Educational Institutions (3 credit hours); CET 758 Advanced Instructional Programming (2 credit hours); K-12 Educational Technology Endorsement Individuals who hold or are eligible for teaching certification may earn the K-12 Educational Technology Endorsement by completing specified courses within the MSET program.

Features: The Master of Science in Educational Technology (MSET) is an instructional technology program designed to meet the rapidly increasing demand for educators who are trained to integrate computer technologies into the curriculum and instruction. As computers and technology have become a significant part of the teaching and learning process, addressing the information needs of teachers has become the key to integrating technology into the classroom and increasing student learning. The primary emphasis of the masters program is to prepare educators who can create learning environments that integrate computing technology into the teaching and learning process. The MSET degree is an advanced degree designed to equip educators to be: leaders in educational technology current in teaching and learning processes and practices current in research technologies and designs knowledgeable of technologies and programming skills knowledgeable of current, technology-based educational tools and products. Specifically by the end of the program, MSET students will understand the capabilities of the computer and its impact upon education. They will be proficient in the use and application of computer software and will be able to demonstrate proficiency in using computers and related technologies to improve their own and their students learning needs. The program integrates a highly technological environment with a project-based curriculum. Its focus is supported by an institutionally systemic belief that there is a substantial role for technology in teaching and learning in all educational environments.

Admission Requirements: Baccalaureate degree from an institution of higher education with full regional accreditation for that degree. Satisfactory scores on the GRE. The test must have been taken within the last 5 years. The GRE test can be waived if one of the following conditions is met: A cumulative grade point average of 3.25 or higher on a 4.0 scale for a baccalaureate degree from a regionally accredited college or university in the US. Official admission into and demonstrated success in a regionally accredited graduate program in the US demonstrated success is defined as grades of A or B in at least 12 hours of graduate work, or graduation from a regionally accredited college/university in the U.S. at least 15 years ago or more. Other factors (such as student maturity, references, or special expertise) also may be used to determine admission to the program. Also see program specific admission requirements for additional requirements. Demonstrated basic knowledge of computers and their applications for educational purposes. Basic knowledge can be demonstrated in one of the following ways: Technology endorsement from an accredited university; or In-service position as full or part-time technology coordinator in a public school. A personal statement of technological competency. The statement should not exceed two pages and should be accompanied by supporting documentation or electronic references, e.g., URL.

Degree Requirements: The program requires a total of 36 credits beyond the baccalaureate degree. All students must take the following: 25 hours of required courses. 11 hours of electives. It is possible to specialize in either Distance Education or Technology Systems by selecting the designated electives for that specialization. You can also get a K-12 Educational Technology Endorsement. It is also possible to select the thesis option from among the electives. MSET courses are offered using a variety of distance delivery methods. At this time, one required course and one elective course have a limited length hands-on campus requirement. These courses are offered in summer and the residency requirement is limited to 1 week per course. Alternatives may be available for the distance student.

Number of Full Time Faculty: 3; **Number of Other Faculty**: 5.

Degrees awarded in 2010–2011 Academic Year—Masters: 30; **Ph.D.**: 0; **Other**: 0.

Grant Monies awarded in 2010–2011 Academic Year: 4,000.

Name of Institution: Texas A&M University.

Name of Department or Program: Educational Technology Program, Department of Educational psychology.

Address: College of Education and Human Development, College Station, TX 77843-4225, USA.

Phone Number: (979)845-7276; **Fax Number**: (979)862-1256.

Email Contact: zellner@tamu.edu; **URL**: http://educ.coe.tamu.edu/~edtc.

Contact Person: Ronald D. Zellner, Associate Professor, Coordinator Program information/Carol Wagner for admissions materials.

Specializations: M.Ed. in Educational Technology; EDCI Ph.D. program with specializations in Educational Technology and in Distance Education; Ph.D. in Educational Psychology Foundations: Learning & Technology. The purpose of the Educational Technology Program is to prepare educators with the competencies required to improve the quality and effectiveness of instructional programs at all levels. A major emphasis is placed on multimedia instructional material's development and techniques for effective distance education and communication. Teacher preparation with a focus on field-based instruction and school to university collaboration is also a major component. The program goal is to prepare graduates with a wide range of skills to work as professionals and leaders in a variety of settings, including education, business, industry, and the military.

Features: Program facilities include laboratories for teaching, resource development, and production. Computer, video, and multimedia development are supported in a number of facilities. The college and university also maintain facilities for distance education material's development and fully equipped classrooms for course delivery to nearby collaborative school districts and sites throughout the state.

Admission Requirements: M.Ed.: Bachelor's degree (range of scores, no specific cut-offs); 400 GRE Verbal, 550 (213 computer version) TOEFL; Ph.D.: 3.0 GPA, 450 GRE Verbal. Composite score from GRE verbal & Quantitative and GPA, letters of recommendation, general background, and student goal statement.

Degree Requirements: M.Ed.: 39 semester credits, oral exam; Ph.D.: course work varies with student goals—degree is a Ph.D. in Educational Psychology Foundations with specialization in educational technology.

Number of Full Time Faculty: 3; **Number of Other Faculty**: 0.

Degrees awarded in 2010–2011 Academic Year—Masters: 8; **Ph.D.**: 4; **Other**: 0.

Grant Monies awarded in 2010–2011 Academic Year: 876,000.

Name of Institution: The University of Texas at Austin.

Name of Department or Program: Curriculum & Instruction.

Address: 406 Sanchez Building, Austin, TX 78712-1294, USA.

Phone Number: (512)471-5942; **Fax Number**: (512)471-8460.

Email Contact: Mliu@mail.utexas.edu; **URL**: http://www.edb.utexas.edu/education/departments/ci/programs/it/

Contact Person: Min Liu, Ed.D., Professor and IT Program Area Coordinator/ Graduate Advisor.

Specializations: The College of Education at the University of Texas at Austin ranked FIRST among public universities by 2012 U.S. News & World Report. The Instructional Technology (IT) Program is a graduate program and offers degrees at the master and doctoral levels. Masters degrees in IT provide students with knowledge and skills of cutting-edge new media technologies, learning theories, instructional systems design, human-computer interaction, and evaluation. They prepare students to be leaders and practitioners in various educational settings, such as K-12, higher education, and training in business and industry. Ph.D. program provides knowledge and skills in areas such as instructional systems design, learning and instructional theories, instructional materials development and design of learning environments using various emerging technology-based systems and tools. Graduates assume academic, administrative, and other leadership positions such as professors, instructional technologists at school district level, managers, and researchers of instructional design and instructional evaluators.

Features: The program is interdisciplinary in nature, although certain competencies are required of all students. Programs of study and dissertation research are based on individual needs and career goals. Learning resources include state-of-art labs in the Learning Technology Center in the College of Education, and university-wide computer labs. Students can take courses offered by other departments and colleges as relevant to their interests. Students, applying to the program, have diverse backgrounds and pursue careers of their interests. The program caters students with both K-12 as well as corporate backgrounds.

Admission Requirements: Instructional Technology program considers only applications for Fall admission, with the deadline of December 15. November 15: Deadline for consideration of financial award Admission decisions are rendered based on consideration of the entire applicant file, including GPA, test scores, references, experience, and stated goals. No single component carries any more significance than another. However, priority may be given to applicants who meet the following preferred criteria: GPA 3.0 or above GRE 1,100 or above (verbal + quantitative, with at least 400 verbal) TOEFL 213 or above (computer)/550 or above (paper-based)/79 or 80 (Internet-based) TOEFL.

Degree Requirements: see http://www.edb.utexas.edu/education/departments/ci/programs/it/studentinfo/cstudents/grad/degrees/ for details.

Number of Full Time Faculty: 4; **Number of Other Faculty**: 38.

Degrees awarded in 2010–2011 Academic Year—Masters: 4; **Ph.D.**: 8; **Other**: 0.

Grant Monies awarded in 2010–2011 Academic Year: 1,306,456.

Name of Institution: East Tennessee State University.

Name of Department or Program: College of Education, Department of Curriculum and Instruction.

Address: Box 70684, Johnson City, TN 37614-0684, USA.

Phone Number: (423)439-7843; **Fax Number**: (423)439-8362.

Email Contact: danielsh@etsu.edu; **URL**: http://www.etsu.edu/coe/cuai/emet-ma.asp.

Contact Person: Harold Lee Daniels.

Specializations: (1) M.Ed. in School Library Media; (2) M.Ed. in Educational Technology; (3) School Library Media Specialist add on certification for those with current teaching license and a masters degree; (4) M.Ed. in Classroom Technology for those with teaching license.

Features: Two (MAC &PC) dedicated computer labs (45+ computers). Online and evening course offerings for part-time, commuter and employed students. Student pricing/campus licensing on popular software (MS, Adobe, Macromedia, etc.). Off site cohort programs for classroom teacher's Extensive software library (900 + titles) with review/checkout privileges.

Admission Requirements: Bachelor's degree from accredited institution with undergraduate GPA of 3.0 or higher, transcripts, personal application essay, interview, in some cases GRE may be required.

Degree Requirements: 36 semester hours, including 12 hours in common core of instructional technology and media, 18 professional content hours, and 5 credit hour practicum (200 field experience hours).

Number of Full Time Faculty: 4; **Number of Other Faculty**: 4.

Degrees awarded in 2010–2011 Academic Year—Masters: 18; **Ph.D.**: 0; **Other**: 2.

Grant Monies awarded in 2010–2011 Academic Year: 32,000.

Name of Institution: University of Tennessee-Knoxville.

Name of Department or Program: Instructional Technology and Educational Studies, College of Education.

Address: A535 Claxton Addition, Knoxville, TN 37996-3456, USA.

Phone Number: (865)-974-5037; **Fax Number**: –.

Email Contact: ecounts1@utk.edu; **URL**: http://ites.tennessee.edu/

Contact Person: Jay Pfaffman.

Specializations: M.S. Ed.S. and Ph.D. in Ed. Concentrations in Curriculum/ Evaluation/Research and Instructional Technology; M.S. and Ph.D. in Ed. Concentration in Cultural Studies in Education.

Features: course work in media production and management, advanced software production, utilization, research, theory, instructional computing, and instructional development.

Admission Requirements: See Graduate Catalog for current program requirements.

Degree Requirements: See Graduate Catalog for current program requirements.

Number of Full Time Faculty: 0; **Number of Other Faculty**: 0.

Degrees awarded in 2010–2011 Academic Year—Masters: 0; **Ph.D.**: 0; **Other**: 0.

Grant Monies awarded in 2010–2011 Academic Year: 0.

Name of Institution: Texas Tech University.

Name of Department or Program: Instructional Technology.

Address: Box 41071, TTU, Lubbock, TX 79409, USA.

Phone Number: (806)742-1997, ext. 297; **Fax Number**: (806)742-2179.

Email Contact: Steven.Crooks@ttu.edu; **URL**: http://edit.educ.ttu.edu.

Contact Person: Dr. Steven Crooks, Program Coordinator, Instructional Technology.

Specializations: M.Ed. in Instructional Technology; completely online M.Ed. in Instructional Technology; Ed.D. in Instructional Technology.

Features: Program is NCATE accredited and follows ISTE and AECT guidelines.

Admission Requirements: Holistic evaluation based on GRE scores (Doctorate only), GPA, student goals, and writing samples.

Degree Requirements: M.Ed.: 39 hours (21 hours instructional technology core, 12 hours instructional technology electives, 6 hours education foundations and research). Ed.D.: 93 hours (60 hours in educational technology, 21 hours in education or resource area, 12 hours dissertation).

Number of Full Time Faculty: 4; **Number of Other Faculty**: 2.

Degrees awarded in 2010–2011 Academic Year—Masters: 25; **Ph.D.**: 5; **Other**: 0.

Grant Monies awarded in 2010–2011 Academic Year: 200,000.

Name of Institution: University of Houston.

Name of Department or Program: Curriculum & Instruction.

Address: 256 Farish Hall, Mail Code 5027, Houston, TX 77204-5027, USA.

Phone Number: 713-743-4975; **Fax Number**: 713-743-4990.

Email Contact: smcneil@uh.edu; **URL**: http://www.it.coe.uh.edu/

Contact Person: Sara McNeil.

Specializations: Instructional design; Urban community partnerships enhanced by technology; Integration of technology in teacher education; Visual representation of information; Linking instructional technology with content area instruction; Educational uses of digital media (including digital photography, digital video, and digital storytelling); Collaborative design and development of multimedia; Uses of instructional technology in health science education.

Features: The IT Program at the University of Houston can be distinguished from other IT programs at other institutions through our unique philosophy based on a strong commitment to the broad representations of community, the individual, and the collaboration that strengthens the two. We broadly perceive community to include our college, the university, and the local Houston environment. The community is a rich context and resource from which we can solicit authentic learning tasks and clients, and to which we can contribute new perspectives and meaningful products. Our students graduate with real-world experience that can only be gained by experience with extended and coordinated community-based projects, not by contrived course requirements. Our program actively seeks outside funding to promote and continue such authentic projects because we so strongly believe it is the best context in which our students can develop expertise in the field. We recognize that each student brings to our program a range of formal training, career experience, and future goals. Thus, no longer can we be satisfied with presenting a single, static curriculum and still effectively prepare students for a competitive marketplace. Our beliefs have led us to develop a program that recognizes and celebrates student individuality and diversity. Students work with advisors to develop a degree plan that begins from their existing knowledge and strives toward intended career goals. We aim to teach not specific software or hardware operations, but instead focus on transferable technical skills couched in solid problem-solving experiences, theoretical discussions, and a team-oriented atmosphere. Students work throughout the program to critically evaluate their own work for the purpose of compiling a performance portfolio that will accurately and comprehensively portray their individual abilities to themselves, faculty, and future employers. Completing our philosophical foundation is a continuous goal of collaboration. Our faculty operates from a broad collaborative understanding that recognizes how everyone involved in any process brings unique and valuable experiences and perspectives. Within the IT program, faculty, staff, and students rely on each other to contribute relevant expertise. Faculty members regularly seek collaboration with other faculty in the College of Education, especially those involved with teacher education, as well as with faculty in other schools across campus. Collaboration is a focus that has been infused through the design of our courses and our relationships with students. Facebook: http://www.facebook.com/groups/189269174434698/

Admission Requirements: Admission information for graduate programs: http://www.coe.uh.edu/it. Masters program: 3.0 grade point average (GPA) for unconditional admission or a 2.6 GPA or above for conditional admission over the last 60 hours of coursework attempted Graduate Record Exam: The GRE must have been taken within 5 years of the date of application for admission to any Graduate program in the College of Education. Doctoral program: Each applicant must normally have earned a masters degree or have completed 36 semester hours of appropriate graduate work with a minimum GPA of 3.0 (A=4.0). Graduate Record Exam: The GRE must have been taken within 5 years of the date of application for admission to any Graduate program in the College of Education.

Degree Requirements: Masters: Students with backgrounds in educational technology can complete the Master's program with 36 hours of coursework. For the typical student, the M.Ed. in Instructional Technology consists of 9 semester hours of core courses required by the College of Education, and an additional 18 hours core in Instructional Technology as well as 9 hours that are determined by the students' career goals (K-12, higher education, business, and industry). Students take a written comprehensive examination over the program, coursework, and experiences. Doctoral: The minimum hours required in the doctoral program is 66. More details about the courses and requirements can be found online at: http://www.coe.uh.edu/current-students/academic-programs/cuin-ed-instruction-technology/index.php.

Number of Full Time Faculty: 5; **Number of Other Faculty**: 5.

Degrees awarded in 2010–2011 Academic Year—Masters: 15; **Ph.D.**: 8; **Other**: 0.

Grant Monies awarded in 2010–2011 Academic Year: 1,000,000.

Name of Institution: University of North Texas.

Name of Department or Program: Technology & Cognition (College of Education).

Address: Box 311337, Denton, TX 76203-1337 USA.

Phone Number: (940)565-2057; **Fax Number**: (940)565-2185.

Email Contact: iyoung@unt.edu; **URL**: http://www.cecs.unt.edu.

Contact Person: Dr. Mark Mortensen & Mrs. Donna Walton, Computer Education and Cognitive Systems. Dr. Jon Young, Chair, Department of Technology and Cognition.

Specializations: M.S. in Computer Education and Cognitive Systems—two emphasis areas: Instructional Systems Technology & Teaching & Learning with Technology. Ph.D. in Educational Computing. See www.cecs.unt.edu.

Features: Unique applications of theory through research and practice in curriculum integration of technology, digital media production, and web development. See www.cecs.unt.edu.

Admission Requirements: Toulouse Graduate School Requirements, 18 hours in education, acceptable GRE: 405 V, 489 A, 3 Analytical Writing for M.S. Degree. Increased requirements for Ph.D. program.

Degree Requirements: 36 semester hours (12 hours core, 12 hours program course requirement based on M.S. track, 12 hours electives). See www.cecs.unt.edu.

Number of Full Time Faculty: 0; **Number of Other Faculty**: 0.

Degrees awarded in 2010–2011 Academic Year—Masters: 0; **Ph.D.**: 0; **Other**: 0.

Grant Monies awarded in 2010–2011 Academic Year: 0.

Name of Institution: Brigham Young University.

Name of Department or Program: Department of Instructional Psychology and Technology.

Address: 150 MCKB, BYU, Provo, UT 84602, USA.

Phone Number: (801)422-5097; **Fax Number**: (801)422-0314.

Email Contact: andy-gibbons@byu.edu; **URL**: http://www.byu.edu/ipt.

Contact Person: Russell Osguthorpe, Professor, Chair.

Specializations: M.S. degrees in Instructional Design, Research and Evaluation, and Multimedia Production. Ph.D. degrees in Instructional Design, and Research and Evaluation.

Features: Course offerings include principles of learning, instructional design, assessing learning outcomes, evaluation in education, empirical inquiry in education, project management, quantitative reasoning, microcomputer materials production, multimedia production, naturalistic inquiry, and more. Students participate in internships and projects related to development, evaluation, measurement, and research.

Admission Requirements: both degrees: transcript, three letters of recommendation, letter of intent, GRE scores. Apply by Feb 1. Students agree to live by the BYU Honor Code as a condition for admission.

Degree Requirements: Master's: 38 semester hours, including prerequisite (3 hours), core courses (14 hours), specialization (12 hours), internship (3 hours), thesis or project (6 hours) with oral defense. Ph.D.: 94 semester hours beyond the Bachelor's degree, including: prerequisite and skill requirements (21 hours), core course (16 hours), specialization (18 hours), internship (12 hours), projects (9 hours), and dissertation (18 hours). The dissertation must be orally defended. Also, at least two consecutive 6-hour semesters must be completed in residence.

Number of Full Time Faculty: 10; **Number of Other Faculty**: 0.

Degrees awarded in 2010–2011 Academic Year—Masters: 15; **Ph.D.**: 10; **Other**: 0.

Grant Monies awarded in 2010–2011 Academic Year: 250,000.

Name of Institution: Utah State University.

Name of Department or Program: Department of Instructional Technology & Learning Sciences, Emma Eccles Jones College of Education and Human Services.

Address: 2830 Old Main Hill, Logan, UT 84322-2830, USA.

Phone Number: (435)797-2694; **Fax Number**: (435)797-2693.

Email Contact: mimi.recker@usu.edu; **URL**: http://itls.usu.edu.

Contact Person: Dr. Mimi Recker, Professor, Chair.

Specializations: M.S. and M.Ed. with concentrations in the areas of Instructional Technology, Learning Sciences, Multimedia, Educational Technology, and Information Technology/School Library Media Administration. Ph.D. in Instructional Technology & Learning Sciences is offered for individuals seeking to become professionally involved in instructional/learning science's research and development in higher education, corporate education, public schools, community colleges, and government.

Features: M.Ed. programs in Instructional Technology/School Library Media Administration and Educational Technology are also available completely online. The doctoral program is built on a strong Master's and Specialists program in Instructional Technology. All doctoral students complete a core with the remainder of the course selection individualized, based upon career goals.

Admission Requirements: M.S. and Ed.S.: 3.0 GPA, a verbal and quantitative score at the 40th percentile on the GRE or 43 MAT, three written recommendations. Ph.D.: relevant Master's degree, 3.0 GPA, verbal, and quantitative score at the 40th percentile on the GRE, three written recommendations, essay on research interests.

Degree Requirements: M.S.: 39 semester hours; thesis or project option. Ed.S.: 30 semester hours if M.S. is in the field, 40 hours if not. Ph.D.: 60 total hours, dissertation, 3-semester residency, and comprehensive examination.

Number of Full Time Faculty: 10; **Number of Other Faculty**: 1.

Degrees awarded in 2010–2011 Academic Year—Masters: 20; **Ph.D.**: 4; **Other**: 1.

Grant Monies awarded in 2010–2011 Academic Year: 1,800,000.

Name of Institution: George Mason University.

Name of Department or Program: Instructional Technology Programs.

Address: Mail Stop 5D6, 4400 University Dr. Fairfax, VA 22030-4444, USA.

Phone Number: (703)993-3798; **Fax Number**: (703)993-2722.

Email Contact: pnorton@gmu.edu; **URL**: http://it.gse.gmu.edu/

Contact Person: Dr. Priscilla Norton, Coordinator of Instructional Technology Academic Programs.

Specializations: Ph.D. Program Learning Technologies Design Research (with specialization in Instructional Design, Integration of Technology in Schools or Assistive Technology) Masters Degrees—Curriculum and Instruction with emphasis in Instructional Technology—Instructional Design & Development Program—Integration of Technology in Schools Program—Assistive Technology Program Graduate Certificates eLearning Integration of Technology in Schools Teaching Secondary Students in Virtual Environments Assistive Technology.

Features: The Instructional Technology program promotes the theory-based design of learning opportunities that maximize the teaching and learning process using a range of technology applications. Program efforts span a range of audiences, meeting the needs of diverse learners—school-aged, adult learners, and learners with disabilities—in public and private settings. Within this framework, the program emphasizes research, reflection, collaboration, leadership, and implementation and delivery models. The Instructional Technology (IT) program provides professionals with the specialized knowledge and skills needed to apply today's computer and telecommunication technologies to educational goals within school, community, and corporate settings. The IT program serves professional educators as well as those involved in instructional design, development, and training in government and private sectors. Master degrees and certificates can be earned in each of three program tracks. Refer to the IT website (http://it.gse.gmu.edu/) for detailed information on admissions, · Track 1—Instructional Design and Development (IDD)—Students are prepared to craft effective solutions within public, private, and educational contexts to instructional challenges by using the latest information technologies in the design and development of instructional materials. · Track II—Integration of Technology in Schools (ITS)—Students are prepared to effectively integrate technology in the K-12 learning environment. Graduates frequently become the local expert and change agent for technology in schools. · Track III—Assistive/Special Education Technology (A/SET)—Graduates will use technology to assist individuals to function more effectively in school, home, work, and community environments. Graduates are prepared to incorporate technology into the roles of educators, related service providers, Assistive Technology consultants, hardware/software designers, and school based technology coordinators.

Admission Requirements: Masters Program—Teaching or training experience, undergrad GPA of 3.0, TOEFL of 575(written)/230(computer), three letters of recommendation, goal statement. Ph.D. Program—http://gse.gmu.edu/programs/phd/

Degree Requirements: M.Ed. in Curriculum and Instruction Track I and III: 30 hours; practicum, internship, or project. M.Ed. in Curriculum and Instruction Track II: 36 hours; practicum M.Ed. in Special Education: 30 hours Ph.D.: 56–62 hours beyond Master's degree for either specialization. Certificate programs: 15 hours Ph.D. Program—65 hours.

Number of Full Time Faculty: 7; **Number of Other Faculty**: 5.

Degrees awarded in 2010–2011 Academic Year—Masters: 130; **Ph.D.**: 15; **Other**: 0.

Grant Monies awarded in 2010–2011 Academic Year: 2,500,000.

Name of Institution: Virginia Tech.

Name of Department or Program: College of Liberal Arts and Human Sciences.

Address: 144 J Smyth Hall, Blacksburg, VA 24061-0488, USA.

Phone Number: (540)231-5587; **Fax Number**: (540)231-9075.

Email Contact: jburton@vt.edu; **URL**: http://www.soe.vt.edu/idt/

Contact Person: John Burton, Program Area Leader, Instructional Design & Technology, Department of Learning Sciences & Technologies.

Specializations: M.A., Ed.S. Ed.D., and Ph.D. in Instructional Design and Technology. Graduates of our Masters and Educational Specialist programs find themselves applying their expertise in a variety of rewarding, professional venues; for example, as instructional designers, trainers, or performance consultants in industrial settings and as teachers or technology coordinators in preK-12. Graduates of our Doctoral program typically assume exciting roles as faculty in higher education, advancing research in the field and preparing the next generation of instructional technologists for the profession.

Features: Areas of emphasis are Instructional Design, Distance Education, and Multimedia Development. Facilities include computer labs, extensive digital video and audio equipment, distance education classroom, and computer graphics production areas.

Admission Requirements: Ed.D. and Ph.D.: 3.3 GPA from Masters degree, GRE scores, writing sample, three letters of recommendation, transcripts. M.A..: 3.0 GPA Undergraduate.

Degree Requirements: Ph.D.: 90 hours above B.S., 2 year residency, 12 hours. Research classes, 30 hours dissertation; Ed.D.: 90 hours above B.S., 1 year residency, 12 hours research classes; M.A..: 30 hours above B.S.

Number of Full Time Faculty: 6; **Number of Other Faculty**: 5.

Degrees awarded in 2010–2011 Academic Year—Masters: 15; **Ph.D.**: 6; **Other**: 2.

Grant Monies awarded in 2010–2011 Academic Year: 3,500,000.

Name of Institution: University of Virginia.

Name of Department or Program: Instructional Science & Technology Program, Department of Curriculum & Instruction, Curry School of Education.

Address: Bavaro Hall #312, 405 Emmet Street, PO Box 400273, Charlottesville, VA 22904-4273, USA.

Phone Number: (434)924-0831; **Fax Number**: (434)924-7461.

Email Contact: kdg9g@virginia.edu; **URL**: curry.edschool.virginia.edu/it.

Contact Person: Karen Dwier, Department of Curriculum, Instruction, & Special Education, Curry School of Education.

Specializations: In the University of Virginias Curry School of Education's Ph.D. program, Instructional Science & Technology (IT) is not just a program; it is a key theme in the identity of the entire school and is influential across the university. Twenty faculty members from across the Curry School and University come together to focus on IT, and students have rich learning opportunities across a range of focal areas:

Instructional Design and Interactive Development

Web 2.0 Convergence, Educational Multimedia

Technology Leadership, Technology & Teaching

Science, Technology, Engineering, & Mathematics(STEM)Education

Consumer Health Education, Gender & Technology

Games/Play/Flow, Museums & Education

M.Ed., Ed.S., Ed.D., and Ph.D. degrees are offered.

Features: The IT program is situated in a major research university with linkages to multiple disciplines. Faculty in the program hold leadership positions with the Center for Advanced Study of Teaching & Learning (CASTL) and the Center for Technology & Teacher Education, among others.

Our students work closely with faculty in a collegial environment on both time-tested and leading-edge practices. You'll find yourself working with the most talented students from virtually every discipline and background, learning team leadership skills and forming lifelong friendships. The University of Virginia is one of the top-ranked public universities in the nation, and the Curry School is nationally recognized for its leadership and innovation, particularly in IT. We are the recipient of the American Association of Colleges for Teacher Education (AACTE)

Innovative Use of Technology Award for modeling innovative use of technology for others in the profession as well as a recipient of the first International Society for Technology in Education (ISTE) Distinguished Achievement Award for integration of technology into teacher education, among other awards and recognition.

Faculty and students are active in national organizations such as the Association for Educational Communications & Technology (AECT), Society for Information Technology & Teacher Education (SITE), and the American Educational Research Association (AERA). Graduates in IT from the Curry School are creating positive change through positions in research and development and instructional innovation around the world. We invite you to discover, create, and change with us.

Admission Requirements: Admission to any graduate program requires: Undergraduate degree from accredited institution in any field, undergraduate GPA 3.0, and TOEFL (if applicable): 600 paper-based, 250 computer-based.

For admission to the Master of Education (M.Ed.), Educational Specialist (Ed.S.), and Doctor of Education (Ed.D.) degrees, minimum 1,000 GRE (V+Q).

For admission to the Doctor of Philosophy (Ph.D.) program, minimum GRE 1,100 (V+Q). Ph.D. admissions are highly competitive and fully funded, to provide mentored, 4-year program based on research, development, and scholarship.

Degree Requirements: M.Ed.: 36 semester hours. Ed.S.: 60 semester hours beyond undergraduate degree.

Ed.D.: 72 semester hours including 48 hours of coursework, 12 hours of internship experience, and a 12 hours capstone project.

Ph.D.: 76 semester hours of coursework and research internship, plus 24 hours of dissertation research. All graduate degrees require a comprehensive examination. The Ph.D. also requires completion of a preliminary examination and a juried pre-dissertation presentation or publication.

Number of Full Time Faculty: 4; **Number of Other Faculty**: 16.

Degrees awarded in 2010–2011 Academic Year—Masters: 4; **Ph.D.**: 5; **Other**: 2.

Grant Monies awarded in 2010–2011 Academic Year: 1,500,000.

Name of Institution: University of Washington.

Name of Department or Program: College of Education.

Address: 115 Miller Hall, Box 353600, Seattle, WA 98195-3600, USA.

Phone Number: (206)543-1847; **Fax Number**: (206)543-1237.

Email Contact: billwinn@u.washington.edu; **URL**: http://www.educ.washington.edu/COE/c-and-i/c_and_i_med_ed_tech.htm.

Contact Person: William Winn, Professor of Education.

Specializations: M.Ed., Ed.D., and Ph.D. for individuals in business, industry, higher education, public schools, and organizations concerned with education or communication (broadly defined).

Features: Emphasis on design of materials and programs to encourage learning and development in school and non-school settings; research and related activity in such areas as interactive instruction, web-based learning, virtual environments, use of video as a tool for design, and development. Close collaboration with program in Cognitive Studies.

Admission Requirements: M.Ed.: goal statement (2–3 pp.), writing sample, 1,000 GRE (verbal plus quantitative), undergraduate GPA indicating potential to success-fully accomplish graduate work. Doctoral: GRE scores, letters of reference, tran-scripts, personal statement, Master's degree or equivalent in field appropriate to the specialization with 3.5 GPA, 2 years of successful professional experience, and/or experience related to program goals desirable.

Degree Requirements: M.Ed.: 45 qtr. hours (including 24 in technology); thesis or project recommended, exam optional. Ed.D.: see http://www.educ.washington.edu/COEWebSite/programs/ci/EdD.html; Ph.D.: http://www.educ.washington.edu/COEWebSite/students/prospective/phdDescrip.html.

Number of Full Time Faculty: –; **Number of Other Faculty**: –.

Degrees awarded in 2010–2011 Academic Year—Masters: 5; **Ph.D.**: –; **Other**: –.

Grant Monies awarded in 2010–2011 Academic Year: –.

Name of Institution: University of Alaska Southeast.

Name of Department or Program: Educational Technology Program.

Address: 11120 Glacier Hwy, HA1, Juneau, AK 99801, USA.

Phone Number: (907)-796-6050; **Fax Number**: (907)-796-6059.

Email Contact: marsha.gladhart@uas.alaska.edu; **URL**: http://uas.alaska.edu/education/experienced.

Contact Person: Marsha Gladhart.

Specializations: Educational Technology.

Features: *distance program, *standards-based learning, *integration of the most current technologies, *collaboration with other teachers, *instructors with k-12 teaching experience, *focus on improving student learning, *use of technology as a tool to assist learning.

Admission Requirements: #A completed graduate application and $60 process-ing fee. #Official academic transcript indicating baccalaureate degree and a GPA of 3.0. #Two (2) general recommendations written by former or current professors, employers, or supervisors who are familiar with your work and performance. Each recommendation must be submitted using the Letter of Recommendation for

Graduate Programs form. #A recommendation documenting your ability to meet the educational technology standards required for entry to the program. This recommendation should be completed by an administrator, supervisor, or technology leader. #Statement of Professional Objectives. #A copy of a current teaching or administrative certificate.

Degree Requirements: Official academic transcript indicating baccalaureate degree and a GPA of 3.0.

Number of Full Time Faculty: 2; **Number of Other Faculty**: 5.

Degrees awarded in 2010–2011 Academic Year—Masters: 11; **Ph.D.**: 0; **Other**: 0.

Grant Monies awarded in 2010–2011 Academic Year: 0.

Name of Institution: University of South Alabama.

Name of Department or Program: Department of Behavioral Studies and Educational Technology, College of Education.

Address: University Commons 3700, Mobile, AL 36688, USA.

Phone Number: (251)380-2861; **Fax Number**: (251)380-2713.

Email Contact: jdempsey@usouthal.edu; **URL**: http://www.southalabama.edu/coe/bset/

Contact Person: Daniel W. Surry, IDD Program Coordinator; Mary Ann Robinson, Ed Media Program Coordinator.

Specializations: M.S. and Ph.D. in Instructional Design and Development. M.Ed. in Educational Media (Ed Media). Online master's degrees in ED Media and IDD are available for qualified students. For information about online master's degree programs, see http://usaonline.southalabama.edu.

Features: The IDD masters and doctoral programs emphasize extensive education and training in the instructional design process, human performance technology and multimedia—and online-based training. The IDD doctoral program has an additional emphasis in research design and statistical analysis. The Ed Media master's program prepares students in planning, designing, and administering library/media centers at most levels of education, including higher education.

Admission Requirements: For the ED Media & IDD Masters: undergraduate degree in appropriate academic field from an accredited university or college; admission to Graduate School; satisfactory score on the GRE. ED Media students must have completed requirements for a certificate at the baccalaureate or masters level in a teaching field. For IDD Ph.D.: Masters degree, all undergraduate & graduate transcripts, three letters of recommendations, written statement of purpose for pursuing Ph.D. in IDD, satisfactory score on GRE.

Degree Requirements: Ed Media masters: satisfactorily complete program requirements (minimum 33 semester hours), 3.0 or better GPA, satisfactory score on comprehensive exam. IDD masters: satisfactorily complete program requirements (minimum 40 semester hours), 3.0 or better GPA; satisfactory complete comprehensive exam. Ph.D.: satisfactory complete program requirements (minimum 82 semester hours of approved graduate courses), 1-year residency, satisfactory score on examinations (research and statistical exam and comprehensive exam), approved dissertation completed. Any additional requirements will be determined by student's doctoral advisory committee.

Number of Full Time Faculty: 0; **Number of Other Faculty**: 0.

Degrees awarded in 2010–2011 Academic Year—Masters: 0; **Ph.D.**: 0; **Other**: 0.

Grant Monies awarded in 2010–2011 Academic Year: 0.

Name of Institution: University of Arkansas.

Name of Department or Program: Educational Technology.

Address: 101 Peabody Hall, Fayetteville, AR 72701, USA.

Phone Number: (479)-575-5111; **Fax Number**: 479-575-2493.

Email Contact: cmurphy@uark.edu; **URL**: http://etec.uark.edu.

Contact Person: Dr. Cheryl Murphy.

Specializations: The program prepares students for a variety of work environments by offering core courses that are applicable to a multitude of professional venues. The program also allows for specific emphasis area studies via open-ended assignments and course electives that include courses particularly relevant to higher education, business/industry, or K-12 environments. The primary focus of the program is on the processes involved in instructional design, training and development, media production, and utilization of instructional technologies. Because technology is continually changing, the program emphasizes acquisition of a process over the learning of specific technologies. Although skills necessary in making Educational Technology products are taught, technology changes rapidly; therefore, a primary emphasis on making technological products would lead to the acquisition of skills that are quickly outdated. However, learning the principles and mental tools critical to producing successful training and education will endure long after "new" technologies have become obsolete. That is why the University of Arkansas ETEC program focuses on the processes as opposed to specific technologies.

Features: The Educational Technology Program is a 33-hour non-thesis online master's program that prepares students for professional positions as educational technologists of education, business, government, and the health professions. Because the program is offered online, there are no on-campus requirements for the completion of this degree.

Admission Requirements: The Educational Technology online master's program admits students in the fall, spring, and summer. Applications and all accompanying documents must be submitted within 3 months of the desired starting semester to ensure adequate processing time. To qualify for admission, applicants must have an earned bachelor's degree and an undergraduate GPA of 3.0 within the last 60 hours of coursework. Specific application materials can be found at http://etec.uark. edu/1069.htm. Applicants for the M.Ed. degree must have met all requirements of Graduate School admission, completed a bachelor's degree, and earned a 3.0 GPA in all undergraduate coursework or obtain an acceptable score on the Graduate Record Examinations or Miller Analogies Test. A Graduate School application, ETEC Program Application, writing sample, autobiographical sketch, and letters of recommendation are required for admission consideration.

Degree Requirements: Beginning Fall 2012, in addition to general admission requirements students must complete a minimum of 34 hours to include 22 semester hours of educational technology core courses; nine semester hours of educational technology electives; and three semester hours of research. Additionally, a Culminating Student Portfolio must be successfully completed during the last semester of coursework. There are no on-campus requirements for the completion of this degree, although approved courses that meet the research requirements may be taken on campus if desired.

Number of Full Time Faculty: 2; **Number of Other Faculty**: 3.

Degrees awarded in 2010–2011 Academic Year—Masters: 9; **Ph.D.**: 0; **Other**: 0.

Grant Monies awarded in 2010–2011 Academic Year: 100,000.

Name of Institution: University of Arkansas at Little Rock.

Name of Department or Program: Learning Systems Technology.

Address: 2801 S University, Little Rock, AR 72204, USA.

Phone Number: (501)-569-3267; **Fax Number**: (501)569-3547.

Email Contact: eivaughn@ualr.edu; **URL**: http://ualr.edu/med/LSTE/

Contact Person: Elizabeth Vaughn-Neely, Ph.D., Chair.

Specializations: The Learning Systems Technology master's degree prepares you for the design, production, and application of these new methods, including creating and designing the following learning products: *documents and electronic displays, *interactive tutorials for web-based delivery, *instructional blogs, *useful web pages, *complete instructional packages using digital images and film clips, *courses using a variety of online course management systems, *learning resource centers.

Features: This program is offered entirely online.

Admission Requirements: Admission to the LSTE master's program requires: *A baccalaureate degree from a regionally accredited institution with substantially the same undergraduate programs as the University of Arkansas at Little Rock with an overall GPA of 3.0 or 3.25 for the last 60 hours. *A 3.0 GPA on the last 60 hours (including postbaccalaureate hours or a 2.7 GPA on all undergraduate hours taken for the baccalaureate degree). *Successful application to the UALR graduate school.

*Academic evaluation by the LSTE program coordinator: After you have completed your online application to the Graduate School, your folder with all of your transcripts will be sent to the program coordinator for evaluation. The program coordinator will then send you a letter with your status in the process. Once you get your letter of acceptance you will be able to start the program in any semester: Fall, Spring, or Summer. If you have any questions, please contact the program coordinator.

Degree Requirements: The 36 graduate credit hours include: *9 Educational Foundations hours, *18 Learning Technologies hours, *Up to 3 elective courses (Foundations, English writing, Learning Technologies or other content area approved by the adviser). No more than 6 hours earned within the last 3 years of transfer credit will be accepted in the program.

Number of Full Time Faculty: 1; **Number of Other Faculty**: 5.

Degrees awarded in 2010–2011 Academic Year—Masters: 7; **Ph.D.**: 0; **Other**: 0.

Grant Monies awarded in 2010–2011 Academic Year: 0.

Name of Institution: California State Polytechnic University.

Name of Department or Program: Educational Multimedia Design.

Address: 3801 West Temple Avenue, Pomona, CA 91768, USA.

Phone Number: (909)-869-2255; **Fax Number**: 909-869-5206.

Email Contact: slotfipour@csupomona.edu; **URL**: www.csupomona.edu/emm.

Contact Person: Dr. Shahnaz Lotfipour.

Specializations: Design and production of eLearning materials and educational multimedia software (including audio, video, animation, web programming (3 levels), graphics, etc.) for educational and corporate training environments using the sound instructional principles and strategies.

Features: Hands-on training, project-based, combination of online and hybrid courses, internship possibilities in educational and corporate settings.

Admission Requirements: Undergraduate GPA of 3.0, three strong letters of recommendations for this program, and satisfying graduate writing test (GWT) within the first couple of quarters.

Degree Requirements: B.A. or B.S. in any area.

Number of Full Time Faculty: 3; **Number of Other Faculty**: 5.

Degrees awarded in 2010–2011 Academic Year—Masters: 32; **Ph.D.**: 2; **Other**: 0.

Grant Monies awarded in 2010–2011 Academic Year: 0.

Name of Institution: California State University Monterey Bay (CSUMB).

Name of Department or Program: Master of Science in Instructional Science and Technology (IST).

Address: 100 Campus Center, Seaside, CA 93955, USA.

Phone Number: (831)-582-4790; **Fax Number**: 831-582-4484.

Email Contact: mist@csumb.edu; **URL**: http://itcd.csumb.edu/mist.

Contact Person: Bude Su, Ph.D.

Specializations: x.

Features: Interdisciplinary collaboration that integrates learning science and information technology is the hallmark of the IST graduate program and a CSUMB core value. Recognizing that the use of technology is critical to the design, development, and delivery of instruction in the twenty-first century, IST integrates modern learning technology and pedagogy to create educational experiences adequate for the contemporary world. This technology infusion models best practices to learners. Rather than setting aside one course that deals solely with ethics and social responsibility, our curriculum integrates ethical reflection and practice throughout the program. All required courses incorporate the basic concepts and concerns of ethics into their design, development, and delivery. Multiculturalism and globalism are infused into the IST curriculum, including discussion of diversity in the conduct of instructional design and diversity in the understanding of ethics. Applied learning is critical to the IST program, and we use an integrated pedagogy that builds on each semester's outcome. Please see the program curriculum outline in the Degree Requirements section, and visit our website for more details at http://www.csumb.edu/mist/

Admission Requirements: (a) Complete and submit an application form at CSUMENTOR.edu and $55.00 application fee payable to CSUMB. (A) Select Fall 2012 as the application term. B. Select MS in Instructional Science and Technology program to continue. (b) Submit all required supporting documents. All supporting documents should be submitted to: School of Information Technology and Communication Design Attention: MIST Program, Building 18, Room 150 100 Campus Center Seaside, CA 93955. (A) Submit two (2) official copies of each of the following: (1) Transcripts of all college coursework taken. *Have two (2) officialtranscripts from all colleges and universities you have attended mailed directly to the MIST Program at the address listed above. (We recommend that you request that an additional copy be mailed directly to you at home and that you leave that envelope unopened until you have confirmation that we have received our copies.) *A GPA of 3.0 is expected for the most recent 60 units of college-level work attempted. GPA between 2.5 and 3.0 may be considered with substantial alternative demonstration of ability to succeed in the program. (2) Test scores (TOEFL, GRE, etc.), (if applicable). *We recommend that you take the GRE test to improve your competitive standing but it is not required. CSUMB's school code for ETS is 1945. *For those students required to demonstrate English proficiency: the IST program requires a TOEFL score of 575 for admission. Selected applicants with TOEFL scores between 525 and 574 and applicants demonstrating English proficiency with test scores other than TOEFL must pass a writing workshop offered by ITCD before the first day of classes as a condition of admission. Applicants with TOEFL scores below 525 will not be considered. *CSUMB minimum requirements for English proficiency for applicants with degrees from foreign universities are listed on the Admissions & Recruitment website at: http://ar.csumb.edu/site/x5362. xml#requirements. (3) Foreign Credential Evaluation (if applicable). *All transcripts from schools outside the United States must be sent, at the applicant's expense, to a foreign credential evaluation service. A detailed "course-by-course" report is required for all programs. Three credential evaluation services accepted by CSU Monterey Bay are: (1) World Education Services, WES, http://www.wes.org/. (2) American Association of Collegiate Registrars and Admissions Offices, AACRAO, http://www.aacrao.org/credential/. (c) International Education Research Foundation, IERF, http://www.ierf.org/. *CSUMB minimum requirements for foreign credential evaluation for applicants with degrees from foreign universities are listed on the Admissions & Recruitment website at: http://ar.csumb.edu/site/x5362. xml#requirements. (B) Submit an original "Statement of Purpose" (one copy is sufficient). *Include a 1,000–2,000 word Statement of Purpose (statement of educational and professional goals) that demonstrates your writing ability. (C) Submit two (2) or three (3) letters of reference (one copy of each is sufficient). *Include two or three letters of recommendation from individuals familiar with your professional and academic work. For more detailed information, please visit our website at: http://www.csumb.edu/mist.

Degree Requirements: Outcomes, Courses, and Assessment The Master of Science in Instructional Science and Technology degree requires 24 semester hours of core courses, four semester hours of an elective, and four semester hours for the culminating Capstone experience or thesis. [Learn more at CSUMB.EDU/capstone]. As the title signifies, the core courses are a cluster of instructional design, instructional systems, and best educational practices that represent the core of the collaborative program. By guiding you toward the Learning Outcomes (LOs) listed below, these courses provide you with the skills necessary to become an effective instructional designer and e-learning developer in today's high-tech, global marketplace. Given the complexities that emanate from strong and growing global forces and conflicting values, we discuss international and ethical issues in all courses. The IST program consists of four terms that must be taken sequentially covering the following courses and outcomes. IST 522: Instructional Design IST 524: Instructional Technology LO 1 Instructional Technology LO 2 Instructional Design Students are introduced to the field and profession of Instructional Science and Technology. Topics include but not limited to history, current issues, future trends, and an overview of how the components of the field fit together. Students investigate and apply instructional design models to carry out small scale projects and generate a detailed instructional design document. Students are encouraged to incorporate projects from their current employment into the class assignments. Term II Courses IST 520: Learning Theories IST 526: Interactive Multimedia Instruction LO 3 Learning Theories LO 4 Interactive Multimedia Students learn to evaluate and select appropriate learning theories and instructional principles. And apply them for the design and implementation of instruction and training. Students construct a functioning learning module using interactive multimedia software, information technology, and media. Term III Courses IST 622: Assessment & Evaluation IST 626: Advanced Instructional Design LO 2 Instructional Design LO 5 Assessment and Evaluation Students work on authentic instructional design projects individually or in small groups. Students engage in a real world design experience that deals with and balancing numerous additional variables, including project management, effective communication with clients, time management, application of professional knowledge and skills, and producing professional level products. Students are introduced to the theoretical framework of assessment as it applies to learner performance, effectiveness of curriculum design, and effectiveness of instructional delivery. Students develop techniques for judging the performance of instructional delivery and conduct appropriate usability, reliability, and efficiency tests of instructional and learning management systems. Term IV Courses IST 699: Graduate Capstone Minimum of 4 elective upper-division or graduate-level credits, approved by program coordinator and faculty advisor, related to the field of instructional science and technology. LO 6 Breadth of Knowledge LO 7 Instructional Science and Technology Capstone Project or Thesis Students complete a Capstone project or thesis that connects with their careers as the culminating experience. Examples include a field study, a client-driven project or applied research.

Number of Full Time Faculty: 8; **Number of Other Faculty**: 12.

Degrees awarded in 2010–2011 Academic Year—Masters: 24; **Ph.D.**: 0; **Other**: 50.

Grant Monies awarded in 2010–2011 Academic Year: 60,000.

Name of Institution: California State University, East Bay.

Name of Department or Program: Online Teaching & Learning.

Address: 25800 Carlos Bee Boulevard, Hayward, CA 94542, USA.

Phone Number: (510)-885-4384; **Fax Number**: (510)-885-4498.

Email Contact: nan.chico@csueastbay.edu; **URL**: http://www.ce.csueastbay.edu/degree/education/index.shtml?intid=fhome_otlm.

Contact Person: Nan Chico.

Specializations: A professional development degree for experienced K-12, college/university faculty and corporate or non-profit trainers at institutions creating new, or building on old, online course and program degrees, workshops, trainings. A major focus is learning how to design courses around accessibility issues.

Features: Courses are in Blackboard, students are given a Blackboard shell of their own to design in or may choose among other course management systems. We focus on best practices in online teaching and learning, using a CMS and varieties of other social media. Not cohort-based, admission is quarterly; maximum two courses per quarter; may skip one to two consecutive quarters.

Admission Requirements: B.A. or B.S. degree from a regionally accredited US institution, in any major; GPA 3.0 in last 60 semester units or last 90 quarter units. Selection is also based on mandatory Letter of Intent.

Degree Requirements: Four 5-week courses taken over two quarters (which earn the Certificate in Online Teaching & Learning); two 10-week electives, four 10-week required courses, the last of which is a Capstone Project. Each course earns 4.5 quarter units; all required courses must earn a "B" or better, overall GPA must be 3.0 or better. Total of 10 courses, 45 units.

Number of Full Time Faculty: 0; **Number of Other Faculty**: 9.

Degrees awarded in 2010–2011 Academic Year—Masters: 45; **Ph.D.**: 0; **Other**: 0.

Grant Monies awarded in 2010–2011 Academic Year: 0.

Name of Institution: California State University, Fresno.

Name of Department or Program: M.A. in Education & Certificate of Advanced Study in Educational Technology.

Address:5005 N Maple Avenue, MS2, Fresno, CA 93740, USA.

Phone Number: (559)-278-0245; **Fax Number**: (559)-278-0107.

Email Contact: royb@csufresno.edu; **URL**: http://www.csufresno.edu/kremen/ci/graduate/ma-education.html.

Contact Person: Dr. Roy M. Bohlin.

Specializations: None.

Features: None.

Admission Requirements: None.

Degree Requirements: Bachelors degree.

Number of Full Time Faculty: 6; **Number of Other Faculty**: 4.

Degrees awarded in 2010–2011 Academic Year—Masters: 9; **Ph.D.**: 0; **Other**: 6.

Grant Monies awarded in 2010–2011 Academic Year: 0.

Name of Institution: Metropolitan State College of Denver.

Name of Department or Program: Department of Special Education, Early Childhood Education, Reading, and Educational Technology.

Address:Teacher Education, Campus Box 21, PO Box 173362, Denver, CO 80217, USA.

Phone Number: (303)556-3322; **Fax Number**: (303) 556–5353.

Email Contact: mchung3@mscd.edu; **URL**: http://www.mscd.edu/~ted.

Contact Person: Dr. Miri Chung.

Specializations: x.

Features: x.

Admission Requirements: x.

Degree Requirements: x.

Number of Full Time Faculty: 2; **Number of Other Faculty**: 1.

Degrees awarded in 2010–2011 Academic Year—Masters: 0; **Ph.D.**: 0; **Other**: 0.

Grant Monies awarded in 2010–2011 Academic Year: 0.

Name of Institution: Regis University.

Name of Department or Program: School of Education and Counseling.

Address: 3333 Regis Boulevard, Denver, CO 80221, USA.

Phone Number: (800)-388-2366; **Fax Number**: (303)-964-5053.

Email Contact: chruskoc@regis.edu; **URL**: www.regis.edu.

Contact Person: Dr. Carole Hruskocy.

Specializations: Instructional Technology Curriculum, Instruction, and Assessment Professional Leadership Adult Learning, Training, and Development Self-Designed Reading Space Studies.

Features: The majority of our programs are offered in the online format.

Admission Requirements: Essay Letters of Recommendation Minimum GPA of 2.75.

Degree Requirements: x.

Number of Full Time Faculty: 15; **Number of Other Faculty**: 150.

Degrees awarded in 2010–2011 Academic Year—Masters: 200; **Ph.D.**: 0; **Other**: 0.

Grant Monies awarded in 2010–2011 Academic Year: 0.

Name of Institution: University of Bridgeport.

Name of Department or Program: Instructional Technology.

Address:126 Park Avenue, Bridgeport, CT 06604, USA.

Phone Number: (203)576-4217; **Fax Number**: (203)576-4633.

Email Contact: jcole@bridgeport.edu; **URL**: http://www.bridgeport.edu/imsit.

Contact Person: Jerald D. Cole.

Specializations: Masters and Professional Diploma (6th Year) Instructional Technology Tracks: (1) Teacher; (2) Trainer; (3) Developer; (4) Technology Education; (5) Technology Leadership.

Features: (1) Open Source Curriculum and Software Model. (2) Cross Platform Mobil Tablet Computing Initiative. (3) Social Constructionist Pedagogy. (4) Hybrid and online courses. (5) Cohort-based. (6) Tuition-free internships for Teacher track.

Admission Requirements: Online Application Essay on experience and objectives for study; Two letters of reference Praxis 1 for teacher track TOEFL for non-native English speakers Transcripts Phone interview.

Degree Requirements: 4 core courses, 2 distribution requirements, 1 research, 1 practicum, 4 electives.

Number of Full Time Faculty: 14; **Number of Other Faculty**: 21.

Degrees awarded in 2010–2011 Academic Year—Masters: 294; **Ph.D.**: 15; **Other**: 117.

Grant Monies awarded in 2010–2011 Academic Year: 350,000.

Name of Institution: University of Florida.

Name of Department or Program: School of Teaching and Learning.

Address: 2403 Norman Hall, Gainesville, FL 32611-7048 USA.

Phone Number: (352)-392-9191, X261; **Fax Number**: (352)-392-9193.

Email Contact: kdawson@coe.ufl.edu; **URL**: http://www.coe.ufl.edu/school/edtech/index.htm (Hybrid programs); http://www.coe.ufl.edu/online/edtech/index.html (Online programs).

Contact Person: Kara Dawson.

Specializations: Hybrid Program: Educational technology students may earn M. Ed., Ed.S., Ed.D., or Ph.D. degrees and have an opportunity to specialize in one of two tracks: (1) Teaching and teacher education or (2) Design and Production of educational materials. Many students merge these tracks. Teacher education students and students in other degree programs may also elect to specialize in Educational Technology. Online Programs: We offer an online Masters, Ed.S., and Ed.D. degrees in "Teaching, learning and facilitating change with educational technology" http://www.coe.ufl.edu/online/edtech/index.html.

Features: Students take core courses listed on our Educational Technology website and then select an area of specialization. Opportunities to collaborative research, write and design with faculty members. Strong community of graduate students.

Admission Requirements: Please see the Educational Technology website for the most up-to-date information.

Degree Requirements: Please see the Educational Technology website for the most up-to-date information. Program and college requirements must be met, but there is considerable flexibility for doctoral students to plan an appropriate program with their advisors.

Number of Full Time Faculty: 5; **Number of Other Faculty**: 3.

Degrees awarded in 2010–2011 Academic Year—Masters: 20; **Ph.D.**: 5; **Other**: 15.

Grant Monies awarded in 2010–2011 Academic Year: 1,000,000.

Name of Institution: University of West Florida.

Name of Department or Program: Instructional and Performance Technology.

Address: 11000 University Parkway, Pensacola, FL 32514, USA.

Phone Number: (850)-474-2300; **Fax Number**: (850)-474-2804.

Email Contact: krasmuss@uwf.edu; **URL**: http://uwf.edu/ect/graduate.cfm#IPT.

Contact Person: Karen Rasmussen.

Specializations: M.Ed., Instructional Technology: Curriculum and Technology Telecommunications and Distance Learning Technology Leadership Human Performance Technology M.S.A., H.P.T.: Human Performance Technology Ed.S., Instructional Technology Performance Technology Distance Learning Ed.D., Curriculum and Instruction, Instructional Technology Specialization: Performance Technology Distance Learning.

Features: Fully online programs at masters-level Small classes Recognized nationally as a "Best Buy" in Online Degree Programs in Human Performance Technology based on quality and affordability.

Admission Requirements: GRE or MAT Score Official Transcripts Letter of Intent See Department Website for additional information for specific programs.

Degree Requirements: M.Ed., 36 credit hours; M.S.A., 33 credit hours; Ed.S., 36 credit hours; Ed.D., minimum 66 credit hours.

Number of Full Time Faculty: 4; **Number of Other Faculty**: 2.

Degrees awarded in 2010–2011 Academic Year—Masters: 17; **Ph.D.**: 0; **Other**: 5.

Grant Monies awarded in 2010–2011 Academic Year: 260,000.

Name of Institution: Ball State University.

Name of Department or Program: Masters of Arts in Curriculum and Educational Technology.

Address: Teachers College, Muncie, IN 47306, USA.

Phone Number: (765)285-5461; **Fax Number**: (765)285-5489.

Email Contact: jmclaus@bsu.edu; **URL**: http://www.bsu.edu/edstudies/edtech/

Contact Person: Jon M. Clausen.

Specializations: Specialization tracks in curriculum or educational technology.

Features: The Masters of Arts in Curriculum and Educational Technology is a 30-hour program designed for educators seeking to integrate technology into K12 curriculum and other instructional contexts where teaching and learning occur. Graduates are prepared to become leaders within their instructional contexts by coursework and experiences that focus on development of a conceptual framework in which technology is an embedded aspect of the teaching and learning process. The program prepares graduates to utilize technology to meet learning needs of students and to critically examine technology's ever-changing presence within schools and society.

Admission Requirements: Prospective students should apply to the Graduate College and provide official transcripts from all universities/colleges attended. A student seeking admittance for a Masters degree must meet the following minimum criteria: Hold an earned bachelors degree from a college or university that is accredited by its regional accrediting association:: Have one of the following: An undergraduate cumulative GPA of at least 2.75 on a scale of 4.0: A cumulative GPA of at least 3.0 on a 4.0 scale in the latter half of the baccalaureate. Additional Information regarding application and admission to the graduate college can be found at the following website. http://www.bsu.edu/gradschool.

Degree Requirements: Successful completion of 30 graduate hours.

Number of Full Time Faculty: 8; **Number of Other Faculty**: 4.

Degrees awarded in 2010–2011 Academic Year—Masters: 15; **Ph.D.**: 0; **Other**: 0.

Grant Monies awarded in 2010–2011 Academic Year: 0.

Name of Institution: Indiana University.

Name of Department or Program: Instructional Systems Technology, School of Education.

Address: WW Wright Education Building, Room 2276, 201 N Rose Avenue, Bloomington, IN 47405-1006, USA.

Phone Number: (812)856-8450; **Fax Number**: (812)856-8239.

Email Contact: istdept@indiana.edu; **URL**: http://education.indiana.edu/~ist/

Contact Person: Theodore Frick, Chair, Department of Instructional Systems Technology.

Specializations: The M.S. and Ed.S. degrees are designed for individuals seeking to be practitioners in the field of Instructional Technology. The M.S. degree is also offered in a web-based format with instructional product and portfolio requirements, with specializations in Workplace Learning and Performance Improvement; Instructional Systems Design Practice; and Learning Technologies. A Studio specialization is available to residential students. Online certificate and licensure programs are also available.

An online Ed.D. was approved by the Indiana Commission for Higher Education in August, 2011, and applications are being accepted for an August, 2012, launch date. The emphasis of the Ed.D. is the application of theory to practice.

The Ph.D. degree features a heavy research emphasis via faculty-mentored research groups and student dossiers for assessing research, teaching, and service competencies.

Features: Requires computer skills as a prerequisite and makes technology utilization an integral part of the curriculum; eliminates separation of various media formats; and establishes a series of courses of increasing complexity integrating production and development. The latest in technical capabilities have been incorporated, including teaching, computer, and laptop-ready laboratories, a multimedia laboratory, and video and audio production studios. Residential master's students have a studio facility available for their exclusive use for two semesters.

Ph.D. students participate in faculty-mentored research groups throughout their program. Students construct dossiers with evidence of research, teaching, and service that are evaluated by faculty on three occasions during the program. The second and third dossier reviews replace the traditional written and oral examinations.

Admission Requirements: M.S.: Bachelor's degree from an accredited institution, 1350 GRE (3 tests required) or 900 plus 3.5 analytical writing (new format), 2.75 undergraduate GPA. Ed.S., Ed.D., and Ph.D.: 1650 GRE (3 tests required) or 1100 plus 4.5 analytical writing (new format), 3.5 graduate GPA.

Degree Requirements: M.S.: 36 credit hours (including 15 credits in required courses); an instructional product; 9 credits in outside electives, and portfolio. Ed.S.: 65 hours, capstone project with written report and a portfolio. Ed.D.: 60 hours postmasters (MS credits not counted towards 60 hours), with written and oral qualifying exams, and dissertation. Ph.D.: 90 hours, dossier reviews, and thesis.

Number of Full Time Faculty: 10; **Number of Other Faculty**: 12.

Degrees awarded in 2010–2011 Academic Year—Masters: 17; **Ph.D.**: 10; **Other**: 1.

Grant Monies awarded in 2010–2011 Academic Year: 1,237,755.

Name of Institution: Purdue University.

Name of Department or Program: College of Education, Department of Curriculum and Instruction.

Address: 100 N University Street, West Lafayette, IN 47907-2098, USA.

Phone Number: (765)494-5669; **Fax Number**: (765)496-1622.

Email Contact: edtech@soe.purdue.edu; **URL**: http://www.edci.purdue.edu/et/

Contact Person: Dr. Tim Newby, Professor of Educational Technology.

Specializations: Master's degree and Ph.D. in Educational Technology. Master's program started in 1982; Ph.D. in 1985.

Features: Vision Statement: The Educational Technology Program at Purdue University nurtures graduates who are effective designers of learning experiences and environments that incorporate technology to engage learners and improve learning.

Admission Requirements: Master's and Ph.D.: 3.0 GPA, three letters of recommendation, statement of personal goals. A score of 550 (paper-based) or 213 (computer-based) or above on the Test of English as a Foreign Language (TOEFL) for individuals whose first language is not English. Ph.D. Additional Requirement: 1,000 GRE (V + Q); Verbal score of at least 500 preferred.

Degree Requirements: Master's: minimum of 32 semester hours (17 in educational technology, 6–9 in research, development, and exit requirements, 6–9 electives); thesis optional. Ph.D.: 60 semester hours beyond the Master's degree (15–18 in educational technology, 27–30 in education and supporting areas; 15 dissertation research hours).

Number of Full Time Faculty: 0; **Number of Other Faculty**: 0.

Degrees awarded in 2010–2011 Academic Year—Masters: 3; **Ph.D.**: 0; **Other**: 0.

Grant Monies awarded in 2010–2011 Academic Year: 0.

Name of Institution: Purdue University Calumet.

Name of Department or Program: Instructional Technology.

Address: 2200 169th Street, Hammond, IN 46323, USA.

Phone Number: (219)-989-2692; **Fax Number**: (219)-989-3215.

Email Contact: buckenme@purduecal.edu; **URL**: http://www.purduecal.edu/education/grad/it.html.

Contact Person: Janet Buckenmeyer.

Specializations: Instructional Technology and Instructional Design.

Features: The Instructional Technology program at Purdue University Calumet is a practitioner-based program. Students entering the program may be teachers but do not need a teaching license to enroll. The program does not lead to PK-12 licensure.

Admission Requirements: 3.0 GPA; Three (3) letters of recommendation; Essay; Two (2) official copies of all transcripts.

Degree Requirements: x.

Number of Full Time Faculty: 3; **Number of Other Faculty**: 1.

Degrees awarded in 2010–2011 Academic Year—Masters: 14; **Ph.D.**: 0; **Other**: 1.

Grant Monies awarded in 2010–2011 Academic Year: 125,000.

Name of Institution: Emporia State University.

Name of Department or Program: Instructional Design and Technology.

Address: 1200 Commercial Street, Campus Box 4037, Emporia, KS 66801 USA.

Phone Number: (620)-341-5829; **Fax Number**: (620)-341-5785.

Email Contact: mchildre@emporia.edu; **URL**: http://idt.emporia.edu.

Contact Person: Dr. Marcus D. Childress, Chair.

Specializations: Distance learning, online learning, corporate education, P-12 technology integration.

Features: All program courses are offered online. The online Master of Science in Instructional Design and Technology program prepares individuals for leadership in the systematic design, development, implementation, evaluation, and management of technology-rich learning in a variety of settings. Individuals obtaining the IDT degree serve as instructional designers/trainers in business, industry, health professions, and the military and are charged with training, development, and eLearning programs within their organizations. Other graduates hold leadership positions in P-12 and post-secondary institutions. In addition to positions in the workplace, graduates regularly choose to pursue their Ph.D. degrees in IDT at top-ranked universities. IDT faculty members hold leadership positions on the Association for Educational Communications and Technology (AECT) board of directors, executive committee, and research & theory division. Forms and application materials available at the website, http://idt.emporia.edu. Other social media contacts, Ning: http://idtesu.ning.com/. Twitter: http://twitter.com/idtesu. Blogspot: http://idtesu.blogspot.com/. YouTube: http://www.youtube.com/idtesu.

Admission Requirements: Graduate application, official transcripts, GPA of 2.75, or more based on a 4-point scale in the last 60 semester hours of undergraduate study, resume, two current recommendations, writing competency. The program admits on a rolling basis. The departmental admission committee reviews and decides on applications as they are received, until there are no remaining openings.

Degree Requirements: 36 credit hours: 21 credit core, 6 credit research, 9 credit electives.

Number of Full Time Faculty: 6; **Number of Other Faculty**: 4.

Degrees awarded in 2010–2011 Academic Year—Masters: 48; **Ph.D.**: 0; **Other**: 0.

Grant Monies awarded in 2010–2011 Academic Year: 10,000.

Name of Institution: Pittsburg State University.

Name of Department or Program: Masters Degree in Educational Technology.

Address: 1701 S Broadway, Pittsburg, KS 66762, USA.

Phone Number: (620)-235-4484.

Email Contact: jstidham@pittstate.edu; **URL**: http://www.pittstate.edu.

Contact Person: Dr. Sue Stidham.

Specializations: Library Media licensure.

Features: x.

Admission Requirements: x.

Degree Requirements: x.

Number of Full Time Faculty: 3; **Number of Other Faculty**: 0.

Degrees awarded in 2010–2011 Academic Year—Masters: 0; **Ph.D.**: 0; **Other**: 0.

Grant Monies awarded in 2010–2011 Academic Year: 0.

Name of Institution: Morehead State University.

Name of Department or Program: Educational Technology Program.

Address: Ginger Hall, Morehead, KY 40351, USA.

Phone Number: (606)-783-2040.

Email Contact: c.miller@morehead-st.edu; **URL**: www.moreheadstate.edu/education.

Contact Person: Christopher T. Miller.

Specializations: Master of Arts in Education degree focuses on technology integration, multimedia, distance education, educational games, and instructional design. Educational Leadership Doctor of Education in Educational Technology Leadership is a practitioner-based doctoral degree program focused on the development of leaders in the field of educational technology.

Features: Master's program is fully online. Ed.D. program is fully online, but requires a 1 week face-to-face seminar course each year.

Admission Requirements: Admission requirements for Master's degree: *Standard or provisional teaching certification, a statement of eligibility for teaching, or letter describing your role as educational support. Those students who fit the criteria of educational support will be able to obtain the masters degree, but it cannot be used for initial teacher certification. *A GRE minimum combined score of 750 (verbal and quantitative) and 2.5 on the analytic writing portion or a minimum 31 raw score (381–386 Scaled Score) on the Miller Analogies Test. *For students who have not met testing requirements for admission into the program, but who have successfully completed 12 hours of coursework required for the program with a 3.5 or above GPA, the department chair may waive the testing requirement. *The testing requirement is waived for students who have already completed a masters degree. *A minimum of 2.75 undergraduate GPA. *Demonstrated competency of computer fluency (i.e., undergraduate or graduate computer competency course or computer competency assessment). Ed.D. admission requirements: *GRE, Miller Analogies Test (MAT), or GMAT scores including GRE writing score or on-demand writing sample.

*Official transcripts of all undergraduate and graduate coursework. *Documentation of a master's degree from an institution accredited by a nationally recognized accreditation body. *Resume or vita documenting years of related professional/ leadership or educational technology, instructional design, and training experience. *Letter of introduction/interest stating professional goals, leadership style, and educational philosophy. *Recommendation forms: at least three professional references from persons in a position to evaluate the applicant's potential for success in a doctoral program. At least one to be completed by immediate or up-line supervisor or (for Ed. Tech track) professional familiarity with candidates use of technology, instructional design, and training. Other recommendation forms to be completed by professional colleagues or university faculty who are familiar with the applicant. *Documentation of previous statistical methodology, research related coursework, or evidence of use and application of data-informed decision making to determine possible need for statistical methodology coursework. *International students and ESL students must meet university minimum TOEFL score or its equivalent. *No more than 24 hours of previously completed postgraduate work from MSU may be counted in the Ed.D. program.

Degree Requirements: Masters program degree requirements *Satisfy general degree requirements. *Must submit a professional portfolio demonstrating work completed within the program during the final semester of graduate work. *Must apply for graduation in the Graduate Office, 701 Ginger Hall, in the beginning of the term that completion is anticipated. *Maintain a 3.0 GPA in all courses taken after completing the bachelor's degree. *Must be unconditionally admitted. Ed.D. Degree Requirements: *Satisfy all degree requirements. *The student must successfully complete and defend a qualifying examination to enroll in Ed.D. 899 capstone courses and continue within the doctoral program. *Students are required to successfully complete and defend a doctoral capstone. *Students must apply for graduation with the Graduate Office at the beginning of the semester in which they intend to complete. *Maintain a cumulative 3.0 GPA in all courses taken. Must be unconditionally admitted. If a student is not unconditionally admitted after completing 12 graduate hours, he/she will not be permitted to register for additional credit hours. *Students are encouraged to complete the program within the cohort time limit. The maximum allowed time for completion is 10 years. *A total of 18 hours will be permitted to be transferred from other universities.

Number of Full Time Faculty: 2; **Number of Other Faculty**: 2.

Degrees awarded in 2010–2011 Academic Year—Masters: 12; **Ph.D.**: 0; **Other**: 0.

Grant Monies awarded in 2010–2011 Academic Year: 0.

Name of Institution: University of Massachusetts, Amherst.

Name of Department or Program: Learning, Media and Technology Masters Program/Math Science and Learning Technology Doctoral Program.

Address: 813 N Pleasant Street, Amherst, MA 01003, USA.

Phone Number: (413)-545-0246; **Fax Number**: (413)-545-2879.

Email Contact: fsullivan@educ.umass.edu; **URL**: http://www.umass.edu/education/academics/tecs/ed_tech.shtml.

Contact Person: Florence R. Sullivan.

Specializations: The Master of Education concentration in Learning, Media and Technology prepares students to understand, critique, and improve technology- and media-based learning and teaching. The program is structured such that students construct solid knowledge of theories of learning and instruction, as well as theories of the design and use of educational technologies and media. Just as importantly, we offer a number of courses and research experiences through which students develop facility with applied aspects of technology-centered educational practices (e.g., authoring software systems, utilizing tools such as Director and Flash). By encountering multiple opportunities for the analysis, design and testing of educational technology/media, students develop a principled approach to technology- and media-based instruction and learning. The Math, Science and Learning Technology doctoral program prepares graduate students to improve the learning and instruction of Science, Technology, Engineering, and Mathematics (STEM) disciplines. To achieve that goal, we are deeply committed to research and scholarship, using both basic and applied research. We put a premium on developing principled approaches to affect educational practice and pursuing rigorous theory building about educational phenomena. We apply such knowledge in developing state of the art instructional designs. These efforts grow from an understanding of educational practice and close work with practitioners in both formal and informal learning settings. Importantly, we recognized that certain social groups have been historically marginalized from STEM disciplines, education, and work. We seek to understand the processes and structures contributing to the systematic exclusion of these groups and to actively contribute to correcting such inequities. Our work draws from a variety of disciplines including cognitive science, sociology, anthropology, the learning sciences, psychology, and computer science.

Features: In the master's program, we consider media and technology both as tools in learning and teaching specific disciplines (e.g., mathematics and science) and as objects of study in and of themselves. With regard to the former, and in line with the affiliated faculty's expertise, students explore the educational uses of a variety of technological forms (e.g., robotics systems for learning engineering, physics, programming, and the arts) and computer-based environments (e.g., software systems for learning scientific image processing). As for the latter, students actively engage in designing and using various learning technologies and media, including Web-based environments, computer-mediated communications systems, computer-based virtual worlds, and new media for new literacies. The features of the doctoral program of study are the following: *Provide an interconnected locus of intellectual activity for graduate students and faculty; *increase equity (in gender, ethnicity, and opportunities) in recruitment, admission, and retention of students and faculty and pursue issues of equity in science education; *teach relevant courses, seminars, and independent studies in mathematics and science education; *conduct pertinent research studies in mathematics and science learning, teaching, curriculum development, and assessment; *build a base of scholarship, disseminate new knowledge, and apply it actively in education; *provide apprenticeship opportunities for graduate students; *understand and support effective practice in mathematics and science education; *coordinate outreach efforts with K-12 schools and related projects; *collaborate with faculty in the Department, School, and University as well as in the wider profession throughout the Commonwealth of Massachusetts, nationally, and internationally.

Admission Requirements: For the master's program—GPA of 2.75 or higher, TESOL test score of 80 points or higher, excellent letters of recommendation, clear statement of purpose. For the doctoral program—earned masters degree in math, natural sciences, learning technology or education, GPA of 2.75 or higher, TESOL test score of 80 points or higher, excellent letters of recommendation, clear statement of purpose.

Degree Requirements: Master's degree—33 credit hours and thesis. Doctoral degree—36 credit hours beyond the masters degree, 18 dissertation credit hours, successful completion of comprehensive exams, successful completion of doctoral dissertation.

Number of Full Time Faculty: 8; **Number of Other Faculty**: 2.

Degrees awarded in 2010–2011 Academic Year—Masters: 22; **Ph.D.**: 4; **Other**: 0.

Grant Monies awarded in 2010–2011 Academic Year: 10,700,000.

Name of Institution: Oakland University.

Name of Department or Program: Master of Training and Development Program.

Address: 2200 North Squirrel Road, Rochester, MI 48309-4494, USA.

Phone Number: (248)-370-4171; **Fax Number**: (248)-370-4095.

Email Contact: ouhrdmtd@gmail.com; **URL**: www2.oakland.edu/sehs/hrd/

Contact Person: Dr. Chaunda L. Scott: Graduate Coordinator.

Specializations: The Master of Training and Development Program at Oakland University provides a unique blend of knowledge and skills in all aspects of training and development. Students can choose between two areas of emphasis: *Instructional Design and Technology *Organizational Development and Leadership.

Features: The Master of Training and Development Program develops practitioners with the knowledge and skills required to enhance individual performance. Graduates of the program will be able to lead interventions associated with diagnosing performance problems and opportunities. Graduates will also be able to design and implement individual and organizational solutions and evaluate results. All courses are taught by outstanding faculty who have diverse backgrounds and experience in business and academia. The Master of Training and Development Program and be completed in two and one half years. Graduates of the program will be qualified to work as human resource development professionals. Including directors of training centers, organizational development consultants, instructional designers, and performance technologists.

Admission Requirements: Official transcripts for undergraduate and graduate coursework showing a bachelors degree from a regionally accredited institution and a cumulative GPA of 3.0 or higher. A formal statement, between 100 and 1,500 words, highlighting work and life experience—preferably 1 year or longer that have led to desire to pursue the Master of Training and Development Degree. Three letters of recommendations to attest to the quality and scope of the applicants academic and professional ability and an interview will be required.

Degree Requirements: The completion of 36 credits approved credits with an overall GPA of 3.0 or better and a grade of 2.8 or above in each additional course. The completion of five core courses is also required; HRD 530 Instructional Design, HRD 506 Theoretical Foundations of Training and Development, HRD 507 Needs Assessment, HRD 605 Program Evaluation, and HRD 611 Program Administration.

Number of Full Time Faculty: 4; **Number of Other Faculty**: 2.

Degrees awarded in 2010–2011 Academic Year—Masters: 15; **Ph.D.**: 0; **Other**: 0.

Grant Monies awarded in 2010–2011 Academic Year: 0.

Name of Institution: University of Michigan.

Name of Department or Program: Department of Educational Studies.

Address: 610 East University, Ann Arbor, MI 48109-1259, USA.

Phone Number: (734)763-7500; **Fax Number**: (734)615-1290.

Email Contact: fishman@umich.edu; **URL**: http://www.soe.umich.edu/learning-technologies/

Contact Person: Barry J. Fishman.

Specializations: Ph.D. in Learning Technologies; M.A. in Educational Studies with a focus on Digital Media & Education.

Features: The Learning Technologies Program at the University of Michigan integrates the study of technology with a focus in a substantive content area. A unique aspect of the program is that your learning and research will engage you in real-world educational contexts. You will find that understanding issues related to a specific content area provides an essential context for meaningful research in learning. Your understanding of technology, school contexts, and a content area will place you among the leaders who design and conduct research on advanced technological systems that change education and schooling. The Doctoral specialization in Learning Technologies must be taken in conjunction with a substantive concentration designed in consultation with your advisor. Current active concentrations include: Science, Literacy, Culture and Gender, Teacher Education, Design and Human-Computer Interaction, Policy, and Social Studies. Other areas are possible.

The Master's Degree in Educational Studies with a focus on Digital Media & Education at the University of Michigan prepares professionals for leadership roles in the design, development, implementation, and research of powerful technologies to enhance learning. Our approach to design links current knowledge and research about how people learn with technological tools that enable new means of organizing and evaluating learning environments. Course and project work reflects the latest knowledge and practice in learning, teaching, and technology. Core courses prepare students to use current understandings about learning theory, design principles, research methodologies, and evaluation strategies in educational settings ranging from classrooms to Web-based and distributed learning environments. Faculty work with students to shape programs that meet individual interests. Practical experience is offered through internships with area institutions.

Admission Requirements: GRE, B.A. for M.A., or Ph.D.; TOEFL (minimum score of 84) for students from countries where English is not the primary language.

Degree Requirements: M.A.: 30 hours beyond B.A. Ph.D.: 60 hours beyond B.A. or 30 hours beyond Masters plus research paper/qualifying examination, and dissertation.

Number of Full Time Faculty: 3; **Number of Other Faculty**: 5.

Degrees awarded in 2010–2011 Academic Year—Masters: 3; **Ph.D.**: 2; **Other**: 0.

Grant Monies awarded in 2010–2011 Academic Year: 0.

Name of Institution: Bemidji State University.

Name of Department or Program: Professional Education.

Address: 1500 Birchmont Drive NE, Bemidji, MN 56601, USA.

Phone Number: (218)-755-3734.

Email Contact: solson@bemidjistate.edu; **URL**: http://www.bemidjistate.edu.

Contact Person: Shari Olson.

Specializations: x.

Features: x.

Admission Requirements: x.

Degree Requirements: x.

Number of Full Time Faculty: 0; **Number of Other Faculty**: 0.

Degrees awarded in 2010–2011 Academic Year—Masters: 0; **Ph.D.**: 0; **Other**: 0.

Grant Monies awarded in 2010–2011 Academic Year: 0.

Name of Institution: University of Missouri: Columbia.

Name of Department or Program: School of Information Science & Learning Technologies.

Address: 303 Td Hall, Columbia, MO 65211, USA.

Phone Number: (573)-882-4546; **Fax Number**: (573)-884-2917.

Email Contact: sislt@missouri.edu; **URL**: www.coe.missouri.edu/~sislt.

Contact Person: John Wedman.

Specializations: The Educational Technology emphasis area prepares educators and technologists for excellence and leadership in the design, development, and implementation of technology in education, training, and performance support. The program offers three focus areas: Technology in Schools Networked Learning Systems Training Design and Development Each focus area has its own set of competencies, coursework, and processes.

Features: All three focus areas are available online via the Internet or on the MU campus. The Technology in Schools focus area is based on the ISTE competencies and culminates in an online portfolio based on these competencies. Several courses are augmented by technical resources developed at MU, including a technology integration knowledge repository and online collaboration tools. The Networked Learning Systems focus area offers a truly challenging and innovative set of technical learning experiences. Students have opportunities to work on large-scale software development projects, acquiring valuable experience and broadening their skill-set. The Digital Media ZONE supports anytime/anywhere technical skill development. The Training and Development focus area links to business, military, and government contexts. The curriculum is offered by faculty with extensive experience in these contexts and is grounded in the problems and processes of today's workplace. Ed.S. and Ph.D. programs are also available.

Admission Requirements: Bachelor's degree with 3.0 in last 60 credit hours of course work. GRE (V >500; A >500; W >3.5); TOEFL of 540 (207 computer-based test) (if native language is not English); Letters of reference.

Degree Requirements: Masters: 30–34 credit hours; 15 hours at 400 level. Specific course requirements vary by focus area.

Number of Full Time Faculty: 0; **Number of Other Faculty**: 0.

Degrees awarded in 2010–2011 Academic Year—Masters: 72; **Ph.D.**: 0; **Other**: 0.

Grant Monies awarded in 2010–2011 Academic Year: 0.

Name of Institution: University of Missouri-Kansas City.

Name of Department or Program: Curriculum and Instructional Leadership.

Address: 4100 Oak Street, Kansas City, MO 64101, USA.

Phone Number: (314)210-6996; **Fax Number**: (816)235-5270.

Email Contact: russelldl@umkc.edu; **URL**: http://r.web.umkc.edu/russelldl/

Contact Person: Donna Russell.

Specializations: 3D Virtual Learning Environments.

Features: x.

Admission Requirements: x.

Degree Requirements: x.

Number of Full Time Faculty: 30; **Number of Other Faculty**: 15.

Degrees awarded in 2010–2011 Academic Year—Masters: 60; **Ph.D.**: 3; **Other**: 0.

Grant Monies awarded in 2010–2011 Academic Year: 700,000.

Name of Institution: East Carolina University.

Name of Department or Program: Mathematics, Science, and Instructional Technology Education.

Address: 342 Flanagan, Greenville, NC 27858, USA.

Phone Number: (252)-328-9353; **Fax Number**: (252)-328-9371.

Email Contact: sugarw@coe.ecu.edu; **URL**: http://www.ecu.edu/educ/msite/it/.

Contact Person: William Sugar.

Specializations: MS in Instructional Technology, M.A.Ed. in Instructional Technology (see corresponding Educational Media & Technology Yearbook entry), Certificates in Computer-based Instruction, Distance Learning and Administration; Performance Improvement and Virtual Reality.

Features: All required and elective courses are offered online. Courses include innovative approaches to online instruction.

Admission Requirements: MAT or GRE exam score.

Degree Requirements: Bachelor's degree.

Number of Full Time Faculty: 7; **Number of Other Faculty**: 3.

Degrees awarded in 2010–2011 Academic Year—Masters: 20; **Ph.D.**: 0; **Other**: 0.

Grant Monies awarded in 2010–2011 Academic Year: 0.

Name of Institution: University of North Carolina, Wilmington.

Name of Department or Program: Master of Science in Instructional Technology, Department of Instructional Technology, Foundations & Secondary Education.

Address: 601 South College Road, Wilmington, NC 28403, USA.

Phone Number: (910)-962-4183; **Fax Number**: (910)-962-3609.

Email Contact: moallemm@uncw.edu; **URL**: http://www.uncw.edu/ed/mit.

Contact Person: Mahnaz Moallem.

Specializations: The Master of Science degree in Instructional Technology (MIT) program provides advanced professional training for teachers and school technology coordinators; business and industry personnel such as executives, trainers, and human resource development employees; persons in the health care field; and community college instructors. The program focuses on the theory and practice of design and development, utilization, management, and evaluation of processes and resources for learning. It emphasizes product development and utilization of advanced technology and provides applied training in the total design, development, implementation, and evaluation of educational and training programs.

Features: As an exciting and innovative program, MIT provides students the opportunity to gain skills and knowledge from educational and applied psychology, instructional systems design, computer science, systems theory, and communication theory, allowing for considerable flexibility to tailor individual needs across other academic disciplines. Students from diverse fields can plan programs which are consistent with their long-range academic and professional goals. MIT courses are offered both on campus and online, allowing professionals to earn their degrees and/or certificates by taking MIT on-campus courses, or MIT online courses, or a combination of both types. In addition, the MIT program is directed toward preparing students to function in a variety of roles to be performed in a broad range of settings, including business and industry, human services, health institutions, higher education, government, military, and public and private K-12 education.

Admission Requirements: Students desiring admission into the graduate program in instructional technology must present the following: A bachelor's degree from an accredited college or university or its equivalent from a foreign institution of higher education based on a 4-year program. A strong academic record (an average GPA of 3.0 or better is expected) in the basic courses required in the area of the proposed graduate study. Academic potential as indicated by satisfactory performance on standardized test scores (e.g., Miller Analogy Test or Graduate Record Examination). The MAT or GRE must have been taken within the last 5 years. Three recommendations from individuals who are in a position to evaluate the student's professional competence as well as potential for graduate study. A statement of career goals and degree objectives. A letter describing educational and professional experiences, their reasons for pursuing graduate study, and the contributions that the student hopes to make after completing the degree. North Carolina essential and advanced technology competencies. Individuals who fall below a specified criterion may be admitted if other factors indicate potential for success. Individuals with identified deficiencies may be accepted provisionally with specified plans and goals for the remediation of those deficiencies. Such remediation may include a requirement of additional hours beyond those normally required for the degree.

Degree Requirements: Applicants should submit the following to the UNCW Graduate School: —Official graduate application (Use the following link https://app.applyyourself.com/?id=uncw-grad to apply electronically.) —Official transcripts of all college work (undergraduate and graduate). The transcripts should be mailed directly to UNCW Graduate School. —Official scores on the Miller Analogy Test (MAT) or Graduate Record Examination (GRE). Scores more than 5 years old will not be accepted. The UNCW institution code for the MAT and GRE is 5,907. —Three recommendations from individuals in professionally relevant fields, addressing the applicants demonstrated academic skills and/or potential for successful graduate study. —Evidence of a bachelors degree at the time of entrance. —International students: TOEFL score of 550 or higher or IELTS (International English Language Testing System) score of 217 or better (computerized test), 550 or better (paper test), or a minimum score of 79 on the Internet-based test (TOEFL iBT) or IELTS minimum score of 6.5 or 7.0 to be eligible for a teaching assistantship. —Letter of application and a statement of professional goals describing applicant's educational and professional experiences, reasons for pursuing a master's degree in instructional technology, and contributions that applicant hopes to make after degree completion.

Number of Full Time Faculty: 5; **Number of Other Faculty**: 6.

Degrees awarded in 2010–2011 Academic Year—Masters: 10; **Ph.D.**: 0; **Other**: 0.

Grant Monies awarded in 2010–2011 Academic Year: 1,199,546.

Name of Institution: University of North Dakota.

Name of Department or Program: Instructional Design & Technology.

Address: 231 Centennial Drive, Stop 7189, Grand Forks, ND 58202, USA.

Phone Number: (701)-777-3574; **Fax Number**: (701)-777-3246.

Email Contact: richard.vaneck@und.edu; **URL**: http://idt.und.edu.

Contact Person: Richard Van Eck.

Specializations: Serious Games, Game-Based Learning K-12 Technology Integration Human Performance Technology eLearning Problem-Based Learning.

Features: Online Hybrid with synchronous and asynchronous learning Masters and Certificates fully available at a distance Three graduate certificates (K-12 Technology Integration; Corporate Training & Performance; eLearning) M.S. and M.Ed. Ph.D. Interdisciplinary studies Research Opportunities: Northern Plains Center for Behavioral Research Odegard School of Aerospace Sciences (Aviation & Radar simulators; Unmanned Aerial Systems Training).

Admission Requirements: See idt.und.edu.

Degree Requirements: See idt.und.edu.

Number of Full Time Faculty: 3; **Number of Other Faculty**: 1.

Degrees awarded in 2010–2011 Academic Year—Masters: 5; **Ph.D.**: 0; **Other**: 2.

Grant Monies awarded in 2010–2011 Academic Year: 50,000.

Name of Institution: Valley City State University.

Name of Department or Program: School of Education and Graduate Studies.

Address: 101 College Street, Valley City, ND 58072, USA.

Phone Number: (701)-845-7303; **Fax Number**: (701)-845-7305.

Email Contact: terry.corwin@vcsu.edu; **URL**: www.vcsu.edu/graduate.

Contact Person: Terry Corwin.

Specializations: The Master of Education program has four concentrations that focus on technology and the learner: Teaching and Technology concentration, Technology Education concentration, Library and Information Technologies concentration, Teaching English Language Learners concentration.

Features: This is a completely online program which focuses on how technology can be used in a school setting to enhance student learning.

Admission Requirements: (1) Baccalaureate degree with a 3.0 undergraduate GPA or a test is required. (2) Three letters of recommendation. (3) Written goals statement. (4) Resume. (5) $35 fee for application.

Degree Requirements: Completion of 32–37 credits depending on concentration. Action Research report. Final portfolio demonstrating program core values.

Number of Full Time Faculty: 12; **Number of Other Faculty**: 5.

Degrees awarded in 2010–2011 Academic Year—Masters: 37; **Ph.D.**: 0; **Other**: 0.

Grant Monies awarded in 2010–2011 Academic Year: 19,950.

Name of Institution: New York Institute of Technology.

Name of Department or Program: Department of Instructional Technology and Educational Leadership.

Address: Northern Boulevard/16 61st Street, Old Westbury/New York City, NY 11568/10023, USA.

Phone Number: (516)686-7777/(212)261-1529; **Fax Number**: (516)686-7655.

Email Contact: smcphers@nyit.edu; **URL**: http://www.nyit.edu/education.

Contact Person: Sarah McPherson, Chair, Department of Instructional Technology and Educational Leadership.

Specializations: M.S. in Instructional Technology for Educators for Educational Technology Specialist Certification, and for Professional Trainers; Certificates in Computers in Education, Teaching 21st Century Skills, Science Technology Engineering Mathematics (STEM); Advanced Certificate: Virtual Education; Advanced Diploma Educational Leadership and Technology for School Building and Advanced Certificate for District Leader; M.S. in Childhood Education.

Features: Courses offered in Long Island, New York City and upstate New York in partnership with NYS Teacher Centers, School Districts, and related to special grant funding graduate courses. Program is offered 100% online statewide, national and internationally. Technology integration in content areas for K-12 teachers; Leadership and Technology for school building and district administrators; Professional Trainer for corporate training, government, and non-profit agencies. All courses are hand-on instruction in technology labs; online courses; hybrid courses; evening, weekend, and summer courses.

Admission Requirements: Bachelor's degree from accredited college with 3.0 cumulative average; Advanced Diploma and Advanced Certificate require Masters for admission.

Degree Requirements: 36 credits with 3.0 GPA for Master of Science, 18 credits with 3.0 GPA for Certificates; Advanced Diploma 33 credits and Advanced Certificate, 15 credits.

Number of Full Time Faculty: 6; **Number of Other Faculty**: 50.

Degrees awarded in 2010–2011 Academic Year—Masters: 130; **Ph.D.**: 0; **Other**: 0.

Grant Monies awarded in 2010–2011 Academic Year: 0.

Name of Institution: Richard Stockton College of New Jersey.

Name of Department or Program: Master of Arts in Instructional Technology (MAIT).

Address: Jimmie Leeds, Pomona, NJ 08240, USA.

Phone Number: (609)-652-4688; **Fax Number**: (609)-626-5528.

Email Contact: leej@stockton.edu; **URL**: http://intraweb.stockton.edu/eyos/page.cfm?siteID=73&pageID=47.

Contact Person: Jung Lee.

Specializations: The Master of Arts in Instructional Technology offered by The Richard Stockton College of New Jersey is designed to bring the best instructional technologies into both public and corporate curricula. With a strong theoretical foundation, the degree enables graduates to use technology as a tool to enhance learning and training.

Features: The program serves (1) students who seek or will continue employment in the P-12 schools; (2) students who wish to pursue coordinator or supervisor positions in P-12 schools and districts; and (3) students seeking or holding careers in business, industry, or non-profit organizations.

Admission Requirements: Minimum 3.0 GPA, relevant experience, reference letters, and GRE General Exam scores or MAT (Miller Analogies Test scores).

Degree Requirements: 11 graduate courses (33 credits) including capstone project course.

Number of Full Time Faculty: 3; **Number of Other Faculty**: 5.

Degrees awarded in 2010–2011 Academic Year—Masters: 22; **Ph.D.**: 0; **Other**: 0.

Grant Monies awarded in 2010–2011 Academic Year: 0.

Name of Institution: Seton Hall University.

Name of Department or Program: College of Education and Human Services.

Address: 400 South Orange Avenue, South Orange, NJ 07079, USA.

Phone Number: (973)-761-9393; **Fax Number**: (973)-313-6036.

Email Contact: edstudies@shu.edu; **URL**: http://www.shu.edu/academics/education/ma-instructional-design/index.cfm.

Contact Person: Rosemary W. Skeele.

Specializations: The Instructional Design program assists teachers to improve their professional performance as educators, instructional and curriculum designers, and to assume instructional leadership roles in their place of employment. Students are accepted from many instructional environments, including K-12, college, and adult education. The program emphasizes a theoretical base for instructional design and exposure to a broad array of the most current instructional methods, strategies, technologies, and materials. Seton Hall University is a recognized leader in the use of a variety of modern techniques and computer-based technologies for teaching and learning.

Features: The Instructional Design Program is nationally recognized by the Association for Educational Communications and Technology. The program is structured to meet the specific goals of each student and provide them with an opportunity to acquire content knowledge and skills that are state of the art, enabling them to expand their personal competence and to achieve higher levels of professional excellence. The program is unique in that it allows students, under the guidance of faculty mentors, to design a master's program that satisfies their interests and career objectives.

Admission Requirements: Official undergraduate and graduate transcripts from each accredited college or university attended; two letters of reference from professional and/or academic contacts attesting to your academic abilities and personal qualifications; a two-page, double-spaced, typed statement of goals; current professional vitae/resume; Miller Analogies Test (MAT) or Graduate Record Examination (GRE) scores, within the past 5 years (note: Candidates who already possess an advanced degree do not need to submit entrance exam scores); a $50 non-refundable fee.

Degree Requirements: The Instructional Design Program is a 36-credit program that yields a Master of Arts degree. Students are engaged in concentration courses, electives, as well as a capstone course that must be taken during their final semester. Throughout the program, students gain knowledge and experiences in the foundations of education, professional education, and technology studies, which enhance the professional preparation of teachers and trainers.

Number of Full Time Faculty: 0; **Number of Other Faculty**: 0.

Degrees awarded in 2010–2011 Academic Year—Masters: 0; **Ph.D.**: 0; **Other**: 0.

Grant Monies awarded in 2010–2011 Academic Year: 0.

Name of Institution: Montclair State University.

Name of Department or Program: Department of Curriculum & Teaching.

Address: 1 College Avenue, Montclair, NJ 07043, USA.

Phone Number: (973)655-5187; **Fax Number**: (973)655-7084.

Email Contact: dominev@mail.montclair.edu; **URL**: http://cehs.montclair.edu.

Contact Person: Dr. Vanessa Domine, Professor of Educational Technology.

Specializations: MSU offers (1) an M.Ed. degree program in Educational Technology (EDTC); (2) a post-bac certification program for Associate School Library Media Specialists (ALMS); and (3) an advanced certification program for School Library Media Specialists (SLMS).

Features: All three programs draw from the same pool of educational technology courses and can be completed together in a carefully assembled program of approximately 46 graduate credits. Three areas comprise coursework: Philosophical foundations, Pedagogical design and integration, and Practical design and application. In the M.Ed. program, students can choose to emphasize in one of three areas: (a) Administration, Policy and Leadership; (b) Organizational Planning and Development; and (c) Curriculum and Technology Integration.

Admission Requirements: Students can apply in person or online to the Graduate School (http://www.montclair.edu/graduate). The M.Ed. program requires submission of GRE scores, letters of recommendation, and a project sample. The ALMS program requires a bachelor's degree and standard NJ teaching license. The SLMS program requires a master's degree, a standard NJ teaching license, and at least 1 year of successful teaching as an associate school library media specialist.

Degree Requirements: The M.Ed. program requires 33 credits of coursework and field experience. The ALMS program requires 18–21 credits of coursework and field experience. The SLMS program requires 36 credits of coursework and field experience.

Number of Full Time Faculty: 0; **Number of Other Faculty**: 0.

Degrees awarded in 2010–2011 Academic Year—Masters: 0; **Ph.D.**: 0; **Other**: 0.

Grant Monies awarded in 2010–2011 Academic Year: 0.

Name of Institution: New York University.

Name of Department or Program: Educational Communication and Technology Program (Ph.D.) and Digital Media Design for Learning Program (M.A., Adv. Cert.), Steinhardt School of Culture, Education, and Human Development.

Address: 239 Greene Street, Suite 300, New York, NY 10003, USA.

Phone Number: (212)998-5520; **Fax Number**: (212)995-4041.

Email Contact: ectdmdl@nyu.edu; **URL**: http://steinhardt.nyu.edu/alt/ect.

Contact Person: Christopher Hoadley (Program Director); Jan Plass (Doctoral Program Coordinator).

Specializations: M.A., Advanced Certificate, in Digital Media Design for Learning, and Ph.D. in Educational Communication and Technology: for the preparation of individuals as educational media designers, developers, media producers, and/or researchers in education, business and industry, health and medicine, community services, government, museums, and other cultural institutions; and to teach or become involved in administration in educational communications and educational technology or learning science programs in higher education, including instructional television, multimedia, Web 2.0, serious games, and simulations. The program also offers a post-M.A. 30-point Certificate of Advanced Study in Education.

Features: emphasizes theoretical foundations, especially a cognitive science and learning sciences perspective of learning and instruction, and their implications for designing media-based learning environments and materials. All efforts focus on video, multimedia, instructional television, web-based technology and simulations and games; participation in special research and production projects and field internships. Uses an apprenticeship model to provide doctoral students and advanced M.A. students with research opportunities in collaboration with faculty.

Admission Requirements: M.A.: Bachelor's degree or international equivalent required. Typically 3.0 undergraduate GPA, statement of purpose (no GRE required). Ph.D.: Master's degree or international equivalent required. 3.0 GPA, 1,100 GRE, responses to essay questions, interview related to academic or professional preparation and career goals. (TOEFL required for international students.)

Degree Requirements: M.A.: 36 semester credit hours including specialization, elective courses, thesis, English Essay Examination. Ph.D.: 57 semester credit hours beyond M.A., including specialization, foundations, research, content seminar, and elective course work; candidacy papers; dissertation; English Essay Examination. Full-time or part-time study available; no online option available.

Number of Full Time Faculty: 4; **Number of Other Faculty**: 4.

Degrees awarded in 2010–2011 Academic Year—Masters: 14; **Ph.D.**: 2; **Other**: 0.

Grant Monies awarded in 2010–2011 Academic Year: 1,500,000.

Name of Institution: Syracuse University.

Name of Department or Program: Instructional Design, Development, and Evaluation Program, School of Education.

Address: 330 Huntington Hall, Syracuse, NY 13244-2340, USA.

Phone Number: (315)443-3703; **Fax Number**: (315)443-1218.

Email Contact: nlsmith@syr.edu; **URL**: http://idde.syr.edu.

Contact Person: Nick Smith, Professor and Department Chair.

Specializations: Certificates in Educational Technology and Adult Lifelong Learning, M.S., M.S. in Instructional Technology, C.A.S., and Ph.D. degree programs in Instructional Design, Educational Evaluation, Human Issues in Instructional Development, Technology Integration, and Educational Research and Theory (learning theory, application of theory, and educational media research). Graduates are prepared to serve as curriculum developers, instructional designers, program and project evaluators, researchers, resource center administrators, technology coordinators, educational technology specialist, distance learning design and delivery specialists, trainers and training managers, and higher education faculty.

Features: The courses and programs are typically project-centered. Collaborative project experience, field work, and internships are emphasized throughout. There are special issue seminars, as well as student- and faculty-initiated mini-courses, seminars and guest lecturers, faculty–student formulation of department policies, and multiple international perspectives. International collaborations are an ongoing feature of the program. The graduate student population is highly diverse.

Admission Requirements: Certificates and M.S.: undergraduate transcripts, recommendations, personal statement, interview recommended; TOEFL for international applicants; GRE recommended. Certificate of Advanced Study: Relevant Masters degree from accredited institution or equivalent, GRE scores, recommendations, personal statement, TOEFL for international applicants; interview recommended. Doctoral: Relevant Masters degree from accredited institution or equivalent, GRE scores, recommendations, personal statement, TOEFL for international applicants; interview strongly encouraged.

Degree Requirements: Certificates: 15 and 24 semester hours. M.S.: 36 semester hours, portfolio required. M.S. in Instructional Technology: 37 semester hours, practicum and portfolio required. C.A.S.: 60 semester hours, exam and project required. Ph.D.: 90 semester hours, research apprenticeship, portfolio, qualifying exams, and dissertation required.

Number of Full Time Faculty: 4; **Number of Other Faculty**: 6.

Degrees awarded in 2010–2011 Academic Year—Masters: 13; **Ph.D.**: 1; **Other**: 16.

Grant Monies awarded in 2010–2011 Academic Year: 489,134.

Name of Institution: East Stroudsburg University.

Name of Department or Program: Instructional Technology, Media Communication and Technology Department.

Address: 200 Prospect Street, East Stroudsburg, PA 18301, USA.

Phone Number: (470)-422-3621; **Fax Number**: (570)422-3876.

Email Contact: bsockman@po-box.esu.edu; **URL**: www.esu.edu/gradmcom.

Contact Person: Beth Rajan Sockman.

Specializations: The graduate programs are designed to develop the technology literacy of educators, prepare specialists to work in K-12 schools, school districts, or instructional technology personnel in education, business, or industry. Students can obtain a Masters of Education degree in Instructional Technology and/or a Pennsylvania Instructional Technologist Specialist Certificate. Students interested in PK-12 education may choose to concentrate in Technology Integration.

Features: The program provides students with an opportunity to take courses from ESU University. Students who successfully complete the program become proficient in using technology in teaching. Students can choose courses that explore that following areas: *Desktop publishing, *Interactive web design (Including Web 2.0 applications) *Graphics, *Video, *New and emerging technologies, *Instructional design, *Learning theories, *Research in Instructional Technology.

Admission Requirements: For M.Ed. degree: *Two letters of recommendation, *Portfolio or interview (Interview is granted after the application is received) *For full admission, a minimum overall undergraduate 2.5 QPA *Rolling deadline For certification: *Contact the graduate coordinator for additional admission information to comply with Pennsylvania Department of Education requirements. *Minimum overall undergraduate QPA 3.0 (Pennsylvania Act 354), *If not 3.0 QPA, then completion of nine credits of Media Communication and Technology Department courses with prior written approval of department faculty adviser, *Two letters of recommendation, *Rolling deadline.

Degree Requirements: Total = 33 credits #Take courses and learn — Take 30 credits of courses for the master's and learn based on your needs. You will learn to use and implement technologies outside average person's experience. #Create, Submit and Present your Portfolio — This is the time to display your learning in a professional manner. In the portfolio you articulate your goals and may identify learning goals for your internship. Click here for the Portfolio Guidelines. #Complete an Internship — You complete a 90 hours internship that extends your knowledge base — 3 credits. #Complete Portfolio and Graduate.

Number of Full Time Faculty: 7; **Number of Other Faculty**: 3.

Degrees awarded in 2010–2011 Academic Year—Masters: 6; **Ph.D.**: 0; **Other**: 0.

Grant Monies awarded in 2010–2011 Academic Year: 3,400.

Name of Institution: Penn State Great Valley School of Graduate Professional Studies.

Name of Department or Program: Education Division/Instructional Systems Program.

Address: 30 E Swedesford Road, Malvern, PA 19355, USA.

Phone Number: (610)-725-5250; **Fax Number**: (610)-725-5232.

Email Contact: ydl1@psu.edu; **URL**: http://www.sgps.psu.edu.

Contact Person: Doris Lee.

Specializations: Instructional Systems/Designs.

Features: x.

Admission Requirements: on-line application, MAT/GRE scores, 2 letters of recommendations.

Degree Requirements: 36 credit.

Number of Full Time Faculty: 10; **Number of Other Faculty**: 15.

Degrees awarded in 2010–2011 Academic Year—Masters: 45; **Ph.D.**: 0; **Other**: 0.

Grant Monies awarded in 2010–2011 Academic Year: 0.

Name of Institution: Temple University.

Name of Department or Program: Department of Psychological Studies in Education.

Address: 1301 Cecil B Moore Avenue, Philadelphia, PA 19122, USA.

Phone Number: (215)204–4497; **Fax Number**: (215)204–6013.

Email Contact: susan.miller@temple.edu; **URL**: http://www.temple.edu/education/

Contact Person: Susan Miller, Ph.D.

Specializations: Instructional and Learning Technology (ILT) is a new master's program within the Educational Psychology Program in the Department of Psychological Studies in Education. As such, ILT is designed to address conceptual as well as technical issues in using technology for teaching and learning. Program areas include (a) instructional theory and design issues, (b) application of technology, and (c) management issues.

Features: Instructional Theory and Design topics include psychology of the learner, cognitive processes, instructional theories, human development, and individual differences as well as psychological and educational characteristics of technology resources, and identification of strengths and weaknesses of instructional technology resources. The Application of Technology area focuses on clarification of instructional objectives, identification of resources to facilitate learning, operation and application of current and emergent technologies, facility using graphic design, multimedia, video, distributed learning resources, WWW and print publishing. Management and Consultation is structured around defining instructional needs, monitoring progress, and evaluating outcomes, designing technology delivery systems, preparing policy statements, budgets, and facility design criteria, managing skill assessment and training, understanding legal and ethical issues, and managing and maintaining facilities.

Admission Requirements: Bachelors Degree from an accredited institution, GRE(MAT) scores, three letters of recommendation, transcripts from each institution of higher learning attended (undergraduate and graduate), goal statement.

Degree Requirements: Coursework (33 hours: 5 core courses, 3 technology electives, 3 cognate area courses) Practicum in students area of interest Comprehensive Exam Portfolio of Certification Competencies (for students interested in PA Department of Ed Certification as Instructional Technology Specialist).

Number of Full Time Faculty: –; **Number of Other Faculty**: –.

Degrees awarded in 2010–2011 Academic Year—Masters: –; **Ph.D.**: –; **Other**: –.

Grant Monies awarded in 2010–2011 Academic Year: –.

Name of Institution: University of Memphis.

Name of Department or Program: Instructional Design and Technology.

Address: 406 Ball Hall, Memphis, TN 38152, USA.

Phone Number: (901)-678-5672; **Fax Number**: (901)-678-3881.

Email Contact: emartndl@memphis.edu; **URL**: http://idt.memphis.edu.

Contact Person: Dr. Trey Martindale.

Specializations: Instructional Design, Educational Technology, Technology Integration, Web 2.0 and Social Media, Web-Based Instruction, Computer-Based Instruction, Mobile Learning, K-12 NTeQ Model, Professional Development, Pedagogical Agents.

Features: Twitter: https://twitter.com/#!/umidt; Facebook: http://www.facebook.com/idtmemphis; IDT Program News: http://idtmemphis.wordpress.com/; Our masters degree is 30 credit hours, and is completely online. The IDT Studio (http://idtstudio.org), staffed and run by IDT faculty and students, serves as an R&D space for coursework and research involving technologies such as digital media, WBT/CBT, pedagogical agents, gaming, and simulation. The IDT program and IDT Studio are connected to the Center for Multimedia Arts in the FedEx Institute of Technology. The IDT Studio brings in outside contract work from corporate partners to provide real-world experience to students. The IDT program is an active partner in the Martin Institute for Teaching Excellence (http://martininstitute.org). We have also partnered with the Institute for Intelligent Systems and the Tutoring Research Group (www.autotutor.org) to work on intelligent agent development and research.

Admission Requirements: Minimum standards which identify a pool of master's level applicants from which each department selects students to be admitted: An official transcript showing a bachelors degree awarded by an accredited college or university with a minimum GPA of 2.0 on a 4.0 scale, competitive MAT or GRE scores, GRE writing test, two letters of recommendation, graduate school, and departmental application. Doctoral students must also be interviewed by at least two members of the program.

Degree Requirements: M.S.: 30 hours total. Internship, master's project or thesis, 3.0 GPA. Ed.D.: 54 hours total. 45 in major, 9 in research; residency project; comprehensive exams; dissertation.

Number of Full Time Faculty: 6; **Number of Other Faculty**: 8.

Degrees awarded in 2010–2011 Academic Year—Masters: 4; **Ph.D.**: 3; **Other**: 2.

Grant Monies awarded in 2010–2011 Academic Year: 750,000.

Name of Institution: Texas A&M University-Commerce.

Name of Department or Program: Department of Educational Leadership.

Address: PO Box 3011, Commerce, TX 75429-3011, USA.

Phone Number: (903)886-5607; **Fax Number**: (903)886-5507.

Email Contact: Sue_Espinoza@tamu-commerce.edu; **URL**: http://www.tamu-commerce.edu/

Contact Person: Dr. Sue Espinoza, Professor, Program Coordinator.

Specializations: M.S. or M.Ed. degrees in Educational Technology-Leadership and in Educational Technology-Library Science Certification programs—School Librarian, and Technology Applications, both approved by the Texas State Board for Educator Certification.

Features: Programs may be completed totally online, although some courses may also be offered in web-enhanced formats, and one or more electives may be offered only face-to-face.

Admission Requirements: Apply to the Graduate School at Texas A&M University-Commerce. For school library certification, must also apply to the professional certification program.

Degree Requirements: 36 hours for each Master's Degree; each program contains core courses, and specialization area courses are selected in consultation with advisor, who is assigned when each student is admitted to the program.

Number of Full Time Faculty: 3; **Number of Other Faculty**: 6.

Degrees awarded in 2010–2011 Academic Year—Masters: 19; **Ph.D.**: 0; **Other**: 0.

Grant Monies awarded in 2010–2011 Academic Year: 0.

Name of Institution: University of Texas at Brownsville.

Name of Department or Program: Educational Technology.

Address: 80 Fort Brown, Brownsville, TX 78520, USA.

Phone Number: (956)882-7540; **Fax Number**: (956)882-8929.

Email Contact: Rene.Corbeil@UTB.edu; **URL**: http://edtech.utb.edu.

Contact Person: J. Rene Corbeil, Ed.D.

Specializations: E-Learning Instructional Design Web-Based Instruction Multimedia Design.

Features: The Online M.Ed. in Educational Technology is a 36-hour program designed to prepare persons in K-12, higher education, corporate, and military settings to develop the skills and knowledge necessary for the classrooms of tomorrow. Graduates of this program will have a much better understanding of the uses of technology and how they can be applied in instructional/training settings. The program focuses on the theory, research, and applications related to the field of educational technology and is intended to help individuals: use instructional technology (computers, telecommunications, and related technologies) as resources for the delivery of instruction, serve as facilitators or directors of instructional technology in educational settings, and/or be developers of instructional programs and materials for new technologies, design instructional materials in a variety of media. In addition to earning an M.Ed. in Educational Technology, students working in K-12 environments also have the opportunity to complete the Master Technology Teacher (MTT) Program and test for the MTT Certificate. The program is provided through the four MTT elective courses offered as an option in the degree program. An E-Learning Certificate is also available for individuals working in higher education or at e-learning industries.

Admission Requirements: Proof of a baccalaureate degree from a 4-year institution which has regional accreditation. GPA of 2.5 or higher (3.0 GPA for "unconditional" admission. Between 2.5 and 2.9 for "conditional" admission). Application Essay/Statement of Goals. Please provide a carefully considered statement of: (1) your academic and professional objectives and (2) explain how graduate study will help you to attain your goals. Note: The GRE is no longer required.

Degree Requirements: The M.Ed. in Educational Technology consists of 24 hours from core courses plus 12 hours of electives for a total of 36 hours. Students can select the 12 hours of electives based upon their professional needs and academic interests (e.g., Master Technology Teacher—MTT Certificate, e-Learning Certificate, or 12 hours in a specific content area such as reading, mathematics, science) with advisor approval. Core Courses: (24 hours) EDTC 6320—Educational Technology EDTC 6321—Instructional Design EDTC 6323—Multimedia/Hypermedia EDTC 6325—Educational Communications EDTC 6329—Selected Topics in Educational Technology EDTC 6332—Practicum in Educational Technology EDCI 6300—Foundations of Research in Education EDCI 6304—Learning and Cognition Electives: (12 hours) EDCI 6301—Instructional Technology in Teaching EDCI 6336—Problems in Education: International Technology Issues EDTC 6340—Applications of Advanced Technologies in the Pk-12 Classroom EDTC 6341—Student-Centered Learning Using Technology EDTC 6342—Technology Leadership EDTC 6343—Master Teacher of Technology Practicum*EDTC 6351—Web-Based Multimedia in Instruction EDTC 6358—Theory and Practice of e-Learning.

Number of Full Time Faculty: 4; **Number of Other Faculty**: 2.

Degrees awarded in 2010–2011 Academic Year—Masters: 42; **Ph.D.**: 0; **Other**: 0.

Grant Monies awarded in 2010–2011 Academic Year: 0.

Name of Institution: Old Dominion University.

Name of Department or Program: Instructional Design & Technology.

Address: Education 228, Norfolk, VA 23529, USA.

Phone Number: (757)-683-6275; **Fax Number**: (757)-683-5862.

Email Contact: gmorriso@odu.edu; **URL**: http://education.odu.edu/eci/idt/

Contact Person: Gary R. Morrison.

Specializations: Our faculty engages students in a rigorous course of study tailored to meet individual educational and career interests. Research opportunities and course work ensure that all students receive a solid foundation in Instructional Design Instructional Design Theory Human Performance Technology Gaming and Simulation Distance Education Evaluation & Assessment Trends and Issues in Instructional Technology Quantitative and Qualitative Research.

Features: All of our courses are offered via distance using a hybrid format. Classroom instruction uses a virtual classroom that allows all students to participate in a face-to-face classroom. A reduced tuition rate is available for students living outside of Virginia who are accepted into the program.

Admission Requirements: MS degree: GRE scores or MAT scores; transcripts for undergraduate and graduate courses; Ph.D.: GRE scores, transcripts for undergraduate and graduate courses, letters of recommendation, and an essay describing professional goals.

Degree Requirements: MS program is 30–36 hours Ph.D. program is a post-master degree consisting of 60 hours.

Number of Full Time Faculty: 4; **Number of Other Faculty**: 0.

Degrees awarded in 2010–2011 Academic Year—Masters: 2; **Ph.D.**: 2; **Other**: 0.

Grant Monies awarded in 2010–2011 Academic Year: 0.

Name of Institution: Concordia University Wisconsin.

Name of Department or Program: Educational Technology.

Address: 12800 N Lakeshore Drive, Mequon, WI 53092, USA.

Phone Number: (262)-243-4595; **Fax Number**: (262)-243-3595.

Email Contact: bernard.bull@cuw.edu; **URL**: http://www.cuw.edu/go/edtech.

Contact Person: Dr. Bernard Bull.

Specializations: Digital culture, designing digital age learning experiences, and social/spiritual/ethical implications of technology.

Features: Courses are available via e-learning or face-to-face. Some cohorts are also offered at off-campus sites in Wisconsin and beyond. In addition, we run occasional thematic cohorts where a group of students work through the program together over an 18–24 month period, all agreeing to focus their thesis or culminating project upon the cohort theme (e.g., new literacies, bridging the digital divide, global education, discipleship in the digital age).

Admission Requirements: To be considered for admission, a student must: Have a bachelor's degree from an accredited college or university. Have a minimum GPA of 3.00 in the undergraduate program.

Degree Requirements: Required Courses EDT 970: Integrating Technology in the Classroom (3) EDT 889—Applying Technology in the Content Areas (3) EDT 908—Critical Issues in Educational Technology (3) EDT 892—Instructional Design (3) EDT 893—Theories of Learning and Design (3) EDT 815—Research in Educational Technology (3) EDT 927, 928, 929—Portfolio I, II, and III (0) EDT 895—Capstone Project (3) OR EDT 890—Thesis Completion Seminar (3) Electives EDT 805—Online Teaching and Learning (3) EDT 814—Educational Ministry in the Digital World (3) EDT 894—Digital Literacy (3) EDT 907—Multimedia for the Classroom (3) EDT 939—School Leadership in Technology (3) EDT 940—Networking, Support, and Delivery Systems for Schools (3) EDT 957—Building Online Learning Communities (Web 2.0 / Learning 2.0) (3) EDT 971—Grants and Funding for Educational Technology Initiatives (3) EDT 804—Strategies for Teaching and Learning with Interactive Whiteboards (1) Other electives as approved by the program director.

Number of Full Time Faculty: 3; **Number of Other Faculty**: 6.

Degrees awarded in 2010–2011 Academic Year—Masters: 0; **Ph.D.**: 0; **Other**: 0.

Grant Monies awarded in 2010–2011 Academic Year: 0.

Name of Institution: University of Wisconsin-Madison.

Name of Department or Program: Curriculum and Instruction, School of Education.

Address: 225 North Mills Street, Madison, WI 53706, USA.

Phone Number: (608)263-4670; **Fax Number**: (608)263-9992.

Email Contact: kdsquire@wisc.edu; **URL**: http://www.education.wisc.edu/ci/

Contact Person: Kurt D. Squire.

Specializations: M.S. and Ph.D. degree programs to prepare Educational Technology faculty and professionals. On-going research includes: studying the impact of contemporary gaming practices on learning, schooling, and society, understanding ways in which online play spaces align (or fail to align) with practices valued outside the game (i.e., informal scientific reasoning, collaborative problem-solving, and media literacy), interrogating the implementation of technology-rich innovations in local and international schools as well as the role of culture in the design of instruction, using photography as a research method in education.

Features: Educational Technology courses are processed through social, cultural, historical, and design-based frames of reference. Current curriculum emphasizes new media theories, critical cultural and visual culture theories, and constructivist theories of instructional design and development. Many courses offered in the evening.

Admission Requirements: Master's and Ph.D.: previous experience in Instructional Technology preferred, previous teaching experience, 3.0 GPA on last 60 undergraduate credits, acceptable scores on GRE, 3.0 GPA on all graduate work.

Degree Requirements: M.S.: 24 credits plus thesis and exam (an additional 12 credits of Educational Foundations if no previous educational background); Ph.D.: 1 year of residency beyond the Bachelor's, major, minor, and research requirements, preliminary exam, dissertation, and oral exam.

Number of Full Time Faculty: 4; **Number of Other Faculty**: 0.

Degrees awarded in 2010–2011 Academic Year—Masters: 1; **Ph.D.**: 1; **Other**: 0.

Grant Monies awarded in 2010–2011 Academic Year: 1,000,000.

Part V
Mediagraphy: Print and Non-Print Resources

Chapter 16
Introduction

Jinn-Wei Tsao

16.1   Contents

This resource lists journals and other resources of interest to practitioners, researchers, students, and others concerned with educational technology and educational media. The primary goal of this section is to list current publications in the field. The majority of materials cited here were published in 2011 or mid-2012. Media-related journals include those listed in past issues of EMTY, as well as new entries in the field. A thorough list of journals in the educational technology field has been updated for the 2012 edition using Ulrich's Periodical Index Online and journal Websites. This chapter is not intended to serve as a specific resource location tool, although it may be used for that purpose in the absence of database access. Rather, readers are encouraged to peruse the categories of interest in this chapter to gain an idea of recent developments within the field. For archival purposes, this chapter serves as a snapshot of the field of instructional technology publications in 2011. Readers must bear in mind that technological developments occur well in advance of publication and should take that fact into consideration when judging the timeliness of resources listed in this chapter.

J.-W. Tsao (✉)
Learning, Design, and Technology Program, The University of Georgia, Athens, GA, USA
e-mail: miketsao@uga.edu

M. Orey et al. (eds.), *Educational Media and Technology Yearbook*, Educational
Media and Technology Yearbook 37, DOI 10.1007/978-1-4614-4430-5_16,
© Springer Science+Business Media New York 2013

16.2   Selection

Items were selected for the Mediagraphy in several ways. The EBSCO Host Databases were used to locate most of the journal citations. Others were taken from the journal listings of large publishing companies. Items were chosen for this list when they met one or more of the following criteria: reputable publisher, broad circulation, coverage by indexing services, peer review, and coverage of a gap in the literature. The author chose items on subjects that seem to reflect the instructional technology field as it is today. Because of the increasing tendency for media producers to package their products in more than one format and for single titles to contain mixed media, titles are no longer separated by media type. The author makes no claims as to the comprehensiveness of this list. It is, instead, intended to be representative.

16.3   Obtaining Resources

Media-related periodicals: The author has attempted to provide various ways to obtain the resources listed in this Mediagraphy, including telephone and fax numbers, Web and postal addresses, as well as email contacts. Prices are also included for student, individual, and institutional subscriptions. The information presented reflects the most current information available at the time of publication.

ERIC documents: As of December 31, 2003, ERIC was no longer funded. However, ERIC documents can still be read and copied from their microfiche form at any library holding an ERIC microfiche collection. The identification number beginning with ED (e.g., ED 332 677) locates the document in the collection. Document delivery services and copies of most ERIC documents can also continue to be available from the ERIC Document Reproduction Service. Prices charged depend on format chosen (microfiche or paper copy), length of the document, and method of shipping. Online orders, fax orders, and expedited delivery are available.

To find the closest library with an ERIC microfiche collection, contact: ACCESS ERIC, 1600 Research Blvd, Rockville, MD 20850-3172, USA; (800) LET-ERIC (538-3742); email: acceric@inet.ed.gov.

To order ERIC documents, contact

ERIC Document Reproduction Services (EDRS)
7420 Fullerton Rd, Suite 110, Springfield, VA 22153-2852, USA
(800)433-ERIC (433-3742); (703)440-1400
Fax: (703) 440–1408
Email: service@edrs.com

Journal articles: Photocopies of journal articles can be obtained in one of the following ways: (1) from a library subscribing to the title, (2) through interlibrary loan,

(3) through the purchase of a back issue from the journal publisher, or (4) from an article reprint service such as ProQuest Microfilm.

ProQuest Microfilm, 789 E. Eisenhower Parkway, PO Box 1346
Ann Arbor, MI 48106-1346, USA
(734)761-4700
Fax: (734)997-4222
Email: sandra.piver@proquest.com

Journal articles can also be obtained through the Institute for Scientific Information (ISI).

ISI Document Solution
P.O. Box 7649
Philadelphia, PA 19104-3389, USA
(800)336-4474, option 5
Fax: (215)222-0840 or (215)386-4343
Email: ids@isinet.com

16.4 Arrangement

Mediagraphy entries are classified according to major subject emphasis under the following headings:

- Artificial Intelligence, Robotics, and Electronic Performance Support Systems
- Computer-Assisted Instruction
- Distance Education
- Educational Research
- Educational Technology
- Information Science and Technology
- Instructional Design and Development
- Learning Sciences
- Libraries and Media Centers
- Media Technologies
- Professional Development
- Simulation, Gaming, and Virtual Reality
- Special Education and Disabilities
- Telecommunications and Networking

Chapter 17
Artificial Intelligence, Robotics, and Electronic Performance Support Systems

Jinn-Wei Tsao

Artificial Intelligence Review: Springer Science+Business Media, PO Box 2485, Secaucus, NJ 07096–2485, USA. www.springer.com/journal/10462, tel: 800-777-4643, fax: 201-348-4505, service-ny@springer.com [8/yr; $862 inst (print/online), $1,034 inst (print+online, content through 1997)]. Publishes reports and evaluations, as well as commentary on issues and development in artificial intelligence foundations and current research.

AI Magazine: Association for the Advancement of Artificial Intelligence, 2275 East Bayshore Road, Suite 160, Palo Alto, California 94303. www.aaai.org/ Magazine, tel: 650-328-3123, fax: 650-321-4457, info08@aaai.org [4/yr; $70 stud, $140 indiv, $280 inst]. Proclaimed "Journal of Record for the AI Community," this magazine provides full-length articles on new research and literature, but is written to allow access to those reading outside their area of expertise.

International Journal of Robotics Research: Sage Publications, 2455 Teller Rd, Thousand Oaks, CA 91320, USA. ijr.sagepub.com, tel: 800-818-7243, fax: 800-583-2665, journals@sagepub.com [14/yr; $216 indiv, $2,091 inst (print), $1,921 inst (online), $2,134 inst (online+backfile, content through Volume 1, Issue 1/ print+online), $2,347 inst (print+online+backfile)]. Interdisciplinary approach to the study of robotics for researchers, scientists, and students. The first scholarly publication on robotics research.

Journal of Intelligent and Robotic Systems: Springer Science+Business Media, PO Box 2485, Secaucus, NJ 07096-2485, USA. www.springer.com/journal/10846, tel: 800-777-4643, fax: 201-348-4505, service-ny@springer.com [16/yr; $2,322 inst (print/online), $2,786 inst (print+online, content through 1997)]. Main objective is to provide a forum for the fruitful interaction of ideas and techniques that

J.-W. Tsao (✉)
Learning, Design, and Technology Program, The University of Georgia,
Athens, GA, USA
e-mail: miketsao@uga.edu

M. Orey et al. (eds.), *Educational Media and Technology Yearbook*, Educational   365
Media and Technology Yearbook 37, DOI 10.1007/978-1-4614-4430-5_17,
© Springer Science+Business Media New York 2013

combine systems and control science with artificial intelligence and other related computer science concepts. It bridges the gap between theory and practice.

Journal of Interactive Learning Research: Association for the Advancement of Computing in Education, PO Box 1545, Chesapeake, VA 23327-1545, USA. www. aace.org/pubs/jilr, tel: 757-366-5606, fax: 703-997-8760, info@aace.org [4/yr; $45 for stud, $125 indiv, $195 inst]. Publishes articles on how intelligent computer technologies can be used in education to enhance learning and teaching. Reports on research and developments, integration, and applications of artificial intelligence in education.

Knowledge-Based Systems: Elsevier, Inc., Journals Customer Service, 3251 Riverport Lane, Maryland Heights, MO 63043, USA. www.elsevier.com/locate/ knosys, tel: 877-839-7126, fax: 314-447-8077, journalcustomerservice-usa@ elsevier.com [12/yr; $226 indiv, $1,481 inst]. Interdisciplinary application-oriented journal on fifth-generation computing, expert systems, and knowledge-based methods in system design.

Minds and Machines: Springer Science + Business Media, PO Box 2485, Secaucus, NJ 07096-2485, USA. www.springer.com/journal/11023, tel: 800-777-4643, fax: 201-348-4505, service-ny@springer.com [4/yr; $834 inst (print/online), $1,001 inst (print + online, content through 1997)]. Discusses issues concerning machines and mentality, artificial intelligence, epistemology, simulation, and modeling.

17.1   Computer-Assisted Instruction

AACE Journal: Association for the Advancement of Computing in Education, PO Box 1545, Chesapeake, VA 23327-1545, USA. www.editlib.org/j/aacej, tel: 757-366-5606, fax: 703-997-8760, info@aace.org [4/yr; $45 for stud, $125 indiv, $195 inst]. Publishes articles dealing with issues in instructional technology.

CALICO Journal: Computer Assisted Language Instruction Consortium, 214 Centennial Hall, Texas State University, San Marcos, TX 78666, USA. calico.org, tel: 512-245-1417, fax: 512-245-9089, info@calico.org [3/yr; $40 stud, $50K-12 or community college teacher, $65 indiv, $105 inst]. Provides information on the applications of technology in teaching and learning languages.

Children's Technology Review: Active Learning Associates, 120 Main St, Flemington, NJ 08822, USA. childrenstech.com, tel: 800-993-9499, fax: 908-284-0405, lisa@childrenstech.com [12/yr; $30 online, $120 print + online]. Provides reviews and other information about software to help parents and educators more effectively use computers with children.

Computers and Composition: Elsevier, Inc., Journals Customer Service, 3251 Riverport Lane, Maryland Heights, MO 63043, USA. www.elsevier.com/locate/ compcom, tel: 877-839-7126, fax: 314-447-8077, journalcustomerservice-usa@

elsevier.com [4/yr; $82 indiv, $454 inst]. *International Journal for Teachers of Writing* that focuses on the use of computers in writing instruction and related research.

Computers & Education: Elsevier, Inc., Journals Customer Service, 3251 Riverport Lane, Maryland Heights, MO 63043, USA. www.elsevier.com/locate/compedu, tel: 877-839-7126, fax: 314-447-8077, journalcustomerservice-usa@elsevier.com [8/yr; $404 indiv, $2,139 inst]. Presents technical papers covering a broad range of subjects for users of analog, digital, and hybrid computers in all aspects of higher education.

Computers in Education Journal: American Society for Engineering Education, Port Royal Square, PO Box 68, Port Royal, VA 22535, USA. www.asee.org/papers -and-publications/publications/division-publications/computers-in-education-journal, tel: 804-742-5611, fax: 804-742-5030, ed-pub@crosslink.net [4/yr; $20 stud, $69 indiv, inst prices vary]. Covers transactions, scholarly research papers, application notes, and teaching methods.

Computers in Human Behavior: Elsevier, Inc., Journals Customer Service, 3251 Riverport Lane, Maryland Heights, MO 63043, USA. www.elsevier.com/locate/ comphumbeh, tel: 877-839-7126, fax: 314-447-8077, journalcustomerservice-usa@ elsevier.com [6/yr; $317 indiv, $1,756 inst]. Scholarly journal dedicated to examining the use of computers from a psychological perspective.

Computers in the Schools: Taylor & Francis Group, Customer Service Department, 325 Chestnut Street, Suite 800, Philadelphia, PA 19106, USA. www.tandf.co.uk/ journals/titles/07380569, tel: 800-354-1420, fax: 215-625-2940, subscriptions@ tandf.co.uk [4/yr; $125 indiv (online), $134 indiv (print + online), $699 inst (online), $777 inst (print + online)]. Features articles that combine theory and practical applications of small computers in schools for educators and school administrators.

Converge: e. Republic, Inc., 100 Blue Ravine Rd, Folsom, CA 95630, USA. www. convergemag.com, tel: 800-940-6039 ext 1319, fax: 916-932-1470, subscriptions@ convergemag.com [4/yr; free]. Explores the revolution of technology in education.

Dr. Dobb's Journal: United Business Media LLC, Customer Service, PO Box 1093, Skokie, IL 60076, USA. www.ddj.com, tel: 888-664-3332, fax: 847-763-9606, drdobbsjournal@halldata.com [12/yr; free to qualified applicants]. Articles on the latest in operating systems, programming languages, algorithms, hardware design and architecture, data structures, and telecommunications; in-depth hardware and software reviews.

eWEEK: Ziff Davis Media Inc., PO Box 3402, Northbrook, IL 60065-3402, USA. www.eweek.com, tel: 888-663-8438, fax: 847-564-9453, eweek@ziffdavis.com [36/yr; $125 (print), $85 (online), free to qualified applicants]. Provides current information on the IBM PC, including hardware, software, industry news, business strategies, and reviews of hardware and software.

Instructor: Scholastic Inc., PO Box 420235, Palm Coast, FL 32142-0235, USA. teacher.scholastic.com/products/instructor, tel: 866-436-2455, fax: 212-343-4799, instructor@emailcustomerservice.com [8/yr; $8]. Features articles on applications and advances of technology in education for K-12 and college educators and administrators.

Interactive Learning Environments: Taylor & Francis Group, Customer Services Department, 325 Chestnut St, Suite 800, Philadelphia, PA 19106, USA. www.tandf. co.uk/journals/titles/10494820, tel: 800-354-1420, fax: 215-625-2940, subscriptions@tandf.co.uk [5/yr; $240 indiv, $713 inst (online), $793 inst (print+online)]. Explores the implications of the Internet and multimedia presentation software in education and training environments.

Journal of Computer Assisted Learning: John Wiley & Sons, Inc., Journal Customer Services, 350 Main St, Malden, MA 02148, USA. www.blackwellpublishing.com/journals/JCA, tel: 800-835-6770, fax: 781-388-8232, cs-agency@ wiley.com [6/yr; $230 indiv (print+online), $1,404 inst (print/online), $1,615 inst (print+online)]. Articles and research on the use of computer-assisted learning.

Journal of Educational Computing Research: Baywood Publishing Co., Inc., 26 Austin Ave., Box 337, Amityville, NY 11701-0337, USA. www.baywood.com/ journals/previewjournals.asp?id=0735-6331, tel: 800-638-7819, fax: 631-691-1770, info@baywood.com [8/yr; $235 indiv (online), $245 indiv (print+online), $598 inst (online), $630 inst (print+online)]. Presents original research papers, critical analyses, reports on research in progress, design and development studies, article reviews, and grant award listings.

Journal of Educational Multimedia and Hypermedia: Association for the Advancement of Computing in Education, PO Box 1545, Chesapeake, VA 23327-1545, USA. www.aace.org/pubs/jemh, tel: 757-366-5606, fax: 703-997-8760, info@aace.org [4/yr; $45 for stud, $125 indiv, $195 inst]. A multidisciplinary information source presenting research about and applications for multimedia and hypermedia tools.

Journal of Research on Technology in Education: International Society for Technology in Education, 180 West 8th Ave., Suite 300, Eugene, OR 97401-2916, USA. www.iste.org/jrte, tel: 800-336-5191, fax: 541-434-8948, iste@iste.org [4/yr; $54 member, $155 non-member]. Contains articles reporting on the latest research findings related to classroom and administrative uses of technology, including system and project evaluations.

Language Resources and Evaluation: Springer Science+Business Media, PO Box 2485, Secaucus, NJ 07096-2485, USA. www.springer.com/journal/10579, tel: 800-777-4643, fax: 201-348-4505, service-ny@springer.com [4/yr; $901 inst (print/online), $1,081 inst (print+online, content through 1997)]. Contains papers on computer-aided studies, applications, automation, and computer-assisted instruction.

Learning and Leading with Technology: International Society for Technology in Education, 180 West 8th Ave., Suite 300, Eugene, OR 97401-2916, USA. www.iste. org/LL, tel: 800-336-5191, fax: 541-302-3778, iste@iste.org [8/yr; $54 member, $100 non-member]. Focuses on the use of technology, coordination, and leadership; written by educators for educators. Appropriate for classroom teachers, lab teachers, technology coordinators, and teacher educators.

MacWorld: Mac Publishing, Macworld Subscription Services, PO Box 37781, Boone, IA 50037, USA. www.macworld.com/magazine, tel: 800-288-6848, fax: 515-432-6994, subhelp@macworld.com [12/yr; $19.97]. Describes hardware, software, tutorials, and applications for users of the Macintosh microcomputer.

OnCUE: Computer-Using Educators, Inc., 877 Ygnacio Valley Road, Suite 104, Walnut Creek, CA 94596, USA. www.cue.org/oncue, tel: 925-478-3460, fax: 925-934-6799, cueinc@cue.org [4/yr; $30 stud, $40 indiv]. Contains articles, news items, and trade advertisements addressing computer-based education.

PC Magazine: Ziff Davis Media Inc., 28 E 28th St, New York, NY 10016-7930, USA. www.pcmag.com, tel: 212-503-3500, fax: 212-503-4399, pcmag@ziffdavis. com [12/yr; $19.99]. Comparative reviews of computer hardware and general business software programs.

Social Science Computer Review: Sage Publications, 2455 Teller Rd, Thousand Oaks, CA 91320, USA. ssc.sagepub.com, tel: 800-818-7243, fax: 800-583-2665, journals@sagepub.com [4/yr; $130 indiv, $725 inst (print), $666 inst (online), $740 inst (online+backfile, content through Volume 1, Issue 1/print+online), $814 inst (print+online+backfile)]. Interdisciplinary peer-reviewed scholarly publication covering social science research and instructional applications in computing and telecommunications; also covers societal impacts of information technology.

Wireless Networks: Springer Science+Business Media, PO Box 2485, Secaucus, NJ 07096-2485, USA. www.springer.com/journal/11276, tel: 800-777-4643, fax: 201-348-4505, service-ny@springer.com [8/yr; $879 inst (print/online), $1,055 inst (print+online, content through 1997)]. Devoted to the technological innovations that result from the mobility allowed by wireless technology.

17.2 Distance Education

American Journal of Distance Education: Taylor & Francis Group, Customer Services Department, 325 Chestnut St, Suite 800, Philadelphia, PA 19106, USA. www.tandf.co.uk/journals/titles/08923647, tel: 800-354-1420, fax: 215-625-2940, subscriptions@tandf.co.uk [4/yr; $79 indiv, $291 inst (online), $323 inst (print+online)]. Created to disseminate information and act as a forum for criticism and debate about research on and practice of systems, management, and administration of distance education.

Journal of Distance Education: Canadian Network for Innovation in Education, BCIT Learning & Teaching Centre, British Columbia Institute of Technology, 3700 Willingdon Ave., Burnaby, BC, Canada V5G 3H2. www.jofde.ca, tel: 604-454-2280, fax: 604-431-7267, journalofde@gmail.com [at least 2/yr; $40 (print); free online]. Aims to promote and encourage scholarly work of empirical and theoretical nature relating to distance education in Canada and throughout the world.

Journal of Library & Information Services in Distance Learning: Taylor & Francis Group, Customer Service Department, 325 Chestnut Street, Suite 800, Philadelphia, PA 19106, USA. www.tandf.co.uk/journals/titles/1533290X, tel: 800-354-1420, fax: 215-625-2940, subscriptions@tandf.co.uk [4/yr; $75 indiv (online), $83 indiv (print+online), $199 inst (online), $220 inst (print+online)]. Contains peer-reviewed articles, essays, narratives, current events, and letters from distance learning and information science experts.

Journal of Research on Technology in Education: International Society for Technology in Education, 180 West 8th Ave., Suite 300, Eugene, OR 97401-2916, USA. www.iste.org/jrte, tel: 800-336-5191, fax: 541-434-8948, iste@iste.org [4/yr; $54 member, $155 non-member]. Contains articles reporting on the latest research findings related to classroom and administrative uses of technology, including system and project evaluations.

Open Learning: Taylor & Francis Group, Customer Services Department, 325 Chestnut St, Suite 800, Philadelphia, PA 19106, USA. www.tandf.co.uk/journals/titles/02680513, tel: 800-354-1420, fax: 215-625-2940, subscriptions@tandf.co.uk [3/yr; $116 indiv, $343 inst (online), $382 inst (print+online)]. Academic, scholarly publication on aspects of open and distance learning anywhere in the world. Includes issues for debate and research notes.

17.3   Educational Research

American Educational Research Journal: Sage Publications, 2455 Teller Rd, Thousand Oaks, CA 91320, USA. aer.sagepub.com, tel: 800-818-7243, fax: 800-583-2665, journals@sagepub.com [6/yr; $69 indiv, $421 inst (print), $387 inst (online), $430 inst (online+backfile, content through Volume 1, Issue 1/ print+online), $473 inst (print+online+backfile)]. Reports original research, both empirical and theoretical, and brief synopses of research.

Educational Research: Taylor & Francis Group, Customer Services Department, 325 Chestnut St, Suite 800, Philadelphia, PA 19106, USA. www.tandf.co.uk/journals/titles/00131881, tel: 800-354-1420, fax: 215-625-2940, subscriptions@tandf.co.uk [4/yr; $197 indiv, $542 inst (online), $602 inst (print+online)]. Reports on current educational research, evaluation, and applications.

Educational Researcher: Sage Publications, 2455 Teller Rd, Thousand Oaks, CA 91320, USA. edr.sagepub.com, tel: 800-818-7243, fax: 800-583-2665, journals@ sagepub.com [9/yr; $58 indiv, $386 inst (print), $355 inst (online), $394 inst (online+backfile, content through Volume 1, Issue 1/print+online), $433 inst (print+online+backfile)]. Contains news and features of general significance in educational research.

Journal of Interactive Learning Research: Association for the Advancement of Computing in Education, PO Box 1545, Chesapeake, VA 23327-1545, USA. www. aace.org/pubs/jilr, tel: 757-366-5606, fax: 703-997-8760, info@aace.org [4/yr; $45 for stud, $125 indiv, $195 inst]. Publishes articles on how intelligent computer technologies can be used in education to enhance learning and teaching. Reports on research and developments, integration, and applications of artificial intelligence in education.

Learning Technology: IEEE Computer Society, Technical Committee on Learning Technology, 150 Androutsou Street, Piraeus GR-18352, Greece. http://www.lttf. ieee.org/learn_tech, tel: (+30) 210-4142766, fax: (+30) 210-4142767, sampson@ unipi.gr [4/yr; free]. Online publication that reports developments, projects, conferences, and findings of the Learning Technology Task Force.

Meridian: North Carolina State University, College of Education, Poe Hall, PO Box 7801, Raleigh, NC 27695-7801, USA. www.ncsu.edu/meridian, meridian_ mail@ncsu.edu [2/yr; free]. Online journal dedicated to research in middle school educational technology use.

Research in Science & Technological Education: Taylor & Francis Group, Customer Services Department, 325 Chestnut St, Suite 800, Philadelphia, PA 19106, USA. www.tandf.co.uk/journals/titles/02635143, tel: 800-354-1420, fax: 215-625-2940, subscriptions@tandf.co.uk [3/yr; $373 indiv, $1,765 inst (online), $1,961 inst (print+online)]. Publication of original research in the science and technological fields. Includes articles on psychological, sociological, economic, and organizational aspects of technological education.

17.4   Educational Technology

Appropriate Technology: Research Information Ltd., Grenville Court, Britwell Rd, Burnham, Bucks SL1 8DF, UK. www.researchinformation.co.uk/apte.php, tel: +44 (0) 1628-600499, fax: +44 (0) 1628-600488, info@researchinformation.co.uk [4/yr; $104 indiv, $316 inst]. Articles on less technologically advanced, but more environmentally sustainable solutions to problems in developing countries.

British Journal of Educational Technology: John Wiley & Sons, Inc., Journal Customer Services, 350 Main St, Malden, MA 02148, USA. www.blackwellpub-lishing.com/journals/BJET, tel: 800-835-6770, fax: 781-388-8232, cs-agency@

wiley.com [6/yr; $213 indiv, $1,336 inst (print/online), $1,536 inst (print + online)]. Published by the National Council for Educational Technology, this journal includes articles on education and training, especially theory, applications, and development of educational technology and communications.

Canadian Journal of Learning and Technology: Canadian Network for Innovation in Education (CNIE), 260 Dalhousie St, Suite 204, Ottawa, ON, Canada K1N 7E4. www.cjlt.ca, tel: 613-241-0018, fax: 613-241-0019, cjlt@ucalgary.ca [3/yr; free]. Concerned with all aspects of educational systems and technology.

Educational Technology: Educational Technology Publications, Inc., 700 Palisade Ave., Englewood Cliffs, NJ 07632-0564, USA. www.bookstoread.com/etp, tel: 800-952-2665, fax: 201-871-4009, edtecpubs@aol.com [6/yr; $229]. Covers telecommunications, computer-aided instruction, information retrieval, educational television, and electronic media in the classroom.

Educational Technology Abstracts: Taylor & Francis Group, Customer Services Department, 325 Chestnut St, Suite 800, Philadelphia, PA 19106, USA. www.tandf.co.uk/journals/titles/02663368, tel: 800-354-1420, fax: 215-625-2940, subscriptions@tandf.co.uk [1/yr; $621 indiv, $1,595 inst (online), $1,679 inst (print + online)]. An international publication of abstracts of recently published material in the field of educational and training technology.

Educational Technology Research & Development: Springer Science + Business Media, PO Box 2485, Secaucus, NJ 07096-2485, USA. www.springer.com/journal/11423, tel: 800-777-4643, fax: 201-348-4505, service-ny@springer.com [6/yr; $371 inst (print/online), $445 inst (print + online, content through 1997)]. Focuses on research, instructional development, and applied theory in the field of educational technology.

International Journal of Technology and Design Education: Springer Science + Business Media, PO Box 2485, Secaucus, NJ 07096-2485, USA. www.springer.com/journal/10798, tel: 800-777-4643, fax: 201-348-4505, service-ny@springer.com [4/yr; $456 inst (print/online), $547 inst (print + online, content through 1997)]. Publishes research reports and scholarly writing about aspects of technology and design education.

Journal of Computing in Higher Education: Springer Science + Business Media, PO Box 2485, Secaucus, NJ 07096-2485, USA. www.springer.com/journal/12528, tel: 800-777-4643, fax: 201-348-4505, service-ny@springer.com [3/yr; $150 inst (print/online), $180 inst (print + online, content through 1997)]. Publishes scholarly essays, case studies, and research that discuss instructional technologies.

Journal of Educational Technology Systems: Baywood Publishing Co., Inc., 26 Austin Ave., PO Box 337, Amityville, NY 11701-0337, USA. www.baywood.com/journals/previewjournals.asp?id=0047-2395, tel: 800-638-7819, fax: 631-691-1770, info@baywood.com [4/yr; $408 inst (online), $430 (print + online)]. Deals with systems technological innovations as they apply to education.

17.5   Information Science and Technology

Canadian Journal of Information and Library Science: University of Toronto Press, Journals Division, 5201 Dufferin St, Toronto, ON, Canada M3H 5T8. www. utpjournals.com/cjils, tel: 416-667-7777, fax: 800-221-9985, journals@utpress. utoronto.ca [4/yr; $50 stud, $85 indiv, $125 inst]. Published by the Canadian Association for Information Science to contribute to the advancement of library and information science in Canada.

EContent: Information Today, Inc., 143 Old Marlton Pike, Medford, NJ 08055-8750, USA. www.econtentmag.com, tel: 800-300-9868, fax: 609-654-4309, custserv@infotoday.com [10/yr; free]. Features articles on topics of interest to online database users; includes database search aids.

Information Processing & Management: Elsevier, Inc., Journals Customer Service, 3251 Riverport Lane, Maryland Heights, MO 63043, USA. www.elsevier. com/locate/infoproman, tel: 877-839-7126, fax: 314-447-8077, journalcustomerservice-usa@elsevier.com [6/yr; $370 indiv, $2,157 inst]. International journal covering data processing, database building, and retrieval.

Information Services & Use: IOS Press, Nieuwe Hemweg 6B, 1013 BG Amsterdam, The Netherlands. www.iospress.nl/html/01675265.php, tel: +31-20-688-3355, fax: +31-20-687-0039, info@iospress.nl [4/yr; $140 indiv (online), $560 inst (online), $616 inst (print+online)]. An international journal for those in the information management field. Includes online and offline systems, library automation, micrographics, videotex, and telecommunications.

The Information Society: Taylor & Francis Group, Customer Services Department, 325 Chestnut St, Suite 800, Philadelphia, PA 19106, USA. www.tandf.co.uk/journals/titles/01972243, tel: 800-354-1420, fax: 215-625-2940, subscriptions@tandf. co.uk [5/yr; $185 indiv, $469 inst (online), $521 inst (print+online)]. Provides a forum for discussion of the world of information, including transborder data flow, regulatory issues, and the impact of the information industry.

Information Technology and Libraries: American Library Association, Subscriptions, 50 E Huron St, Chicago, IL 60611-2795, USA. www.ala.org/lita/ital, tel: 800-545-2433, fax: 312-944-2641, subscription@ala.org [4/yr; free]. Articles on library automation, communication technology, cable systems, computerized information processing, and video technologies.

Information Today: Information Today, Inc., 143 Old Marlton Pike, Medford, NJ 08055-8750, USA. www.infotoday.com/it, tel: 609-654-6266, fax: 609-654-4309, custserv@infotoday.com [11/yr; $87.50]. Newspaper for users and producers of electronic information services. Includes articles and news about the industry, calendar of events, and product information.

Information Technology Management: IGI Global, 701 E Chocolate Ave., Suite 200, Hershey, PA 17033-1240, USA. www.igi-pub.com/journals/details.asp?id=200, tel: 866-342-6657, fax: 717-533-8661, cust@igi-global.com [2/yr; $70 indiv, $90 inst]. Designed for library information specialists, this bi-annual newsletter presents current issues and trends in information technology presented by and for specialists in the field.

Internet Reference Service Quarterly: Taylor & Francis Group, Customer Services Department, 325 Chestnut St, Suite 800, Philadelphia, PA 19106, USA. www.tandf.co.uk/journals/WIRS, tel: 800-354-1420, fax: 215-625-2940, subscriptions@tandf.co.uk [4/yr; $85 indiv (online), $90 indiv (print+online), $218 inst (online), $242 inst (print+online)]. Discusses multidisciplinary aspects of incorporating the Internet as a tool for reference service.

Journal of Access Services: Taylor & Francis Group, Customer Services Department, 325 Chestnut St, Suite 800, Philadelphia, PA 19106, USA. www.tandf.co.uk/journals/WJAS, tel: 800-354-1420, fax: 215-625-2940, subscriptions@tandf.co.uk [4/yr; $80 indiv (online), $85 indiv (print+online), $218 inst (online), $242 inst (print+online)]. Explores topics and issues surrounding the organization, administration, and development of information technology on access services and resources.

Journal of the American Society for Information Science and Technology: John Wiley & Sons, Inc., Journal Customer Services, 350 Main St, Malden, MA 02148, USA. onlinelibrary.wiley.com/journal/10.1002/(ISSN)1532-2890, tel: 800-835-6770, fax: 781-388-8232, cs-agency@wiley.com [12/yr; $2,620 inst (print), $2,719 inst (print+online)]. Provides an overall forum for new research in information transfer and communication processes, with particular attention paid to the context of recorded knowledge.

Journal of Database Management: IGI Global, 701 E Chocolate Ave., Suite 200, Hershey, PA 17033-1240, USA. www.idea-group.com/journals/details.asp?id=198, tel: 866-342-6657, fax: 717-533-8661, cust@igi-global.com [4/yr; $210 indiv, $595 inst (print/online), $860 inst (print+online)]. Provides state-of-the-art research to those who design, develop, and administer DBMS-based information systems.

Journal of Documentation: Emerald Group Publishing Inc., Brickyard Office Park, 84 Sherman Street, Cambridge, MA 02140, USA. www.emeraldinsight.com/jd.htm, tel: 617-945-9130, fax: 617-945-9136, america@emeraldinsight.com [6/yr; inst prices vary]. Focuses on theories, concepts, models, frameworks, and philosophies in the information sciences.

Journal of Interlibrary Loan, Document Delivery & Electronic Reserve: Taylor & Francis Group, Customer Services Department, 325 Chestnut St, Suite 800, Philadelphia, PA 19106, USA. www.tandf.co.uk/journals/titles/1072303X, tel: 800-354-1420, fax: 215-625-2940, subscriptions@tandf.co.uk [5/yr; $104 indiv (online), $112 indiv (print+online), $412 inst (online), $458 inst (print+online)]. A forum for ideas on the basic theoretical and practical problems regarding all aspects of library resource sharing faced by planners, practitioners, and users of network services.

Journal of Library Metadata: Taylor & Francis Group, Customer Services Department, 325 Chestnut St, Suite 800, Philadelphia, PA 19106, USA. www.tandf. co.uk/journals/titles/19386389, tel: 800-354-1420, fax: 215-625-2940, subscriptions@tandf.co.uk [4/yr; $82 indiv (online), $88 indiv (print+online), $259 inst (online), $288 inst (print+online)]. A forum for the latest research, innovations, news, and expert views about all aspects of metadata applications and information retrieval in libraries.

17.6   Instructional Design and Development

Human-Computer Interaction: Taylor & Francis Group, Customer Services Department, 325 Chestnut St, Suite 800, Philadelphia, PA 19106, USA. www.tandf. co.uk/journals/titles/07370024, tel: 800-354-1420, fax: 215-625-2940, subscriptions@tandf.co.uk [4/yr; $84 indiv, $687 inst (online), $763 institution (print+online)]. A journal of theoretical, empirical, and methodological issues of user science and of system design.

Instructional Science: Springer Science+Business Media, PO Box 2485, Secaucus, NJ 07096-2485, USA. www.springer.com/journal/11251, tel: 800-777-4643, fax: 201-348-4505, service-ny@springer.com [6/yr; $893 inst (print/online), $1,072 inst (print+online, content through 1997)]. Promotes a deeper understanding of the nature, theory, and practice of the instructional process and the learning resulting from this process.

International Journal of Human-Computer Interaction: Taylor & Francis Group, Customer Services Department, 325 Chestnut St, Suite 800, Philadelphia, PA 19106, USA. www.tandf.co.uk/journals/titles/10447318, tel: 800-354-1420, fax: 215-625-2940, subscriptions@tandf.co.uk [12/yr; $194 indiv (online), $206 indiv (print+online), $1,601 inst (online), $1,779 inst (print+online)]. Addresses the cognitive, social, health, and ergonomic aspects of work with computers. It also emphasizes both the human and computer science aspects of the effective design and use of computer interactive systems.

Journal of Educational Technology Systems: Baywood Publishing Co., Inc., 26 Austin Ave., Box 337, Amityville, NY 11701-0337, USA. www.baywood.com/journals/previewjournals.asp?id=0047-2395, tel: 800-638-7819, fax: 631-691-1770, info@baywood.com [4/yr; $408 inst (online), $430 inst (print+online)]. Deals with systems in which technology and education interface; designed to inform educators who are interested in making optimum use of technology.

Journal of Applied Learning Technology: Learning Technology Institute, 50 Culpeper St, Warrenton, VA 20186, USA. www.salt.org/salt.asp?ss=l&pn=jalt, tel: 540-347-0055, fax: 540-349-3169, info@lti.org [4/yr; $100 member, $45 non-member, $40 inst]. Devoted to the issues, problems, and applications of instructional delivery systems in education, training, and job performance.

Journal of Technical Writing and Communication: Baywood Publishing Co., Inc., 26 Austin Ave., PO Box 337, Amityville, NY 11701-0337, USA. www.baywood.com/journals/previewjournals.asp?id=0047-2816, tel: 800-638-7819, fax: 631-691-1770, info@baywood.com [4/yr; $109 indiv (online), $117 indiv (print+online), $408 inst (online), $430 inst (print+online)]. Essays on oral and written communication, for purposes ranging from pure research to needs of business and industry.

Journal of Visual Literacy: International Visual Literacy Association, Dr. David R. Moore, IVLA Executive Treasurer, Ohio University, 250 McCracken Hall, Athens, OH 45701, USA. www.ohio.edu/visualliteracy, tel: 740-597-1322, jvleditor@ohio.edu [2/yr; $30 student, $60 indiv]. Explores empirical, theoretical, practical, and applied aspects of visual literacy and communication.

Performance Improvement: John Wiley & Sons, Inc., Journal Customer Services, 350 Main St, Malden, MA 02148, USA. www3.interscience.wiley.com/journal/112729556/home, tel: 800-835-6770, fax: 781-388-8232, cs-agency@wiley.com [10/yr; $85 indiv (print/online), $94 indiv (print+online), $376 inst (print/online), $434 inst (print+online)]. Promotes performance science and technology. Contains articles, research, and case studies relating to improving human performance.

Performance Improvement Quarterly: John Wiley & Sons, Inc., Journal Customer Services, 350 Main St, Malden, MA 02148, USA. www3.interscience.wiley.com/journal/117865970/home, tel: 800-835-6770, fax: 781-388-8232, cs-agency@wiley.com [4/yr; $65 indiv, $195 inst (print/online/print+online)]. Presents the cutting edge in research and theory in performance technology.

Training: Lakewood Media Group, PO Box 247, Excelsior, MN 55331, USA. www.trainingmag.com, tel: 877-865-9361, fax: 847-291-4816, ntrn@omeda.com [6/yr; $79, free to qualified applicants]. Covers all aspects of training, management, and organizational development, motivation, and performance improvement.

17.7   Learning Sciences

International Journal of Computer-Supported Collaborative Learning: Springer Science+Business Media, PO Box 2485, Secaucus, NJ 07096-2485, USA. www.springer.com/journal/11412, tel: 800-777-4643, fax: 201-348-4505, service-ny@springer.com [4/yr; $466 inst (print/online), $559 inst (print+online, content through 1997)]. Promote a deeper understanding of the nature, theory, and practice of the uses of computer-supported collaborative learning.

Journal of the Learning Sciences: Taylor & Francis Group, Customer Services Department, 325 Chestnut St, Suite 800, Philadelphia, PA 19106, USA. www.tandf.co.uk/journals/titles/10508406, tel: 800-354-1420, fax: 215-625-2940, subscriptions@tandf.co.uk [4/yr; $78 indiv, $756 inst (online), $840 inst (print+online)]. Provides a forum for the discussion of research on education and learning, with emphasis on the idea of changing one's understanding of learning and the practice of education.

17.8   Libraries and Media Centers

Collection Building: Emerald Group Publishing Inc., Brickyard Office Park, 84 Sherman Street, Cambridge, MA 02140, USA. www.emeraldinsight.com/cb.htm, tel: 617-945-9130, fax: 617-945-9136, america@emeraldinsight.com [4/yr; inst prices vary]. Provides well-researched and authoritative information on collection maintenance and development for librarians in all sectors.

Computers in Libraries: Information Today, Inc., 143 Old Marlton Pike, Medford, NJ 08055-8750, USA. www.infotoday.com/cilmag/default.shtml, tel: 609-654-6266, fax: 609-654-4309, custserv@infotoday.com [10/yr; $99.95]. Covers practical applications of microcomputers to library situations and recent news items.

The Electronic Library: Emerald Group Publishing Inc., Brickyard Office Park, 84 Sherman Street, Cambridge, MA 02140, USA. info.emeraldinsight.com/el.htm, tel: 617-945-9130, fax: 617-945-9136, america@emeraldinsight.com [6/yr; inst prices vary]. International journal for minicomputer, microcomputer, and software applications in libraries; independently assesses current and forthcoming information technologies.

Government Information Quarterly: Elsevier, Inc., Journals Customer Service, 3251 Riverport Lane, Maryland Heights, MO 63043, USA. www.elsevier.com/locate/govinf, tel: 877-839-7126, fax: 314-447-8077, journalcustomerservice-usa@elsevier.com [4/yr; $195 indiv, $680 inst]. *International Journal of Resources, Services, Policies, and Practices.*

Information Outlook: Special Libraries Association, Information Outlook Subscriptions, 1700 Eighteenth Street, NW, Washington, DC 20009-2514, USA. www.sla.org/pubs/serial/io, tel: 703-647-4900, fax: 1-202-234-2442, magazine@sla.org [12/yr; $125]. Discusses administration, organization, and operations. Includes reports on research, technology, and professional standards.

The Journal of Academic Librarianship: Elsevier, Inc., Journals Customer Service, 3251 Riverport Lane, Maryland Heights, MO 63043, USA. www.elsevier.com/locate/jacalib, tel: 877-839-7126, fax: 314-447-8077, journalcustomerservice-usa@elsevier.com [6/yr; $140 indiv, $413 inst]. Results of significant research, issues, and problems facing academic libraries, book reviews, and innovations in academic libraries.

Journal of Librarianship and Information Science: Sage Publications, 2455 Teller Rd, Thousand Oaks, CA 91320, USA. lis.sagepub.com, tel: 800-818-7243, fax: 800-583-2665, journals@sagepub.com [4/yr; $107 indiv, $733 inst (print), $673 inst (online), $748 inst (online + backfile, content through Volume 1, Issue 1/print + online), $823 inst (print + online + backfile)]. Deals with all aspects of library and information work in the United Kingdom and reviews literature from international sources.

Journal of Library Administration: Taylor & Francis Group, Customer Services Department, 325 Chestnut St, Suite 800, Philadelphia, PA 19106, USA. www.tandf.co.uk/journals/titles/01930826, tel: 800-354-1420, fax: 215-625-2940, subscriptions@

tandf.co.uk [8/yr; $211 indiv (online), $234 indiv (print+online), $809 inst (online), $899 inst (print+online)]. Provides information on all aspects of effective library management, with emphasis on practical applications.

Library & Information Science Research: Elsevier, Inc., Journals Customer Service, 3251 Riverport Lane, Maryland Heights, MO 63043, USA. www.elsevier.com/locate/lisres, tel: 877-839-7126, fax: 314-447-8077, journalcustomerservice-usa@elsevier.com [4/yr; $165 indiv, $520 inst]. Research articles, dissertation reviews, and book reviews on issues concerning information resources management.

Library Hi Tech: Emerald Group Publishing Inc., Brickyard Office Park, 84 Sherman Street, Cambridge, MA 02140, USA. www.emeraldinsight.com/lht.htm, tel: 617-945-9130, fax: 617-945-9136, america@emeraldinsight.com [4/yr; inst prices vary]. Concentrates on reporting on the selection, installation, maintenance, and integration of systems and hardware.

Library Hi Tech News: Emerald Group Publishing Inc., Brickyard Office Park, 84 Sherman Street, Cambridge, MA 02140, USA. www.emeraldinsight.com/lhtn.htm, tel: 617-945-9130, fax: 617-945-9136, america@emeraldinsight.com [10/yr; inst prices vary]. Supplements Library Hi Tech and updates many of the issues addressed in-depth in the journal; keeps the reader fully informed of the latest developments in library automation, new products, network news, new software and hardware, and people in technology.

Library Journal: Media Source, Inc., 160 Varick Street, 11th Floor, New York, NY 10013, USA. www.libraryjournal.com, tel: 800-588-1030, fax: 712-733-8019, LJLcustserv@cds-global.com [23/yr; $157.99]. A professional periodical for librarians, with current issues and news, professional reading, a lengthy book review section, and classified advertisements.

Library Media Connection: Linworth Publishing, Inc., PO Box 204, Vandalia, OH 45377, USA. www.librarymediaconnection.com/lmc, tel: 800-607-4410, fax: 937-890-0221, linworth@linworthpublishing.com [6/yr; $69]. *Journal for Junior and Senior High School Librarians*; provides articles, tips, and ideas for day-to-day school library management, as well as reviews of audiovisuals and software, all written by school librarians.

The Library Quarterly: University of Chicago Press, Journals Division, PO Box 37005, Chicago, IL 60637, USA. www.journals.uchicago.edu/LQ, tel: 877-705-1878, fax: 877-705-1879, subscriptions@press.uchicago.edu [$26 students (online), $47 indiv (print), $46 indiv (online), $52 indiv (print+online), inst prices vary]. Scholarly articles of interest to librarians.

Library Resources & Technical Services: American Library Association, Subscriptions, 50 E Huron St, Chicago, IL 60611-2795, USA. www.ala.org/ala/mgrps/divs/alcts/resources/lrts/index.cfm, tel: 800-545-2433, fax: 312-944-2641, subscription@ala.org [4/yr; $100 print, $95 online, $105 print+online]. Scholarly papers on bibliographic access and control, preservation, conservation, and reproduction of library materials.

Library Trends: Johns Hopkins University Press, PO Box 19966, Baltimore, MD 21211-0966, USA. www.press.jhu.edu/journals/library_trends, tel: 800-548-1784, fax: 410-516-3866, jrnlcirc@press.jhu.edu [4/yr; $80 indiv (print), $85 indiv (online), $150 inst (print)]. Each issue is concerned with one aspect of library and information science, analyzing current thought and practice and examining ideas that hold the greatest potential for the field.

Public Libraries: American Library Association, Subscriptions, 50 E Huron St, Chicago, IL 60611-2795, USA. www.ala.org/pla/publications/publiclibraries, tel: 800-545-2433, fax: 312-944-2641, subscription@ala.org [6/yr; $65]. News and articles of interest to public librarians.

Public Library Quarterly: Taylor & Francis Group, Customer Services Department, 325 Chestnut St, Suite 800, Philadelphia, PA 19106, USA. www.tandf.co.uk/journals/WPLQ, tel: 800-354-1420, fax: 215-625-2940, subscriptions@tandf.co.uk [4/yr; $114 indiv (online), $123 indiv (print+online), $373 inst (online), $415 inst (print+online)]. Addresses the major administrative challenges and opportunities that face the nation's public libraries.

Reference and User Services Quarterly: American Library Association, Subscriptions, 50 E Huron St, Chicago, IL 60611-2795, USA. http://www.rusq.org, tel: 800-545-2433, fax: 312-944-2641, subscription@ala.org [4/yr; $33 student, $65 member]. Disseminates information of interest to reference librarians, bibliographers, adult services librarians, those in collection development and selection, and others interested in public services.

The Reference Librarian: Taylor & Francis Group, Customer Services Department, 325 Chestnut St, Suite 800, Philadelphia, PA 19106, USA. www.tandf.co.uk/journals/wref, tel: 800-354-1420, fax: 215-625-2940, subscriptions@tandf.co.uk [4/yr; $251 indiv (online), $278 indiv (print+online), $1,057 inst (online), $1,174 inst (print+online)]. Each issue focuses on a topic of current concern, interest, or practical value to reference librarians.

Reference Services Review: Emerald Group Publishing Inc., Brickyard Office Park, 84 Sherman Street, Cambridge, MA 02140, USA. www.emeraldinsight.com/rsr.htm, tel: 617-945-9130, fax: 617-945-9136, america@emeraldinsight.com [4/yr; inst prices vary]. Dedicated to the enrichment of reference knowledge and the advancement of reference services. It prepares its readers to understand and embrace current and emerging technologies affecting reference functions and information needs of library users.

School Library Journal: Media Source, Inc., 160 Varick Street, 11th Floor, New York, NY 10013, USA. www.slj.com, tel: 800-595-1066, fax: 712-733-8019, slj-custserv@cds-global.com [15/yr; $136.99]. For school and youth service librarians. Reviews about 4,000 children's books and 1,000 educational media titles annually.

School Library Media Activities Monthly: Libraries Unlimited, Inc., PO Box 291846, Kettering OH 45429, USA. www.schoollibrarymedia.com, tel: 800-771-5579, fax: 937-890-0221, schoollibrarymonthly@sfsdayton.com [8/yr; $55].

A vehicle for distributing ideas for teaching library media skills and for the development and implementation of library media skills programs.

School Library Media Research: American Library Association and American Association of School Librarians, Subscriptions, 50 E Huron St, Chicago, IL 60611-2795, USA. www.ala.org/ala/aasl/aaslpubsandjournals/slmrb/schoollibrary.cfm, tel: 800-545-2433, fax: 312-944-2641, subscription@ala.org [annual compilation; free online]. For library media specialists, district supervisors, and others concerned with the selection and purchase of print and non-print media and with the development of programs and services for preschool through high school libraries.

Teacher Librarian: The Scarecrow Press, Inc., 4501 Forbes Blvd, Suite 200, Lanham, MD 20706, USA. www.teacherlibrarian.com, tel: 800-462-6420, fax: 800-338-4550, admin@teacherlibrarian.com [5/yr; $56 indiv]. "The Journal for School Library Professionals"; previously known as Emergency Librarian. Articles, review columns, and critical analyses of management and programming issues.

17.9   Media Technologies

Broadcasting & Cable: NewBay Media, LLC., 28 E. 28th St, 12th Floor, New York, NY 10016, USA. www.broadcastingcable.com, tel: 800-554-5729, fax: 712-733-8019, bcbcustserv@cdsfulfillment.com [47/yr; $199]. All-inclusive news-weekly for radio, television, cable, and allied business.

Educational Media International: Taylor & Francis Group, Customer Services Department, 325 Chestnut St, Suite 800, Philadelphia, PA 19106, USA. www.tandf. co.uk/journals/titles/09523987, tel: 800-354-1420, fax: 215-625-2940, subscriptions@ tandf.co.uk [4/yr; $145 indiv, $530 inst (online), $590 inst (print+online)]. *The Official Journal of the International Council for Educational Media.*

Historical Journal of Film, Radio and Television: Taylor & Francis Group, Customer Services Department, 325 Chestnut St, Suite 800, Philadelphia, PA 19106, USA. www.tandf.co.uk/journals/titles/01439685, tel: 800-354-1420, fax: 215-625-2940, subscriptions@tandf.co.uk [4/yr; $434 indiv, $1,187 inst (online), $1,319 inst (print+online)]. Articles by international experts in the field, news and notices, and book reviews concerning the impact of mass communications on political and social history of the twentieth century.

International Journal of Instructional Media: Westwood Press, Inc., 118 5 Mile River Rd, Darien, CT 06820-6237, USA. www.adprima.com/ijim.htm, tel: 203-656-8680, fax: 212-353-8291, PLSleeman@aol.com [4/yr; $225]. Focuses on quality research on ongoing programs in instructional media for education, distance learning, computer technology, instructional media and technology, telecommunications, interactive video, management, media research and evaluation, and utilization.

Journal of Educational Multimedia and Hypermedia: Association for the Advancement of Computing in Education, PO Box 1545, Chesapeake, VA 23327-1545, USA. www.aace.org/pubs/jemh, tel: 757-366-5606, fax: 703-997-8760, info@aace.org [4/yr; $45 for stud, $125 indiv, $195 inst]. A multidisciplinary information source presenting research about and applications for multimedia and hyper-media tools.

Journal of Popular Film and Television: Taylor & Francis Group, Customer Service Department, 325 Chestnut Street, Suite 800, Philadelphia, PA 19106, USA. www.tandf.co.uk/journals/titles/01956051.asp, tel: 800-354-1420, fax: 215-625-2940, subscriptions@tandf.co.uk [4/yr; $66 indiv, $177 inst (online), $197 (print+online)]. Articles on film and television, book reviews, and theory. Dedicated to popular film and television in the broadest sense. Concentrates on commercial cinema and television, film and television theory or criticism, filmographies, and bibliographies. Edited at the College of Arts and Sciences of Northern Michigan University and the Department of Popular Culture, Bowling Green State University.

Learning, Media & Technology: Taylor & Francis Group, Customer Services Department, 325 Chestnut St, Suite 800, Philadelphia, PA 19106, USA. www.tandf.co.uk/journals/titles/17439884, tel: 800-354-1420, fax: 215-625-2940, subscriptions@tandf.co.uk [4/yr; $475 indiv, $1,657 inst (online), $1,841 inst (print+online)]. *This Journal of the Educational Television Association* serves as an international forum for discussions and reports on developments in the field of television and related media in teaching, learning, and training.

Media & Methods: American Society of Educators, 1429 Walnut St, Philadelphia, PA 19102, USA. www.media-methods.com, tel: 215-563-6005, fax: 215-587-9706, info@media-methods.com [5/yr; $35]. The only magazine published for the elementary school library media and technology specialist. A forum for K-12 educators who use technology as an educational resource, this journal includes information on what works and what does not, new product reviews, tips and pointers, and emerging technologies.

Multichannel News: NewBay Media, LLC., 28 E. 28th St, 12th Floor, New York, NY 10016, USA. www.multichannel.com, tel: 888-343-5563, fax: 712-733-8019, mulcustserv@cdsfulfillment.com [47/yr; $199]. A newsmagazine for the cable television industry. Covers programming, marketing, advertising, business, and other topics.

MultiMedia & Internet@Schools: Information Today, Inc., 143 Old Marlton Pike, Medford, NJ 08055-8750, USA. www.mmischools.com, tel: 609-654-6266, fax: 609-654-4309, custserv@infotoday.com [5/yr; $19.95]. Reviews and evaluates hardware and software. Presents information pertaining to basic trouble-shooting skills.

Multimedia Systems: Springer Science+Business Media, PO Box 2485, Secaucus, NJ 07096-2485, USA. www.springer.com/journal/00530, tel: 800-777-4643, fax:

201-348-4505, service-ny@springer.com [6/yr; $676 inst (print/online), $811 inst (print+online, content through 1997)]. Publishes original research articles and serves as a forum for stimulating and disseminating innovative research ideas, emerging technologies, state-of-the-art methods and tools in all aspects of multimedia computing, communication, storage, and applications among researchers, engineers, and practitioners.

Telematics and Informatics: Elsevier, Inc., Journals Customer Service, 3251 Riverport Lane, Maryland Heights, MO 63043, USA. www.elsevier.com/locate/tele, tel: 877-839-7126, fax: 314-447-8077, journalcustomerservice-usa@elsevier.com [4/yr; $153 indiv, $1,365 inst]. Publishes research and review articles in applied telecommunications and information sciences in business, industry, government, and educational establishments. Focuses on important current technologies, including microelectronics, computer graphics, speech synthesis and voice recognition, database management, data encryption, satellite television, artificial intelligence, and the ongoing computer revolution.

17.10 Professional Development

Journal of Digital Learning in Teacher Education: International Society for Technology in Education, Special Interest Group for Teacher Educators, 180 West 8th Ave., Suite 300, Eugene, OR 97401, USA. www.iste.org/jdlte, tel: 800-336-5191, fax: 541-302-3778, iste@iste.org [4/yr; $32 member, $122 non-member]. Contains refereed articles on preservice and in-service training, research in computer education and certification issues, and reviews of training materials and texts.

Journal of Technology and Teacher Education: Association for the Advancement of Computing in Education, PO Box 1545, Chesapeake, VA 23327-1545, USA. www.aace.org/pubs/jtate, tel: 757-366-5606, fax: 703-997-8760, info@aace.org [4/yr; $45 for stud, $125 indiv, $195 inst]. Serves as an international forum to report research and applications of technology in preservice, in-service, and graduate teacher education.

17.11 Simulation, Gaming, and Virtual Reality

Simulation & Gaming: Sage Publications, 2455 Teller Rd, Thousand Oaks, CA 91320, USA. http://www.sag.sagepub.com, tel: 800-818-7243, fax: 800-583-2665, journals@sagepub.com [6/yr; $147 indiv, $1,047 inst (online), $1,152 inst (online+backfile, content through Volume 1, Issue 1)]. An *International Journal of Theory, Design, and Research* focusing on issues in simulation, gaming, modeling, role-playing, and experiential learning.

17.12   Special Education and Disabilities

Journal of Special Education Technology: Technology and Media Division, JSET, PO Box 3853, Reston, VA 20195, USA. www.tamcec.org/jset, tel: 703-709-0136, fax: 405-325-7661, info@exinn.net [4/yr; $87 indiv, $208 inst]. Provides information, research, and reports of innovative practices regarding the application of educational technology toward the education of exceptional children.

17.13   Telecommunications and Networking

Canadian Journal of Learning and Technology: Canadian Network for Innovation in Education (CNIE), 260 Dalhousie St, Suite 204, Ottawa, ON, Canada K1N 7E4. www.cjlt.ca, tel: 613-241-0018, fax: 613-241-0019, cjlt@ucalgary.ca [3/yr; free]. Concerned with all aspects of educational systems and technology.

Computer Communications: Elsevier, Inc., Journals Customer Service, 3251 Riverport Lane, Maryland Heights, MO 63043, USA. www.elsevier.com/locate/comcom, tel: 877-839-7126, fax: 314-447-8077, journalcustomerservice-usa@elsevier.com [18/yr; $2,319 inst (print/online)]. Focuses on networking and distributed computing techniques, communications hardware and software, and standardization.

EDUCAUSE Review: EDUCAUSE, 4772 Walnut St, Suite 206, Boulder, CO 80301-2536, USA. www.educause.edu/er, tel: 303-449-4430, fax: 303-440-0461, er-subs@educause.edu [6/yr; $35]. Features articles on current issues and applications of computing and communications technology in higher education. Reports on EDUCAUSE consortium activities.

International Journal on E-Learning: Association for the Advancement of Computing in Education, PO Box 1545, Chesapeake, VA 23327-1545, USA. www.aace.org/pubs/ijel, tel: 757-366-5606, fax: 703-997-8760, info@aace.org [4/yr; $45 for stud, $125 indiv, $195 inst]. Reports on current theory, research, development, and practice of telecommunications in education at all levels.

The Internet and Higher Education: Elsevier, Inc., Journals Customer Service, 3251 Riverport Lane, Maryland Heights, MO 63043, USA. www.elsevier.com/locate/iheduc, tel: 877-839-7126, fax: 314-447-8077, journalcustomerservice-usa@elsevier.com [4/yr; $80 indiv, $450 inst]. Designed to reach faculty, staff, and administrators responsible for enhancing instructional practices and productivity via the use of information technology and the Internet in their institutions.

Internet Reference Services Quarterly: Taylor & Francis Group, Customer Services Department, 325 Chestnut St, Suite 800, Philadelphia, PA 19106, USA. www.tandf.co.uk/journals/titles/10875301, tel: 800-354-1420, fax: 215-625-2940, subscriptions@tandf.co.uk [4/yr; $85 indiv (online), $90 indiv (print+online),

$218 inst (online), $242 inst (print+online)]. Describes innovative information practice, technologies, and practice. For librarians of all kinds.

Internet Research: Emerald Group Publishing Inc., Brickyard Office Park, 84 Sherman Street, Cambridge, MA 02140, USA. www.emeraldinsight.com/intr.htm, tel: 617-945-9130, fax: 617-945-9136, america@emeraldinsight.com [5/yr; inst prices vary]. A cross-disciplinary journal presenting research findings related to electronic networks, analyses of policy issues related to networking, and descriptions of current and potential applications of electronic networking for communication, computation, and provision of information services.

Online: Information Today, Inc., 143 Old Marlton Pike, Medford, NJ 08055-8750, USA. www.infotoday.com/online, tel: 609-654-6266, fax: 609-654-4309, custserv@infotoday.com [6/yr; $129.50]. For online information system users. Articles cover a variety of online applications for general and business use.

Index